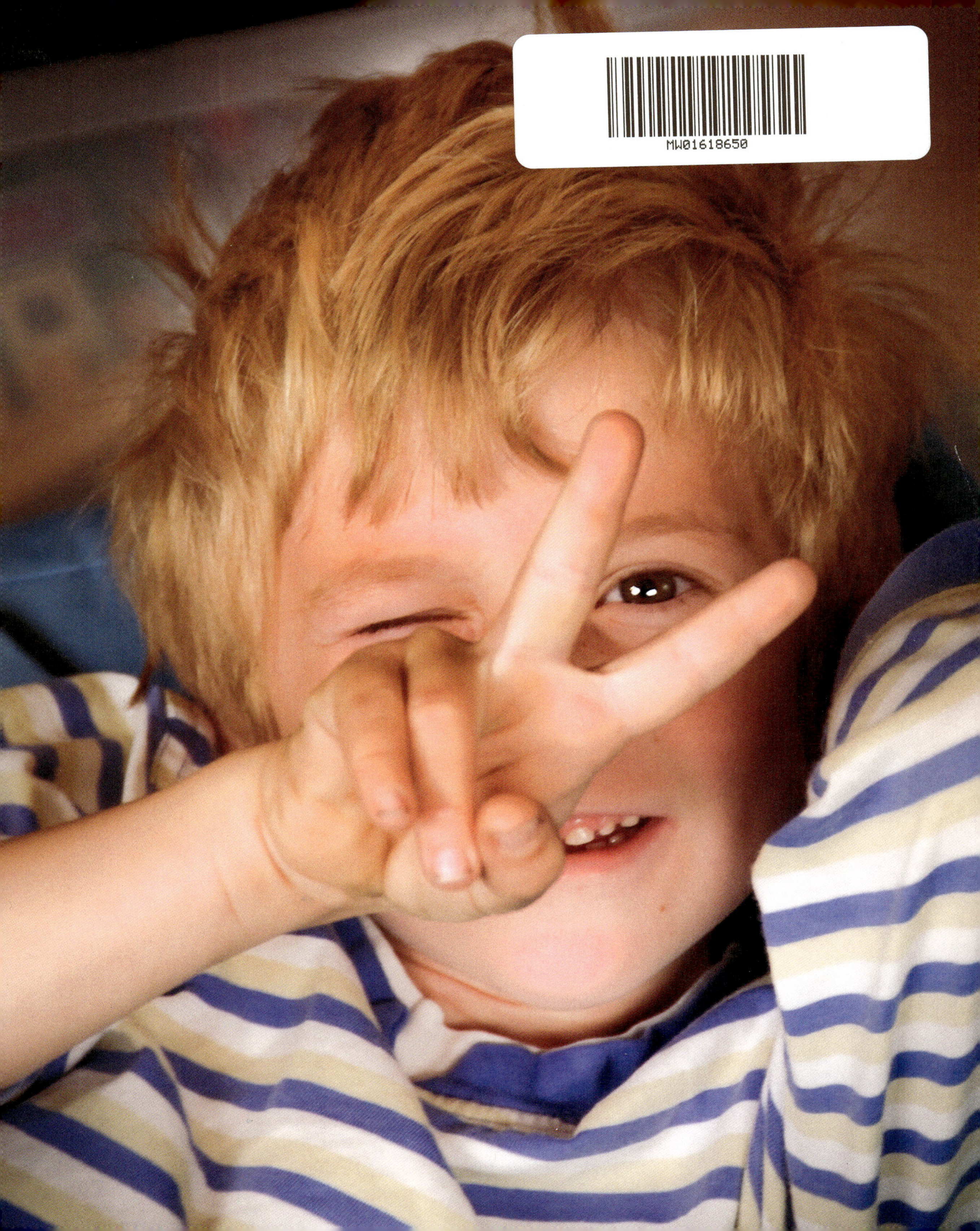

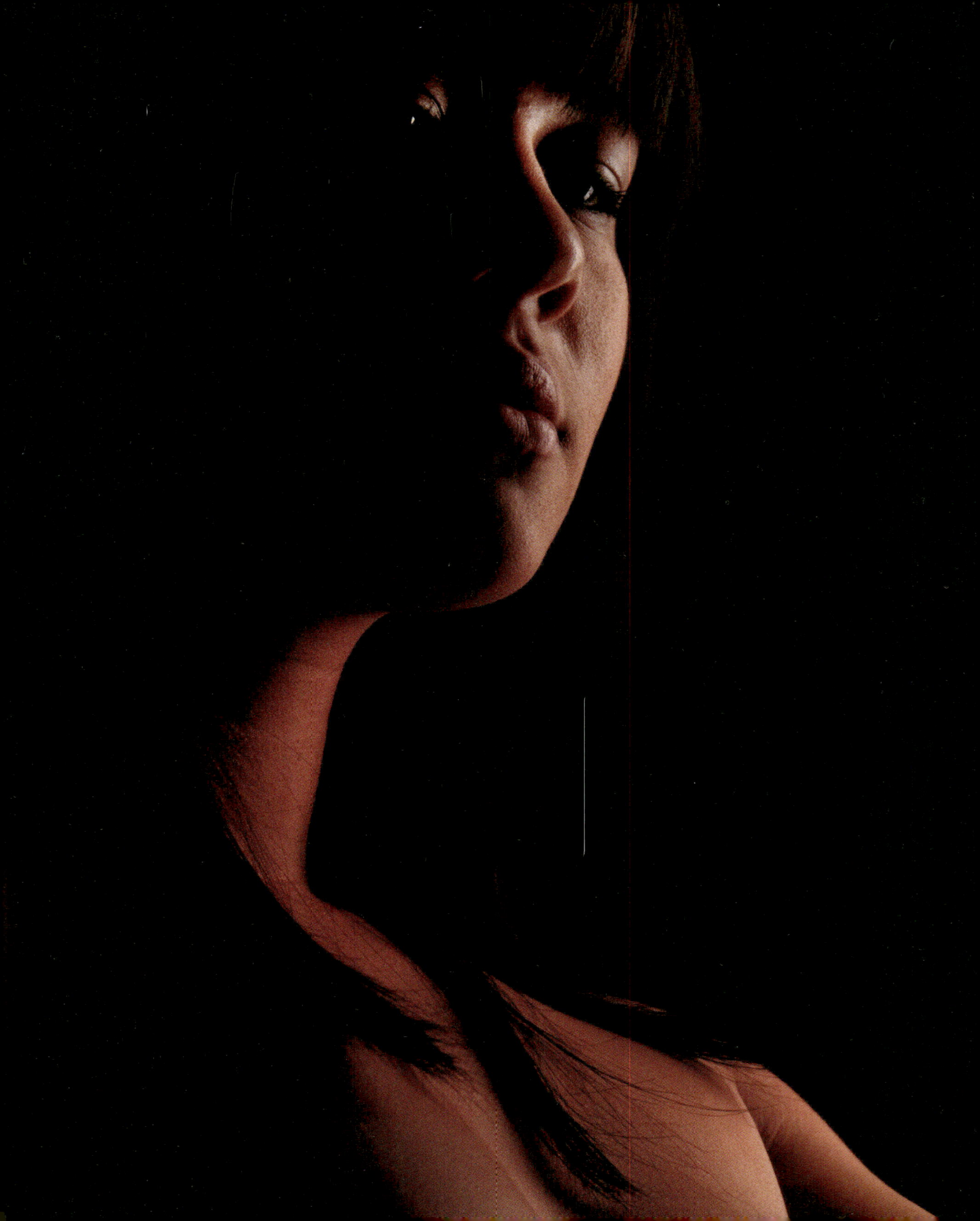

Creative Portraits

Digital Photography Tips & Techniques

Harold Davis

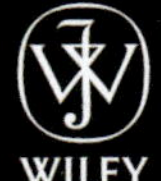

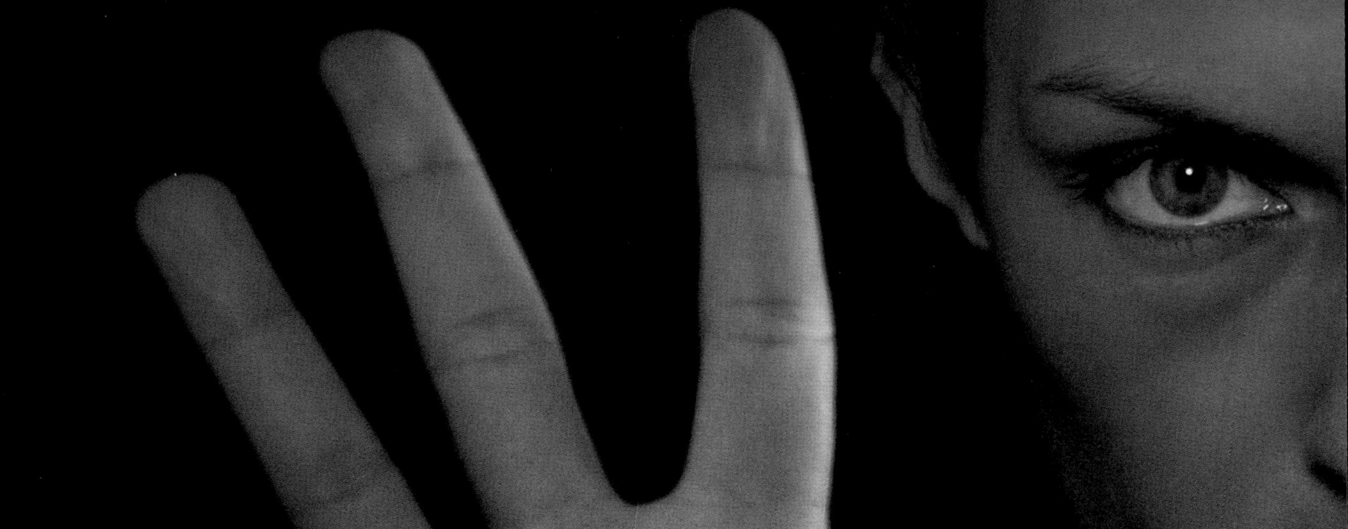

Creative Portraits: Digital Photography Tips & Techniques
by Harold Davis

Published by
Wiley Publishing, Inc.
10475 Crosspoint Boulevard
Indianapolis, IN 46256
www.wiley.com

Published simultaneously in Canada

ISBN: 978-0-470-62326-8

Manufactured in the United States of America

10 9 8 7 6 5 4 3 2 1

For general information on our other products and services or to obtain technical support, please contact our Customer Care Department within the U.S. at (800) 762-2974, outside the U.S. at (317) 572-3993 or fax (317) 572-4002.

Wiley also publishes its books in a variety of electronic formats. Some content that appears in print may not be available in electronic books.

Library of Congress Control Number: 2010931109

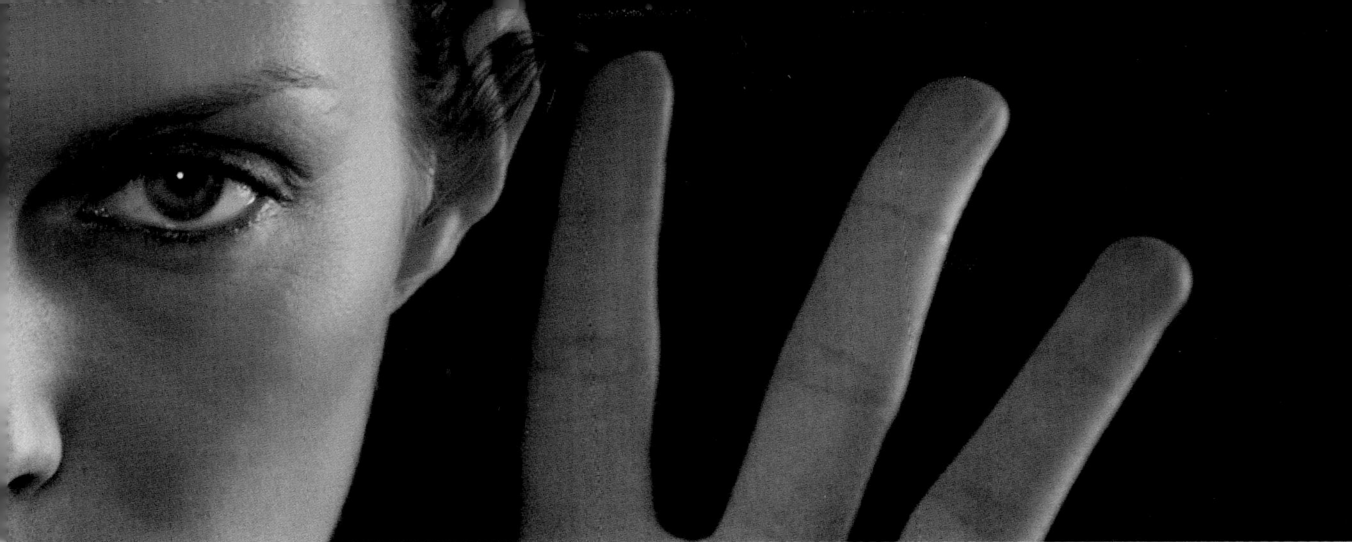

Acknowledgements

A very special thanks to everyone who helped with this book, modeled for me, or sat for their portrait. You know who you are.

Credits

Acquisitions Editor: Courtney Allen

Project Editor: Matthew Buchanan

Technical Editor: Chris Bucher

Copy Editor: Matthew Buchanan

Editorial Manager: Robyn Siesky

Business Manager: Amy Knies

Senior Marketing Manager: Sandy Smith

Vice President and Executive Group Publisher: Richard Swadley

Vice President and Publisher: Barry Pruett

Book Designer: Phyllis Davis

Media Development Project Manager: Laura Moss

Media Development Assistant Project Manager: Jenny Swisher

▲ Front piece: My son Nicky is full of life and always changeable and in motion. The trick in photographing him is to be ready with the camera so I can get the photo while the getting is good.
200mm, 1/15 of a second at f/5.6 and ISO 400, hand held

▲ Title page: Using a single bare studio strobe to selectively light this portrait established a clear demarcation between light and shadow areas.
95mm, 1/200 of a second at f/9 and ISO 100, hand held

▲ Above: In portraiture, the subject's eyes are looked at first because they are the most expressive feature. Hands are a close second, so in this pose I combined hands and eyes.
70mm, 1/100 of a second at f/6.3 and ISO 100, hand held

▼ Page 6: The model in this photo was bored and had an uninteresting expression until I asked her to use a mask. With the mask in place, her eyes conveyed true emotion which helped make a striking portrait.
135mm, 1/60 of a second at f/8 and ISO 100, hand held

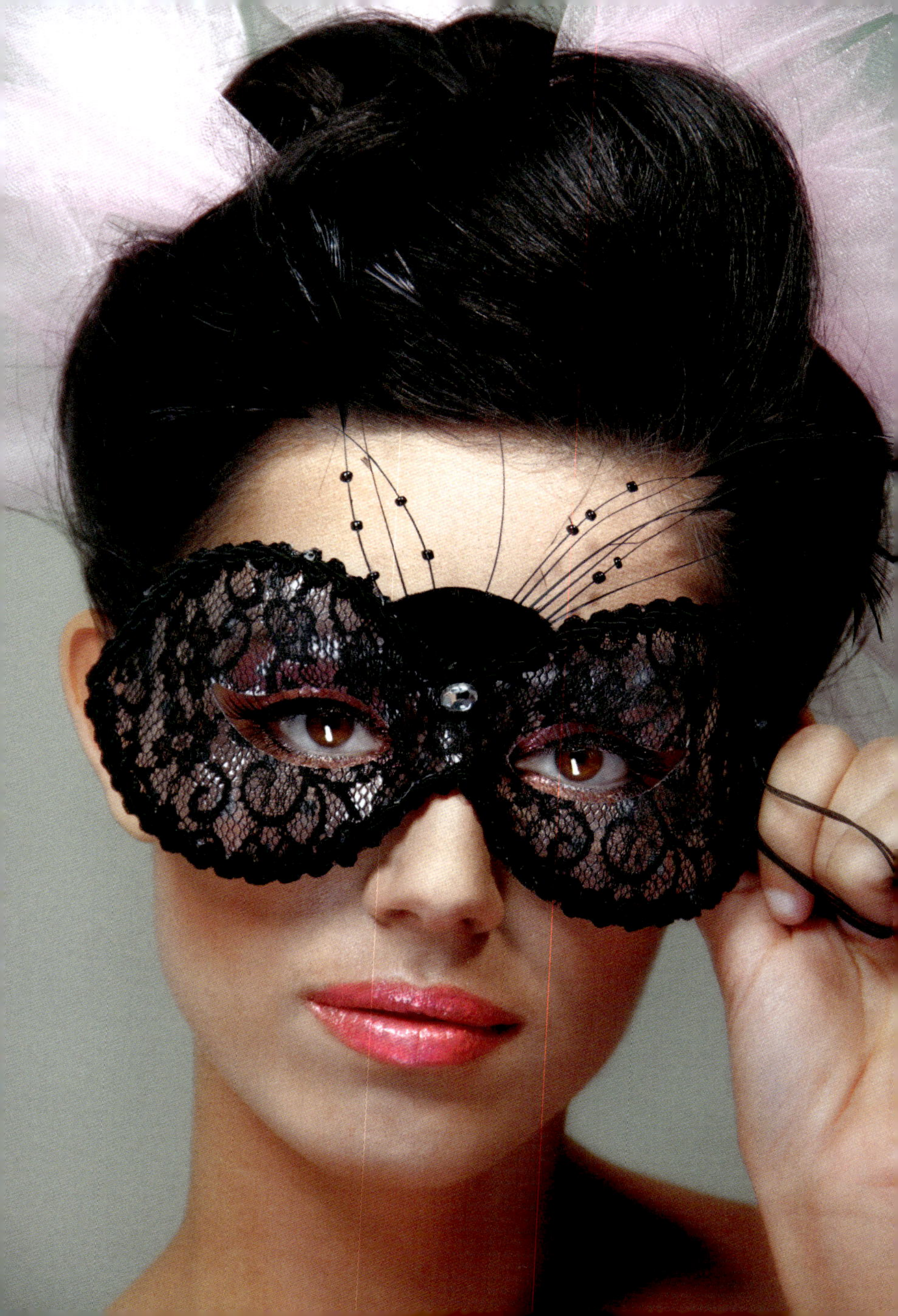

Contents

Introduction

"The proper study of Mankind is Man," wrote Alexander Pope in 1733. Bringing this thought into the context of a modern digital photographer, making portraits of men, women, and children is a passionate undertaking for many of us.

As a well-known proverb says, "the eyes are the window to the soul." It's often believed that by looking into someone's eyes you can see into their core being; and that by observing a face, or a photo of a face, you can understand character. The issues common to all photography—composition, lighting, exposure, and camera technique—come into play when you make a portrait. In portraiture, the variables of character and physiognomy add assumptions about the relationship between reality and portrayal, as well as challenges in rendering character as you see it, and opportunities for creative photography.

To what extent is a photographic portrait "real"? Does the portrait represent the subject fairly and accurately? Put another way, do you know something that is true about the subject after looking at the portrait?

These are excellent questions. If you are not involved in the serious pursuit of making photographs, you're likely to assume that there is a correlation between the photo and the reality of the subject, and that you've learned something about someone by looking at their portrait. But as photographers, we know that many photographic portraits are superficial and plastic—and highly subject to manipulation.

The truth of a portrait depends upon the insight and integrity of the photographer, the honesty of the subject, and the photographic and digital techniques and manipulations used. Not all photographic portraits are intended to be truthful, nor should they be. For example, if you are hunting for a job, there's absolutely nothing wrong with putting "your best foot forward" by using an overtly flattering professional head shot.

My point is that in portrait photography it is crucial to be aware of your intentions and goals. A glamour session in the studio is a very different affair from a gritty portrait that attempts to reveal the truth about a complex personality, warts and all. Also, unlike most other kinds of photography, great portraiture requires collaboration with your subject. If you are taking a photo of a blade of grass or a railroad station, you don't really care what the plant or the building thinks of you. But if you are photographing a person, your relationship with the person—their life experiences, how they feel about photography, and what they think of you—plays an important role in the process of photography.

Speaking of intentions and goals, *Creative Portraits* is unlike other portrait photography books you may have seen. My assumption is that you are seriously interested in photography—or you probably wouldn't have picked up this book. But this isn't primarily a treatise about studio portrait techniques.

Instead, *Creative Portraits* aims squarely at the heart and soul of portrait photography, which is what most of us really care about: how do we create meaningful, interesting, and compelling portraits of our friends, family, and kids?

As with my other *Creative* photography titles, I believe that the two best ways to learn about photography are by looking at photos—and by taking photos. Each photographic portrait in this book is accompanied by a description explaining how and why I made the photo. It's a perfectly reasonable strategy to look at the photos, consider how they were made, and then dip into the text for those topics in which you'd like a little more in-depth information.

Please use *Creative Portraits* as an idea book. If you are moved to try a new technique when photographing someone you care about, then I will have succeeded in my goal for *Creative Portraits*. Enjoy!

Harold Davis

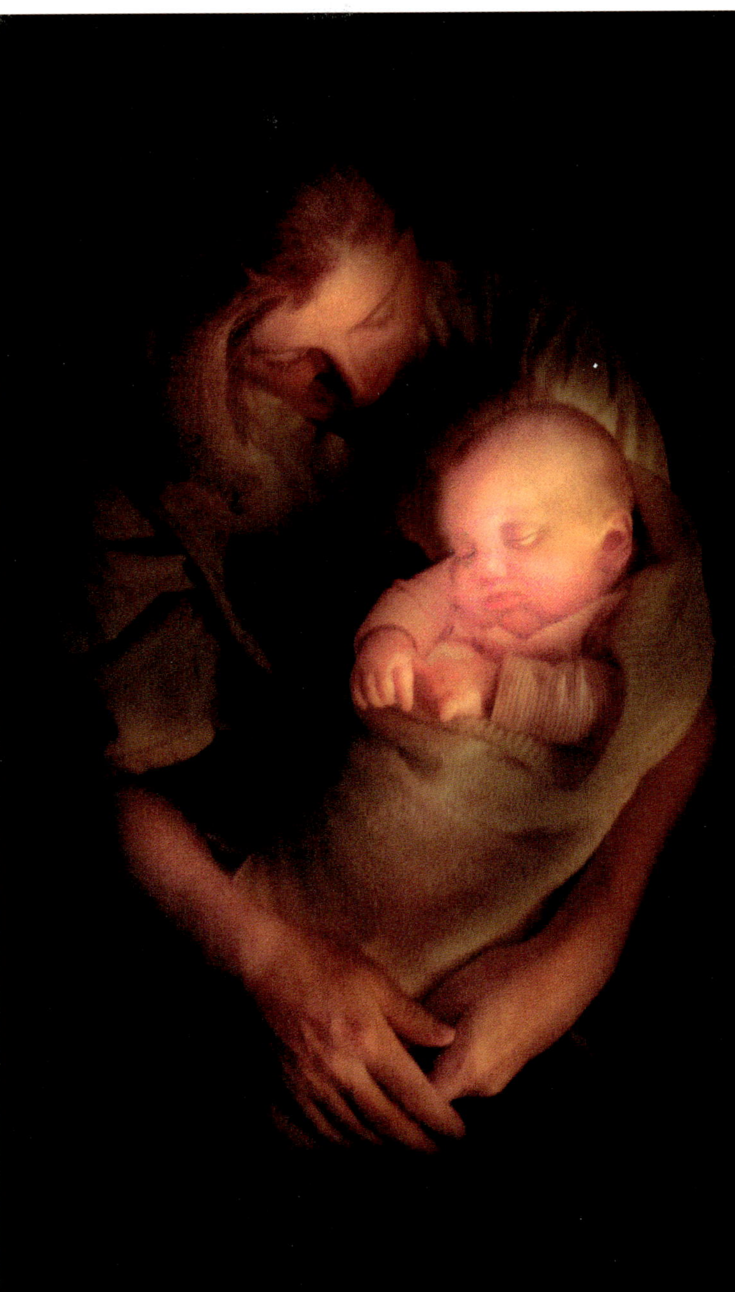

▶ I took this photo of my wife and sleeping baby by the light of a 15-watt bulb. To make the exposure, I needed to boost the ISO to 2000. This led to a noisy capture. Not all digital noise is bad—in this case it adds to the interest of the photo.

32mm, 1/8 of a second at f/4 and ISO 2000, hand held

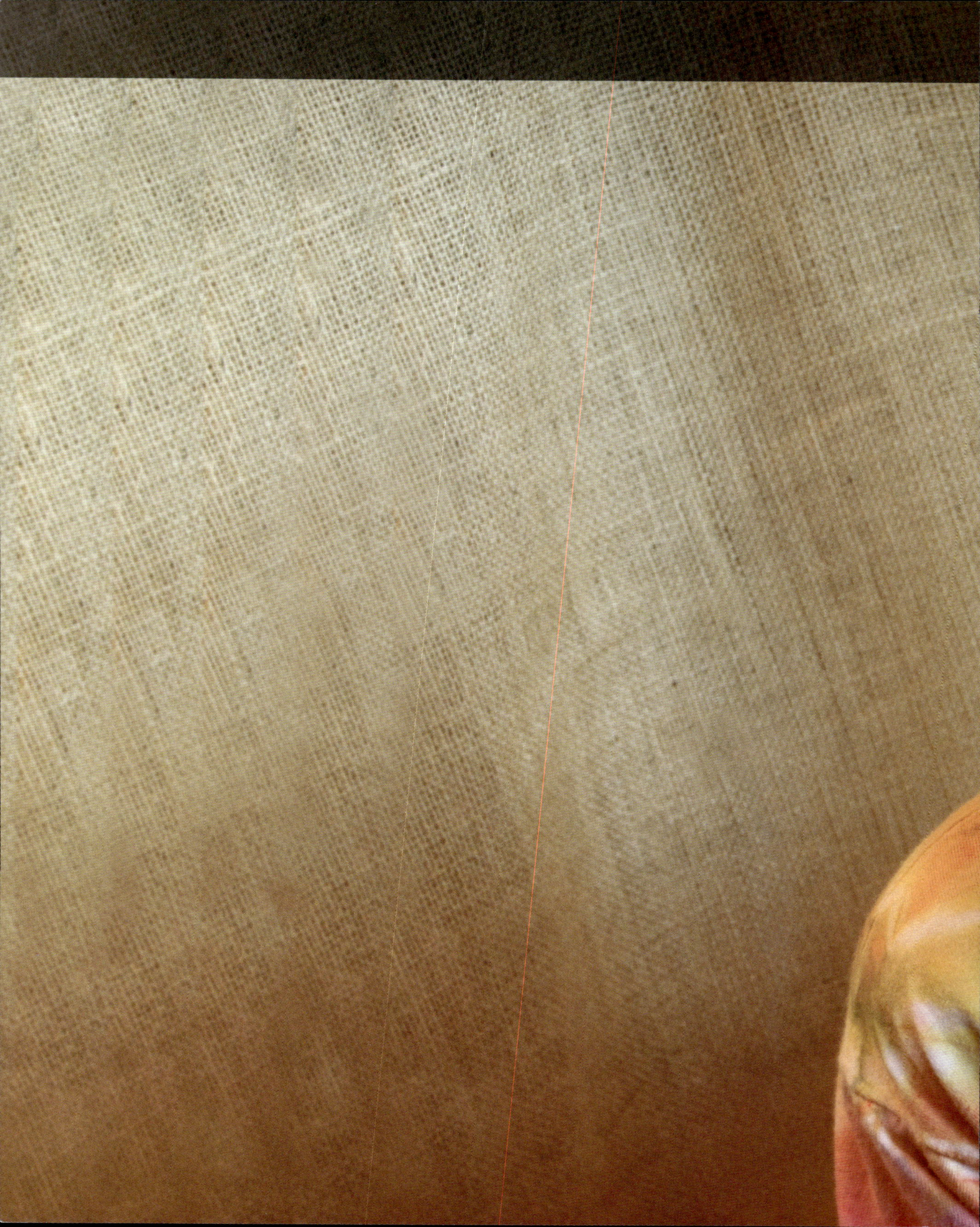

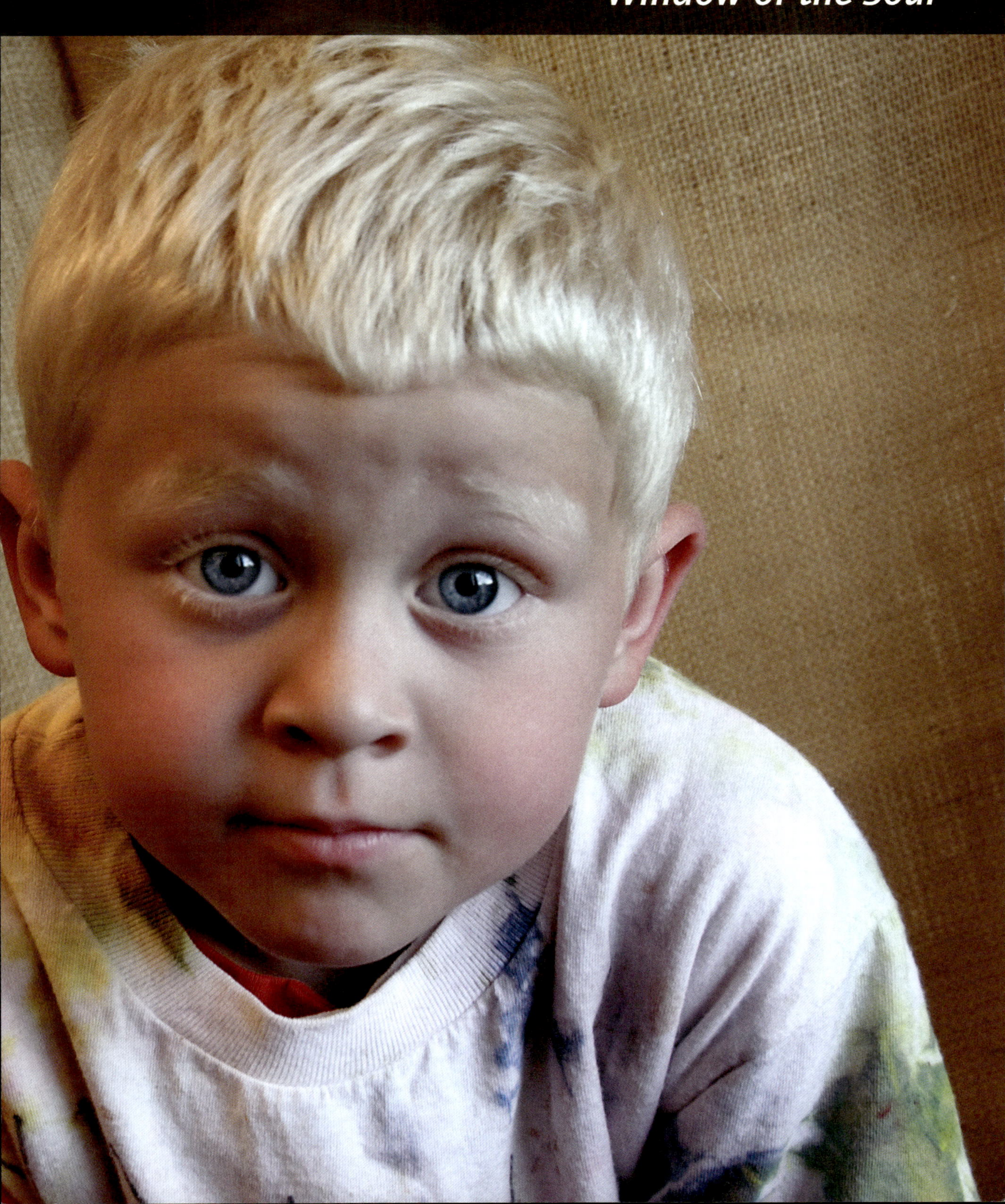

Kinds of Portrait Photos

If you stop to think about it for a moment, you'll realize that there are many different kinds of portrait photographs. While the proof is in the final image, often these differences boil down to the intentions of both the photographer and the subject of the portrait.

Historic European royal court portrait paintings were intended to glorify and flatter their subjects; some modern portrait photography plays a similar role. The portraits of business executives in suits that show up in annual reports are usually intended to show capable executives who are dressed and groomed according to the rules of their station in life, and whom shareholders would trust with money.

Moving away from the realm of the professional photograph, street portraits are often intended to capture a "decisive moment"—to use the phrase coined by the great Henri Cartier-Bresson. While these photographs depict people, they are more about action and composition than character.

Professional photographer, serious amateur, or novice alike, we all want to make portraits of our kids and families in moments of joy. This is a laudable goal—and I'll show you how to have more fun and make better photos of your kids and family starting on page 168.

Whatever kind of portrait photography interests you, the most important thing is to practice making your photos with mindfulness. The goal should be to come up with an image that says something about its subject. At the same time, cameras don't take photos, people do. Making a portrait photo involves two actors: the subject and the photographer. A good portrait is about the subject, and about the impressions and feelings the photographer has for the subject. In this sense, creating a portrait photo can be an extraordinarily intimate act.

▶ To make an interesting portrait, I positioned this professional model on the opposite side of a translucent curtain. Next, I lit this photo with a single studio strobe to the left and above the model. The light was pointed down at the curtain, not at the model, and the effect of bouncing the light off the curtain creates a soft and dreamy effect.

200mm, 1/160 of a second at f/11 and ISO 100, hand held

▲ Pages 10–11: Five-year-old Mathew is a beautiful and affectionate boy who is having a bit of a hard time being the youngest of three boys, along with the birth of his new baby sister. Mathew likes to help when I'm photographing. Together we change lenses and count the seconds for long exposures.

One day in the studio he said to me, "Dad, take my picture." He told me exactly where he wanted to sit and what background he wanted to use. Then he pressed the shutter himself.

I think Mathew's portrait (actually, a self-portrait) shows both sides of the child: the lovely, warm, carefree boy, as well as the troubled gaze of a youngster who always expected to be the baby of the family and doesn't know quite what hit him.

Tungsten light with barn door, 36mm, 1/15 of a second at f/8 and ISO 500, tripod mounted

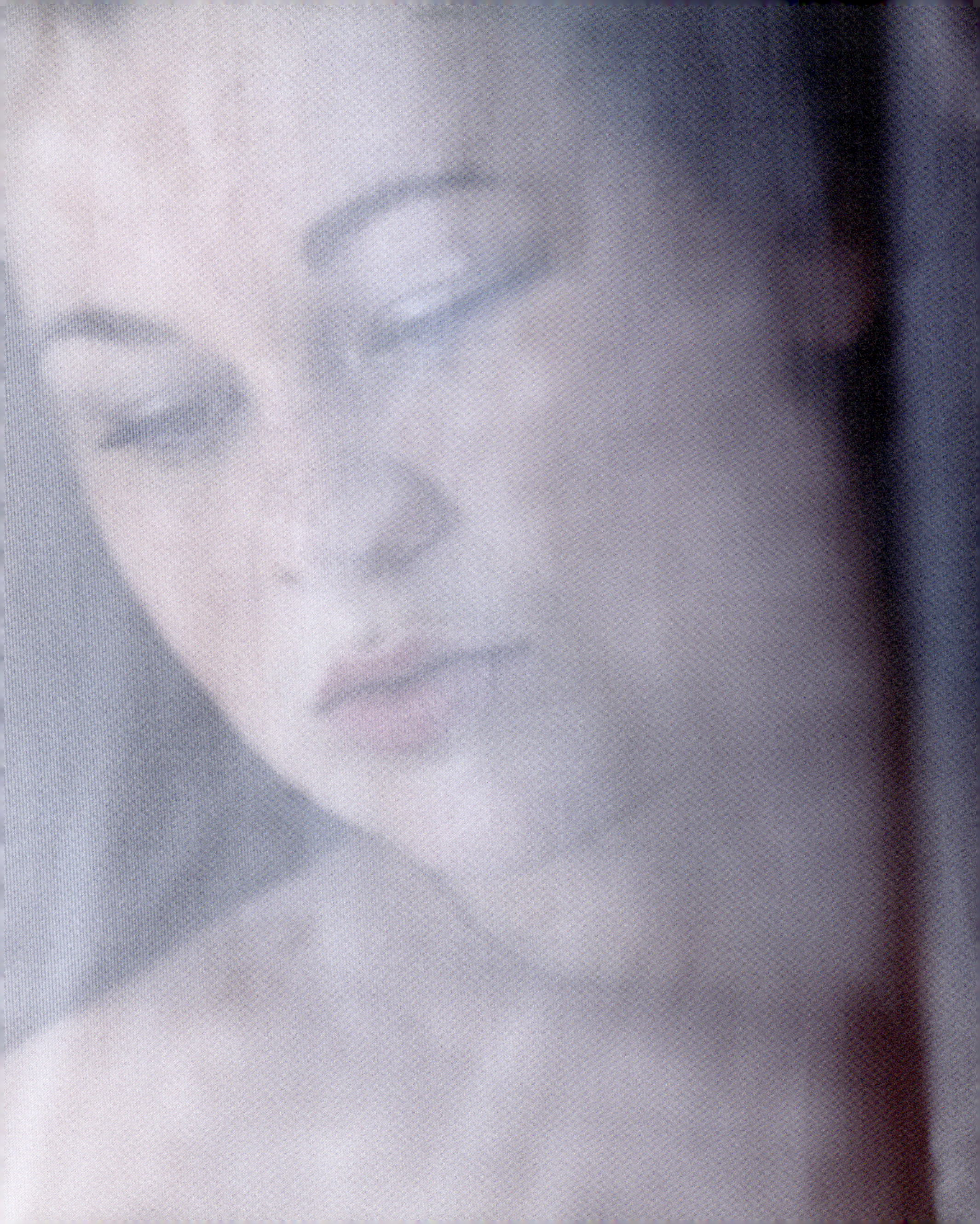

Why People Sit for a Portrait

When you are shooting a portrait, it's important to think about why your subjects are sitting for you.

How many different motivations for being photographed can you list? Here are some:

- To memorialize a record of a special time, for example wedding or maternal portraits
- For professional reasons, for example a head shot to be used with a resume
- As a gift for a loved one
- As an examination of self, and the relationship with the photographer
- For the cash, when a professional model poses
- To have fun

There are many more possible motivations, and some of them overlap (for example, someone could pose for your camera both to have fun and to create a record of the day of a wedding).

Of course, your portrait subjects may not literally be *sitting*. It's often the case that they are running, jumping, lying down—anything but sitting. A subject in motion may be harder to capture because you need to fire the shutter with precise timing, but motion can often show more life than a static pose.

But getting back to the question of why someone allows themselves to be the subject of a portrait, some of the best portraits are done without explicit cooperation of their subjects. For example, if I see an interesting face as I'm walking along the street, I'll often "snap first and ask questions later." By the way, if you follow this approach, be open and forthcoming when you discuss your actions with your subject. For more about street photography of people, see page 68.

As a photographer, it is important to understand the motivation of your subjects. Armed with this understanding, you can deliver what they are looking for in the portrait session.

Never underestimate the power of fun! Even if a subject has come to you for a "very serious" reason—they need a business portrait or head shot—nothing says that you can't have fun during the portrait session. You'll get better portraits if you inject an element of play into your photo session.

▶ The obvious fun shown in this bridal portrait makes up for the mundane background. I used a fast shutter speed (1/1250 of a second) in bright outdoor sunshine to capture and "stop" the motion.

200mm, 1/1250 of a second at f/5.6 and ISO 200, hand held

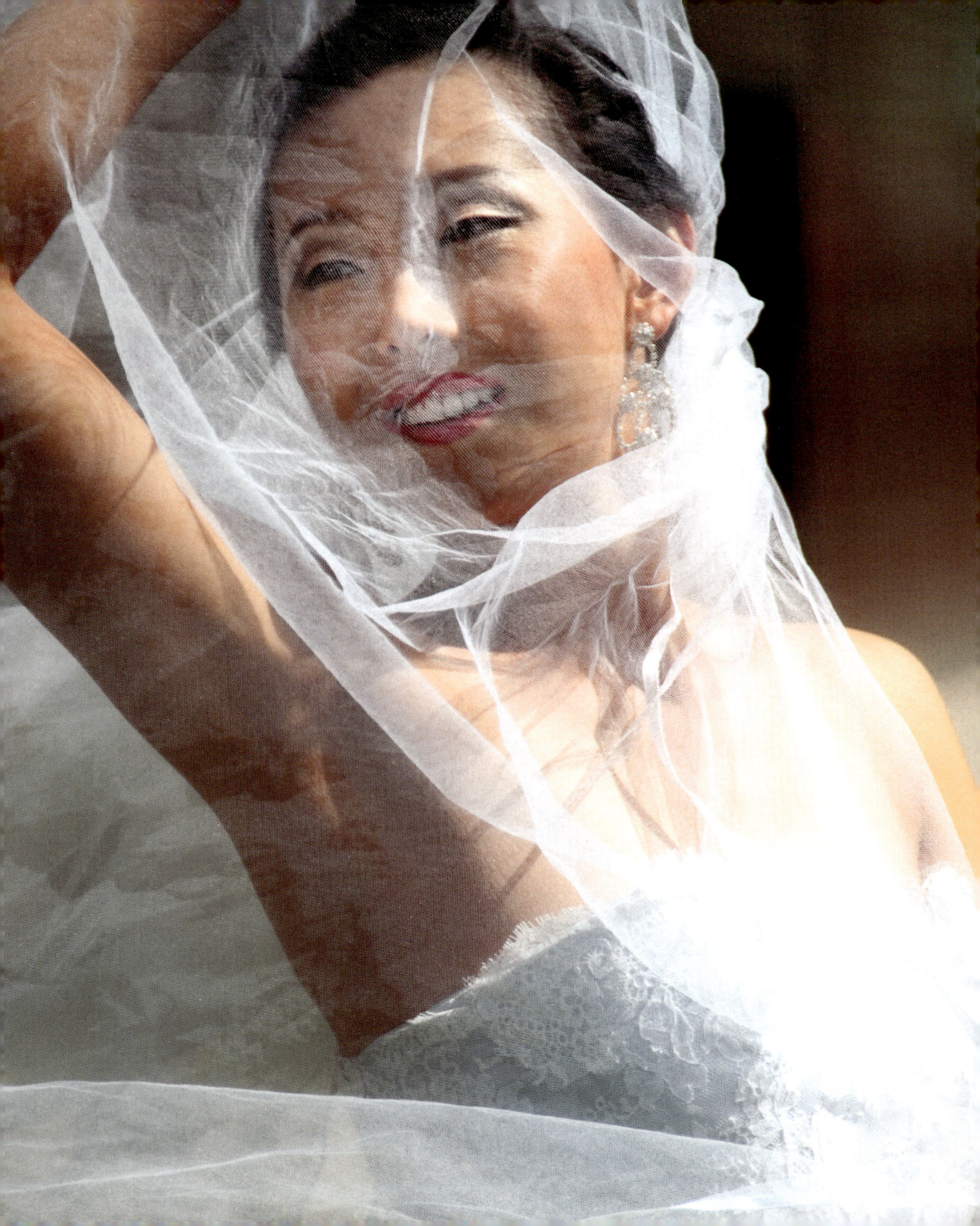

Why Photographers Make Portraits

The reasons photographers take portraits can be as varied as the reasons that subjects sit for them.

It's possible that you may have alternative or additional goals besides those of your subjects—and that's fine. Actually, this happens a great deal of the time. Photographers often have a visual agenda that they don't fully disclose to their portrait subjects.

A good photographer makes an effort to understand their interactions with portrait subjects. This means the photographer needs to constantly monitor their own feelings in relation to the portrait subject. Just as a portrait subject brings emotion to the session, the photographer's motivation impacts the quality of the image making.

Your motivation in making a portrait should help guide your approach both practically and visually. Photographers take pictures of people for many reasons, including:

- The desire to preserve special memories
- Wanting to say something significant about a person
- The need to make a statement
- Because the photographer is getting paid to make the portrait
- As an exercise in image making—either technical or aesthetic

A portrait session involves at least two people—the photographer and the subject. People being people, these two interact, have personal motivations, and feelings for each other. An important part of the equation is the motivation of someone who is being photographed. Next, the intentions and feelings of the photographer towards the subject are very significant. The rubber meets the road—and great portraits emerge—in the final piece of the puzzle: how the motivations, intentions, and mutual feelings of the photographer and subject interact and mesh.

The task of the photographer during the interaction with the subject is to guide

▶ This studio portrait was an intentional re-creation of the glamour effects achieved by Hollywood photographer George Hurrell. Many of Hurrell's most famous photos were created using uncoated lenses that would be considered flawed by modern standards. Hurell used lighting equipment that created harsh light—and required his models to hold still for long periods of time.

Photographer Rafael Hernandez, who has been studying Hurrell's work for many years, directed the lighting in this shoot. Using studio strobes to simulate the Hurrell effects was essentially an act of homage and creative anachronism that required considerable technical expertise with studio lighting equipment. The main ingredient was to use a key light positioned above and pointed down at the model's face. This generated a "butterfly" shadow—so named because the shadow somewhat resembles a butterfly—beneath the model's nose. The butterfly shadow is considered emblematic of Hurrell's work.

By the way, although the lighting in this portrait mimics Hurrell's work, the overall effect remains considerably less harsh than in Hurrell's classic early portraits.

100mm, 1/160 of a second at f/16 and ISO 100, hand held

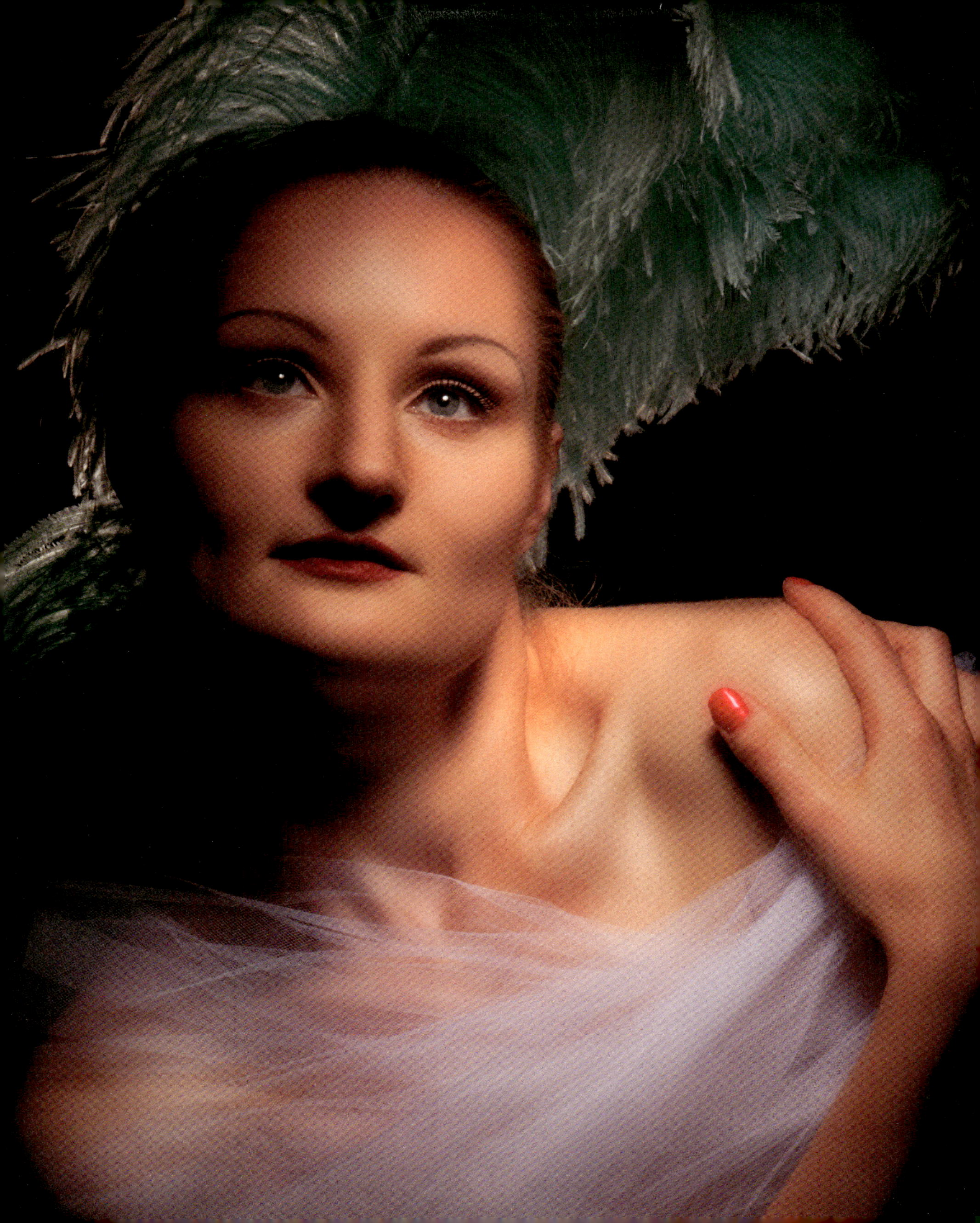

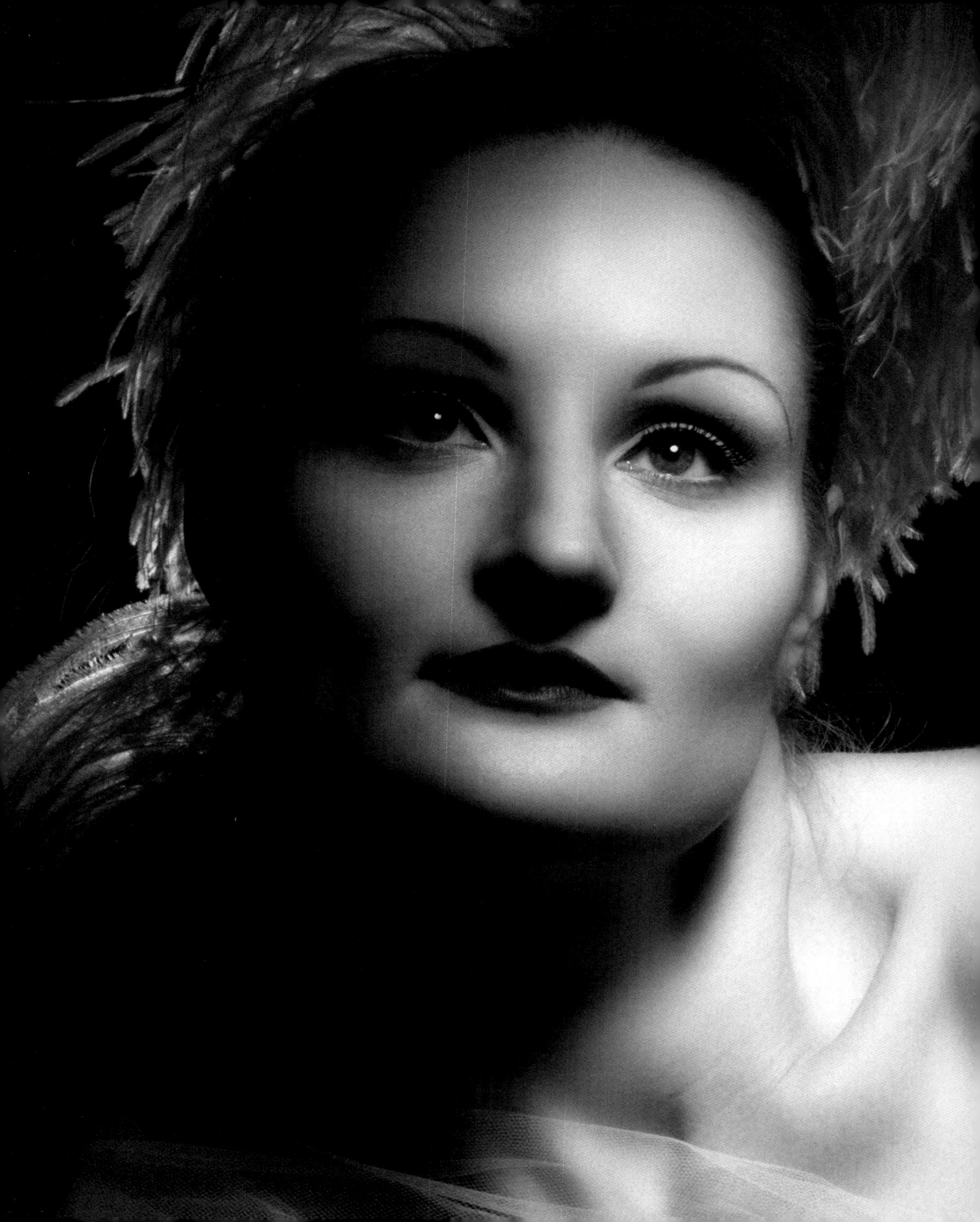

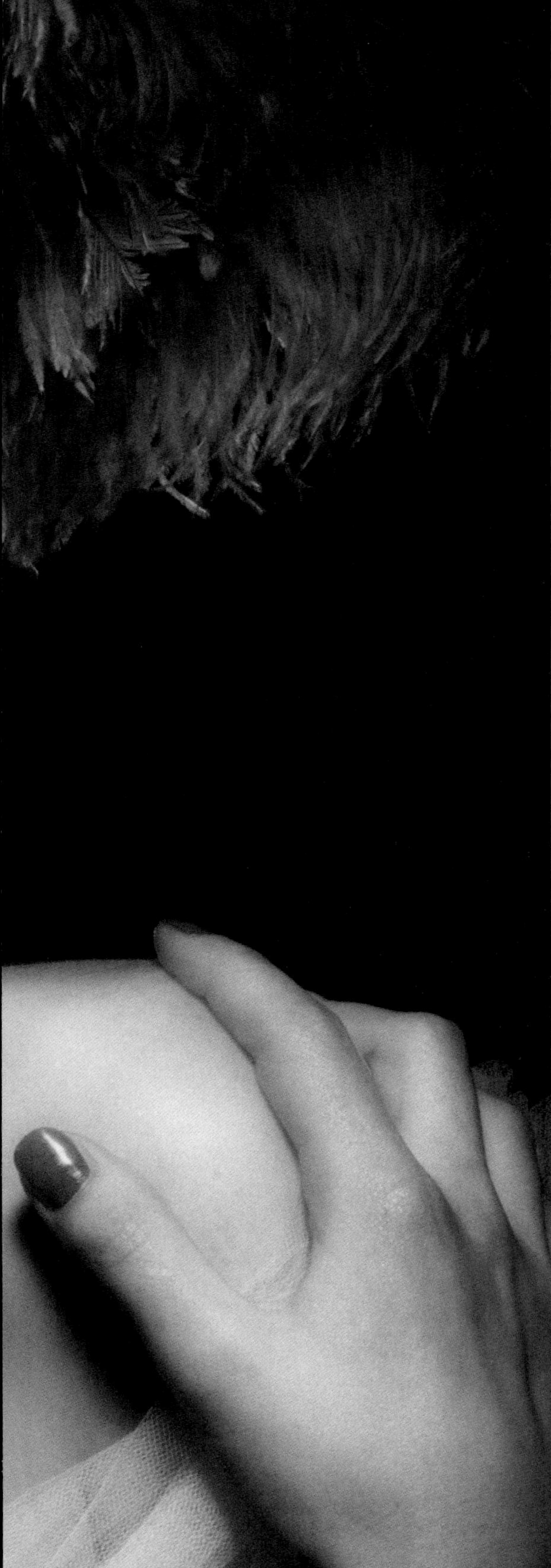

the session to achieve goals that have been mutually agreed upon—as well as the photographer's possibly independent goals.

As with any relationship, if photographer and subject are completely at loggerheads then acceptable portraits are not likely to result.

While sometimes the photographer can be passive in the relationship with a portrait subject, my experience is that the photographer-subject interaction works best when the photographer takes control. You should think of this as a directorial step: the subject cannot see the impact of lighting or the way the image is coming together in the camera viewfinder. By directing and posing the portrait subject, you are not being unreasonably bossy—you are simply using your technical and visual expertise to serve the same role as a film director in helping to make sure that everything comes together.

◀ Hurrell is most famous for his work in the 1930s. He made contact prints directly from 8 x 10 film shot in a view camera, typically at fairly slow shutter speeds (so the models had to be posed to keep still during the exposure process). The orthochromatic film available led to unrealistic renditions of colors as monochromatically translated; for example, lips and cheeks tended to go dark.

Uncoated lenses produced halo effects, and the film stock added halation—increased glow on the highlights. Film was underexposed and overdeveloped, leading to dramatic high contrasts between lights and darks, and much retouching (which was done directly on the 8 x 10 film, very carefully, by the legions of retouchers employed by the movie studios).

Since Hurrell's work was monochromatic—and made using equipment and chemistry from a specific historical era that led to the anomalies I've described—I wanted to convert this photo to black and white and give it a look closer to something that Hurrell might have done.

In Photoshop, I simulated Hurrell's black and white tones and contrast by combining a High Contrast Red preset Black & White adjustment layer with the Nik Silver Efex Antique Plate 1 filter. Photoshop and portraiture is explained starting on page 196.

100mm, 1/160 of a second at f/16 and ISO 100, hand held

The Psychology of Portraiture

The true creative art of portraiture involves a partnership between subject and photographer where neither can be quite sure of the other, but both must trust the other to get good results.

For any transaction between people to be successful, both people have to get something. With portraiture, if the photographer or model is a professional, sometimes money changes hands. But dollars and cents may be the least significant part of the transaction. It's important as a photographer to keep your eye on the emotional content of what you are doing.

Someone who comes to you for a portrait is making themselves potentially vulnerable. As a photographer, you have the power to make your subjects look beautiful or ugly, to tell the truth about them, or to distort their reality. This is a relationship of trust, and one that can easily be abused.

Good portrait subjects like to be photographed, just as good portrait photographers like to make portraits. The emotional psychology of this transaction is similar to the exchange between exhibitionists and voyeurs: the world needs both to work in symbiosis.

Your subjects will not always tell you their innermost thoughts, just as you probably won't—and shouldn't—disclose everything you are seeing and considering. If you are out to capture the truth, literal warts and all, how cooperative can you really expect your subjects to be? On the other hand, completely airbrushed images devoid of character don't disclose anything about their subject.

The psychology of this partnership between photographer and subject walks the knife's edge between daring to tell the truth and remaking the subject as more attractive than reality. The tension between these goals is what makes for interesting portraits. In any case, photographers need to consider these issues, and work with subjects by partly telling their real desires, and partly hiding them. It is up to us as photographers to ferret out the real intention behind modeling or sitting for a portrait.

Armed with this information we must work as directors—by begging, cajoling, ordering, and catering to the psychology of the subject—to get the best results possible from the portrait session. If your subjects are shy in front of the lens, you need to coax them to perform. On the other hand, subjects who are already extroverted may need to be directed so they look their best.

▶ I went to a photo session to photograph a model I had never worked with before. Arriving at the studio, I found that Shelby had a generic blond look, almost like a mid-western stewardess. We started talking and we agreed that we wanted to go for a portrait with character. To get started, I shot some photos of Shelby's basic look. One of them is shown to the right. Then, she went to change...

200mm, 1/160 of a second at f/8 and ISO 200, hand held

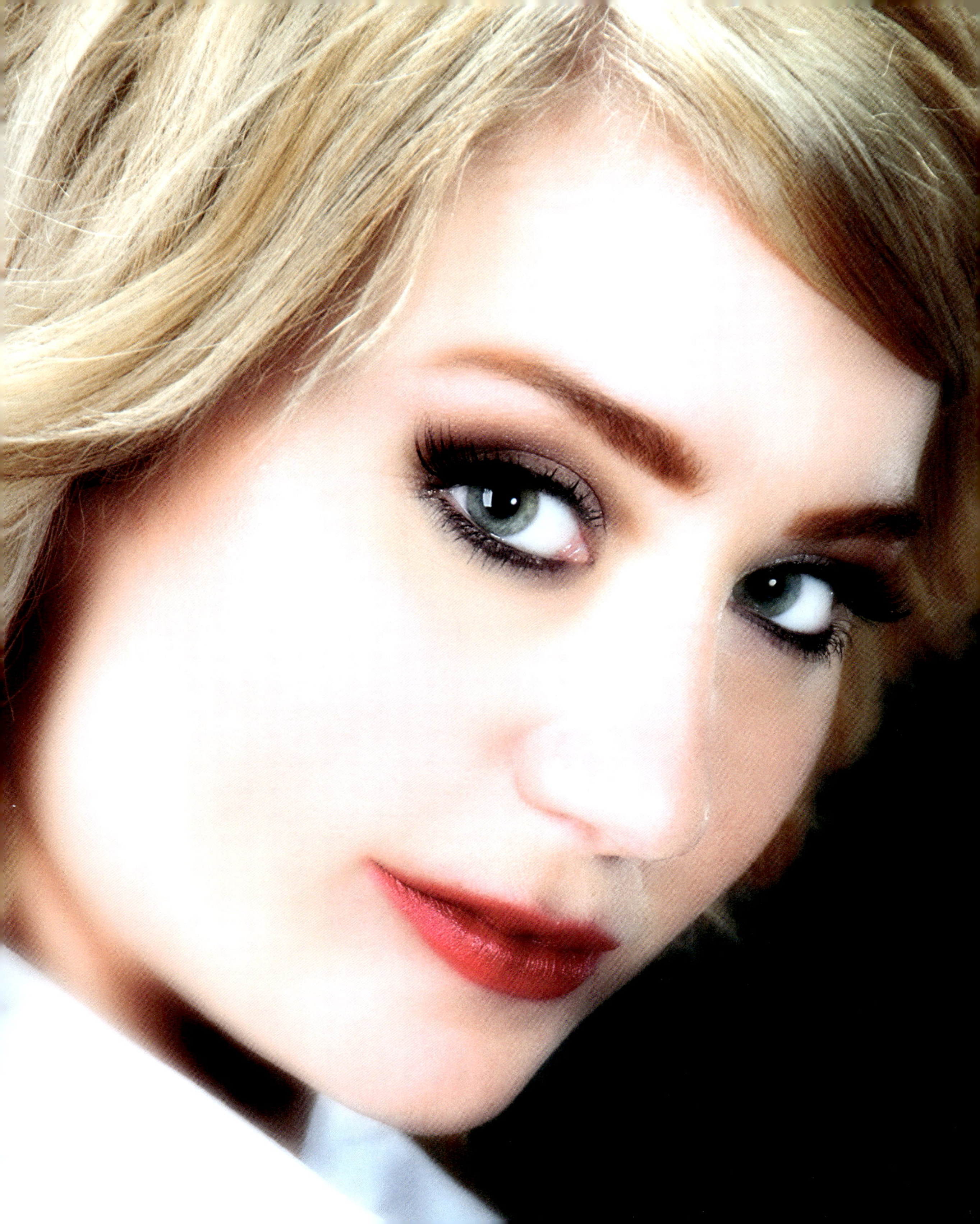

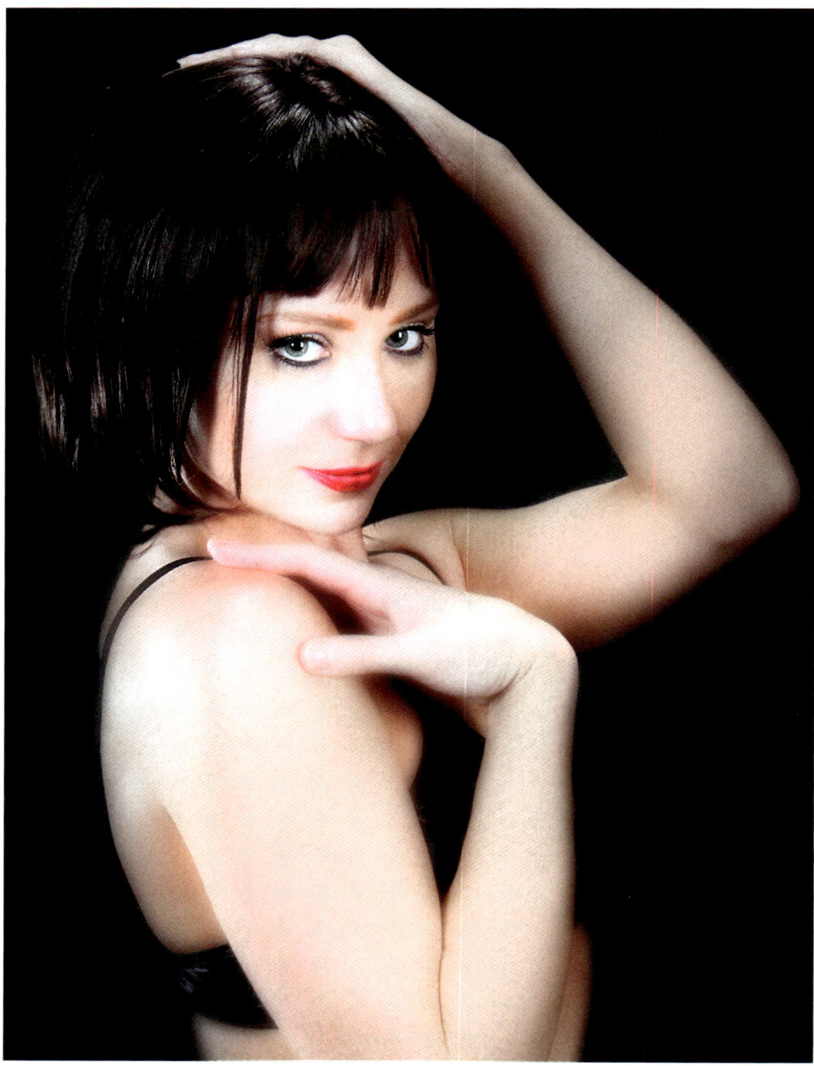

▲ ... After Shelby changed into a black wig and leather halter top, things began to get interesting. Her mood definitely got more edgy with the new styling. Notice how a wardrobe or prop switch can alter the entire gestalt of a portrait.

52mm 1/160 of a second at f/9 and ISO 200, hand held

▶ I then told Shelby to think of someone she both "loved and hated." It had been difficult before for her to demonstrate any strong emotions for the camera. This instruction was easy for her to follow. She immediately thought of someone who fit the bill. The portraits that resulted show considerable drama, conviction, and character.

35mm, 1/160 of a second at f/9 and ISO 200, hand held

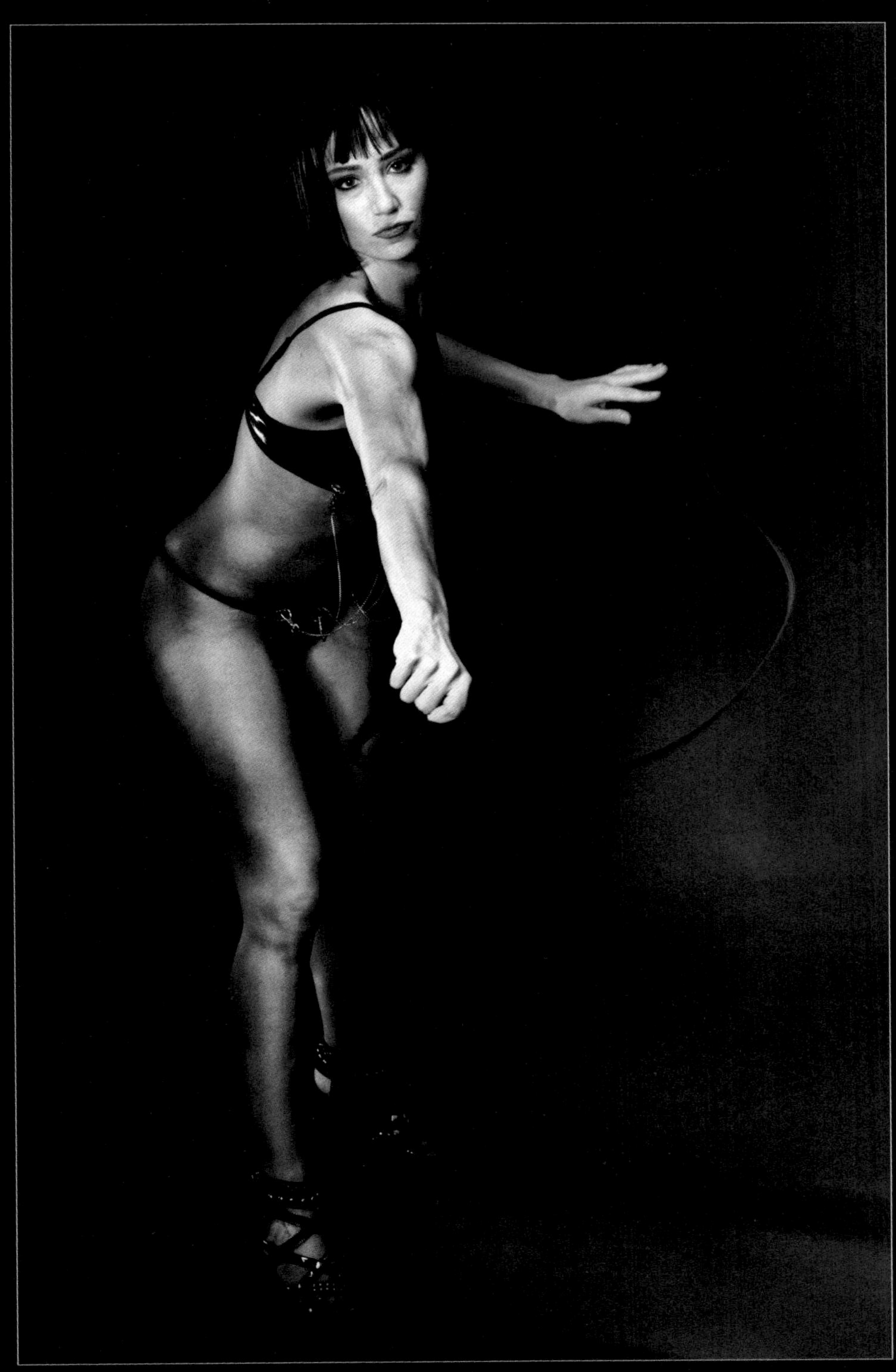

Understanding People

If you are going to make dynamic photos that reveal something about your portrait subjects, first you have to understand something about people. Not just people in general, but your specific subject—the person in front of you who is sitting for a portrait because she or he has paid you to have a photo made, because you want to take their photo, or for whatever reason.

Depending upon the circumstances, you may not know much about your subjects before you begin your portrait session. Of course, the opposite is possible—you may be photographing your family and have a lifetime of knowledge about them.

If you don't know much about your subject, and your time to learn about them is short, then you'll have to rely on your instinct, intuition, and general knowledge of people. You can also fall back on some general techniques for interacting with and learning about people:

- People want to be understood, and to relate to the photographer making their portrait.
- It's important to portrait subjects to have a voice in "their" photos.
- Portrait subjects will usually sense when you are intending to treat them with respect.
- It usually helps to get your subjects to relax in the early stages of a portrait

Playing the People Game

I am always curious about the people around me, and I want to learn more about almost everyone I see even when I'm not photographing them. One way I hone my imaginative people skills is what I call the "people game."

In a public place—like a Starbucks coffee shop—I wait until I find someone interesting looking. I then tell myself their story—where they are from, what they do for a living, what kind of relationship they are in.

Even doing this much of the people game will help you hone your understanding of people over time. But to really get something from the exercise, you should start a conversation and see how close or far off your conjectures are.

▶ This is a portrait of Molly, a beautiful college student who had taken up modeling on the side because she wrecked her car. She was hoping to raise some money to help pay for a replacement. I photographed Molly in a studio often used by camera clubs to photograph models.

The more I talked to Molly, the more I realized that she was nervous in front of the camera. With this understanding, I helped her to relax by talking about family and home. I also understood that she really *wanted* to model—and that the whole story about the wrecked car was an excuse designed to let her overcome her own inhibitions.

When she (literally) let her hair down, we were able to collaborate on a serene, glamorous, and seductive portrait.

200mm, 1/160 of a second at f/8 and ISO 100, hand held

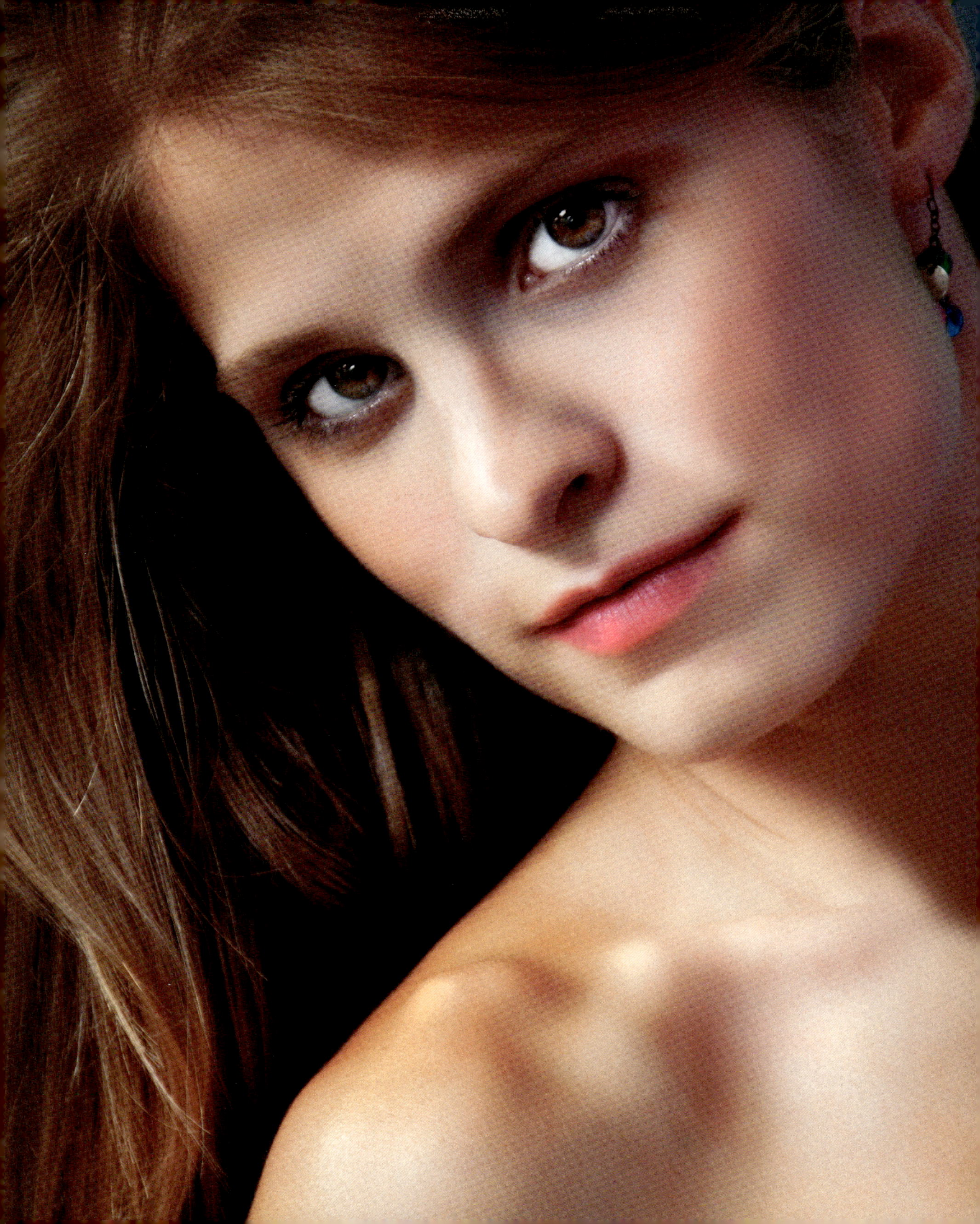

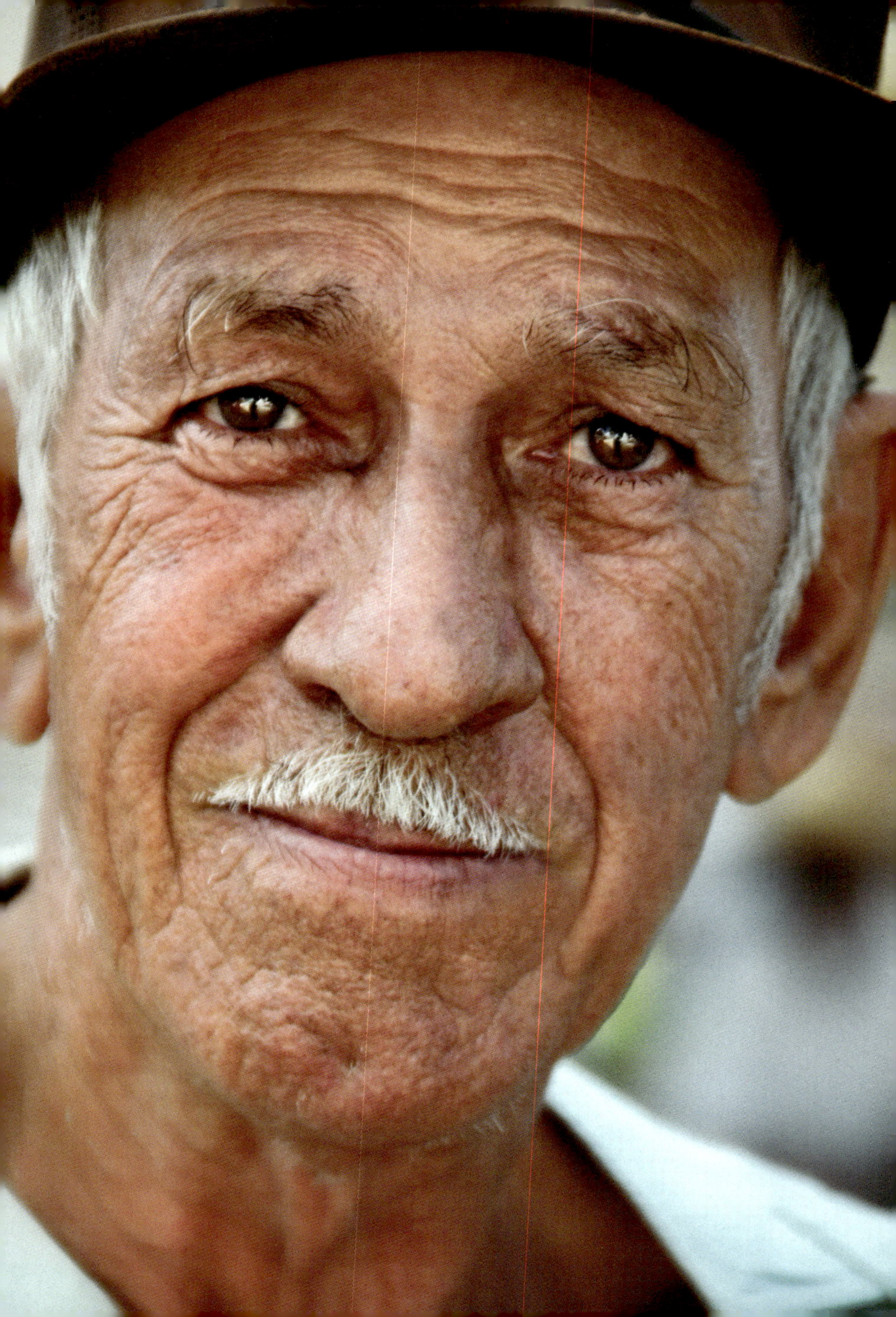

session. Don't take the first few photos in a session too seriously. A technique that helps subjects to relax is to ask them to run or jump. Music that your subject enjoys will also help them relax.

- People like to talk about themselves. It's the rare portrait subject that won't tell you his or her life story if you ask.

To be a good portrait photographer it certainly helps to be curious about people. Start your session by indulging your curiosity.

Begin by asking innocuous questions. Most people will talk about where they are from, what they do for a living, and about their family.

You can move on to more provocative questions gradually. I tend to phrase these as finding out about someone's "loves" and "hates." But be careful here! If you think you've stepped over an unspoken line, you probably have. If you quickly back off, no harm will be done. But be sensitive to the inherent vulnerability in sitting for a portrait, the emotional needs of your portrait subjects, and never press intimate conversations too far.

Every portrait session varies, and everyone who comes in front of your camera will be unique. But here are a few of the common personality profiles you are likely to run into, the specific problem they present to quality portraiture, and some suggestions for overcoming the problem.

- ***Easy and casual:*** Often encountered in street photography situations, these subjects are fine with being photographed, but don't want to reveal much of themselves. You'll get better results if you take the time to start a substantive conversation with these subjects.
- ***Been there, done that:*** People who have been photographed a great deal—especially professional models—tend to take the portraiture process for granted and go on auto-pilot with "moves" they think look good to the camera. The key here is to slow things down. Tell the subject you are looking for a different viewpoint, one that hasn't been photographed before.
- ***Terminally shy:*** Many accomplished people are surprisingly shy in front of the camera. With these people you have to recognize that they are shy and work to gain their trust. A good approach is to show the photos you are making as you go along, and to engage them in the process of figuring out how to incrementally improve results.

◀ I was wandering around an outdoor market in Cienfuegos, a Cuban provincial capital. As is almost always the case in Cuba, a band was performing live music. This gentleman struck up a conversation with me. We talked about our kids, and he told me about his family in the United States and how much he missed seeing some of his family members. Then I asked to take his photo.

Of course, I don't really know the subject of this portrait. But I think having spent the time talking to him helped me to make a casual photo that shows some of the inner nature of the man. This is a better portrait than it would have been if I had just shot it without talking to the subject.

200mm, 1/160 of a second at f/6.3 and ISO 200, hand held

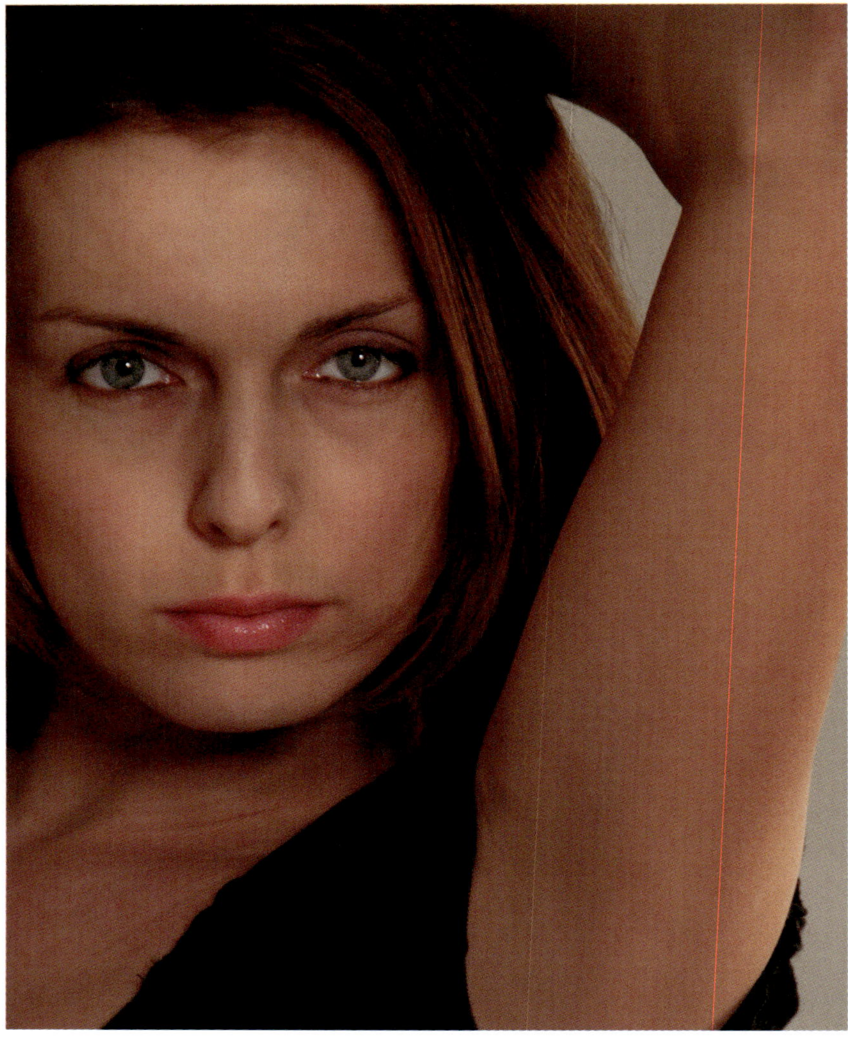

▲ The full measure of the character shown in this portrait comes from the direct and penetrating stare in the model's eyes. In this photo, the forcefulness of the direct gaze is somewhat balanced by the unusual off-center composition showing more of the model than is typical in a head shot. By itself, the face alone here would seem too fierce—it takes contextualizing the gaze within the angle of the model's bent arm to create a balanced portrait.

200mm, 1/125 of a second at f/7.1 and ISO 100, hand held

▶ I began this book by a reference to eyes as windows into someone's soul (page 8). It's an expectation that to get to know someone you must look into their eyes. This studio portrait of Christianna runs counter to this notion. In some cases, when the subject looks down—instead of directly at the camera—it can give the photo a sensitive and poetic feeling, providing a great deal of emotional information about the subject.

200mm, 1/200 of a second at f/6.3 and ISO 100, hand held

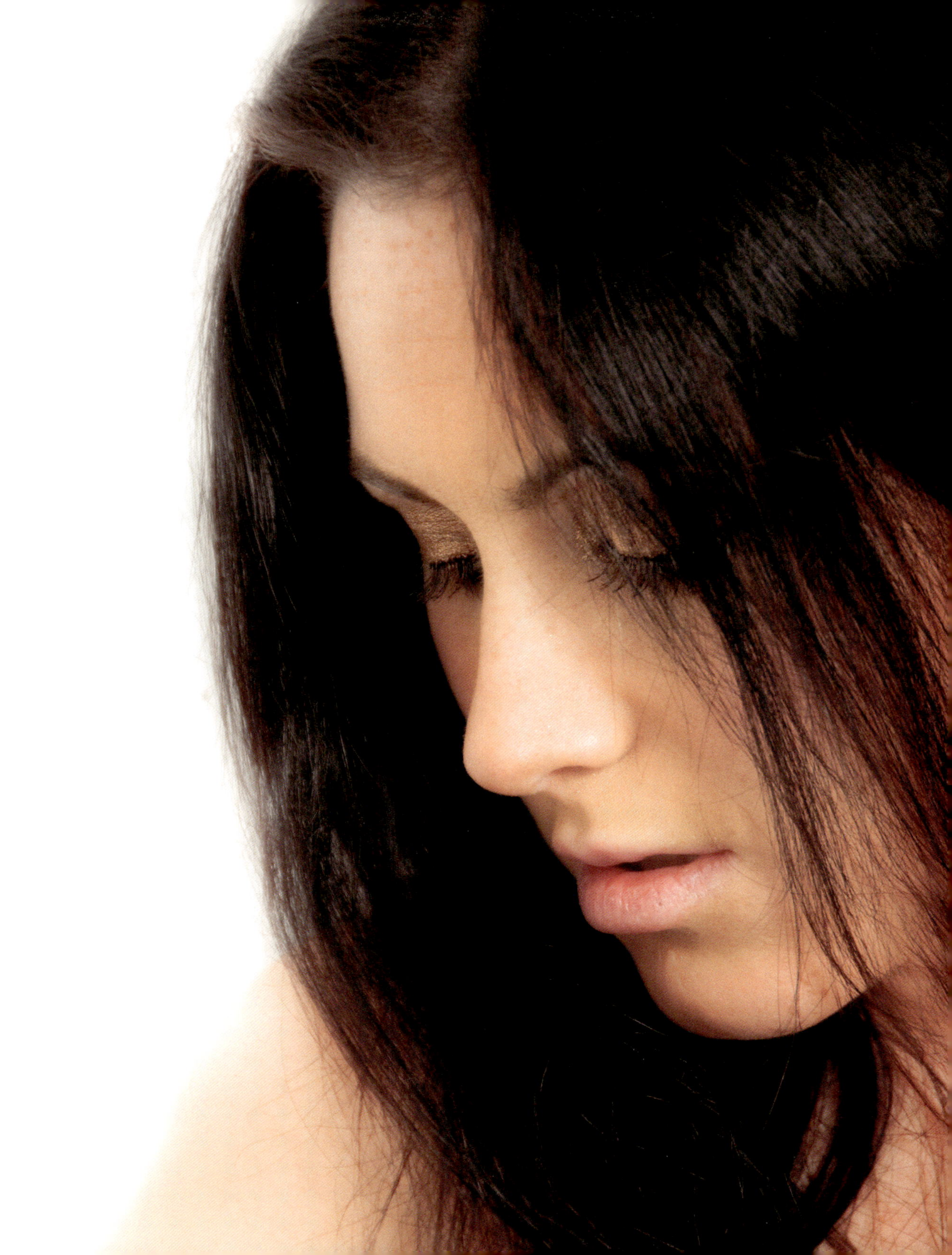

Character is Destiny

To what extent are our futures pre-determined by our character? How much free will do we have in our destiny? These are deep questions about which well-intentioned people can easily disagree. Your attitude towards character and destiny is likely to be shaped by your ethical, moral, and religious outlook—and the society you are part of.

Whatever your beliefs in this area, there's no doubt that character is extremely important—and difficult to capture in a portrait. But, of course, portrait photographers must do their best to render as much of their subject's character as they understand.

By a certain age, it is said, one gets the face one deserves—and there is some truth in this cliché.

Of course, appearance is important—and works in both directions. If someone looks like an authority figure, is it because they are one? Or does looking a certain way help one become what one looks like?

Portrait photographers should be aware that young children rarely show the full measure of their characters in their faces. However, as kids grow, they start to show character. Along with character comes the ability to dissemble and the desire to be cool. You can see the influence of society on older kids—in their faces and body posture as well as the branded clothing they wear.

Fully grown adults and older individuals do often wear their characters "on their face"—although they may not always be happy when this is pointed out to them.

A good portrait photograph, even if made under casual conditions, can show a great deal about the character someone has become—or the possible characters that a younger person may grow into.

At the same time, effective portraits often exaggerate the characteristics shown in the physiognomy that is being captured. If you think your subject is glamorous, and wants to be portrayed as having glamour, then by all means exaggerate this trait. If authority is central to the person you are photographing, then by all means convey this in your photo.

Don't underestimate the ability of propping (see page 96), posing (page 110), and lighting (starting on page 140) to convey information about character. The truth is, people who look at photos pick up on the visual cues you provide. A good part of the art of portraiture is aligning these visual cues with what you want to say about the character of the person you are photographing.

▶ Maria runs a small tourist concession in a Cuban village. I asked for her permission to photograph her because I felt that the lines on her face made a map of her life. You don't need to know the specifics to understand that hers has been a hard life with much sorrow and pain—and that Maria is a survivor.

170mm, 1/40 of a second at f/5.6 and ISO 200, hand held

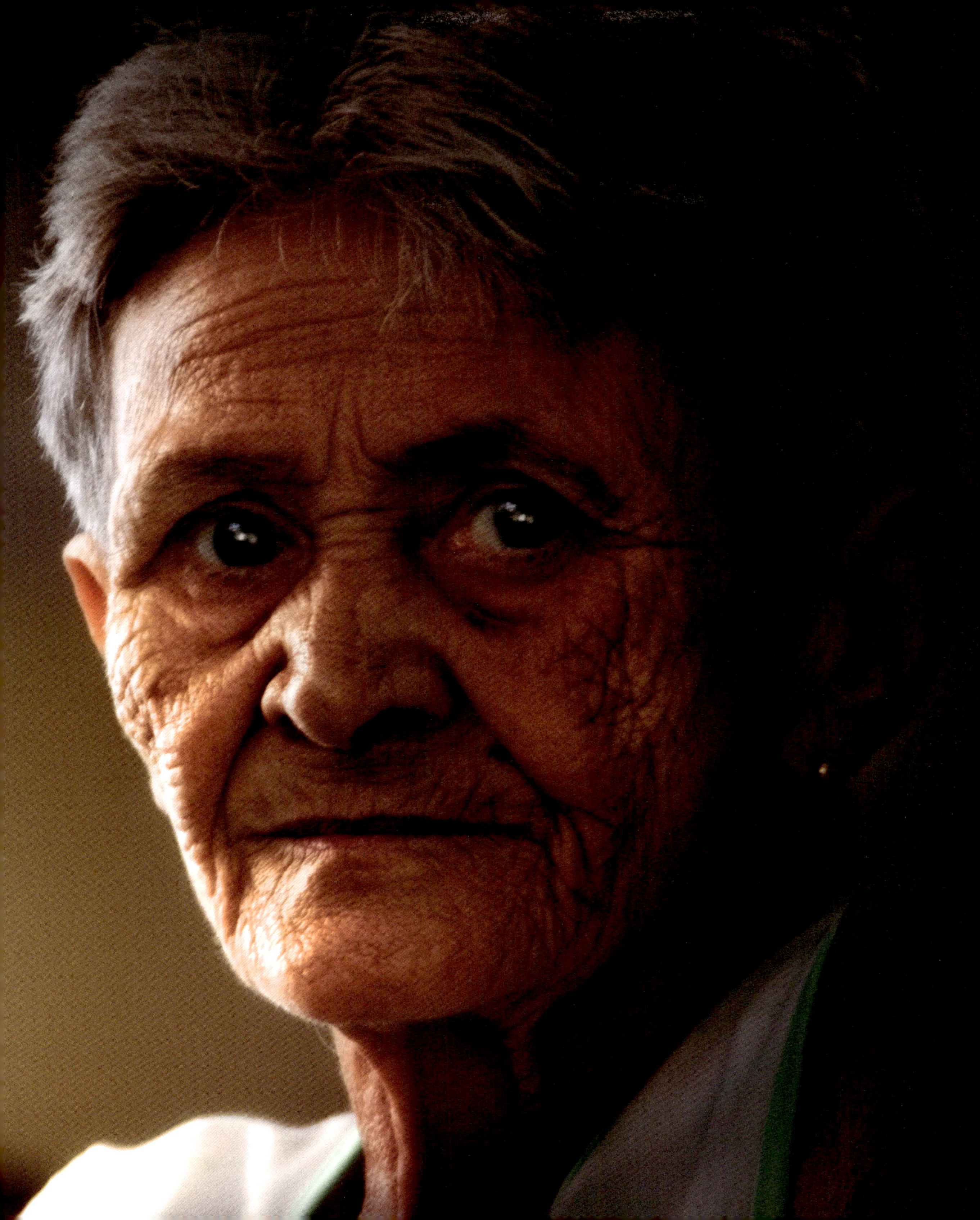

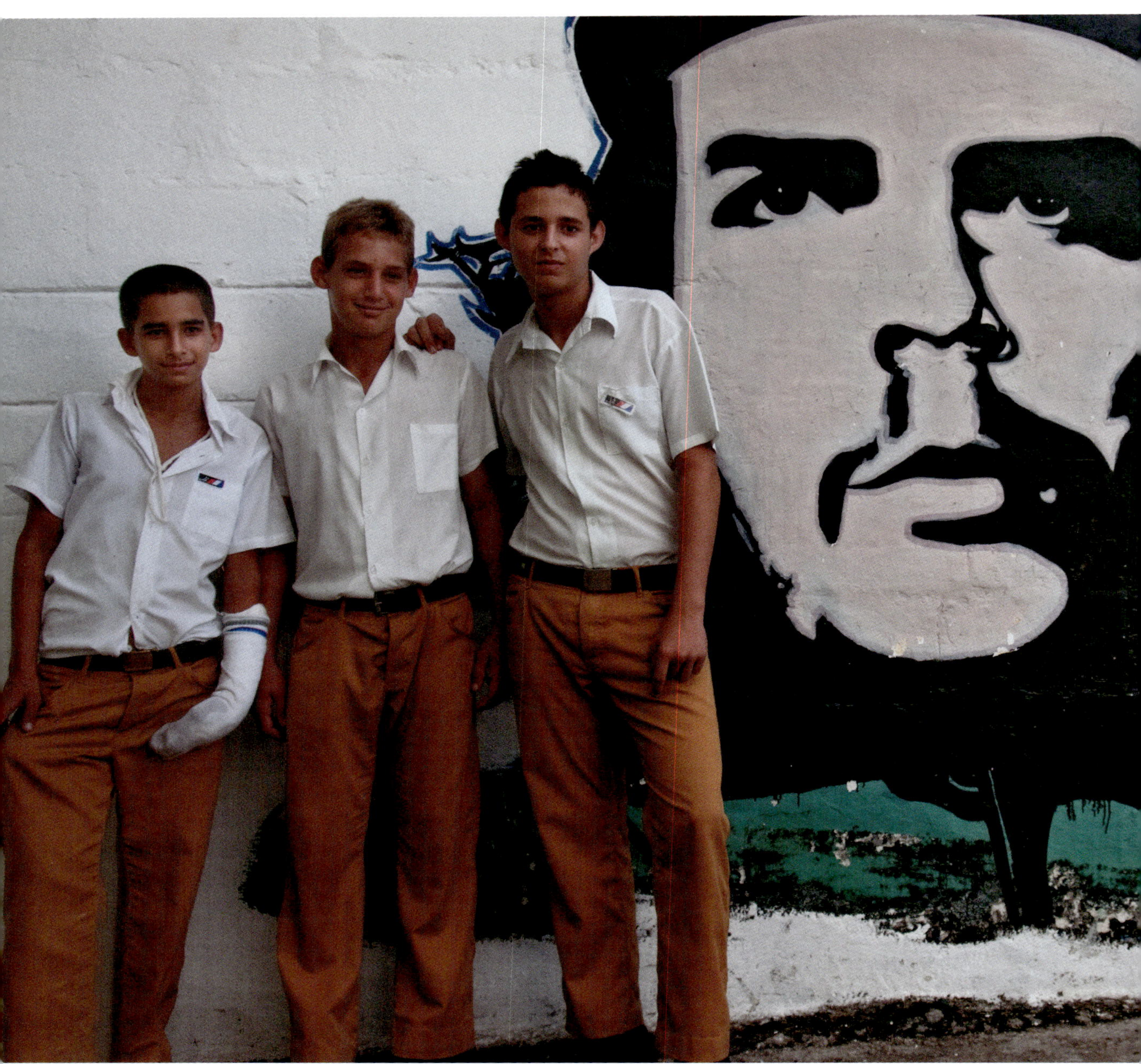

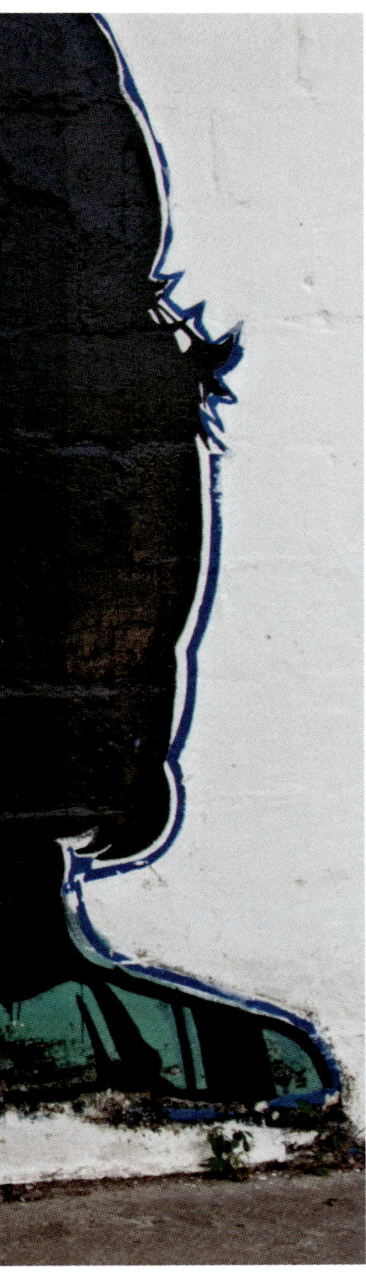

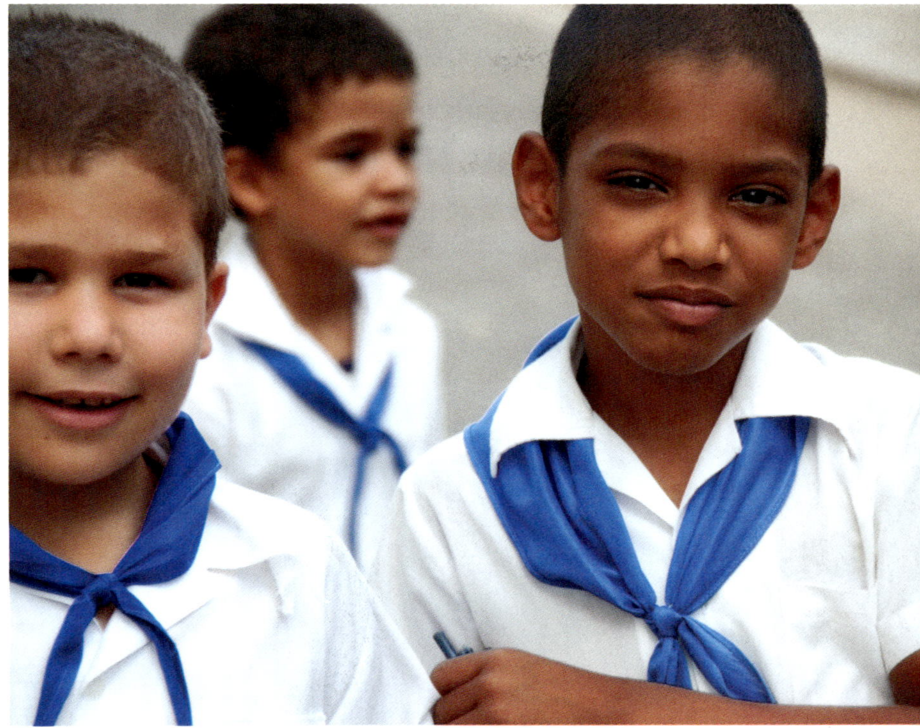

▲ Elementary students the world over haven't yet learned to guard themselves. The Cuban boy on the right is gazing directly at the camera with undisguised interest. It's easy to read the open friendliness of his disposition.

120mm, 1/160 of a second at f/6.3 and ISO 200, hand held

◀ I photographed these nonchalant Cuban middle schoolers beneath an iconic mural of Che Guevara. They are obviously interested in the camera and photographer, but unwilling to make a statement to that effect by staring directly at me. It's important to these boys to be casual. They are wearing the required school uniform, slouched together in youthful solidarity. But one boy guards the cast of his broken arm with a sock.

One wonders how the omnipresent gaze of Che, eyes slightly raised and focused on the distant horizon, has molded these kids. Che seems to look at long range, idealistic goals while the boys in this casual portrait are grounded, and care most about getting on day by day.

28mm, 1/200 of a second at f/7.1 and ISO 200, hand held

Capturing Emotion

Emotion exists apart from character. Evil villains in a melodrama can experience great joy and happiness—perhaps when they've successfully blown up the train that ran over the heroine tied to the tracks. Even brave and chivalrous romantic heroes often wallow in the depths of emotional despair for so long that one gets disgusted with them.

My point is that you can be a paragon of all virtues and still experience "bad" feelings, just as you can be a nasty piece of work and find occasional happiness and emotional fulfillment.

From the photographer's viewpoint, it is important to understand that emotion can clearly be differentiated from character. Character is innate, or perhaps built up over a lifetime of experience. Emotion is fleeting and fickle—it doesn't take much to make emotion "turn on a dime."

"Fleeting" and "fickle" are the watchwords here. There's really not too much a portrait photographer can do about character other than observe and capture it. However, emotions can be manipulated. Give some people a kitten or baby to stroke and they'll be happy. It's almost always possible to make someone angry by speaking to them in a bossy, superior, and irritating way. But these superficial emotions come and go quickly. They aren't as meaningful as the underlying character. To capture emotions as opposed to character you better be ready to move quickly:

- Be prepared to provide propping as necessary to facilitate positive emotions. I don't suggest that you necessarily keep kittens or babies in your studio. But do provide props that tend to make people feel good about themselves—for example, elegant books and comfortable chairs.
- Use verbal manipulation—such as flattery—to get the emotions you'd like to capture. To use this technique effectively, you have to be careful and use all your understanding of people. There's a fine line to tread between being overly manipulative on one side, and not directive or interactive enough on the other.
- Act quickly and be ready to photograph because the play of emotions on a face or body can move swiftly and soon be replaced by a competing emotion.

It's often overlooked that human emotion can be shown using details. A close-up view of hands, or feet, or some specific part of an interaction can yield a great deal of emotional payoff—sometimes more than a full view of the scene.

▶ To take advantage of the radiant expression on the baby's face as she looked at her mother, I needed to be able to shoot quickly in dappled low-light conditions. If I had hesitated, I would have lost this never-to-be-repeated expression and moment.

I boosted my ISO to 800 and proceeded to swiftly capture this intensely happy moment.

32mm, 1/80 of a second at f/5.6 and ISO 800, hand held

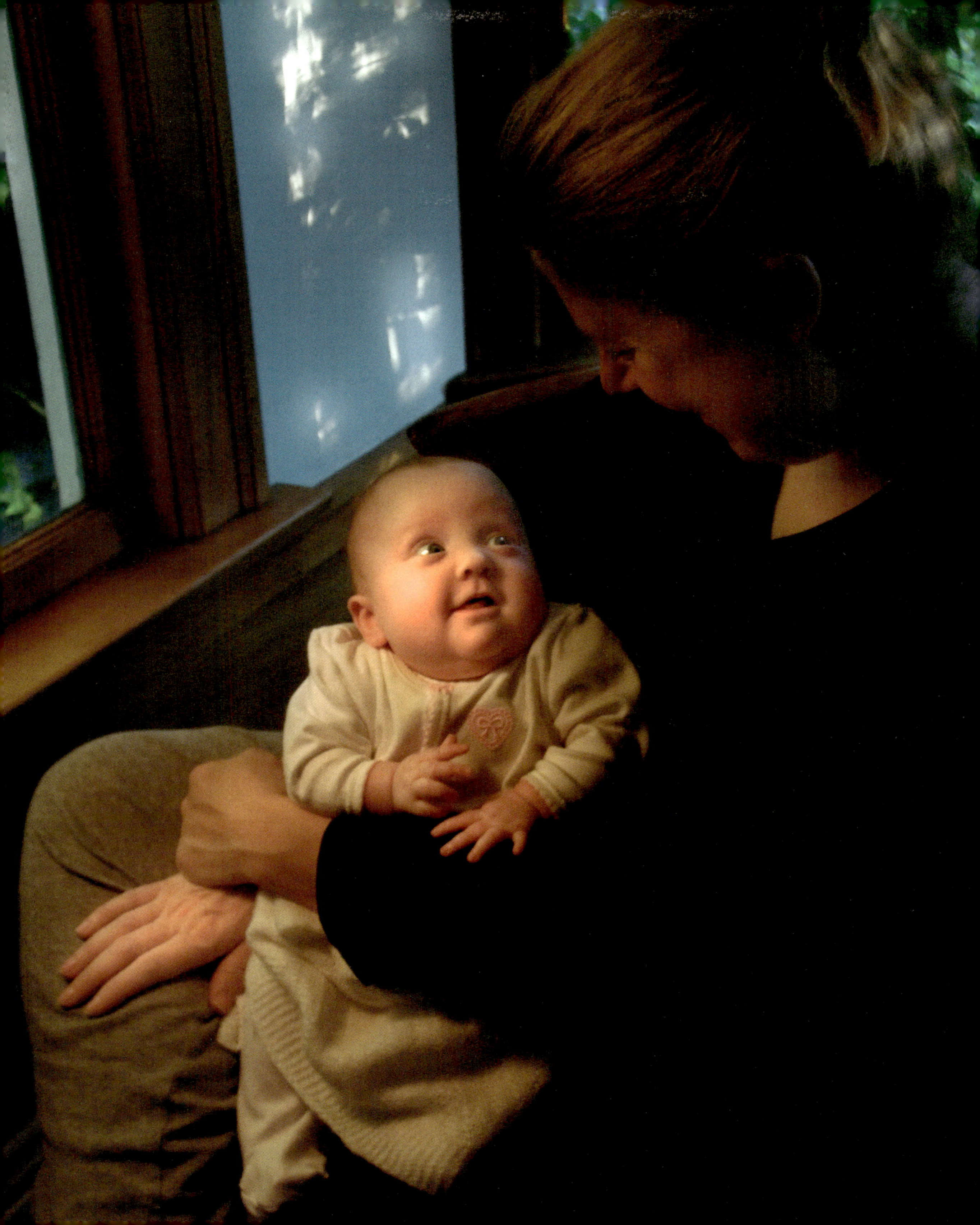

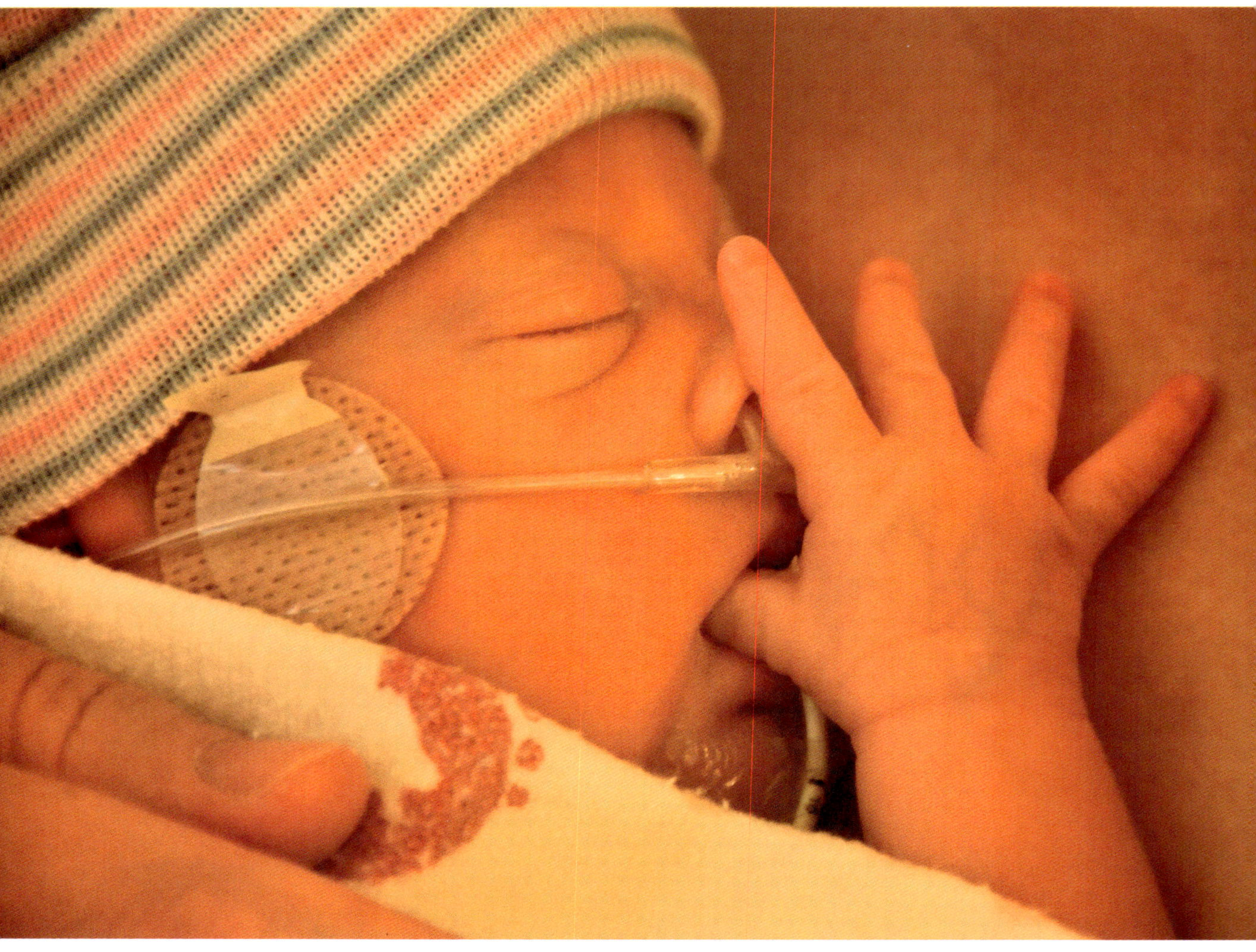

▲ Everyone can relate to a baby sucking its thumb; it is happiness in the moment. This photo shows a baby in the NICU (Newborn Intensive Care Unit) sucking on her thumb—an ordinary, everyday moment in a somewhat extraordinary environment.

200mm 1/15 of a second at f/5.6 and ISO 2500, hand held

▶ It's common to think that a portrait must include someone's face. In fact, you can learn a great deal from photographs of hands or feet—or even someone's shadow.

This portrait of hands shows my daughter Katie Rose holding her mom's far larger hand not that long after Katie's premature birth. By comparing the size of the two hands, a viewer can learn about the situation. In this case, the detail is as revealing as a broader portrait might be.

150mm 1/25 of a second at f/5.6 and ISO 2500, hand held

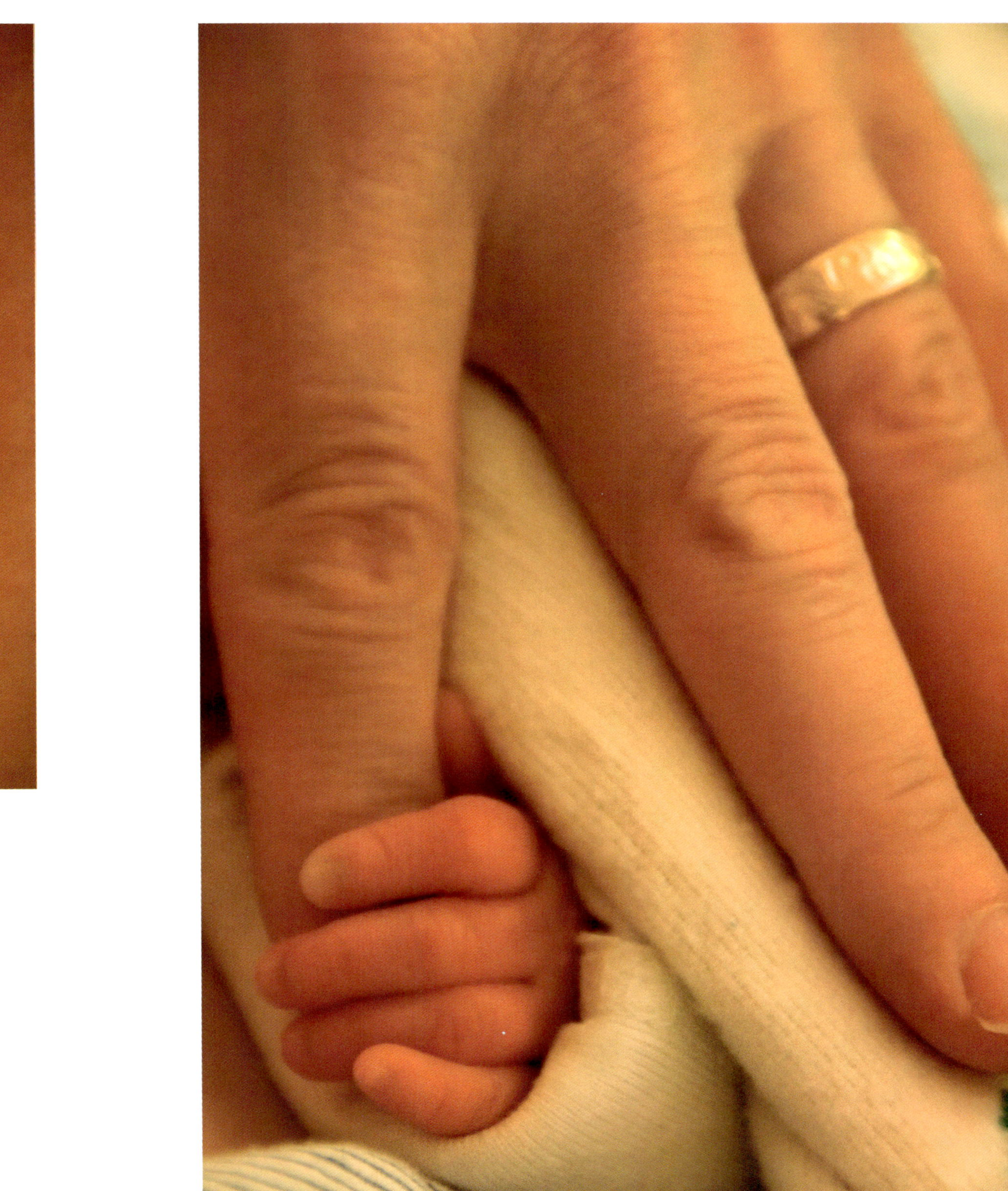

Telling the Truth About Someone

As you gain experience as a portrait photographer, you are likely to begin to size up subjects based on your understanding of people, your ability to read character, and your readiness to adjust for the short term impact of emotional states. So what happens when the truth about someone is mixed, or even downright ugly? Do you have a duty—or desire—to tell the truth about someone?

These are difficult questions, particularly when money is thrown into the mix. Generally, a photographer who is hired wants to give the client what they want, with the familiar motto, "The client is always right."

What happens when the subject of a portrait has an unrealistic idea of what they look like?

This is a common situation because many people have no idea what they really look like. It's quite common to look into the mirror and see someone very different from the person seen by the rest of the world.

Portrait subjects who have an unrealistic impression of how they look are a fact of life. You can often help guide these people into a more realistic visual self-appraisal.

In these days of Photoshop, it is possible to "fix" many flaws in a form of virtual, digital plastic surgery. How much of this should you do? There are no hard and fast answers, and the right calls depend upon the context of the photograph (see page 206 for more on this topic).

If you've been hired to help a client appear in a certain way, and knowingly accepted the engagement despite the challenges, then it is your job to fulfill your commitment and satisfy your client.

On the other hand, documentary or journalistic photography bears no such strictures—and in fact is required to tell the truth.

Many portrait photography sessions lie between these two extremes. Your job is to be aware of the issues, deal with them with integrity, and try to place your portrait on the truth-to-cosmetic-surgery spectrum with tact, dignity, and a sense of responsibility.

▶ The gentleman shown in this photo is a licensed photo model who poses for tourists on the streets of Old Havana, Cuba. You can see from the travel guide resting to the left of the model that he has been featured on the cover of at least one book. The question is, why? Surely, there is no sense that this character is attractive or glamorous.

The appeal here is apparent authenticity. Tourists pay to photograph this fellow, and his visage appears on travel guide books, because he exudes the nitty-gritty of real life in Cuba. You take a picture of him because you want to bring home a real slice of Cuban life.

When I made this portrait, I was careful to include the previous publication credit within the frame of the photo—because a large part of the appeal of this image is the story that this subject *has* in fact been in published photos.

28mm, 1/60 of a second at f/4 and ISO 100, hand held

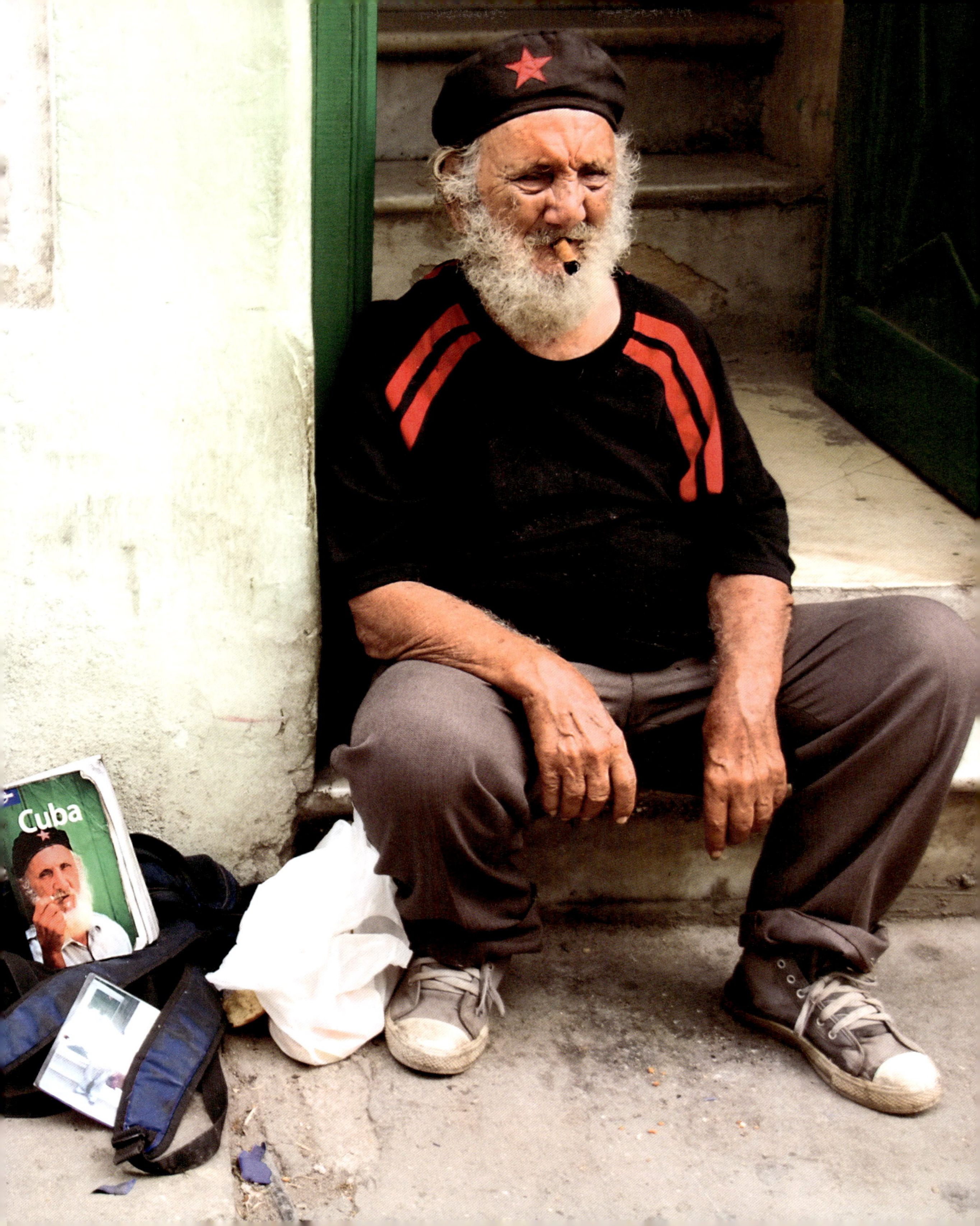
Cuba

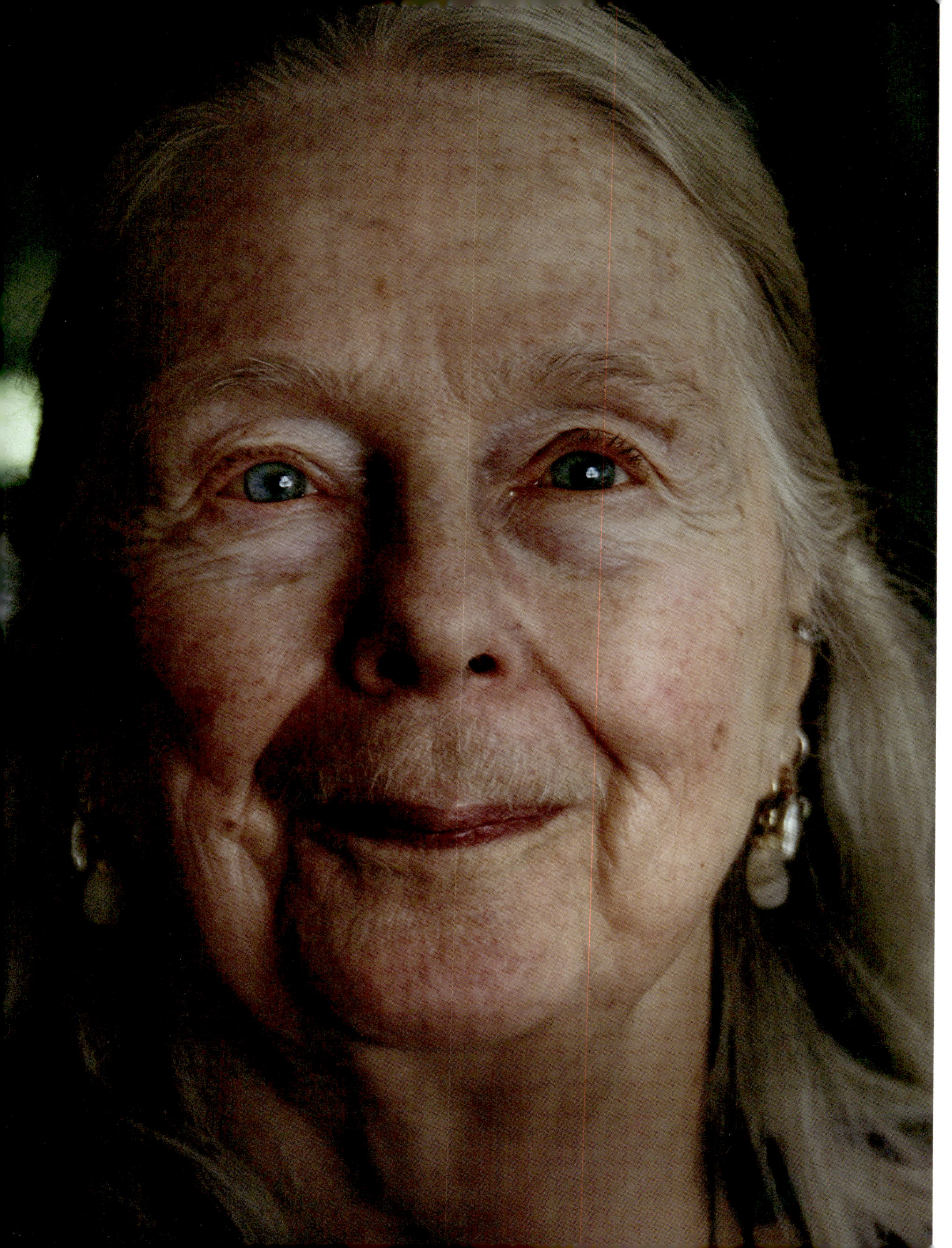

▶ The movie *Avatar* had just come out, and my client told me she wanted to look like one of the denizens of the planet Pandora from the movie. Despite extensive make-up in the studio, this was not going to happen in the normal course of photography. So I "went creative" in Photoshop, and added the effect you see here using a LAB color inversion. While this "look" is not exactly like one of the Na'vi—the inhabitants of Pandora in the movie—it was sufficiently exotic to please the subject of the portrait.

200mm, 1/160 of a second at f/6.3 and ISO 100, hand held, LAB inversion in Photoshop

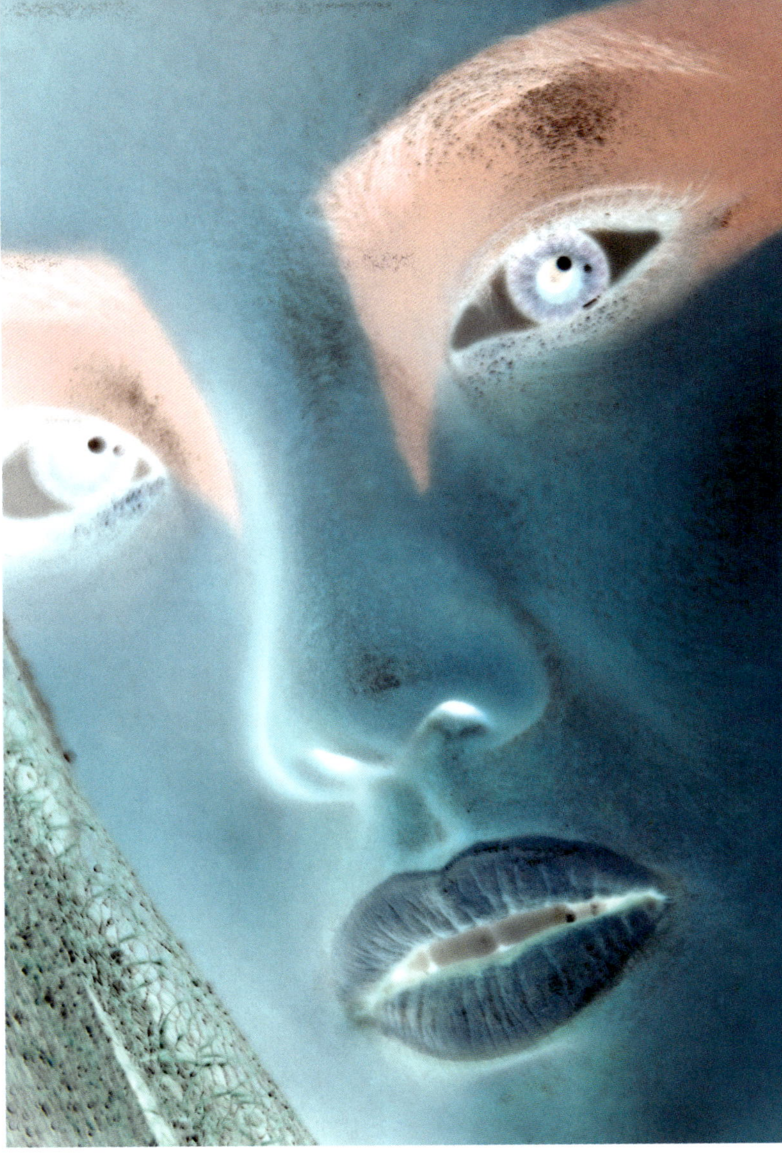

◀ This is a casual portrait of Virginia Davis, taken shortly after her successful eye surgery for cataracts. Virginia is a fiber artist, weaver, and anthropologist with a special interest in the indigenous crafts of Central America, Mexico, and Japan. She also happens to be my mother.

I believe that Virginia's intelligence, and many of the facets of her distinguished and varied career come through in this portrait. However, it must be noted that she doesn't like this portrait and doesn't think it shows her as she really is.

In fact, many times when you create a portrait that you believe tells the truth about your subject, your subject may not consider the photo flattering.

80mm, 1/80 of a second at f/5.0 and ISO 400, hand held

Vanity and Narcissism

"Vanity of vanities, all is vanity," expounds King Solomon in the Bible. Vanity means an unrealistic sense of one's own worth and attractiveness, along with an unhealthy dose of narcissism—or self involvement.

Often there's no practical reason for someone to want or need a portrait. So commissioning a portrait, or sitting for a portrait, is at least in part intrinsically an act of vanity. Oddly enough, this very narcissism can stand in the way of creating a compelling portrait—which may on the surface be what the subject desires, or thinks she desires. This happens because the most compelling portraits do to some degree tell the truth. A subject that is too influenced by vanity may interrupt the creative process—and derail images that have the power of truth.

Dealing with the interference that vanity and narcissism can bring to the portrait photography table requires a multi-prong approach on the part of the photographer. Key points include:

- Be a perfectionist. Try to check details like make-up, hair position, and how clothing fits. If the portrait subject sees that you really care about these things, he or she may be better able to keep narcissistic impulses somewhat in check.
- Figure out your line, and hold firmly to it. You need to know how much truth your photo will reveal, and how much it is to be a staged concoction. When you are clear about where your portrait falls on this spectrum, you will know how to proceed.
- Be prepared to use misdirection and benign manipulation to achieve your goals. Using props that allow your subject to playact will often help you achieve superior results because the subject is focused on playing—and not so much on how they look.

Perhaps the best approach to vanity in a subject is to be calm about it. After all, a portrait session is at least to some degree—and superficially—the subject's show. I like to joke with my subjects that "film is cheap"—of course I don't shoot film, and there's very little cost to making digital exposures. So I go ahead and indulge my subjects and take the photos they want, all the time knowing that in the end I will find a way to make *my* photos. After all, in the end the photographer controls the show.

▶ A fisheye lens pointed an inch or two from someone's nose will usually generate a humorous and grotesque caricature. Depending upon their sense of humor, many people will not appreciate having their portrait taken in this way—although it can be a great icebreaker in many photo sessions.

Fortunately, my young daughter was in no position to object—resulting in the unusual and effective portrait you see here.

10.5mm digital fisheye, 1/250 of a second at f/8 and ISO 400, hand held

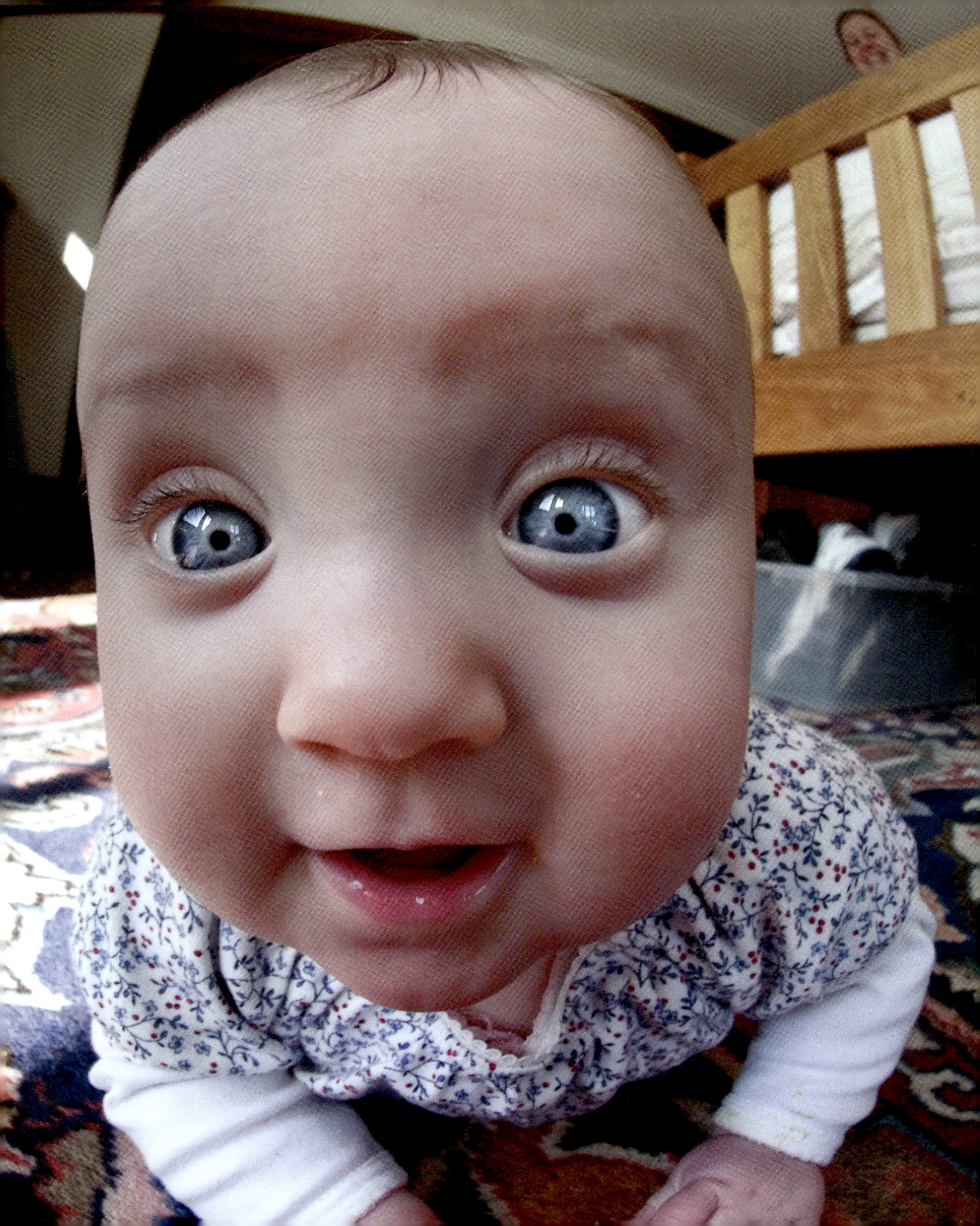

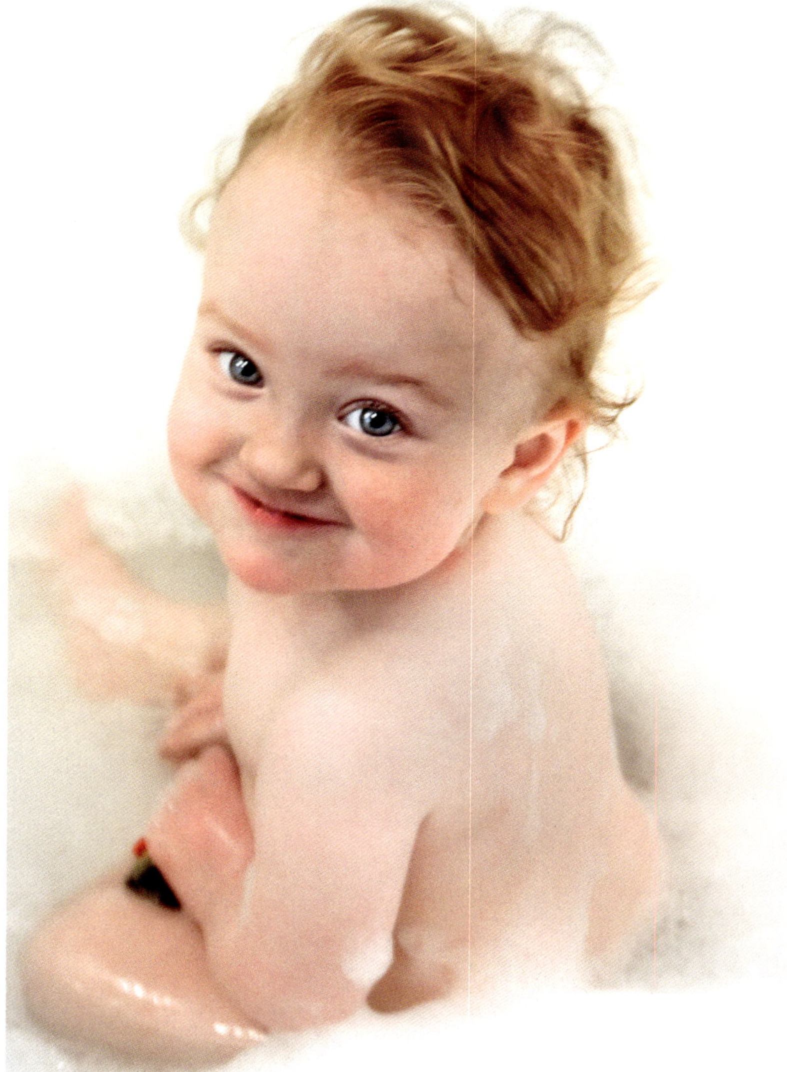

▲ Some kids learn surprisingly early in our society to be media savvy, and to pose for the camera. Even so, if a child trusts you they will mostly go about what they are doing without paying too much attention to a photographer. The catch is that they don't pay attention to instructions either—so you cannot expect a child to hold a pose. You must be ready and in position to make your portraits during the fleeting moments that an attractive photo is possible.

80mm, 1/25 of a second at f/5 and ISO 1000, hand held

► Certain kinds of props can free portrait subjects from worrying too much about how they look. This greater relaxation can lead to more natural and exciting photos. For example, this beautiful woman was somewhat shy and stiff in front of the camera. Once I handed her the mask to use as a prop, she started vamping it up, and her true inner loveliness was able to emerge.

90mm, 1/160 of a second at f/5.6 and ISO 100, hand held

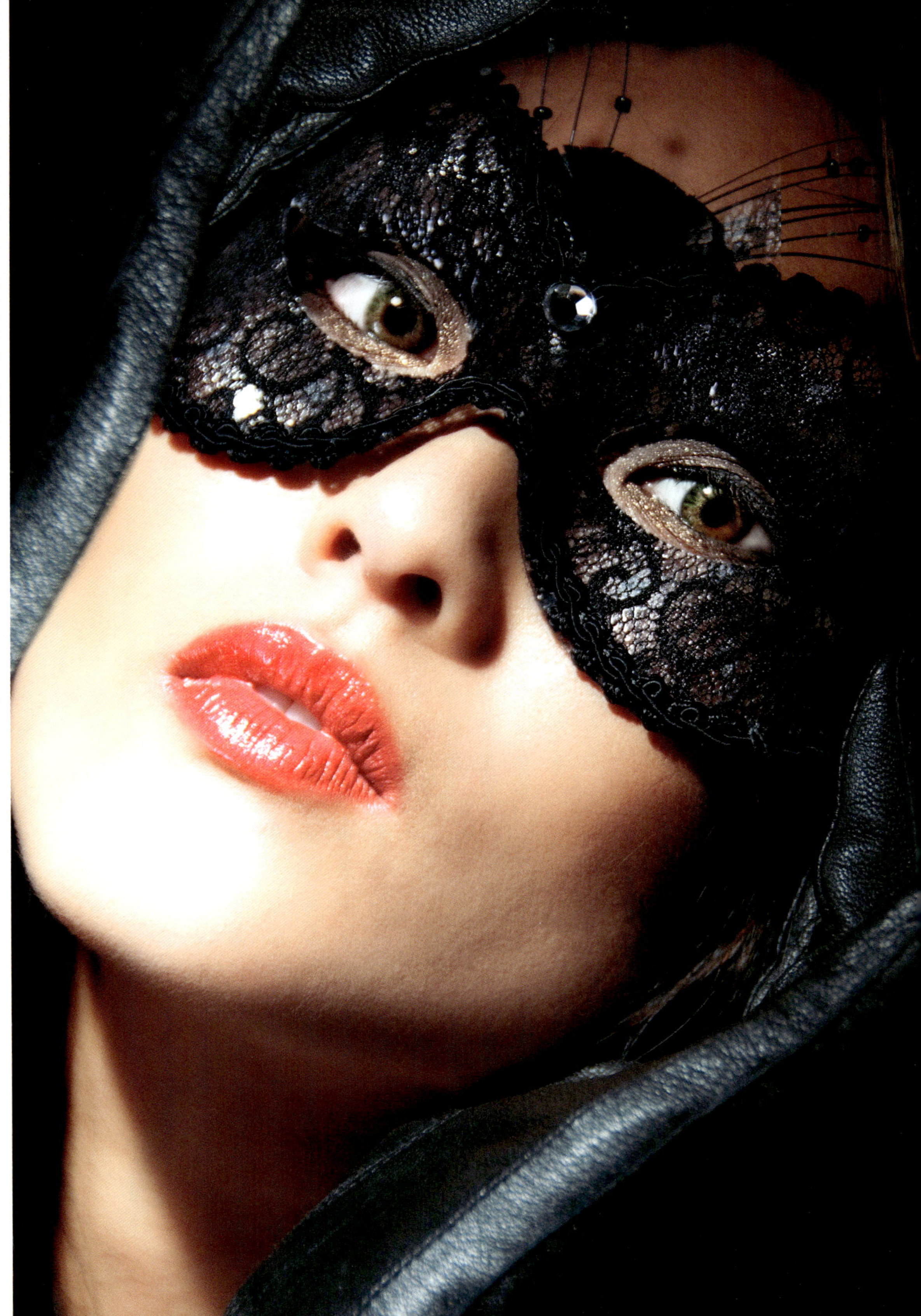

Artifice and Portraiture

At one end of the spectrum is a portrait of a glossy model in a magazine. She looks much too good to be true. In fact, she is too glamorous to be true—she's been primped, made-up, styled, and Photoshopped within an inch of her life.

At the other end of the spectrum, gritty, down-and-out drunks sit hunched over coal braziers in a shanty town, or lie inebriated in the gutter. These down on their luck characters are portrayed in an apparently straightforward way in high contrast black-and-white, exposing the misery in some part of the world.

The artifice in the first kind of portrait photography is very clear to all but the most naïve viewers. Most photographers will recognize considerable artificiality in the second kind of portraiture as well. The "real life" scenes may well have been posed—the compositions created to maximize emotional impact, and the contrast artificially enhanced to increase drama.

Here's the bottom line: portraiture and artifice go hand and hand. All good portraits involve some artifice—in the presentation of the subject, the lighting, and in the way the photograph was made.

If the artifice is too obvious, then the photograph doesn't fully succeed. I like to quote the poet Randall Jarrell, who wrote, "Art, being bartender, is never drunk."

It's almost impossible for a serious photographer to create a portrait without employing some artifice. As a photographer, once you've seen Paris, how are they going to keep you down on the farm? If you've been spending any time at all on photography as a hobby—let alone as a profession—you simply can't go back to the days of artlessly pressing the shutter without giving any thought to craft, content, or presentation.

Since it's a given that there will be artifice in portraiture, and it's also clear that too much artifice is unappealing, you must learn to walk the line between these extremes. Furthermore, there's no compromise that is right for all photographers. Some lean more to glamour, others to candids, and many fall in different postures along the wonderful spectrum of portrait photography.

▶ This cute studio portrait of a model is nicely propped with an umbrella and high-heel shoes. It was shot on a white seamless background. While it's a nice view of the model, who has a rather sweetly amused expression, it's also clear at a moment's glance that this is a highly stylized and artificial photo.

40mm, 1/160 of a second at f/9 and ISO 100, hand held

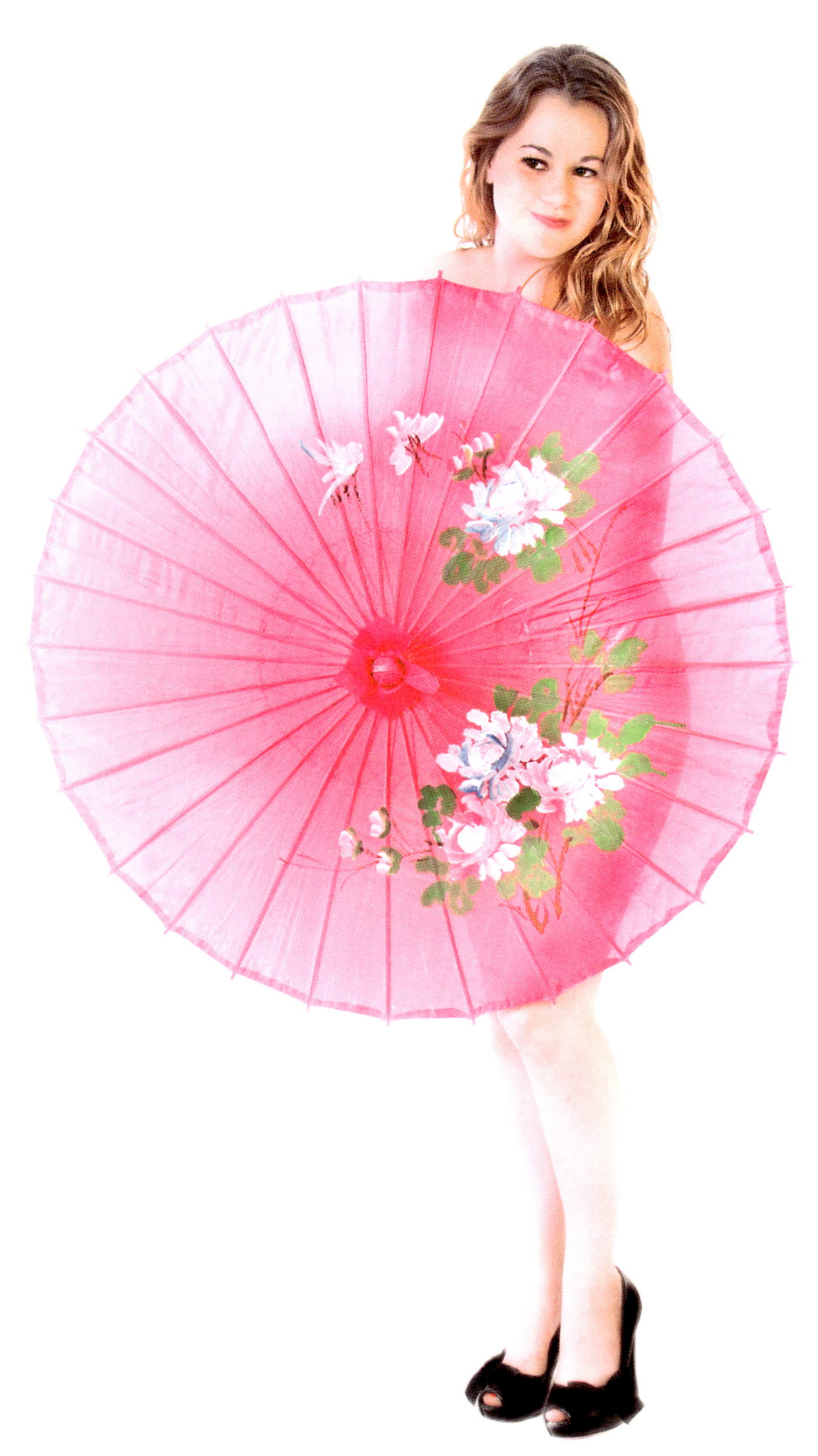

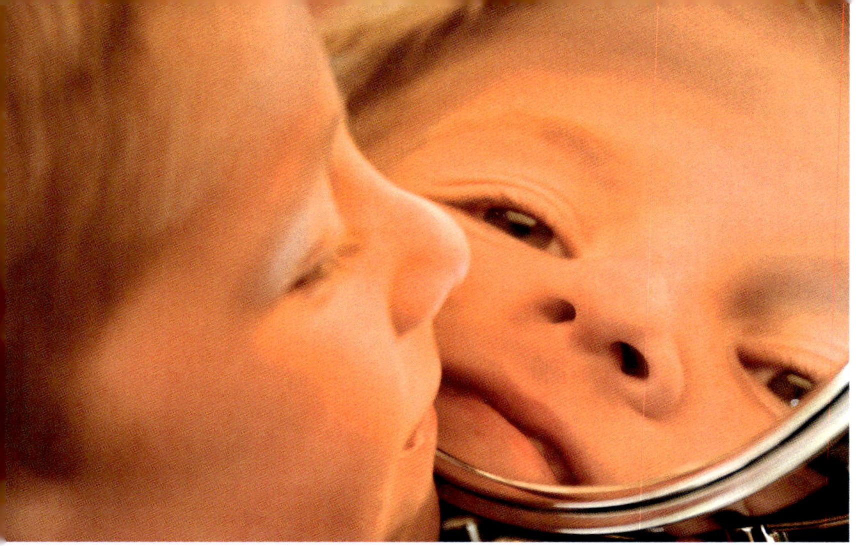

◀ Here, Nicky is shown looking in a mirror following his first haircut. While Nicky is studying himself, it's clear that he is using the mirror to track the photographer—in other words this child is highly aware of the situation that surrounds this portrait. Using the mirror as a prop that enables this child to feel more in control of the portrait session helps to make him feel relaxed—and provides a nice opportunity to create a composition using the reflection.

105mm macro, 1/40 of a second at f/5.3 and ISO 400, hand held

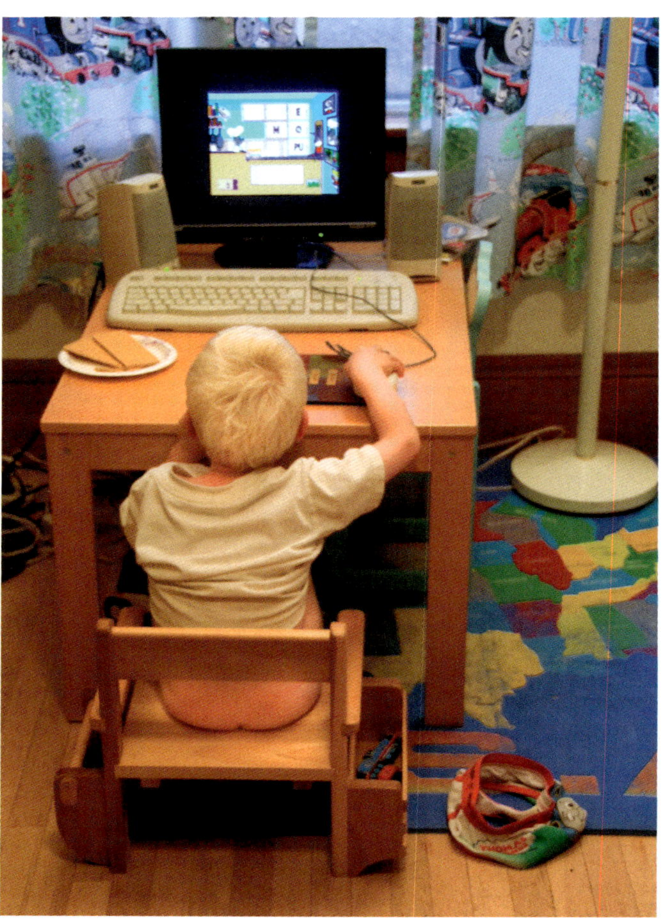

◀ With no self-consciousness whatsoever, Mathew is multitasking in this photo—leading to a very humorous casual portrait.

By the way, this photo was not staged. Mathew decided to multi-task in this way entirely on his own initiative.

42mm, 1/30 of a second at f/4.5 and ISO 1250, hand held

▶ Who is imitating whom? In this case, baby came first. The minute I saw the baby's tongue come out, I knew I had to ask her mom to do the same—and she was willing to oblige me. The result is a casual but humorous portrait of mother and child that feels authentic.

32mm, 1/50 of a second at f/4.2 and ISO 1250, hand held

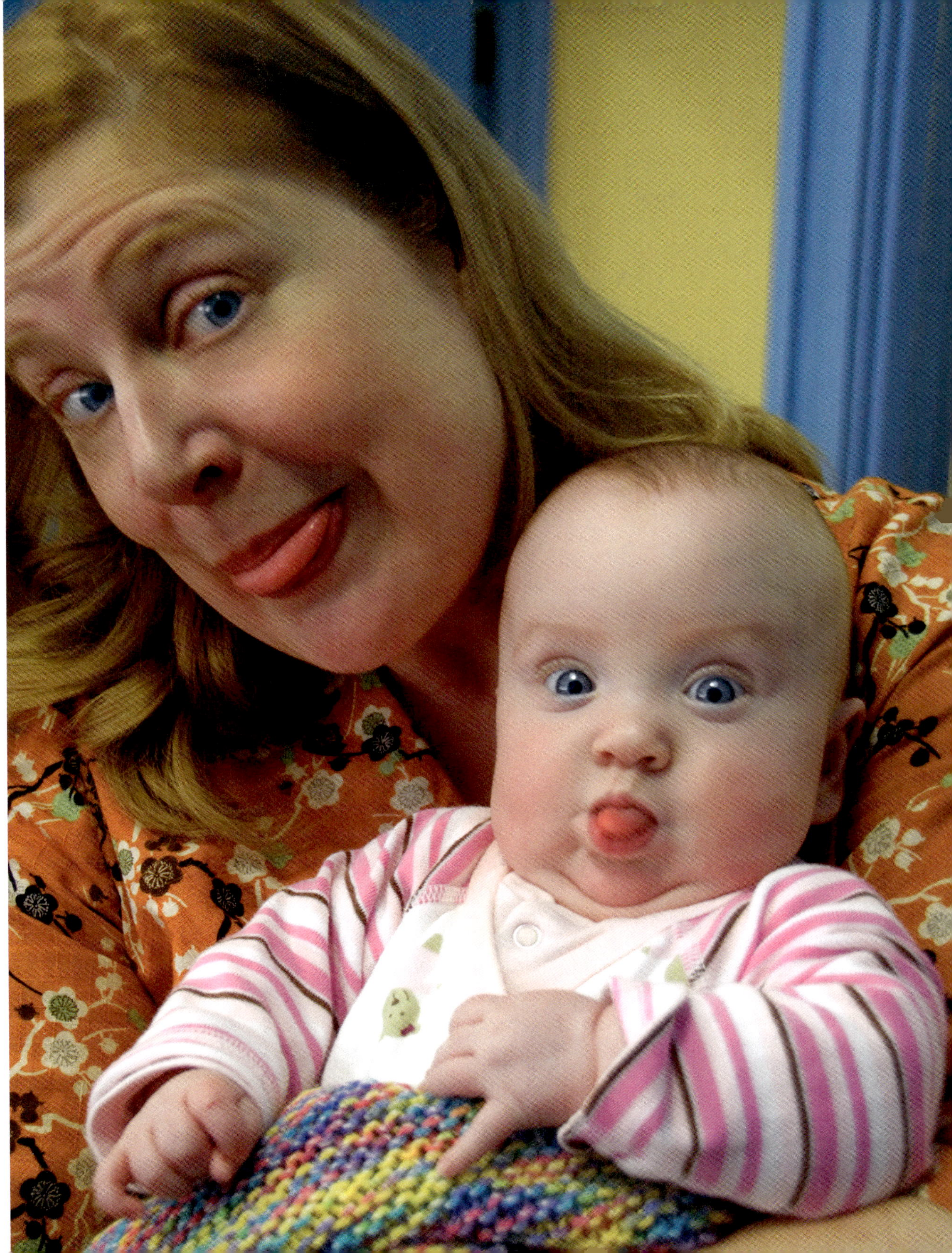

Creating a Self-Portrait

Shooting a self-portrait is often an exercise in futility. This is a very difficult kind of photograph to pull off successfully. It's hard to be both in front of the camera and behind the camera. The straightforward technical issues of getting composition, focus, and exposure right suddenly become much more difficult. Most photographic self-portraits are not great works of art.

However, I suggest taking the time to create one or more self-portraits as a useful exercise for anyone interested in portraiture. It's a very helpful experience to be both the subject of a photo and in control of the photography.

Modeling is a great way to learn what it feels like to be in front of the camera—experience that can help you be a better photographer. Sitting for portraits with other photographers can also be a useful

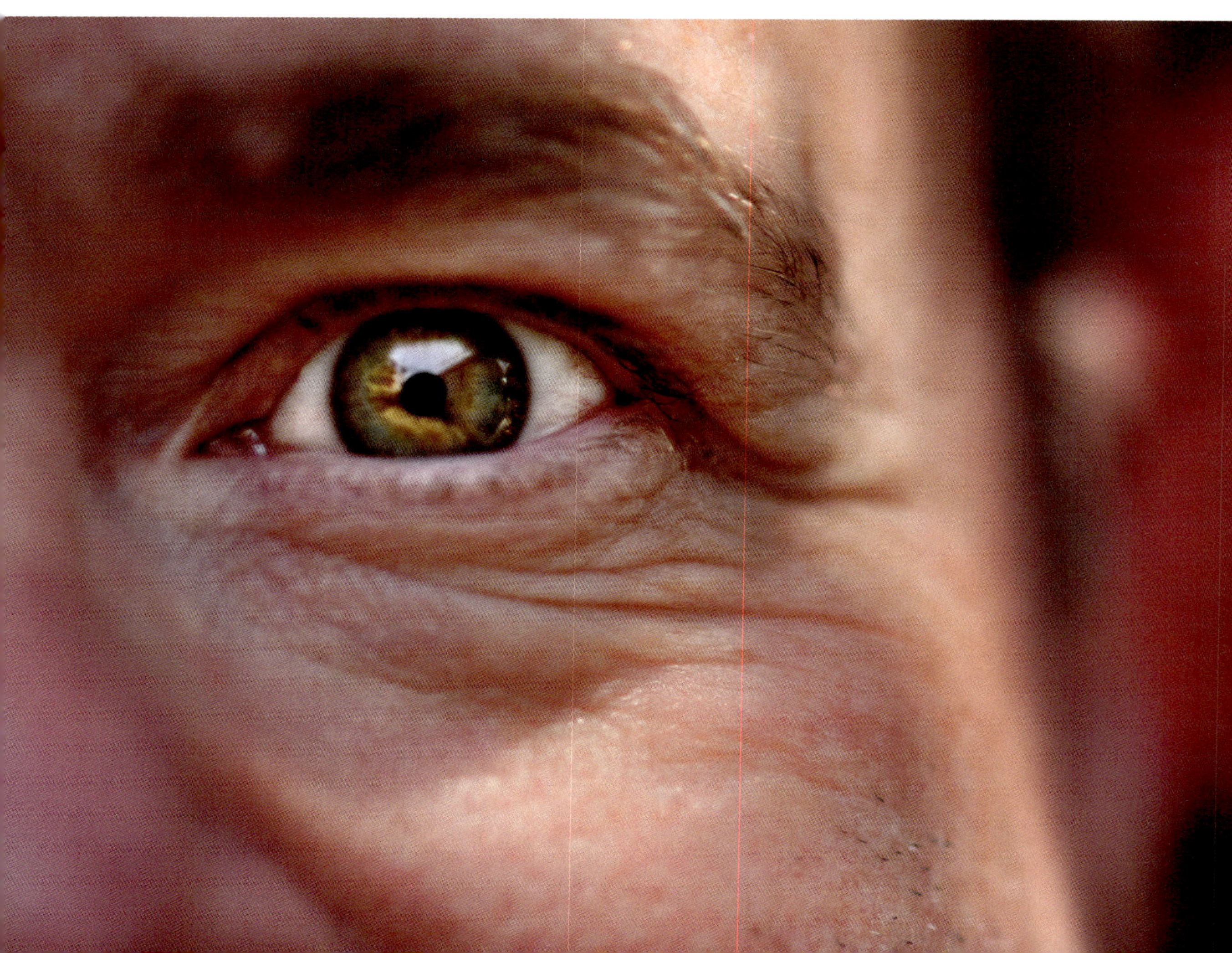

experience for the aspiring portrait photographer. While recommended, neither experience has the same benefits as taking a photo of oneself, by oneself. When I create a self-portrait, I can literally experience the emotional swings depending on whether I'm setting the camera up, or waiting for the shutter to release. Behind the camera I'm cool and analytical. In front, I start mugging right away.

Furthermore, there's nothing like taking your own portrait to really internalize the potential conflict between truth and beauty.

There are three basic techniques for creating a self-portrait:

- Shoot into a mirror
- Put the camera on a tripod
- Hold the camera up with arms extended and point it back at your face

You can use a remote release to trigger the camera if it is on a tripod, provided that the camera isn't too far away. A wireless release will work over longer distances than one that uses a cable. The self-timer works well regardless of how far you are from the camera, and is built into most cameras. However, you do have to run into position and then pose while the self-timer is counting down.

It's also possible to combine self-portrait techniques. For example, you could use a tripod to make a shot that shows you looking into a mirror.

If you try making a self-portrait I guarantee you'll have fun, and also learn something about the dynamics of portrait photography. There's nothing like being both photographer and subject to help you understand the contradictory pulls of voyeurism and exhibitionism, and of narcissism and the desire to tell the truth.

◀ What could be more important to a photographer than his eye? Therefore, I decided to emphasize my eye in this self-portrait. I set the lens to the most wide open aperture (f/2) and used aperture-preferred metering.

I put the camera on a tripod and took up position in dappled shade. I measured the distance from the camera to my eye as best I could and set the focus manually, knowing it would take many tries to get the focus on my eye correct. I used the self-timer to trigger the shutter.

While the self-timer was counting down, looking at my camera on the tripod, I could see brightness from the eye-piece coming through the lens. Therefore, I knew that my eye would at least be in the photo. I tried to keep the light from the eye-piece in the center of the lens as I looked at the camera.

It did indeed take many tries to get this photo right.

100mm, 1/1000 of a second at f/2 and ISO 200, tripod mounted

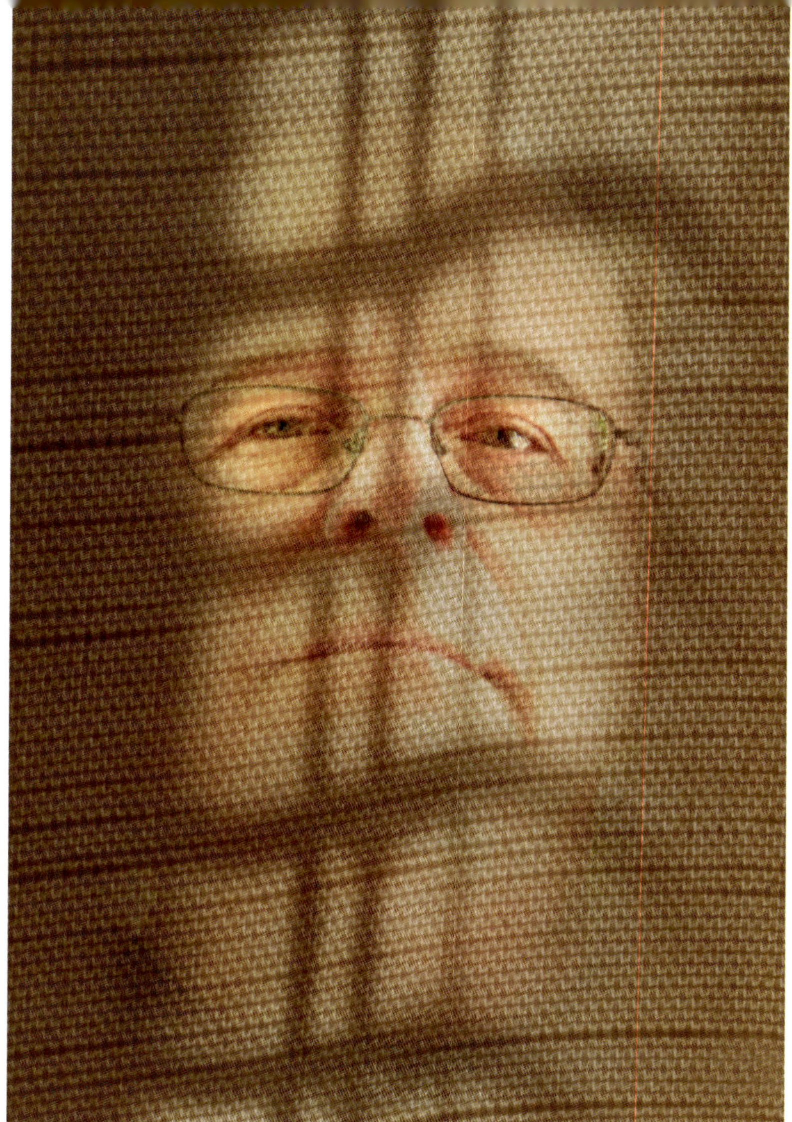

▲ I added a bit of interest to my self-portrait by compositing it with a macro showing shadows on a textured curtain.

95mm, 1/125 of a second at f/5.6 and ISO 250, tripod mounted (self-portrait) and 50mm macro, 1/8 of a second at f/32 and ISO 200, tripod mounted (curtain), combined in Photoshop

▶ I used a single light source, and shot this self-portrait into a rectangular mirror.

70mm, 1/25 of a second at f/5.6 and ISO 640, tripod mounted

Getting a friendly friend to help

Making a self-portrait is much easier if you get a friend to help. The friend can stand in where you intend to pose, or help you focus and compose the camera following your directions. Either way, it's cheating and not quite a solo self-portrait—but then we all need a little help from our friends sometimes, and the important thing is to experience both roles essentially at the same time.

Flickr for self-portrait inspiration

If my self-portraits don't inspire you, and you are having trouble coming up with ideas for your own creative self-portrait, I suggest you go to Flickr, www.flickr.com, and search for "self-portrait." Among the tens of thousands of self-portraits on Flickr, you are sure to come up with something you can use as a starting place.

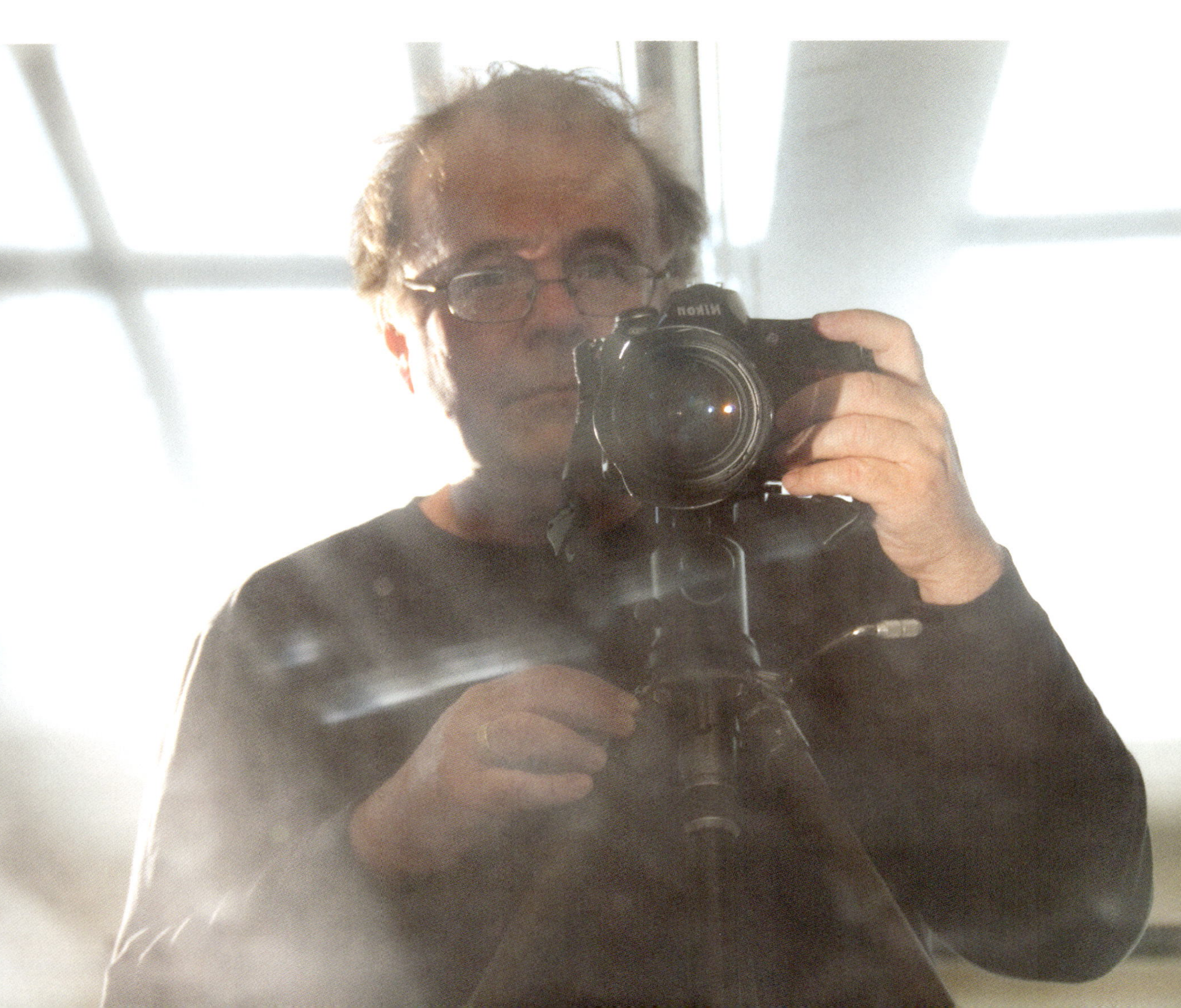

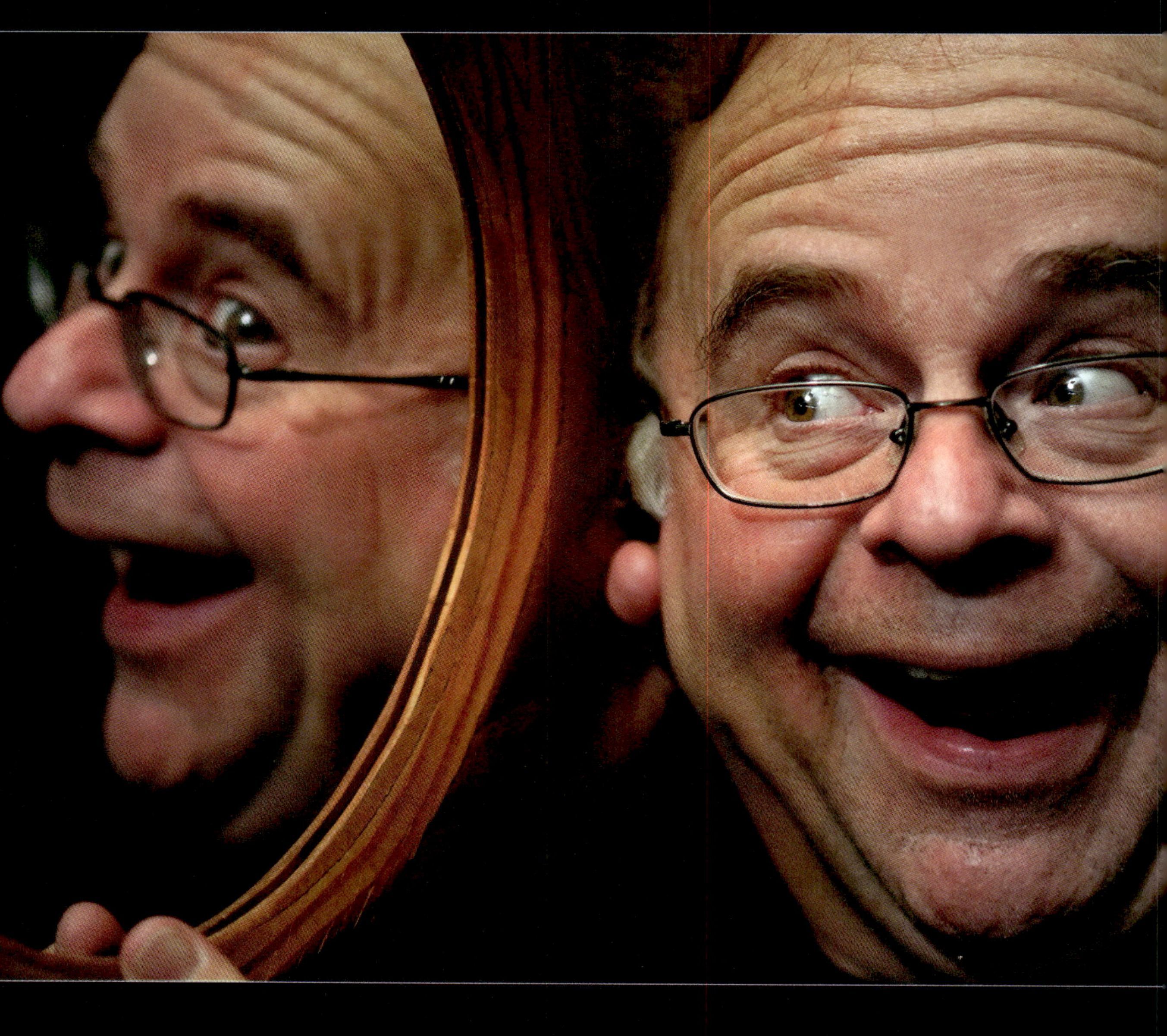

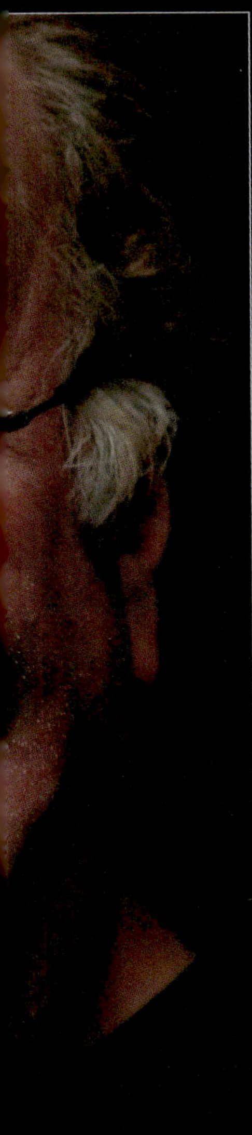

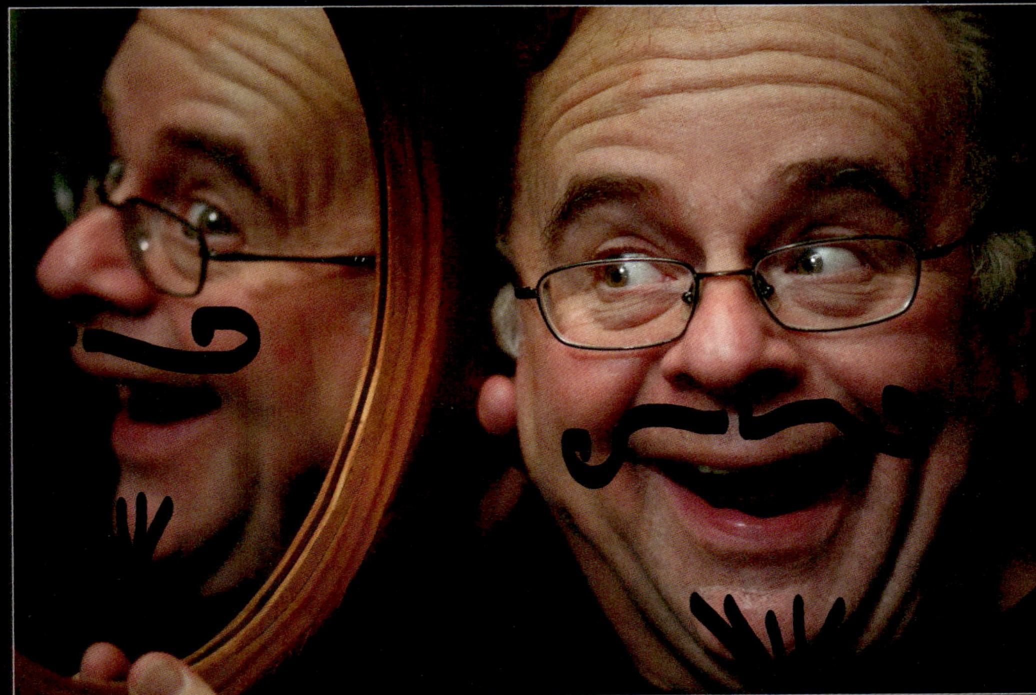

I put the camera on a tripod and used the self-timer to fire the exposure. There was something about the setup with the mirror that made me start wanting to "mug it up." This carried over into post-processing in Photoshop, where I had fun drawing a Dali-esque moustache on myself!

100mm, 1/100 of a second at f/2 and ISO 640, tripod mounted

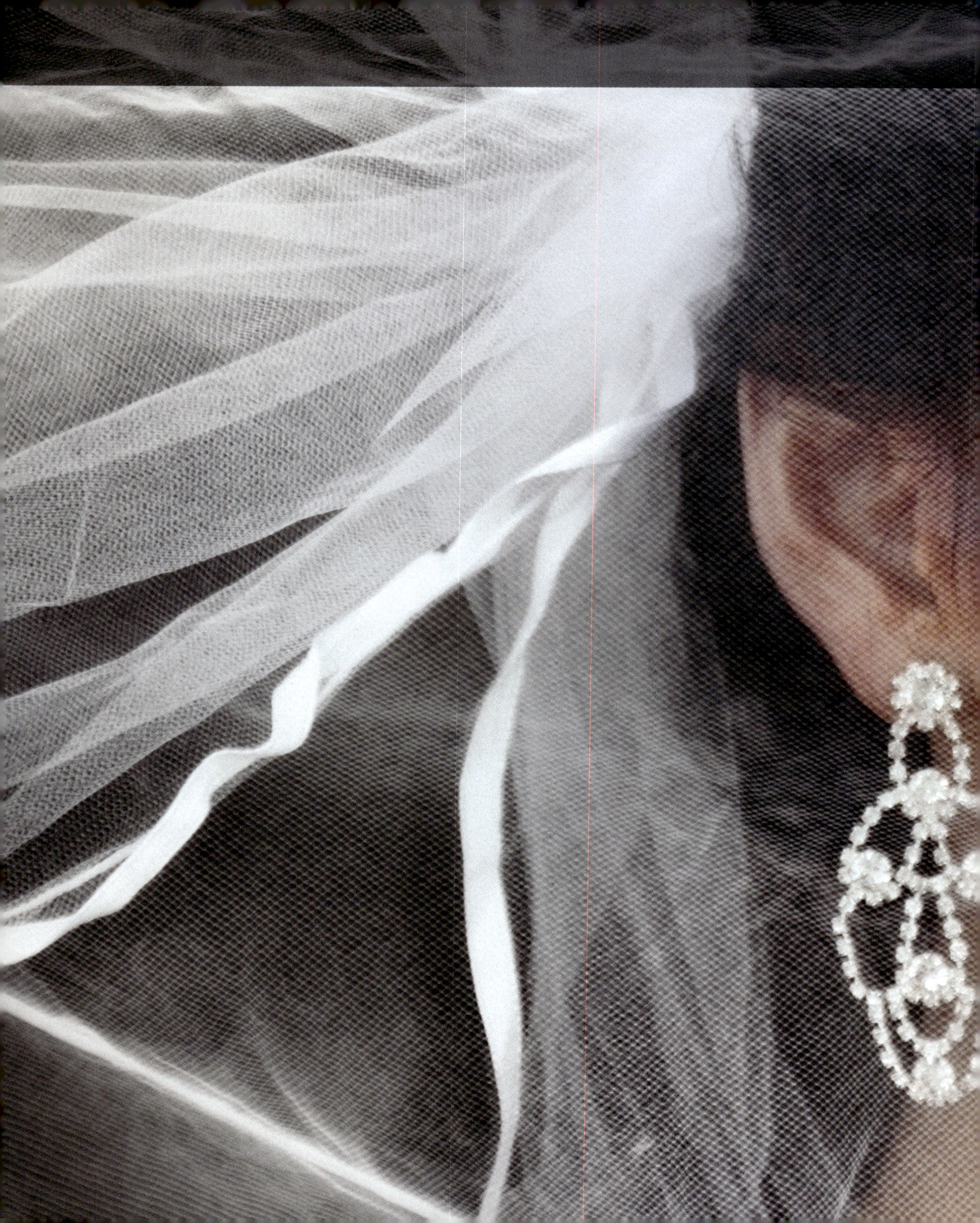

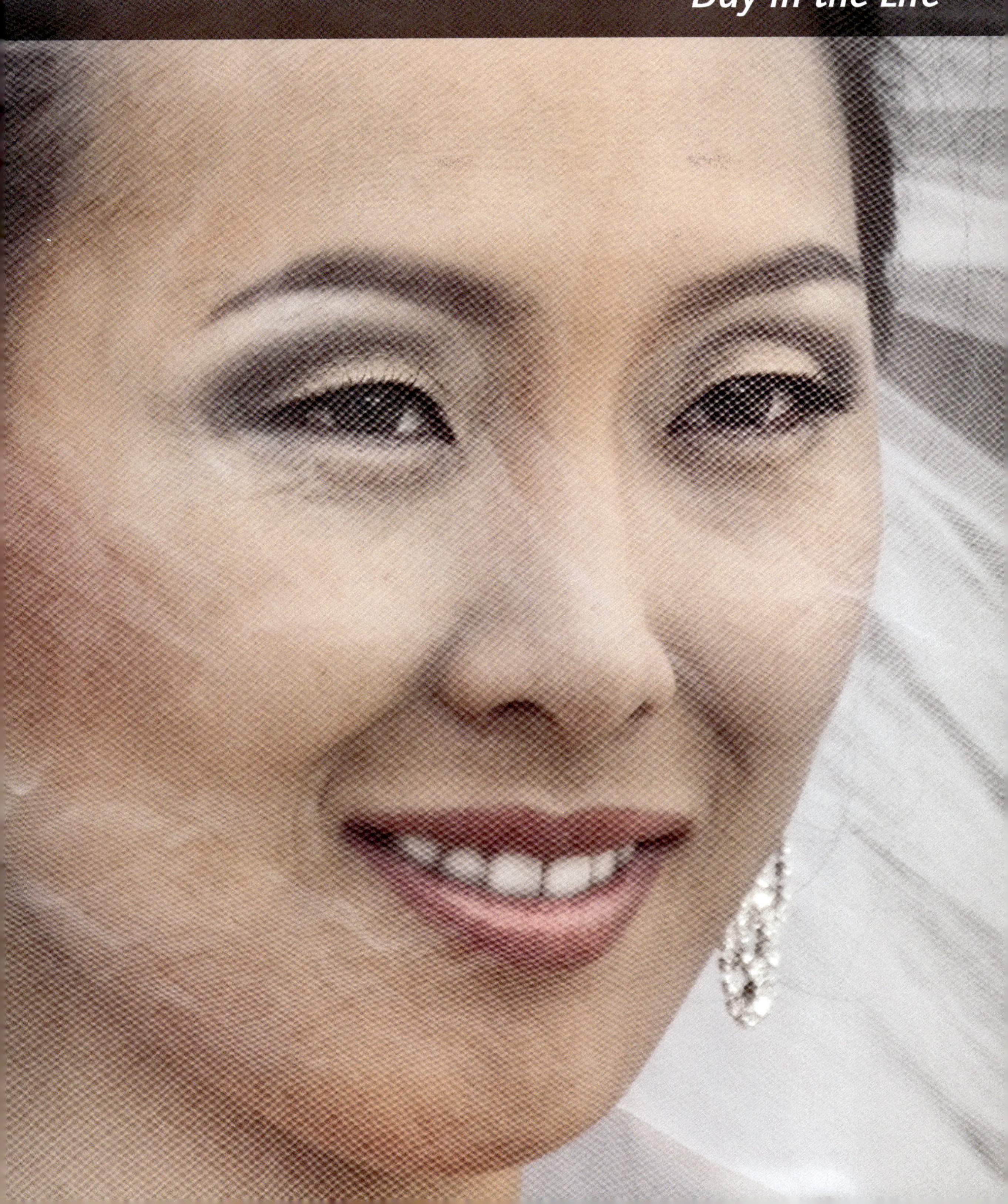

Assignment: People

Photographer Jay Maisel quips that he always carries his camera with him because "it's hard to take a photo without a camera." In a similar spirit, it's hard to make a portrait without a subject. I can see this sung to the tune of the Barbra Streisand lyric "People who need people": if you are going to make photos of people, you need people, or at least a person.

So, it's pretty obvious that as a portrait photographer one must become comfortable photographing people. But unlike flowers, trees, landscapes, and still life subjects, people have their own ideas. People talk back, they move around, and can be smelly, dirty, and loud. People you approach to photograph may think you are flirting with them, rather than approaching on a photographic basis. In short, the interaction between a photographer and a portrait subject is fraught with the entire gamut of complexities that enters into any relationship between people.

In some cases, this interaction between photographer and portrait subject begins in a straightforward way. If someone has hired you to make a portrait, or if you have hired a model, there's certainly no guarantee you can make a great or revealing portrait. But at least the initial parameters of the relationship are clear (see pages 14–27 for more about the psychology of photographer-subject interaction).

It's a whole different story when you photograph a stranger who has not asked to be photographed. If the thought of going up to someone you see who looks interesting and asking whether you can take their photo makes you nervous, then to become an effective portrait photographer you need

▶ My oldest son and I went looking for a firefighter to photograph. Everyone at the first fire station we visited was busy—after all, they do have more important things to do than model for a visiting photographer. But the lieutenant suggested we visit another station in the hills that tended to be less busy.

At the second station, this veteran firefighter graciously donned his full turnout gear and posed for me. I photographed him by the natural light in the garage filled with fire engines.

1/80 of a second at f/4.8 and ISO 640, hand held

▲ Pages 56–57: I like to use gauzy fabrics as a prop in my portraits. Many colors work well, but white is probably best—white transparent fabric adds a nice romantic light. And what could be more romantic than a white wedding veil? The only thing to be careful about is creases in the fabric—these should not cover important facial features.

This bridal portrait was created using natural light against a stone monument, with the breeze blowing the veil around. I selectively desaturated the image in Photoshop (keeping the color in the bride's face) to emphasize the impact of the veil.

1/250 of a second at f/5.6 and ISO 200, hand held

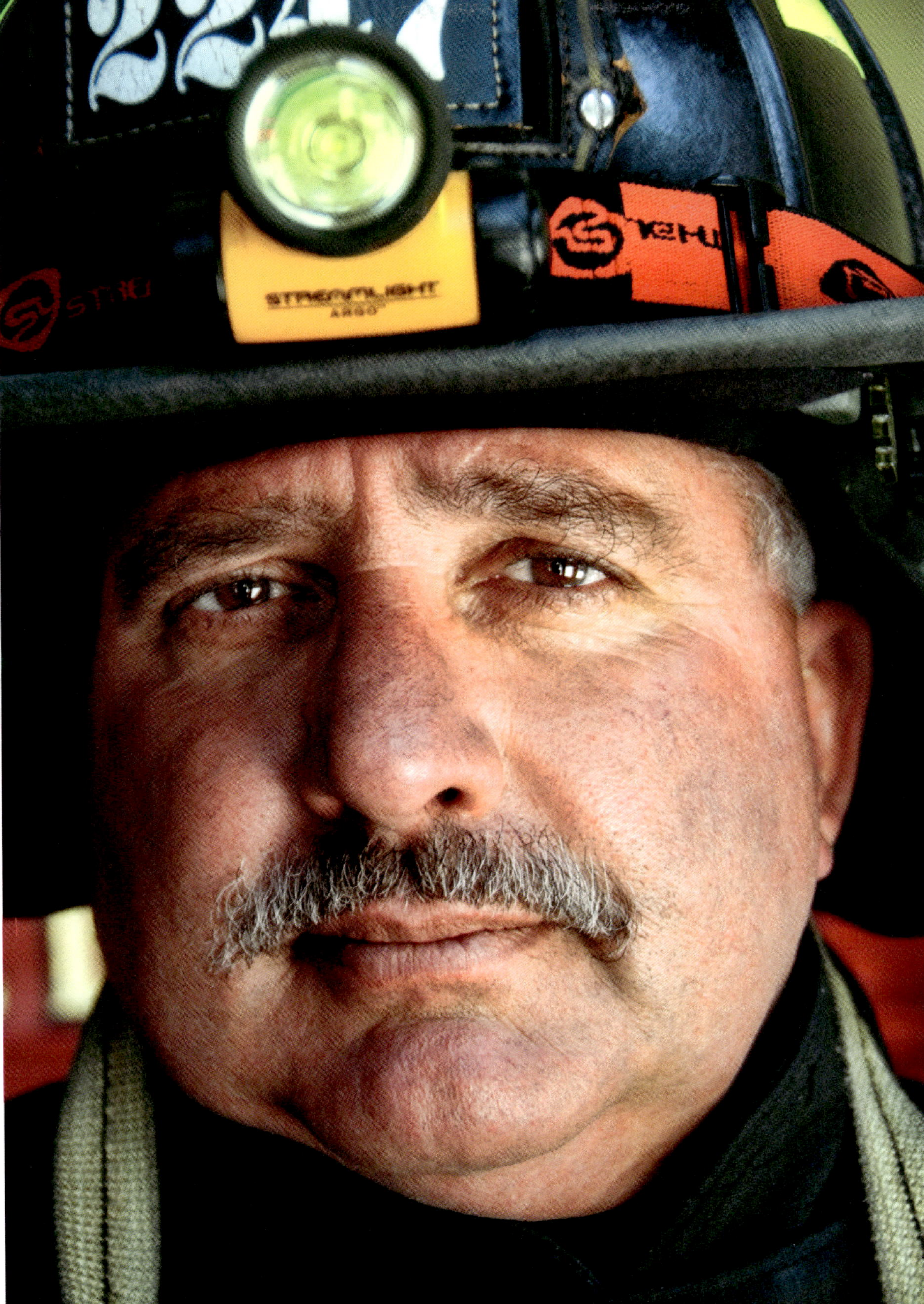
STREAMLIGHT
ARGO

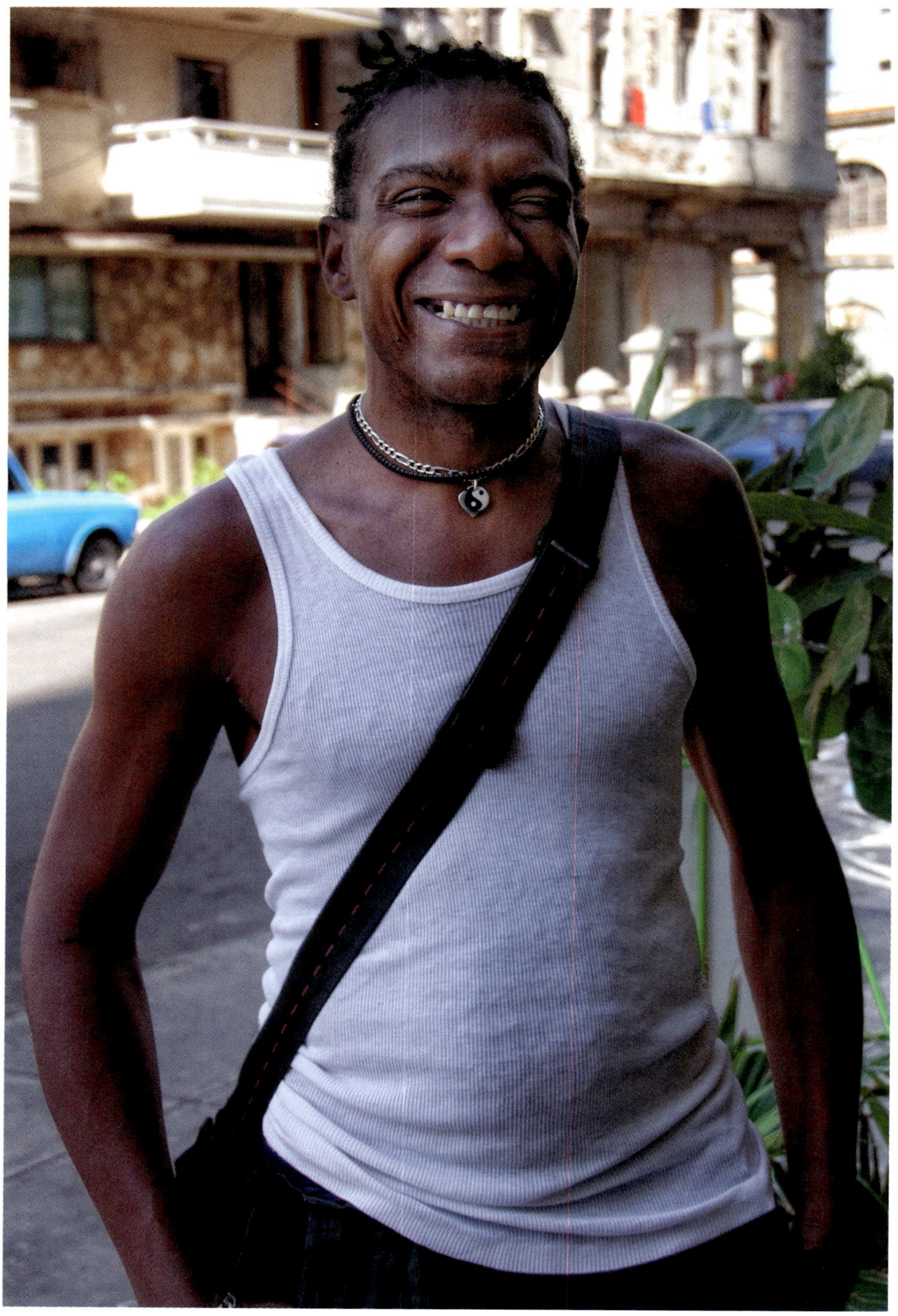

to work on this. A little bit of nervousness is a good thing—it keeps you on your toes—but too much can be paralyzing.

Becoming comfortable photographing people without an official photographer-subject relationship pays dividends across many kinds of photography. Not only will you be better at people photography, you'll also have more confidence in approaching static subjects, and in photographing models. Photographing people you meet casually requires improvisation and the ability to be quick on your feet—good skills for any photographer to have.

Approaching People

The best way to get comfortable approaching people with photography in mind is to get out there and actually approach people. "Gee," I can hear you saying already, "thanks a lot Harold for that pearl of wisdom."

Okay, you don't have to get snippy with me. Here's what I have in mind.

Approaching someone you don't know—or maybe only know slightly—with any request brings up the gamut of emotions we carry around since we were kids in the school yard. Will we be rejected? Will we be taunted? On the other hand, acceptance means cathexis, the creation of an emotional bond between yourself and the other person, however slight and transient. Both rejection and acceptance have powerful effects to our psyche.

The only way to get past fear of rejection and embarrassment is to practice approaching people. There's no substitute for actually going ahead and walking up to someone. Look at it this way: what's the worst that can happen? You might get rejected. So what? There are millions of people out there for you to photograph.

In my workshops, I suggest some simple exercises to get comfortable photographing people. Here are two ideas:

- Take your camera to a busy street corner. Make portraits of five people, asking their permission first.
- Think of a job that involves physicality that interests you; for example, being a fire fighter, carpenter, or cook. Now go to a related work place (fire house, construction site, or restaurant) and ask for permission to photograph (obviously, your shots should include people).

Model Releases

If you are planning to license your photos—or think there is a chance that you might want to license your photos in the future, for example through a stock agency—you need to get a signed model release from your subject. It's usually better to get the model release signed before you start taking photos—or at least to get an

◄ On my first afternoon in Havana, Cuba, I wandered the tropical streets in a bit of a daze. From out of nowhere this man appeared and offered to show me some "things tourists don't usually get to see." I wasn't sure whether to trust him, and I think he sensed my uncertainty—you can see this in his guarded, partially closed eyes and the overly forced smile.

I shot this photo in bright shade, overexposing a bit more than I would have for someone with a lighter skin tone.

36mm, 1/160 of a second at f/6.3 and ISO 100, hand held

agreement in principle that a release will be signed—before you push the shutter.

However, don't let the need for a release stop you from taking photos. Even after the fact it is usually easier to get people to sign model releases than you might expect. It is better to snap first and negotiate for a release later than to miss the opportunity for a great shot.

I carry a small stack of model releases in my camera backpack as part of my kit so I'm always ready to get a release when the situation arises. Don't forget to pack a pen as well, so you aren't wasting time fumbling and trying to find one.

My model releases are printed one per page, so each person I photograph signs their own release. Another viable scheme has the language of the release printed on the top of a form with a list of signature lines for subjects to sign. Sometimes the comfort of having other signatures on the form will help induce reluctant subjects to sign.

I approach the topic of model releases with photographic subjects in a straightforward and open fashion. I explain that I am a professional photographer, and that I have no current specific use for the photos I am taking (assuming this is true). I hand out a business card with the web address for my portfolio. I explain that if I want to use a photo in the future, I'll need to get a release. I try not to make too many specific promises about sending copies of my photos in exchange for the release—frankly, my life is busy enough without adding this commitment to my list—but I will offer to send files if that's what it takes to get the release. I make a note of anything I've said I'll do on the signed release form so that it doesn't get overlooked.

As long as they understand what you are asking, most people are happy to sign your release form.

If you are photographing someone under eighteen, make sure that a parent signs the release.

You can easily find sample model release forms by searching online, or from professional associations such as the American Society of Media Photographers (www.asmp.org), or stock photo agencies such as Getty Images (www.gettyimages.com).

A recent innovation that can make the process of collecting model releases easier is an industry-standard model release application for the iPhone and iPad. To find a mobile model release app, go to http://itunes.apple.com.

▶ Marcus works at Gioia Pizza, the best place for pizza-by-the-slice in Berkeley, California (if you are ever visiting Berkeley, stop by and try a slice). I found his face and friendly nature interesting, and asked if I could photograph him. I used a small flash unit mounted on top of my camera to make this portrait in the low-light conditions of the pizzeria.

Top: This distinctive crop shows Marcus's eyes to good effect. I liked the expression in his eyes a great deal, and to fully capture it I was willing to "break the rules" by cutting off his mouth, though leaving a hint of a smile.

Bottom: As Marcus worked, I pointed the camera down to create a photo that shows someone who is contemplative and focused on his job, not the camera.

Both: 105mm macro, 1/60 of a second at f/6.3 and ISO 200, hand held

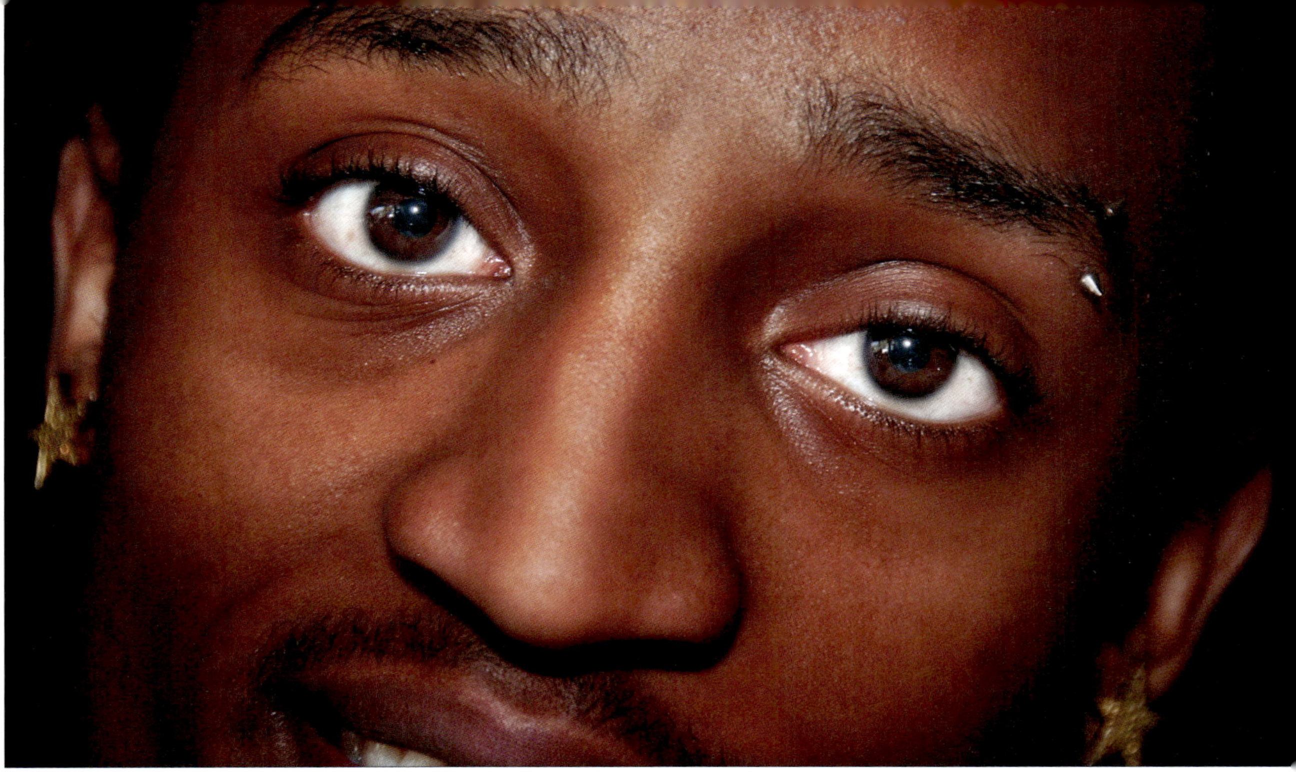

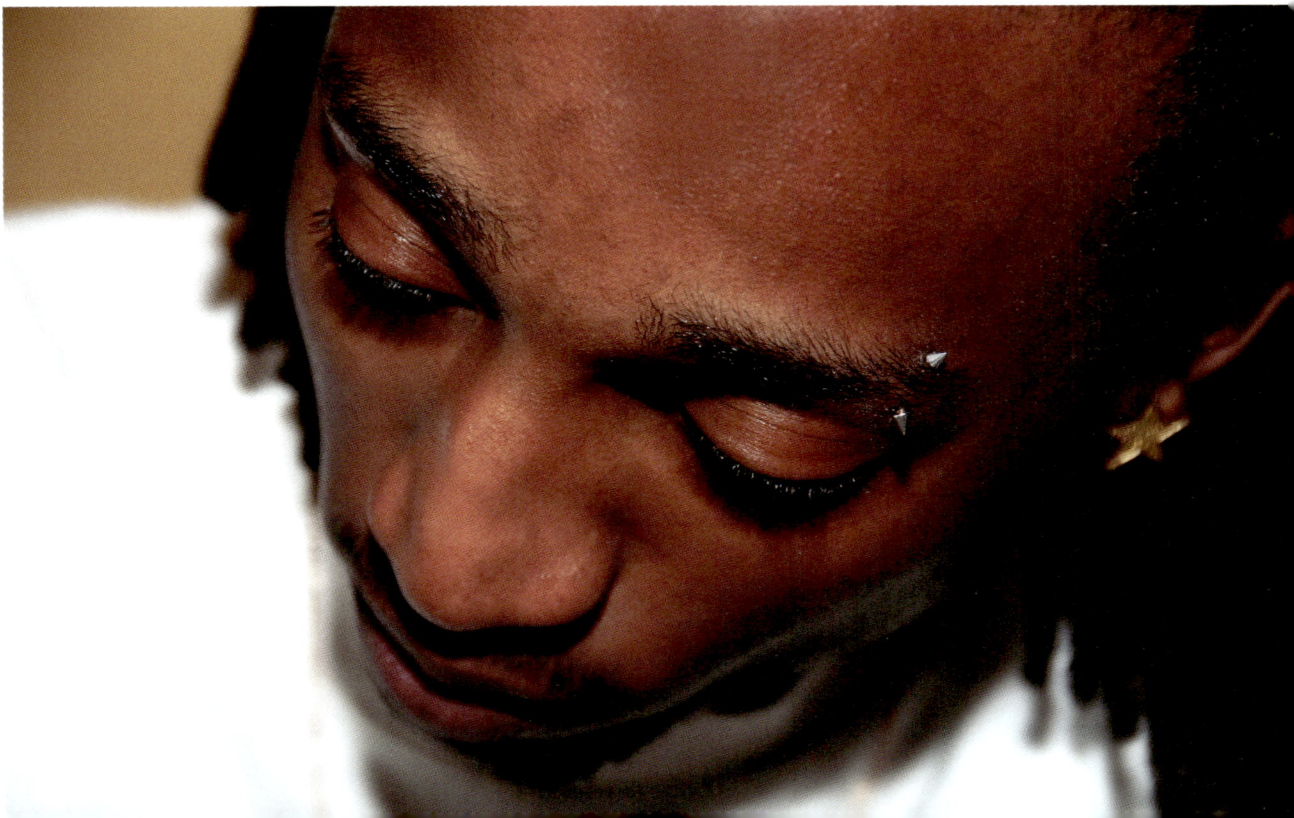

Composing Portraits

Composing portraits is a great deal like composing any photograph. You need to consider the formal aspects of composition: the lines, shapes, patterns, framing, and colors involved. For this aspect of portrait composition, it is often helpful to think of your subject as a landscape. It really doesn't matter whether you are photographing a starlet in a hula hoop or a dramatic mountainside; composition is composition. To learn more about composition generally, check out my book *Creative Composition: Digital Photography Tips & Techniques* (Wiley).

As with any photograph, how you compose your portrait will telegraph to the viewer what is important within the image. You need to take care to place subjects within your frames and in relationship to other elements of the image in a way that is visually interesting and tells a story.

When looking at a photo, a viewer's eye tends to go first to brighter areas that are in focus. It's also natural to first look at the eyes in a portrait. The eyes are a very central element in the composition of any photo that involves portraiture. If there is a face in the photo, probably the eyes of your subject should be in focus.

Don't underestimate the impact of details. Many times jewelry, small things that a person is wearing, or a hand gesture can tell us a great deal about a person. We aren't always conscious of the source of our information, but most of us are able to read these intimate visual cues to form a picture of the complete person.

Photographic composition of photos of people does differ from composition of inanimate subjects such as landscapes in one important way: you can direct, or suggest, that people move to a location or pose in a specific way.

I'd suggest that you not abuse this power. Good professional photographers are used to telling portrait subjects, or groups of people they are photographing, how to arrange themselves for the best results. But they do this with a sense of humor and an awareness of the context of the situation. Oddly, pushy amateur photographers can have a tin ear about when their subjects have had enough—and then are surprised at the mediocre results. The moral here is to be sensitive to the nuances in the responses when you make a suggestion that may enhance your composition.

▶ I got my camera ready on a tripod pointed at the playhouse windows, then directed my three-year-old son Mathew inside. I asked him to open the windows, and quickly snapped the photo using a fast enough shutter speed to stop his motion.

The open window acts as a framing device and helps make the composition of this portrait effective.

95mm, 1/500 of a second at f/5.6 and ISO 200, tripod mounted

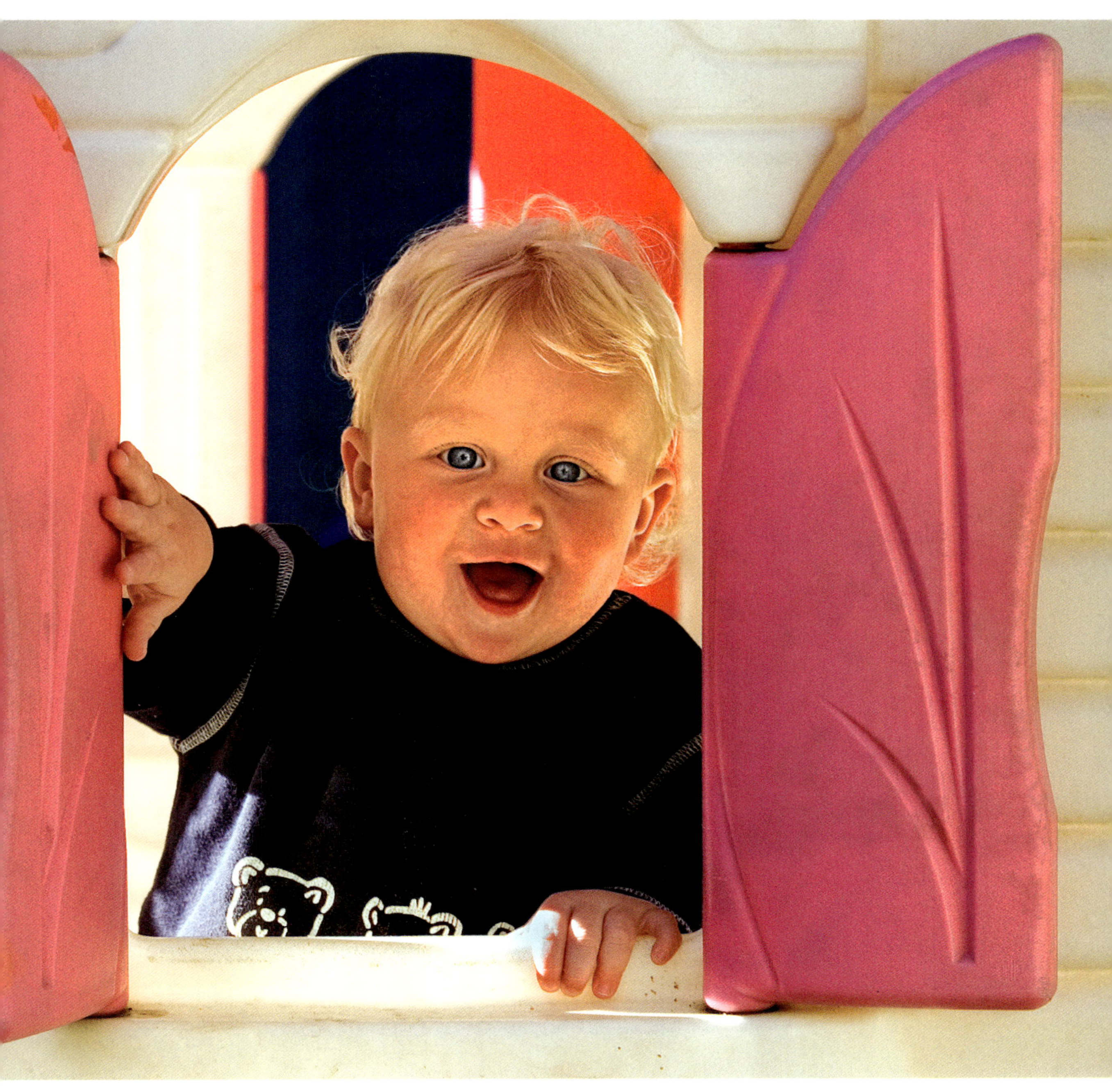

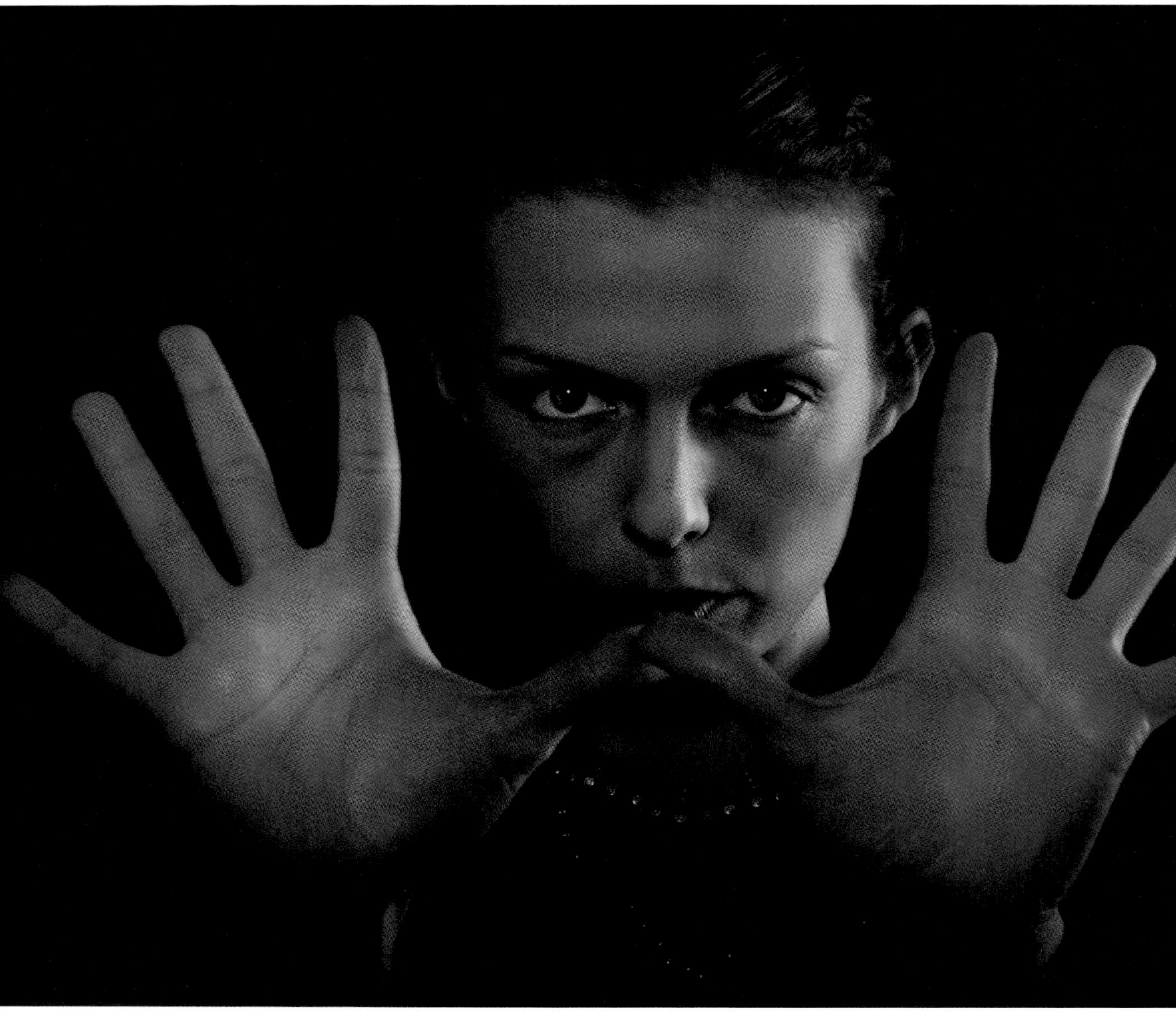

▲ By positioning the model's face so that it is framed by her hands, I created an unusual and striking monochromatic composition in this portrait shot.

70mm, 1/100 of a second at f/6.3 and ISO 100

▶ My idea with this photo was to make as flat a composition as possible using a macro lens. The only distinctive element in an otherwise featureless "landscape" would be the belly button and ornament. I used studio strobe lighting to evenly light this model's stomach.

200mm macro, 1/200 of a second at f/6.3 and ISO 200 tripod mounted

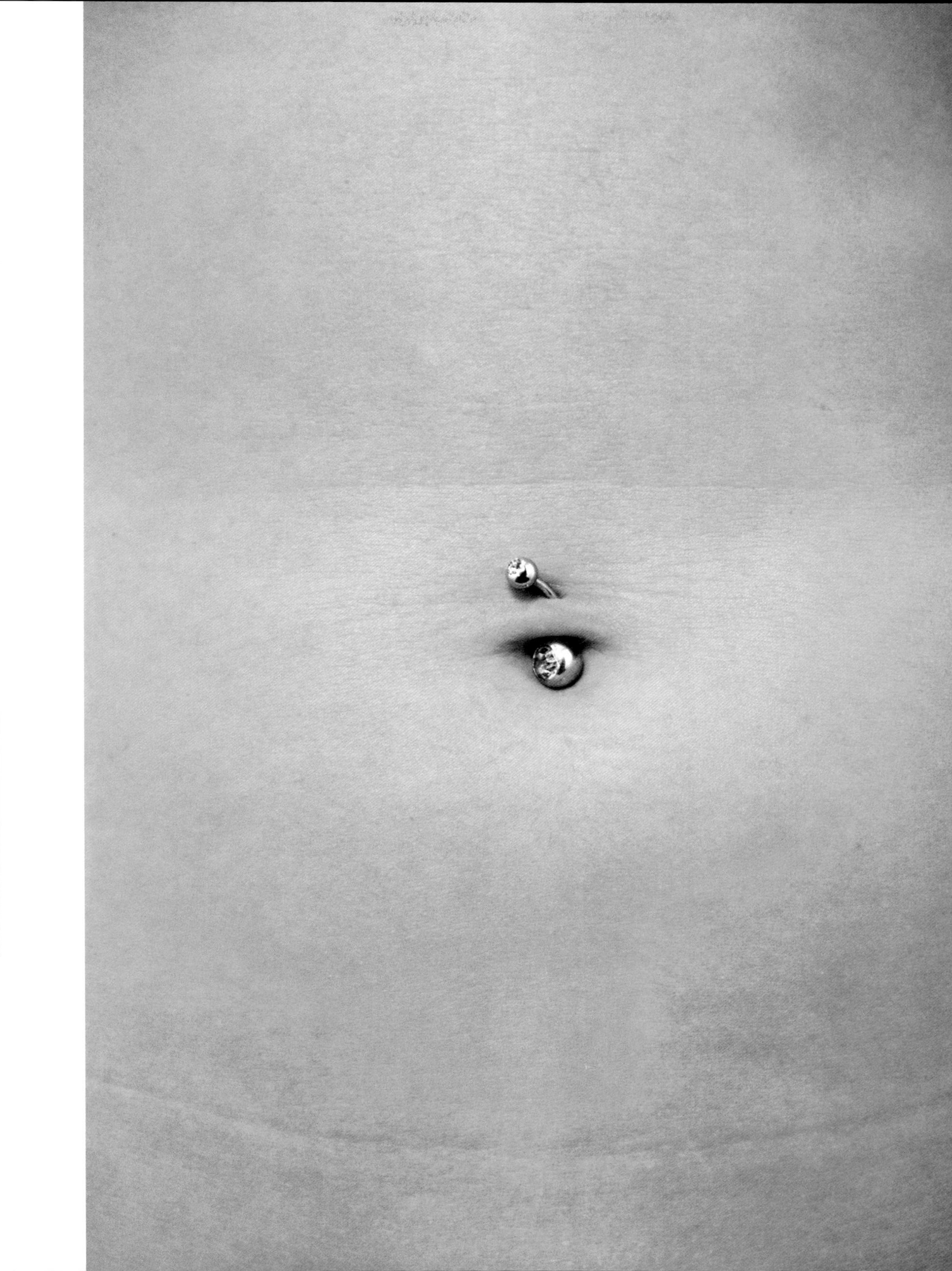

Street Photography

Street photography is portrait photography in public places where the subjects are mostly people you don't know. This tends to be "grab shot" photography—shooting images on the fly. The opportunity is to take advantage of people in their natural environment doing their thing, ultimately creating work that is more natural than photos taken in a posed, artificial environment.

If this approach is to work, then your subjects need to be distracted. Certainly, some street shots work when the subjects have apparently taken some notice of the photographer. But casual, spur-of-the-moment photography on the streets usually doesn't work out so well if you are the only thing that's interesting. What the street photographer needs is distraction. Distraction comes in many forms: farmer's markets, block parties, emergency sirens, other people, stores for window shopping, and so on.

The great photographer Henri Cartier-Bresson helped define the fields of photo-journalism and street photography. He coined the phrase "decisive moment" to describe the elegant, apparently spur-of-the-moment compositions that have come to be emblematic of Cartier-Bresson's style. Often Cartier-Bresson stalked his decisive moments by composing a photo and then waiting for hours with great patience for the additional elements that made his image sublime. He knew his decisive moment when he saw it, and was able to snap his photos accordingly.

You may not have the patience to use a strategy that employs so much waiting. However, street photography inherently does involve recognizing the shot when you see it—and acting without delay. Slight changes in posture, expression, and attitude can make a big difference. If you don't make the photo when you first see it, you will likely lose it—and only have yourself to blame.

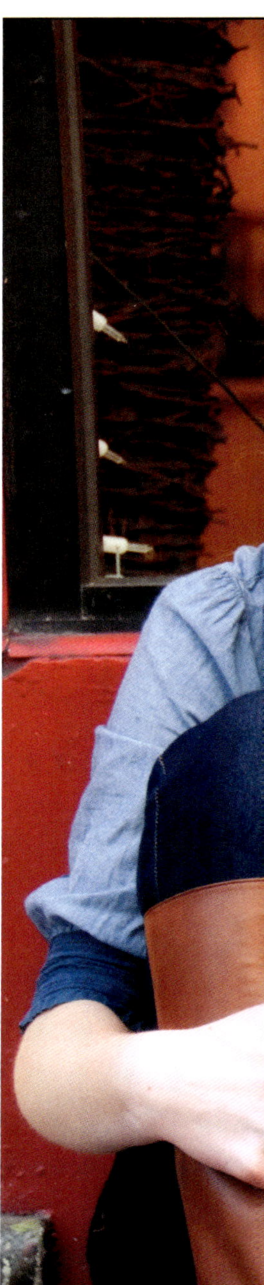

▶ I posed this couple on the sidewalk in front on an art gallery, and asked them to mimic the expression on the statuette's face. The photo works because of the inherent humor in juxtaposing the expression on the sculpture with that on the models' faces. It's also clear that the subjects of this photo are enjoying themselves—and this enjoyment translates into a photo that is fun to look at.

The couple in the photo were hamming it up, and I kept on shooting, trying to capture the best moment. This version is the one that worked best.

62mm, 1/60 of a second at f/4.8 and ISO 500, hand held

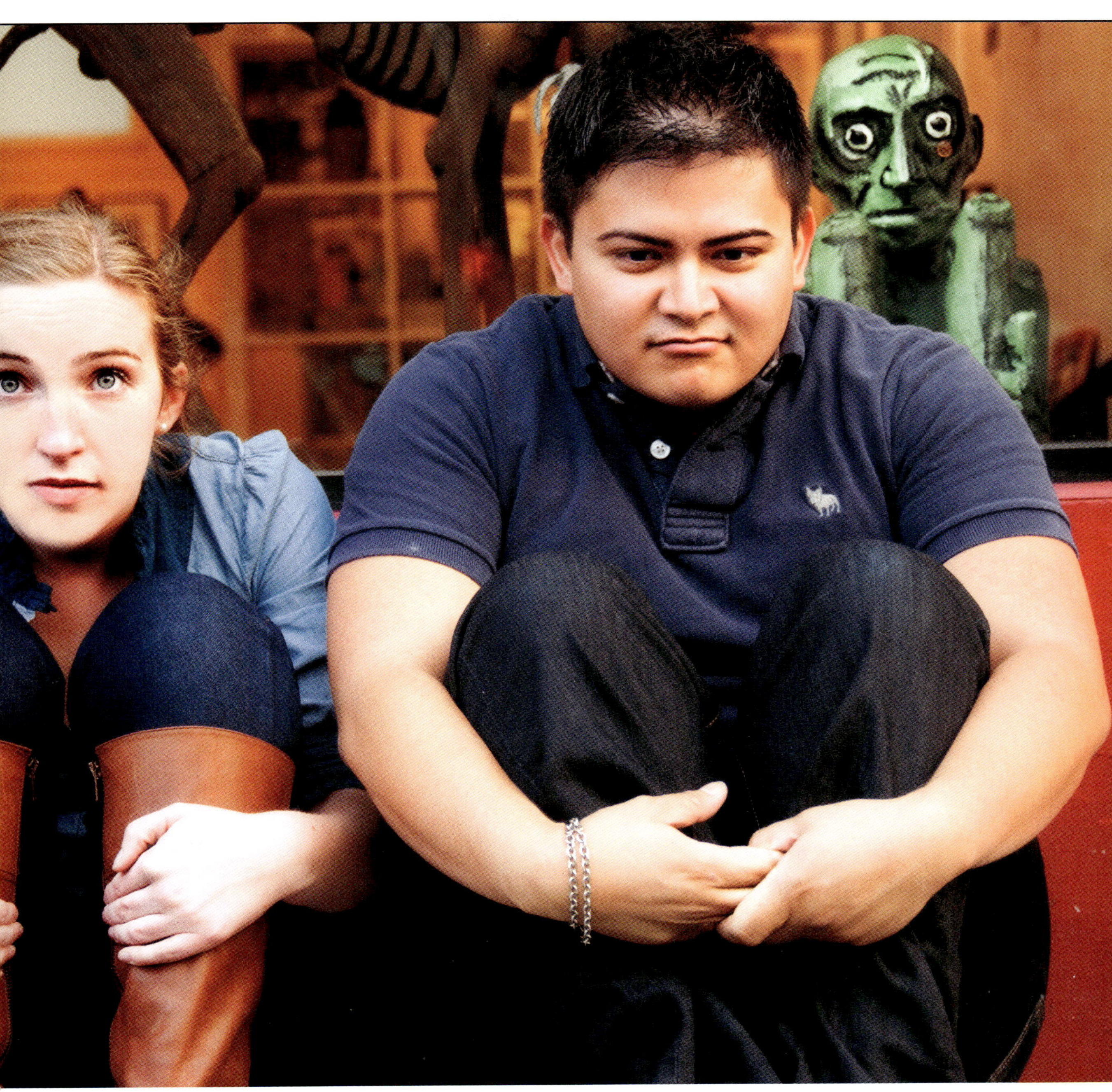

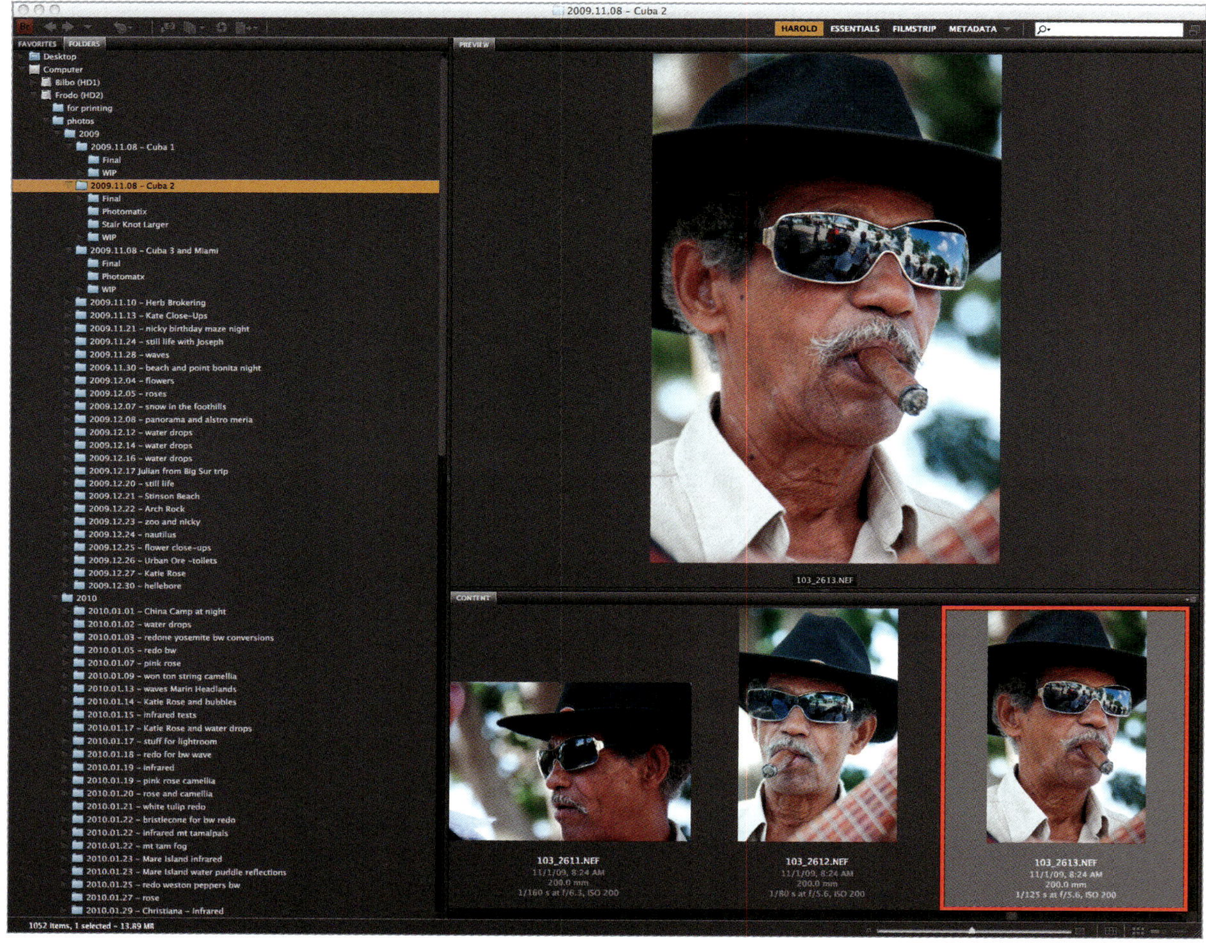

Open air markets, street fairs, and carnivals are among the best places for street photography because everyone is so busy and having such a good time that they don't pay much attention to photographers.

I photographed this guitar player in a small square in Cienfuegos, a provincial Cuban capitol.

Above: The guitar player was moving around as he performed. You can see several of my shots in Adobe Bridge—only one of them was framed to make an interesting composition.

Right: Nearby, a street fair was taking place. In the square, musicians played, kids exercised, and people relaxed. The story of the activity of the square is told in the reflections in the guitar player's sunglasses.

200mm, 1/125 of a second at f/5.6 and ISO 200, hand held

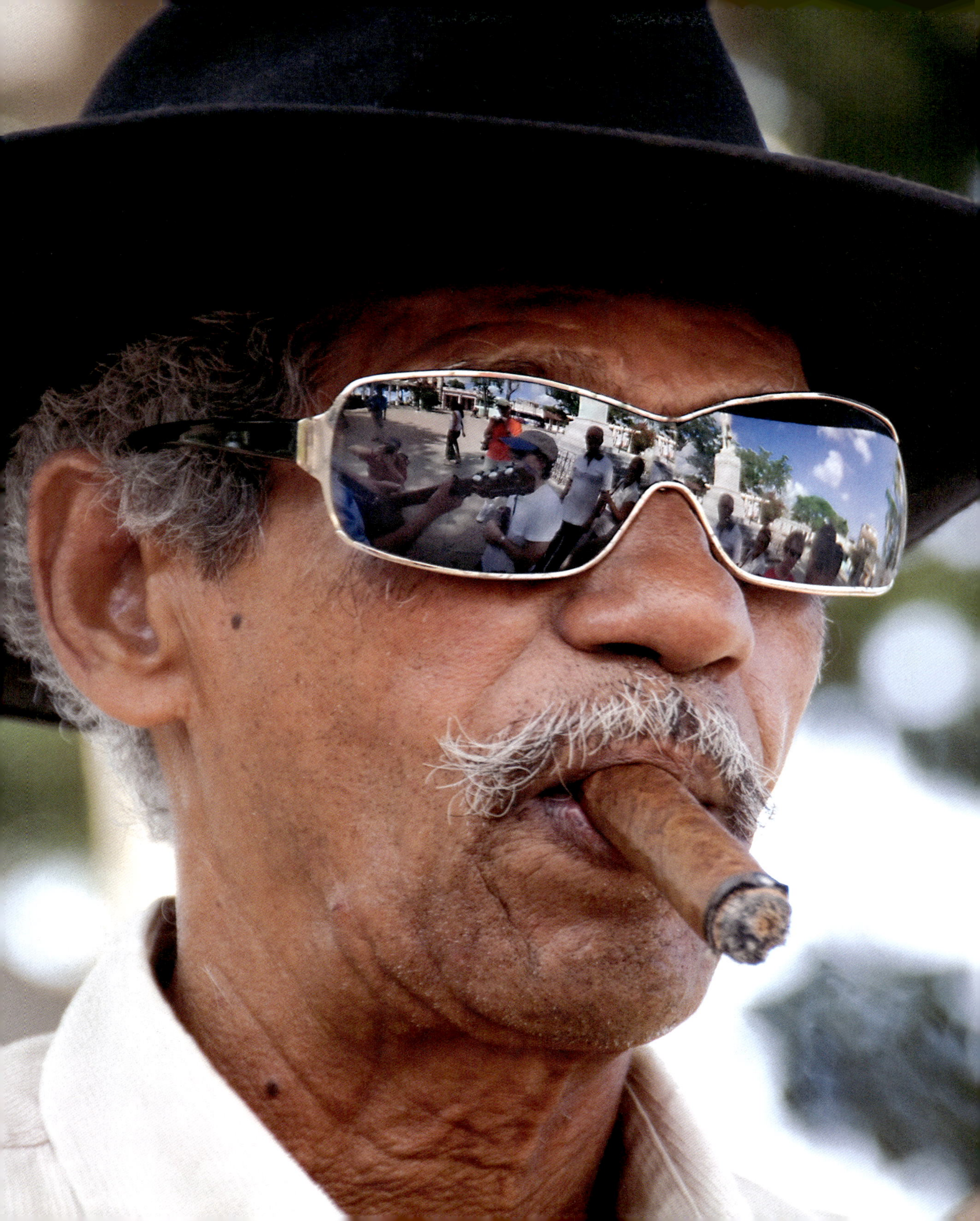

Environmental Portraiture

An environmental portrait is a portrait created in an environment that is significant to the subject. Typically, this is the subject's home or work environment—and not in the photography studio or on the street—although other environments are possible. In any case, the key point is that the environment shown in the photo shows something important about the subject of the portrait. In a good environmental portrait, the background not only adds information, it also brings an entirely new visual dimension to the photo.

It's often a great idea to photograph someone where they live, work, or play. People are more comfortable and therefore more themselves in places they are used to.

When making these kinds of portraits, you should think expansively. Take the idea of an environmental portrait beyond where it normally goes. There's nothing that says that you have to limit the scope of your vision to a boring office or a neatly manicured living room.

It's always important to consider the background in your portraits, how the background relates to your subject, and how the inclusion of an environmental background enriches a given portrait. Considering these questions gives rise to a true sense of what environmental portraiture is about—and will help you create portraits with more depth, even when only a small bit of environmental background is included.

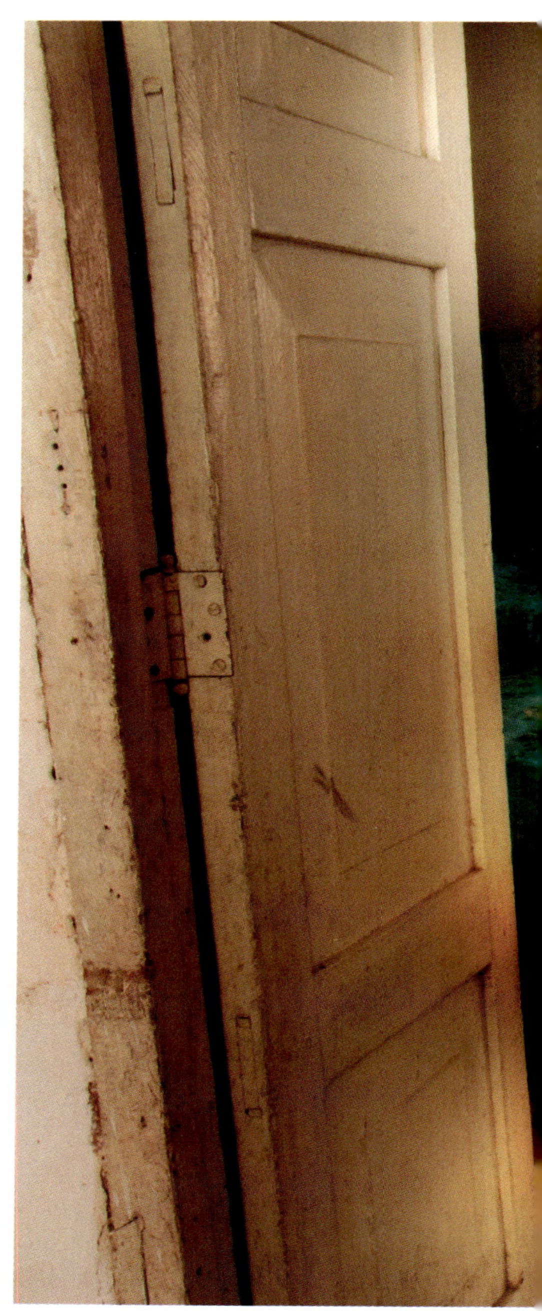

▶ The center of this composition is a woman reading in her home in provincial Cuba. Even though she is the subject of the portrait, she appears quite small in the photograph, which is unusual. Part of the point of showing this woman in the environment of her home is to show the sparseness of possessions, even in relatively well-off Cuban homes.

Two exposures combined in Photoshop, each exposure 20mm, f/22 and ISO 400, tripod mounted; exposed at 1/10 of a second and 1/25 of a second

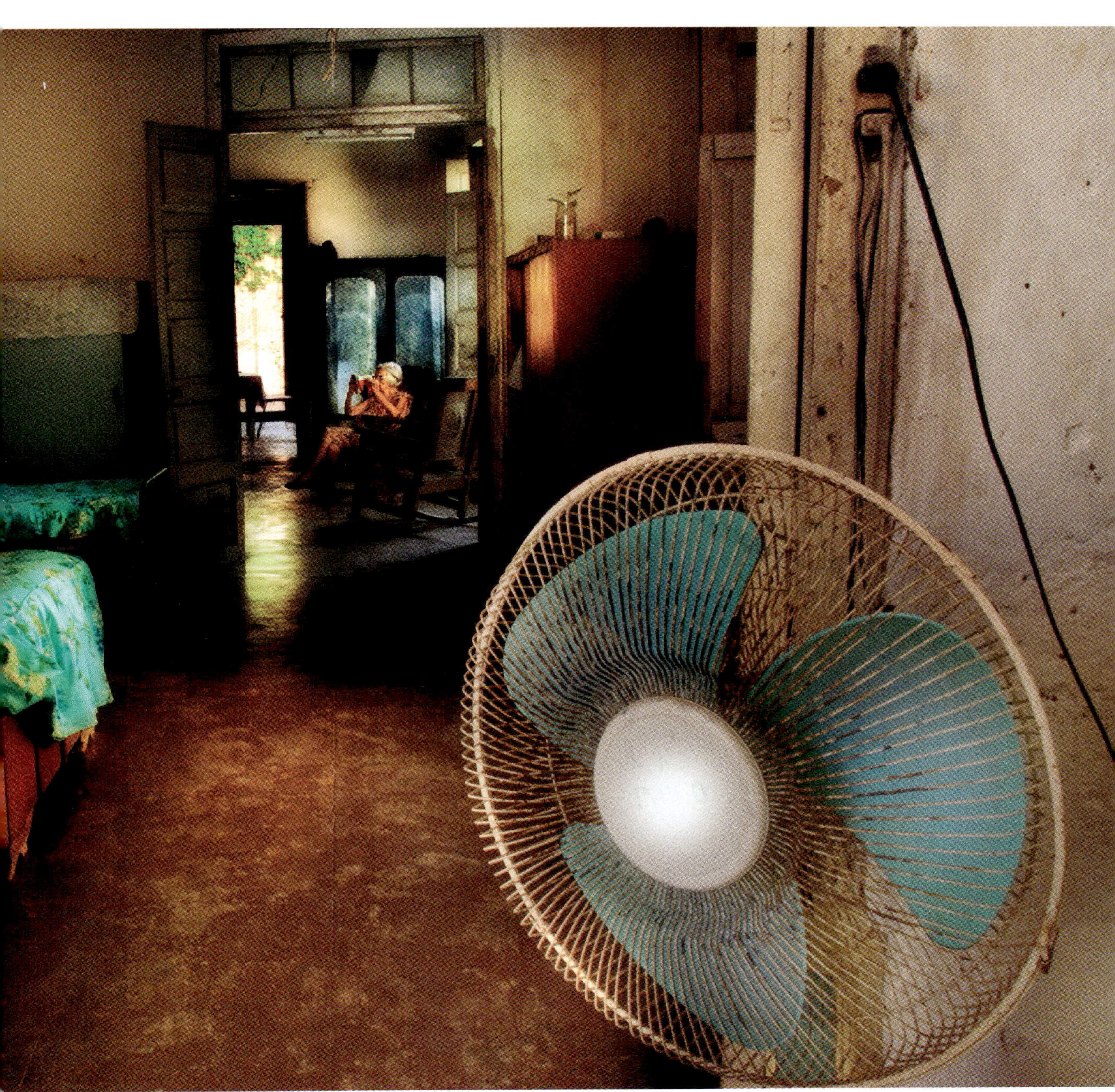

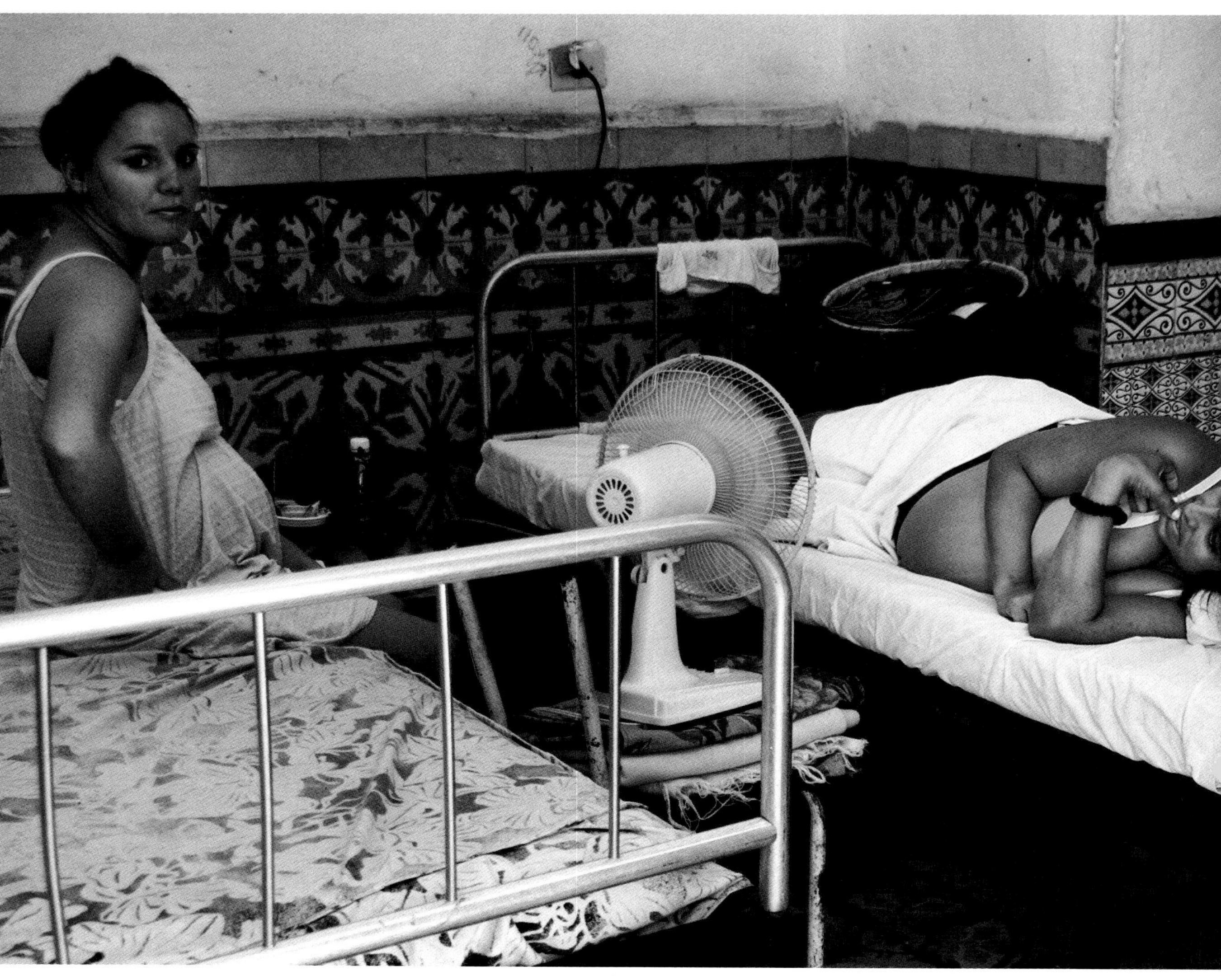

▲ I photographed these women in a high-risk pregnancy ward in Trinidad, Cuba. The physical environment of the ward—with no medical apparatus present—says as much about their situation as the way the women look.

27mm, 1/60 of a second at f/4.5 and ISO 400, hand held

▶ This school teacher was the lonely custodian of a house for visiting teachers. The house was largely destroyed during the last hurricane that passed through Cuba and never fully rebuilt. His expression seemed to echo the emptiness of the facility he was responsible for.

I photographed him using a wide angle lens (12mm) to help emphasize the sparseness of his surroundings.

12mm, 1/100 of a second at f/5.0 and ISO 160, hand held

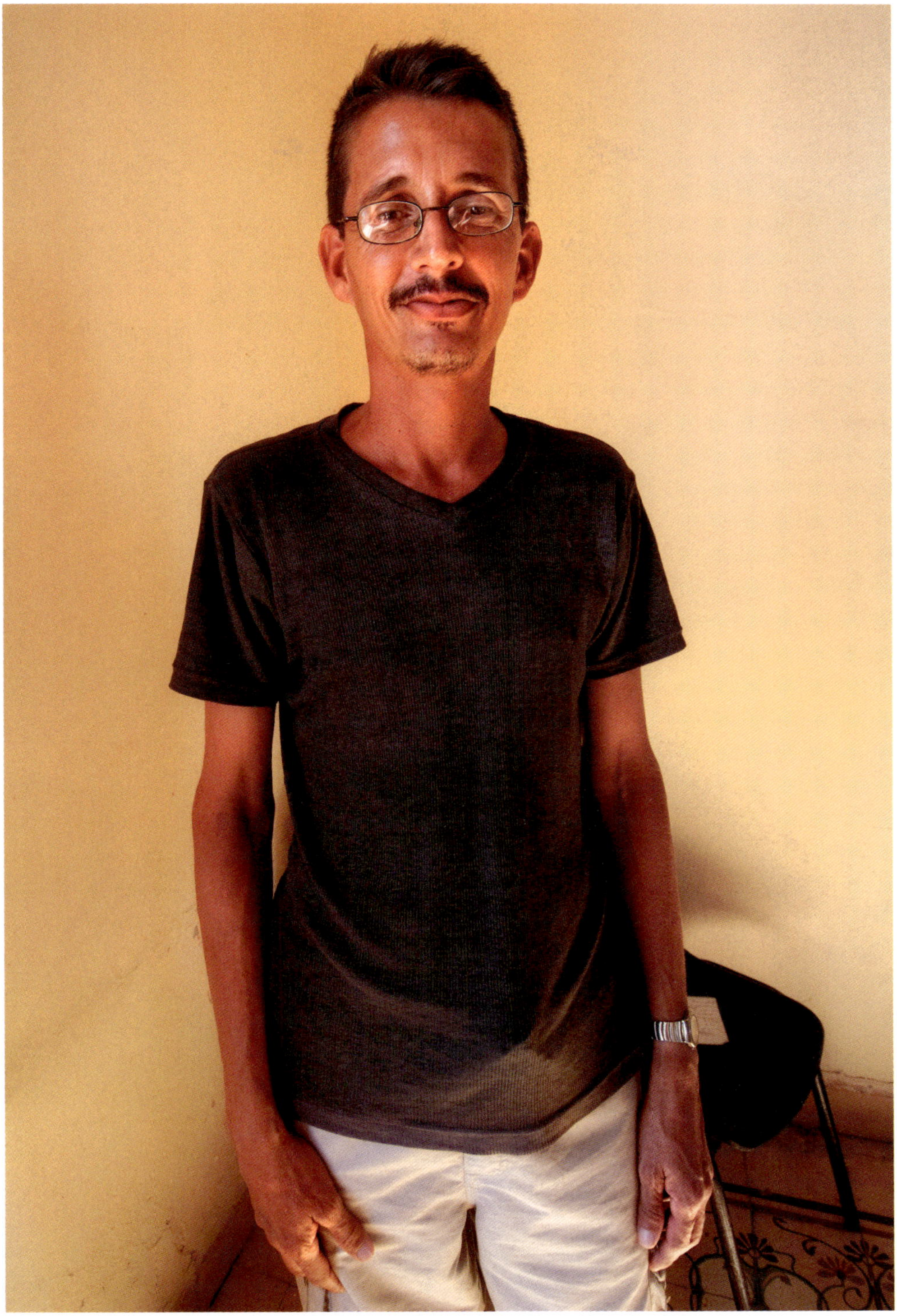

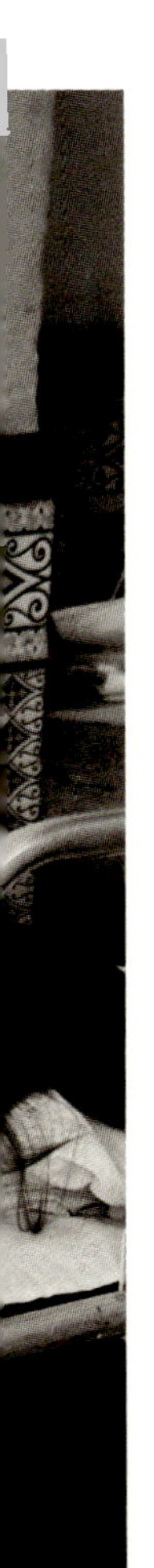

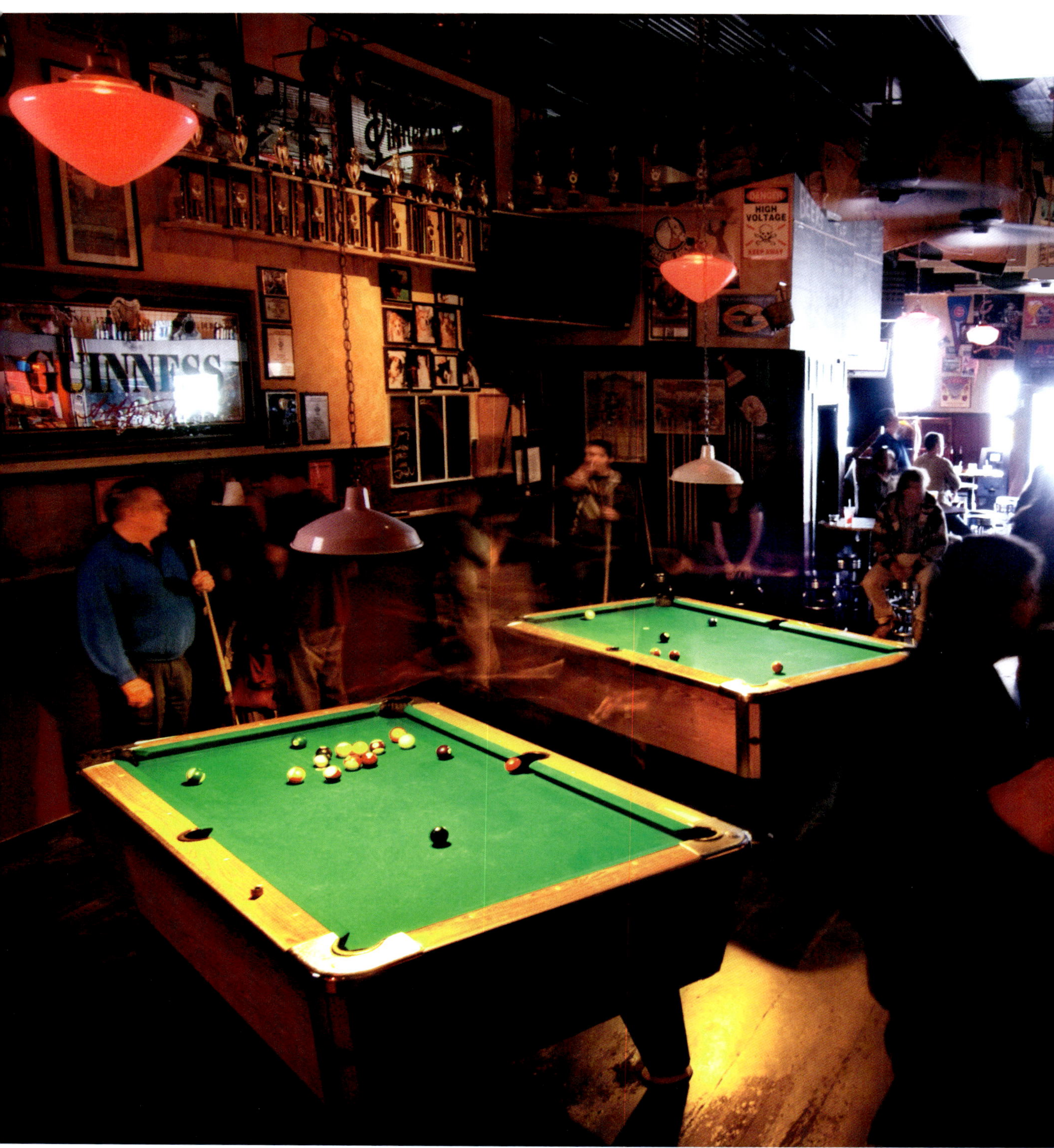
GUINNESS
HIGH VOLTAGE

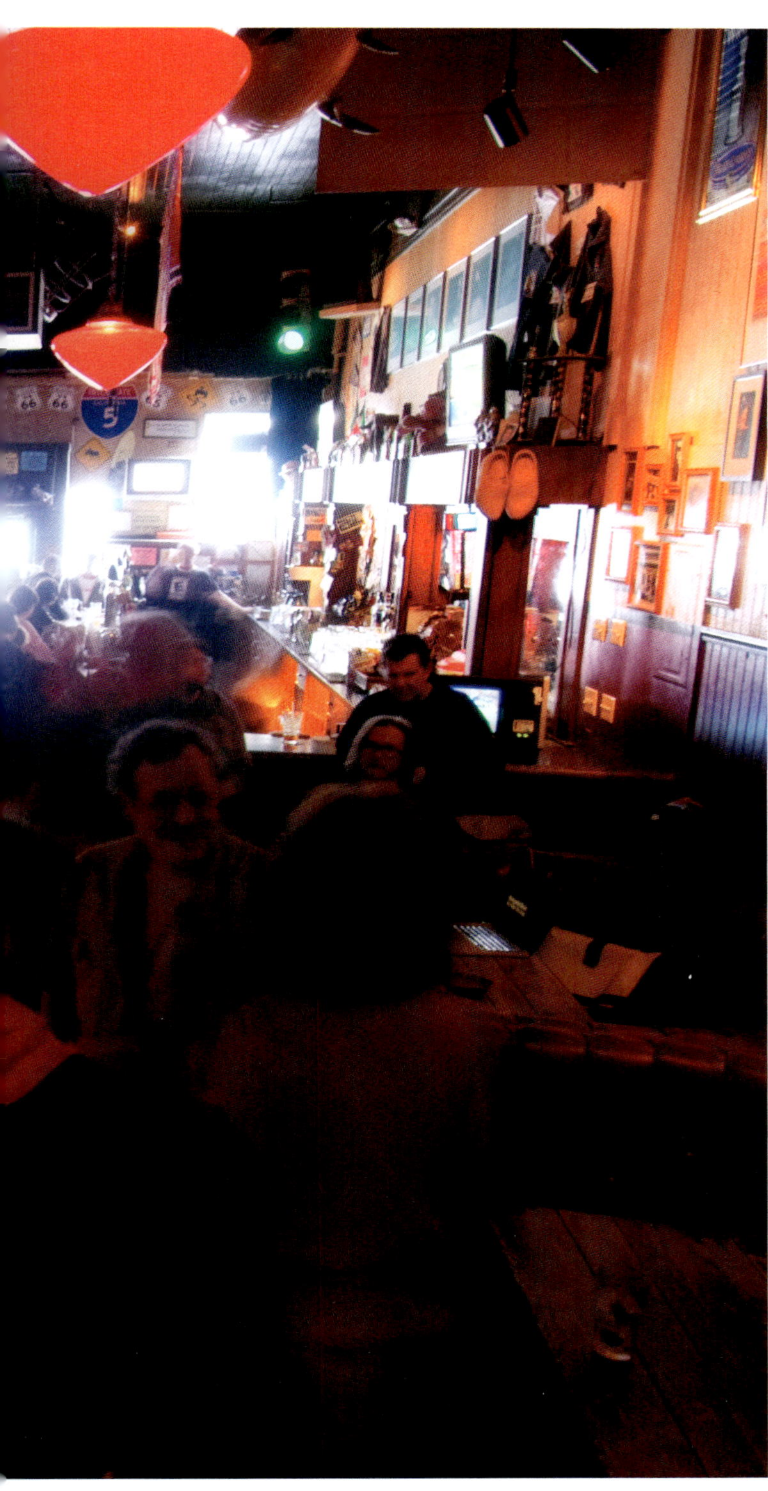

◄ There's no single person distinctly shown in this long exposure (4 seconds) taken inside a pool hall and bar. But the environment itself, even without a clearly delineated portrait, can say a great deal about the people in the bar—at least to the extent that the viewer probably has a pre-conceived notion about the kind of people you are likely to find in this environment.

16mm, 4 seconds at f/10 and ISO 200, tripod mounted

People at Work

For many people, more than half their waking hours are spent working. Much of the most exciting and visually interesting things we do occur while we are at work. For every boring desk job, there is someone professionally blowing glass, fixing cars, or climbing trees—doing something dirty and possibly dangerous that can be photographed.

These jobs may be boring and repetitive to the people doing them, but for us as photographers they represent several opportunities. Someone at work gives a photographer the chance of using the occupation to show something about a portrait subject. The job itself may present great narrative possibilities—even if it is boring, the repetitive routine will hopefully be leavened with bits of humor.

Finally, work is the greatest distraction. Even if you are not particularly interested in the visuals of the job, your subjects will probably be paying at least some attention to what they are doing.

It makes sense to keep your eyes open for opportunities that involve people at work. But why not make your own opportunities? Go out and research an active, physical profession. Then call ahead to get permission to photograph in the workplace.

Don't neglect details related to the paraphernalia and apparatus of a profession. These small things can be very telling. The tools someone uses on a job can narrate a great deal about a person, even if you never see the person themselves—and can help to paint a portrait in someone's mind just based on a few objects.

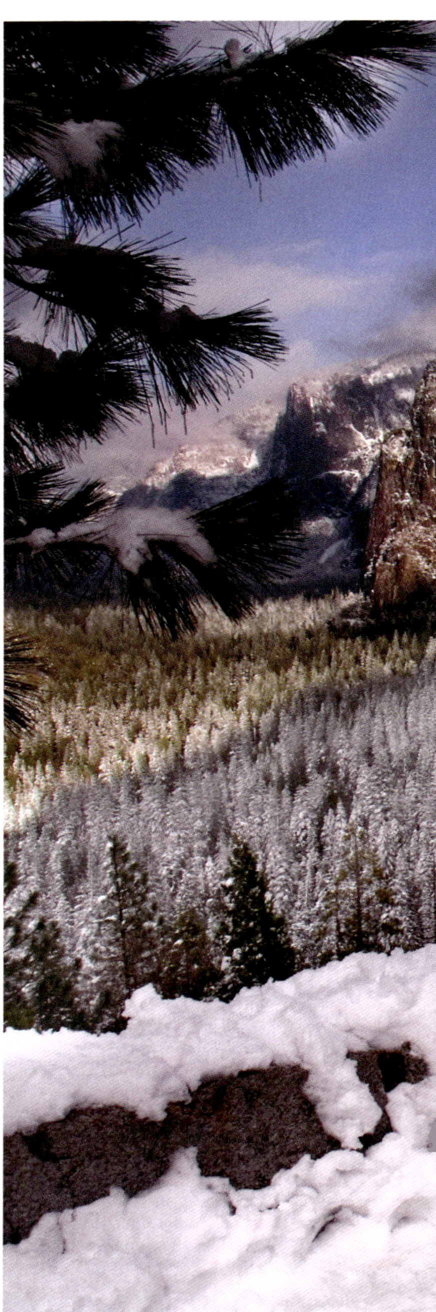

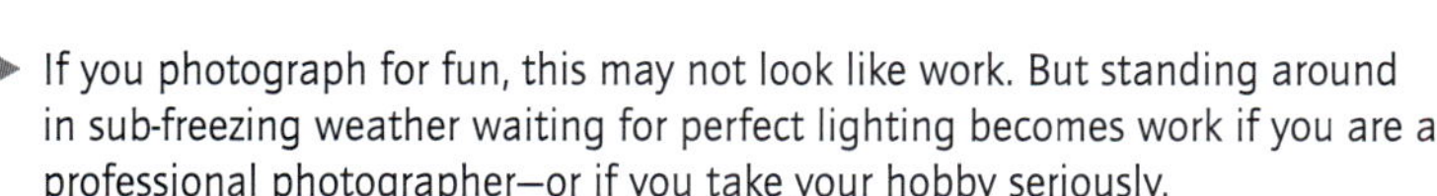

▶ If you photograph for fun, this may not look like work. But standing around in sub-freezing weather waiting for perfect lighting becomes work if you are a professional photographer—or if you take your hobby seriously.

I shot these photographers at Tunnel View in Yosemite Valley, California watching the light on a vista made famous by Ansel Adams. These photographers remind me of "Paparazzi"—with the ideal light of a natural scenic view as the target, rather than a celebrity.

18mm, 1/200 of a second at f/7.1 and ISO 100, hand held

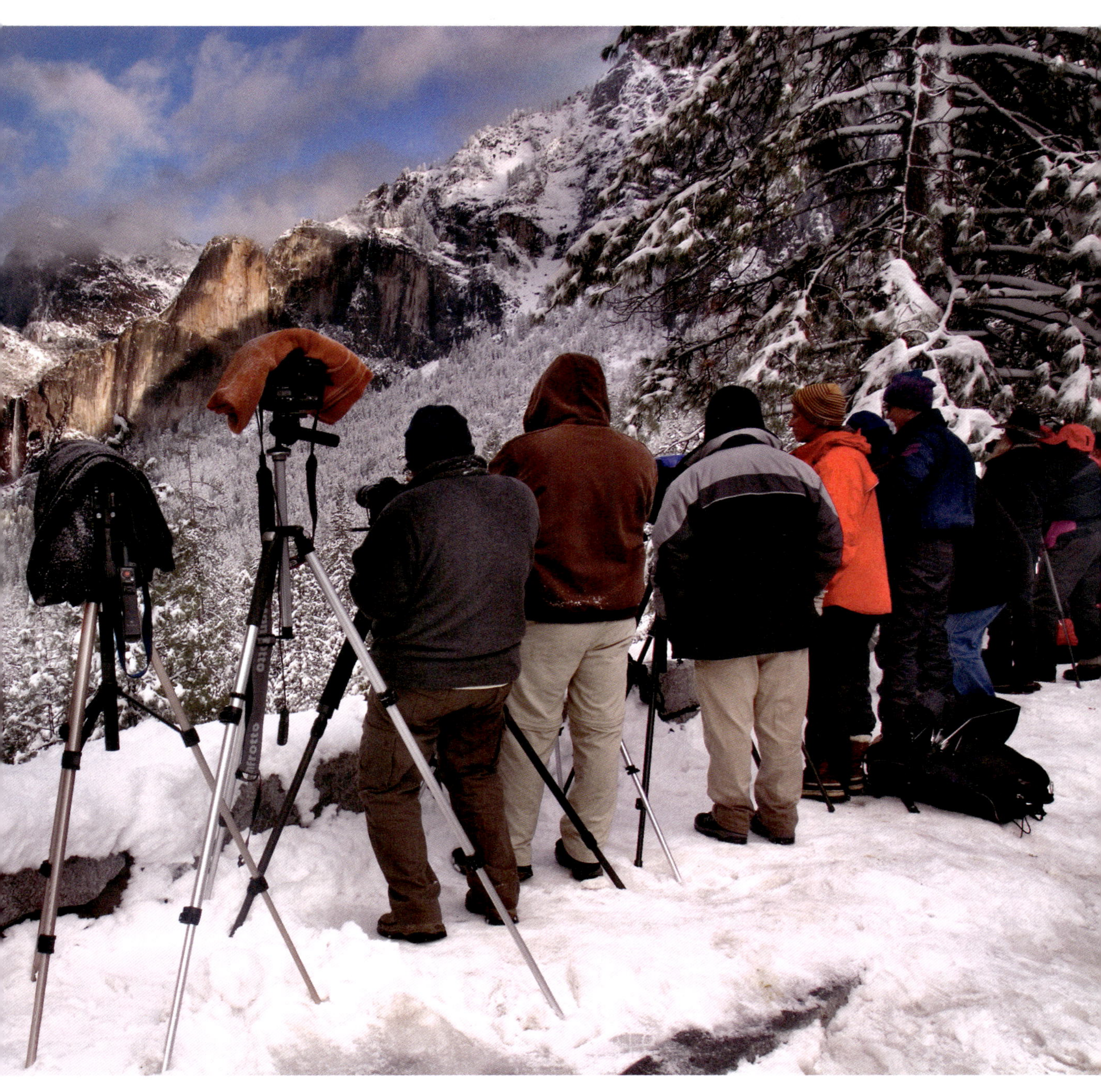

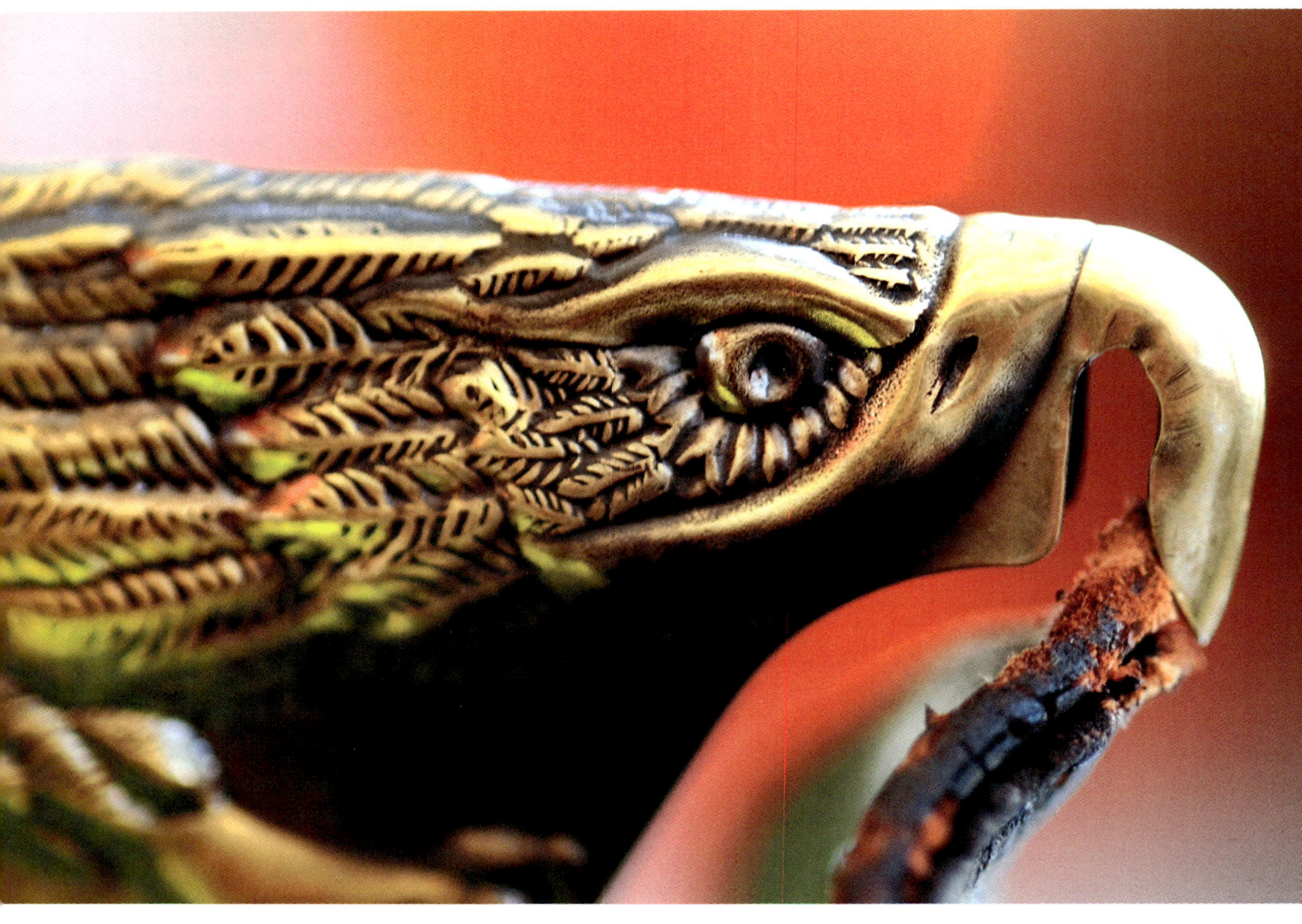

There are no human subjects in this set of three photos. But the paraphernalia shown even without anybody present amounts to a partial portrait of the work-life of a fire fighter.

▲ A surprisingly decorative bird holds a fireman's badge on top of this fire helmet.

105mm macro, 1/50 of a second at f/3.5 and ISO 640, hand held

▶ Top: This photo shows the relationship of the badge to the decorative bird (the beak is shown at the top of the photo).

105mm macro, 1/60 of a second at f/4 and ISO 640, hand held

▶ Bottom: Firefighter's helmet and oxygen mask.

56mm, 1/80 of a second at f/4.8 and ISO 640, hand held

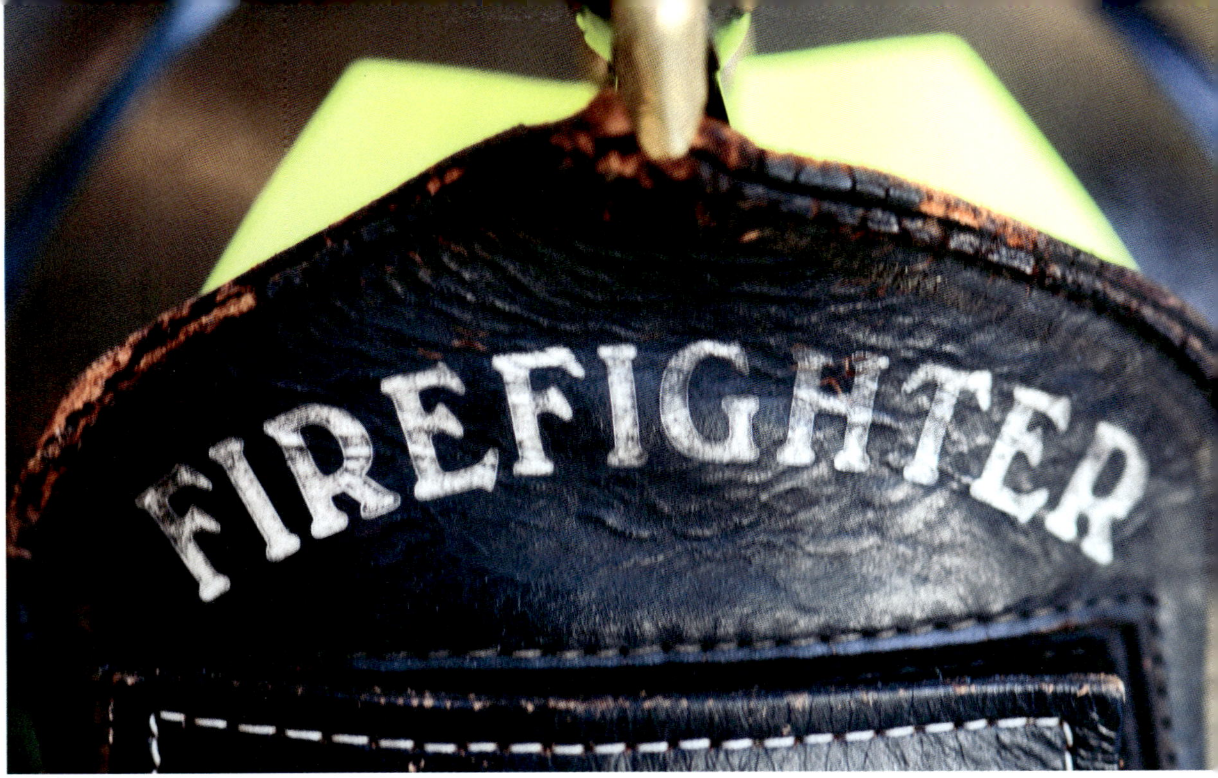

FIREFIGHTER

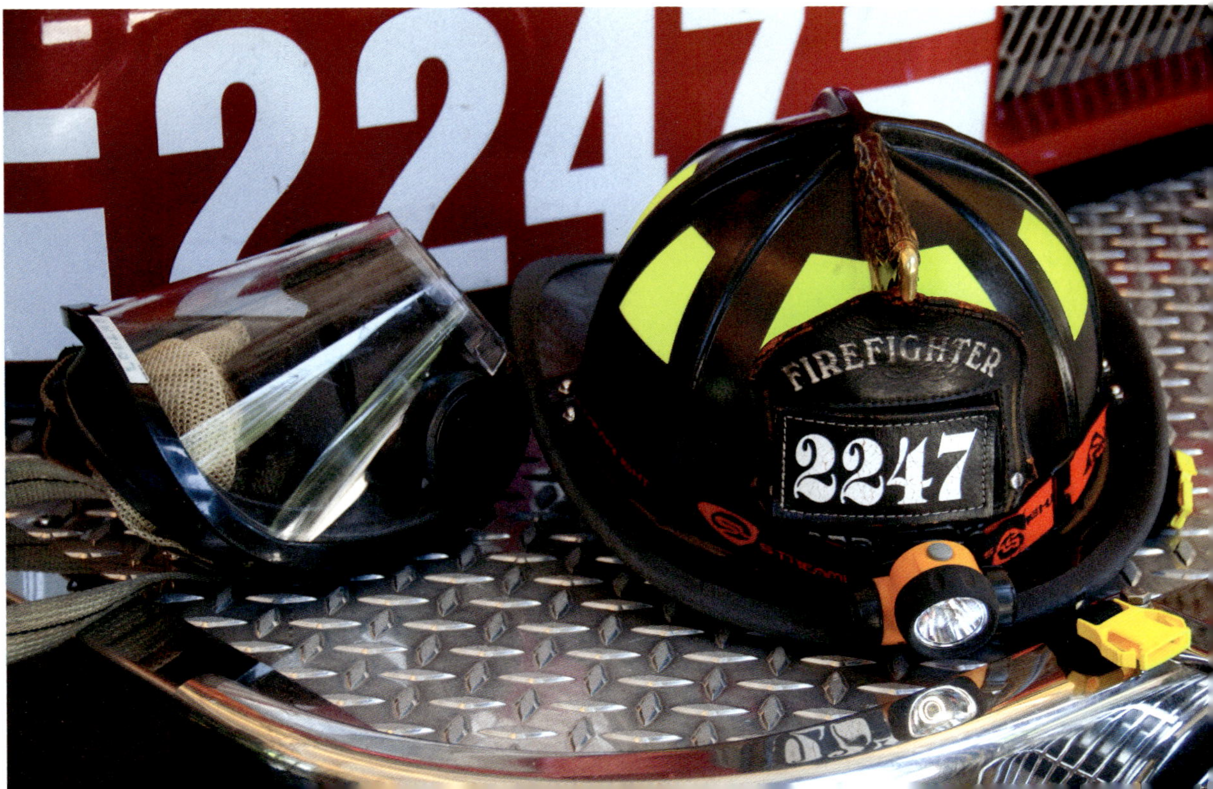

2247
FIREFIGHTER
2247

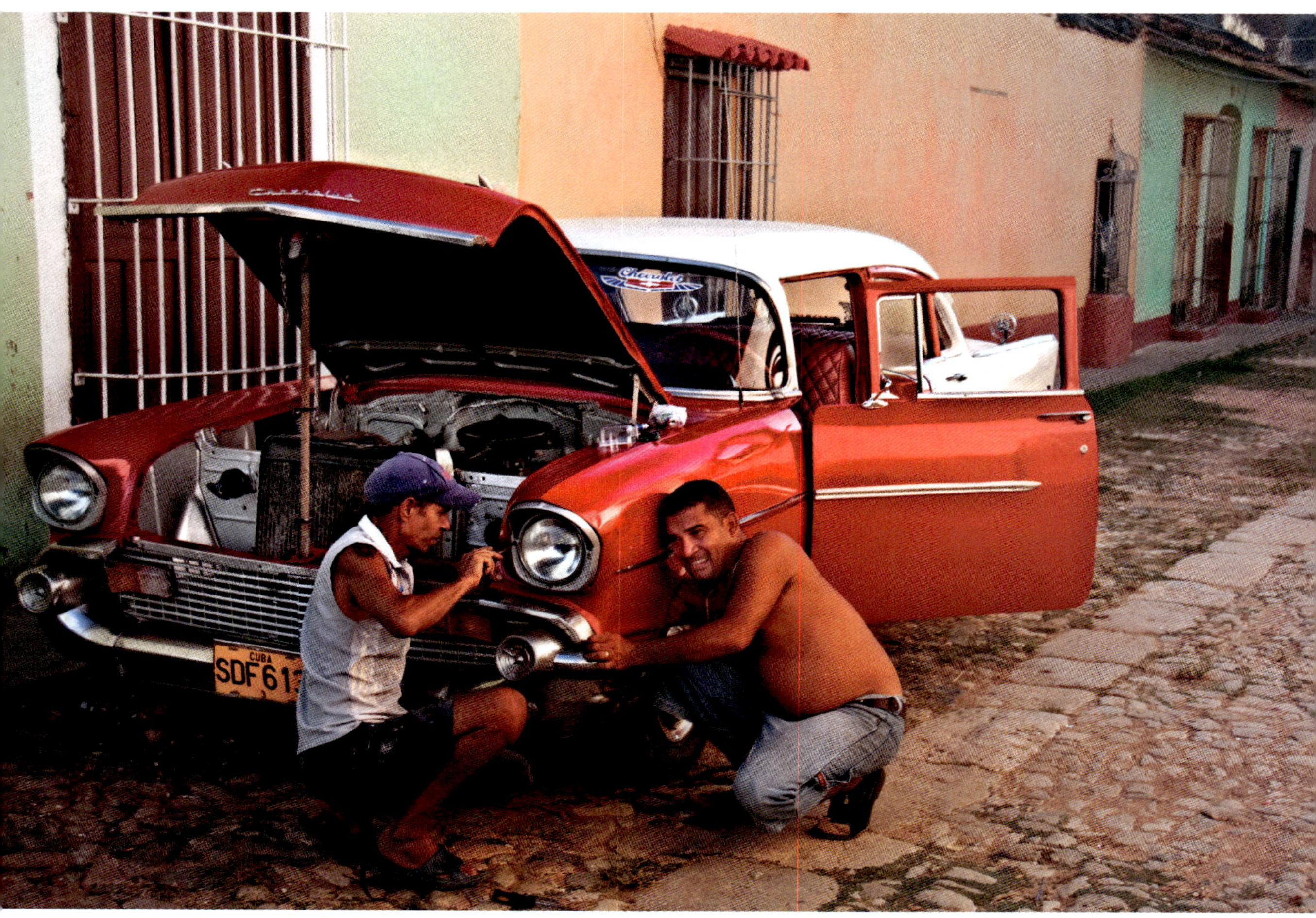

▲ While wandering the back streets of Trinidad, Cuba, I came upon these two men working on this antique car. I thought their relation to the car, and to each other, told an interesting story about concentration, endurance, and the struggle for perfection—note the good shape the car is in—so I snapped the photo.

35mm, 1/100 of a second at f/5 and ISO 100, hand held

▶ This detail shot of a Cuban cowboy at work tells a story: the rope is in everyday use and highly functional, and the rubber boots show that the work is practical—not stylized in the way that the gear belonging to a rodeo cowboy might be.

112mm, 1/250 of a second at f/8 and ISO 100, hand held

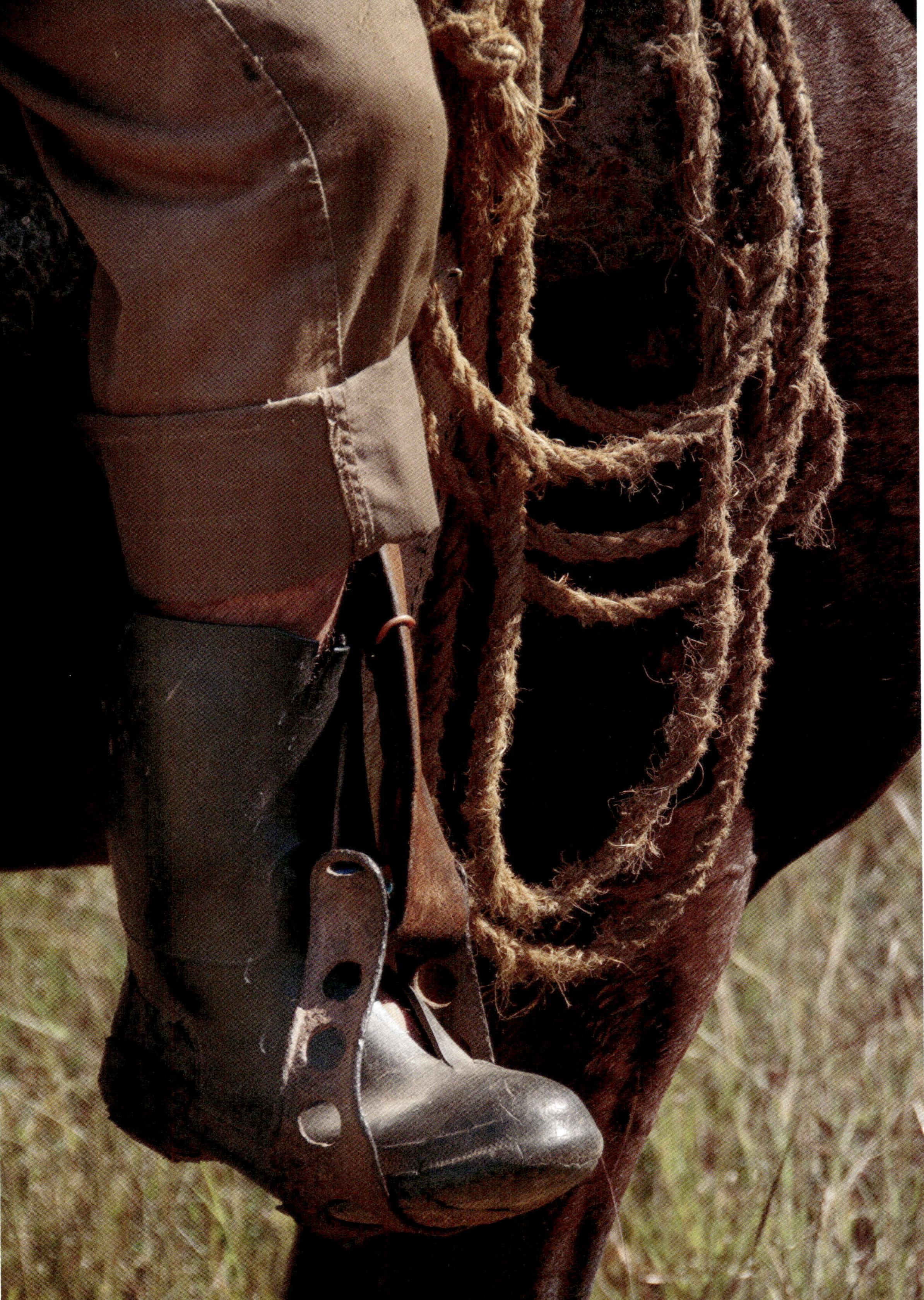

People at Play

Play can mean many things to different people. For some people, play means a game of chess or reading a book. Some simply like to stroll. Others are more active, and like to run, jump, splash—or play organized sports. Acting is play, and travel can be also. Depending on preferences and context, anything that is neither work nor sleep—in other words, leisure time—can be considered play.

Using the verb "to play" in a slightly different sense, playing is what kids do. To play means to have fun, and if you encourage your portrait subjects to play, you are likely to get casual and interesting photos. Photos of people at play can reveal a side of the person not normally seen.

I suggest that you keep an eye out for people playing. Play usually represents a photographic opportunity. Try to conceptualize your photo so that it shows what is special about the play. For example, a slow shutter speed can exaggerate motion—and a fast shutter speed can stop motion crisply.

Furthermore, it's important to bring play into your photographic portraits even if it is not present organically. After all, photography is supposed to be fun. If your portrait subjects are encouraged to "mug it up" some of your shots may be over the top and unusable. But once things settle down, you are likely to get more lively, interesting, and unusual portraits.

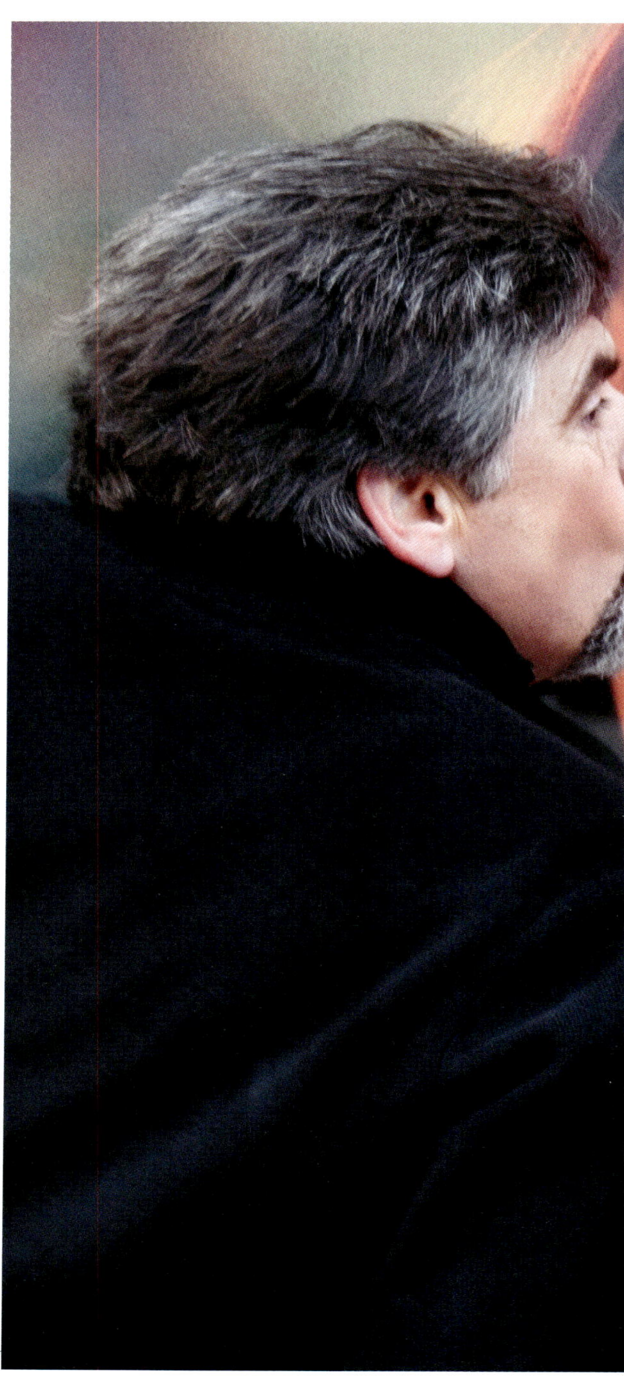

▶ I asked this father and son to kiss the woman on the billboard. They had fun playing along with me, and I got an interesting portrait.

70mm, 1/100 of a second at f/5 and ISO 500, hand held

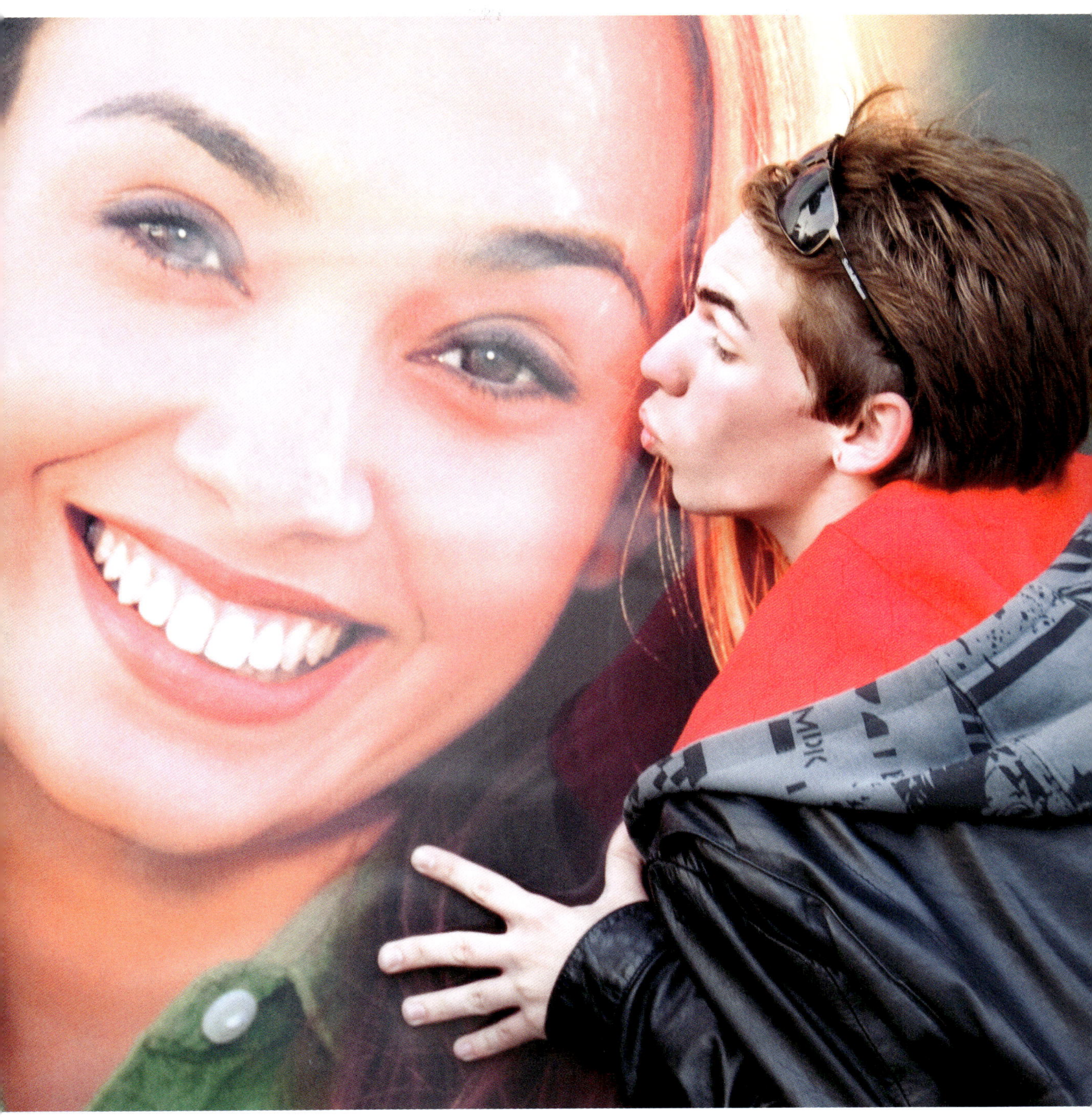

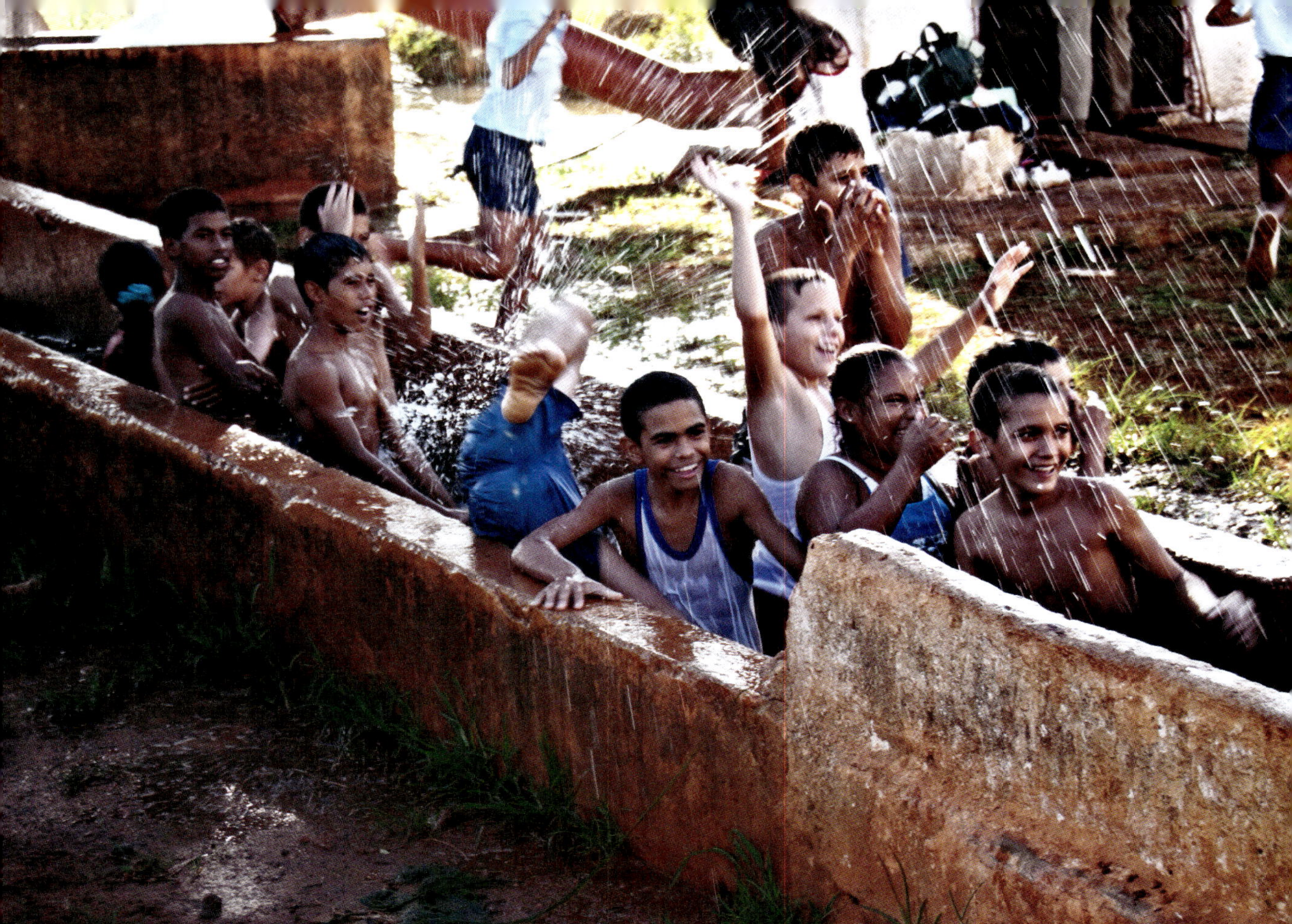

▲ Kids everywhere love to play in water; these youths are cavorting in an irrigation channel in the Cuban countryside.

55mm, 1/60 of a second at f/4.8 and ISO 100

▶ I asked my son Nicky to jump, and was ready to capture him in mid-air as he experienced the exhilarating effects of pretend flight.

12.7mm (about 40mm in 35mm terms), 1/160 of a second at f/8 and ISO 80, hand held (taken with a Canon Powershot G9)

▼ Pages 88–89: Many people in Havana, Cuba live a great part of their life on the waterfront boulevard called the Malecón where the ocean breezes are much cooler than the humid streets of the barrio. Life along the Malecón is a never-ending promenade, with couples embracing, families quarrelling, and people walking back and forth.

I used a long exposure (1.6 seconds) to show this motion as blurs of color.

150mm, 1.6 seconds at f/22 and ISO 100, tripod mounted

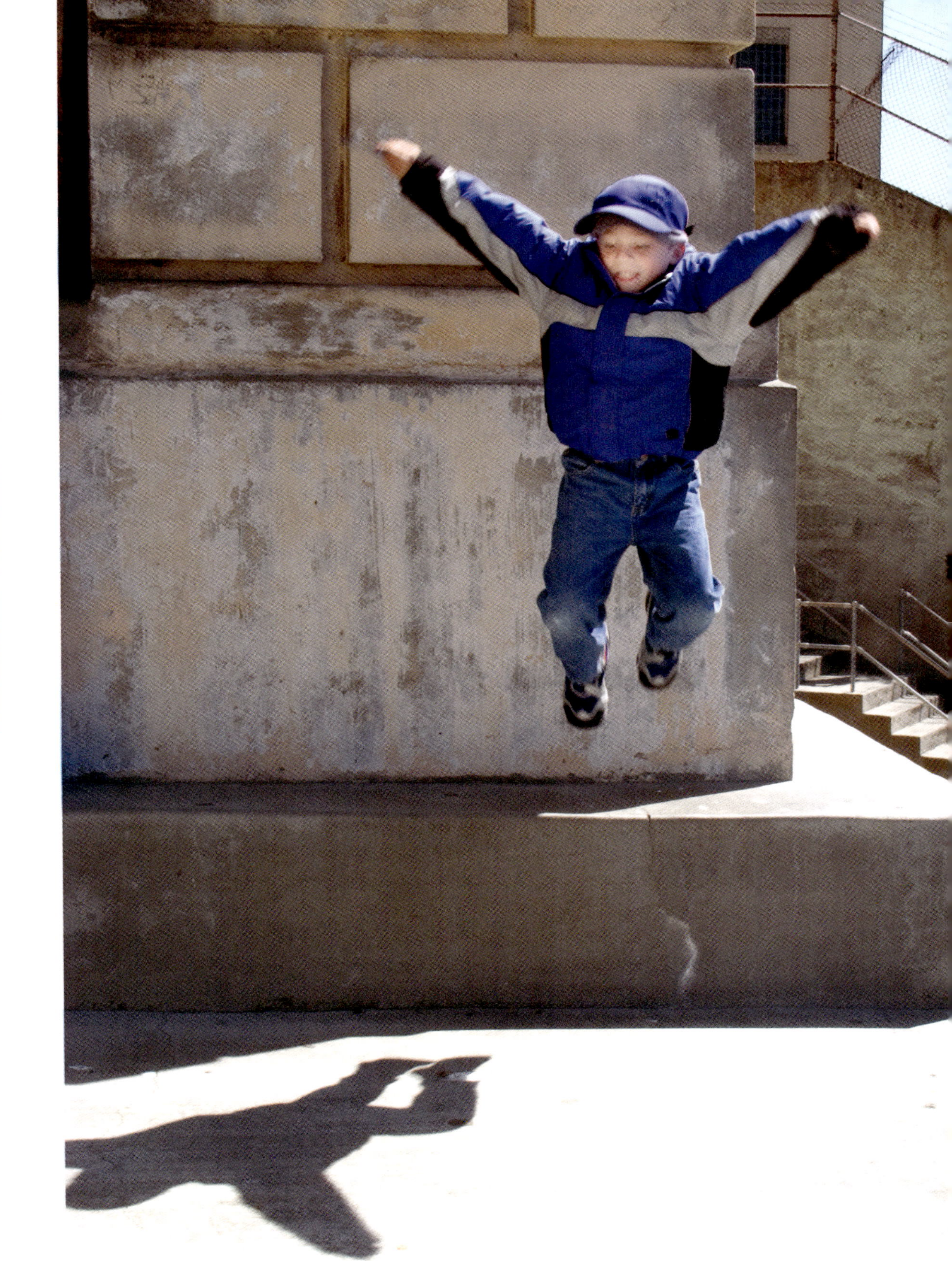

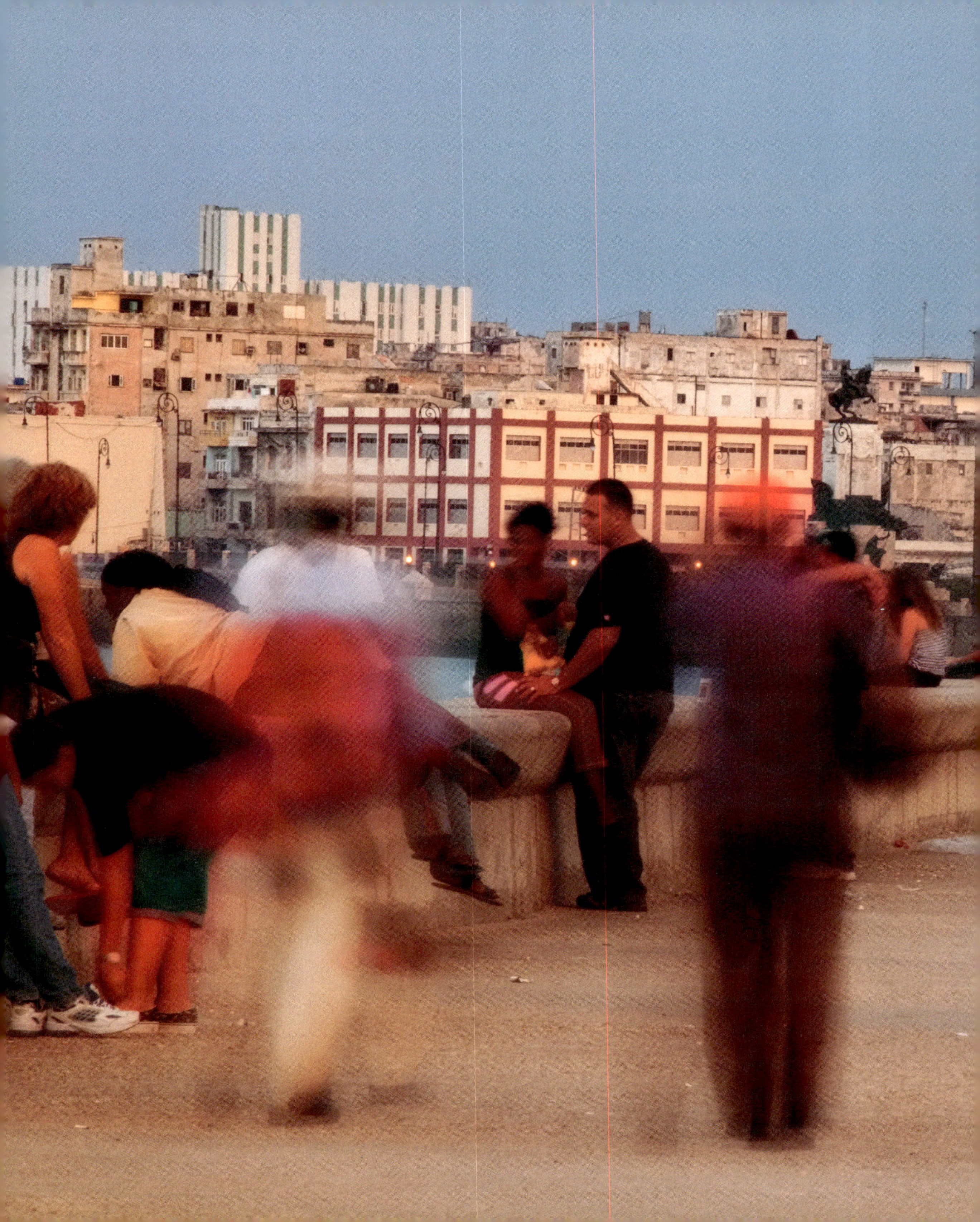

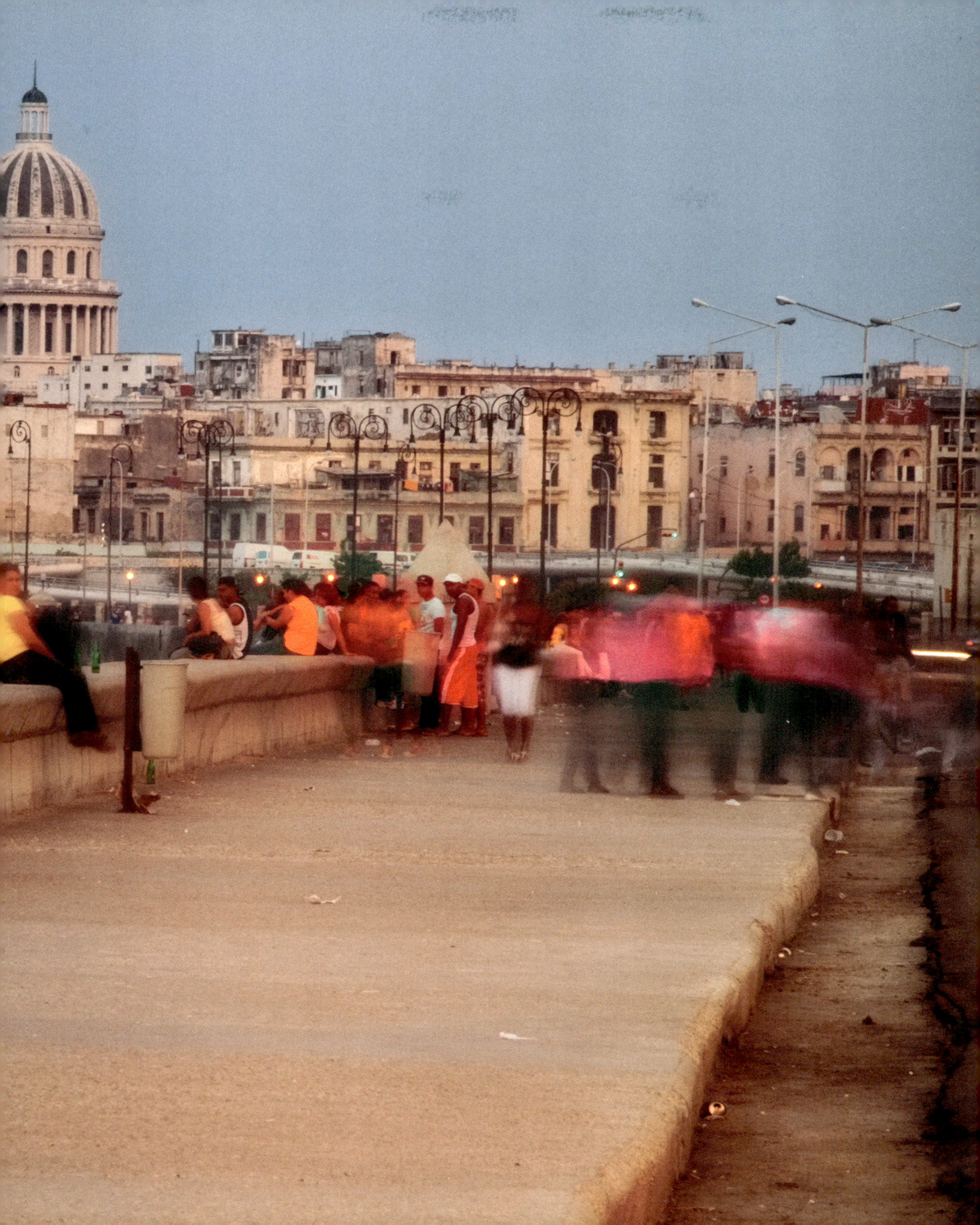

Working with Models

When you work with a model there is a different dynamic in operation than when you are photographing your family, someone you don't know on the street, or when someone has asked you to take their photo. It's the model's job to pose for you, and most professional models have a great deal of experience posing.

While many professional models have a repertoire of poses, it works best in most cases for the photographer to be very involved in posing the model. In other words, you should usually be prepared to tell the model what to do. Be professional and serious about work (although this doesn't mean you can't have fun!). Setting a productive tone, along with clear and supportive direction on the part of the photographer, helps create an effective portraiture session with a model.

Think of it this way: part of your job when photographing a model is to be a director. The model can't see the scene from the camera's viewpoint, but you can. Sometimes it helps to show the model what you've captured on your LCD, but this always takes place after the shot has been made.

Since you're the one in the position to see what impact the choices you've made are having—and since you're the only one to know the look of the photos you've pre-visualized—you need to be the one controlling the ongoing direction of the shoot.

I welcome input from the models I work with, but I realize that I am the one calling the shots. If I do so in a courteous and precise manner, this helps both me and the model relax.

Don't assume that you'll always have to pay a model. Good photographers can sometimes work with models on a trade-for-services basis, where you provide the model with images for use in their portfolio. Be careful to spell out the details of this kind of arrangement in advance. How many digital image files at what resolution will the model get? Will these files be processed and retouched in Photoshop (see *Portraits in the Digital Darkroom* starting on page 196)? Who—model and photographer—will have rights to license the photos? Sometimes trading modeling for photography can be a win-win situation for both parties—but also it's less complicated to pay for a model's time, and have them sign a standard model release (see pages 61-62 for more about releases).

Forget whatever fantasies you may have that all models are gorgeous, tall, and busty blonds. Photographic models come in all genders, shapes, and sizes. Even if you consider glamour models, no two are alike—and models who don't tend towards a stereotypical look can be the most fun to work with.

▶ I posed this model on a black background with low-key lighting in order to create a glamorous effect.

31mm, 1/100 of a second at f/5.6 and ISO 100, hand held

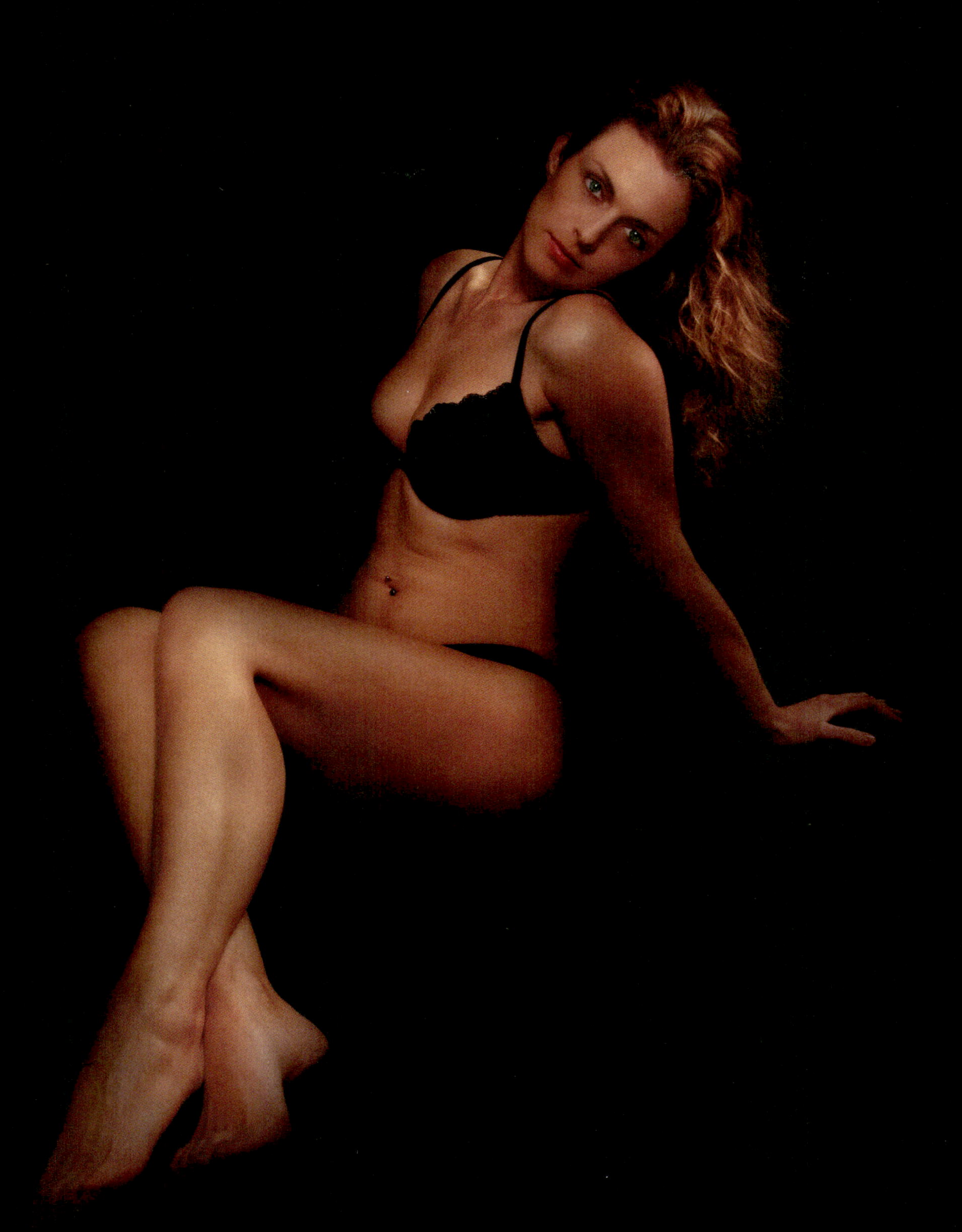

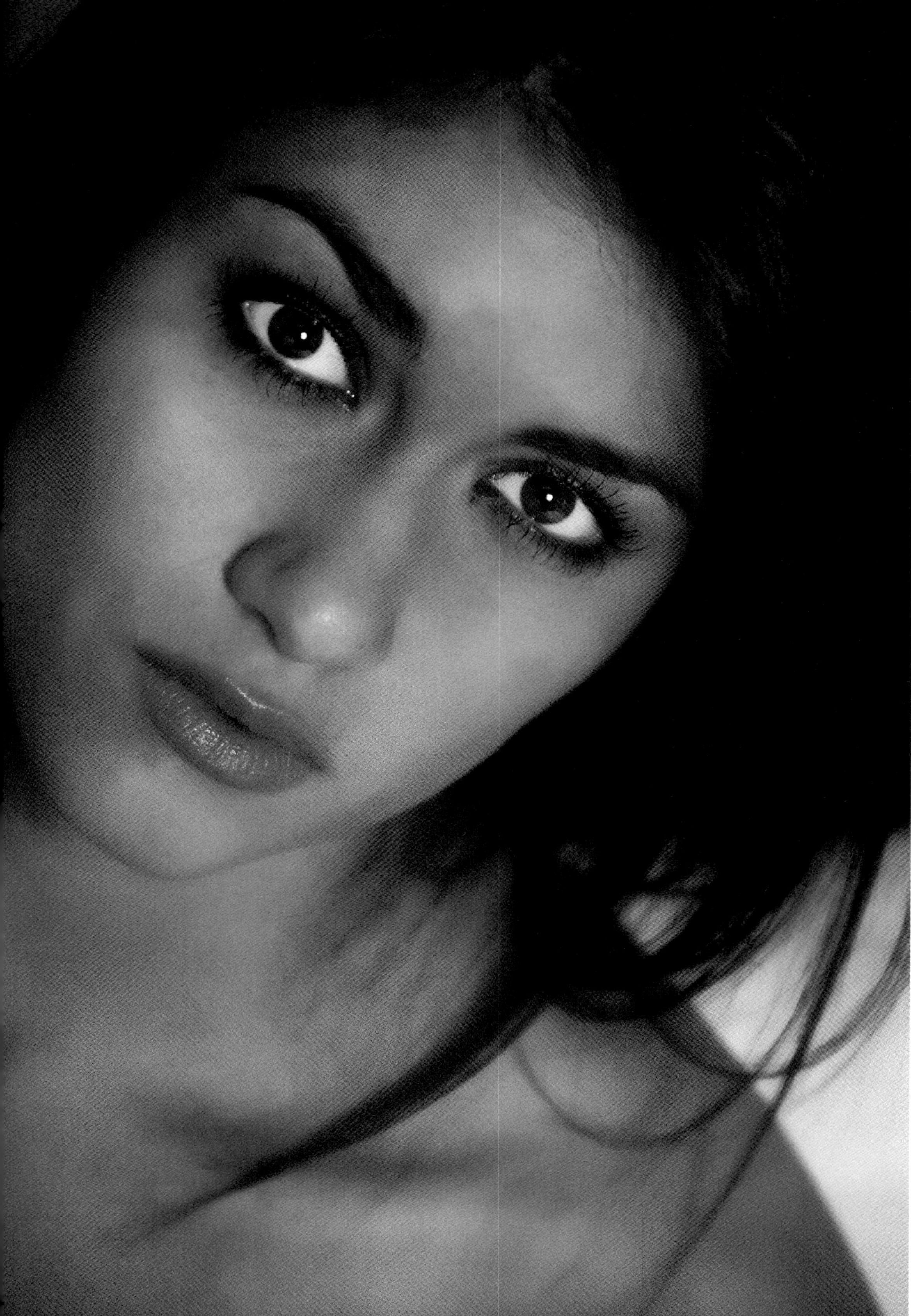

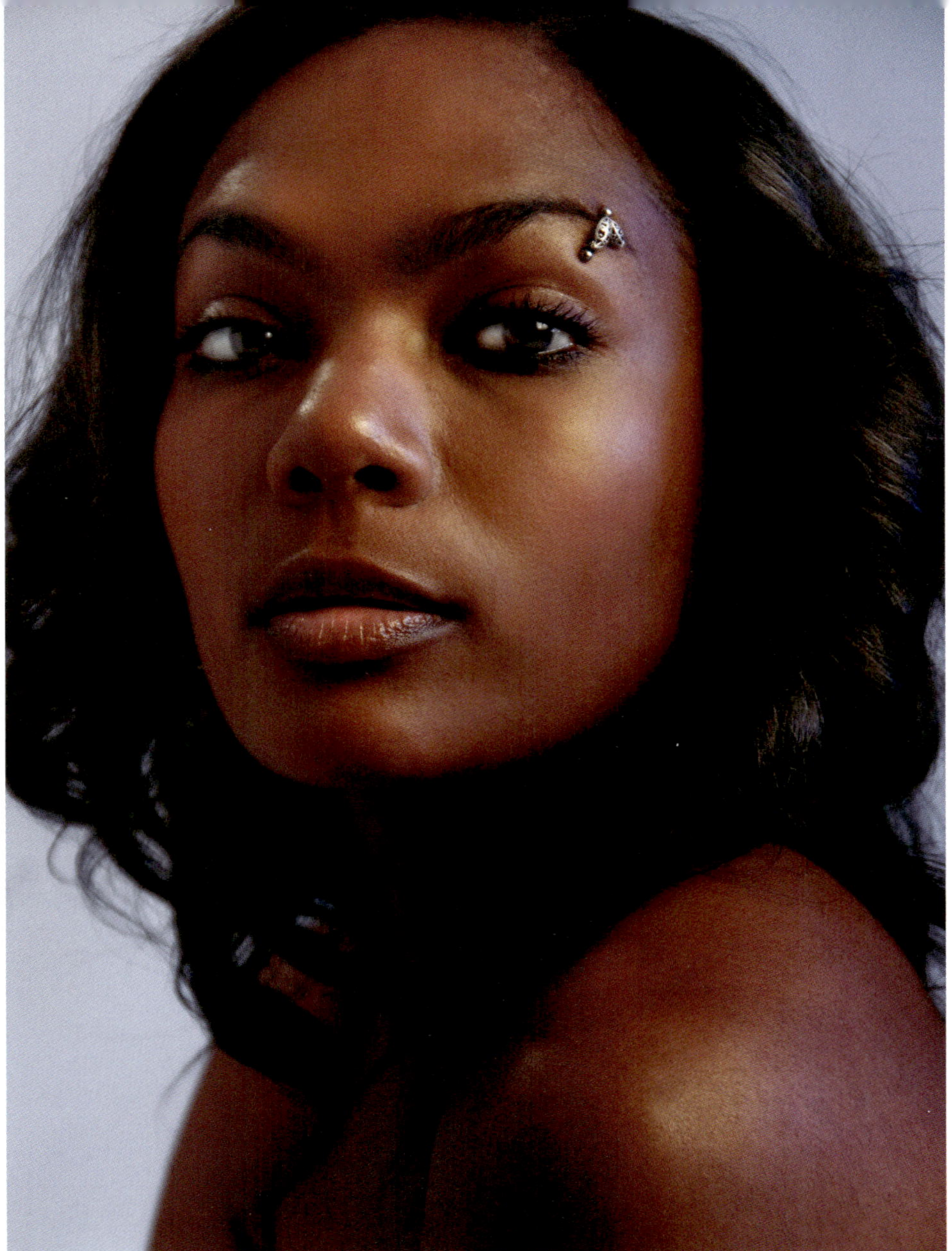

▲ This is a portrait of a striking and attractive figure model who was used to working with artists and photographers. Since her specialty was holding difficult physical poses, I thought it would be interesting instead to create a simple portrait of her face.

105mm, 1/125 of a second at f/7.1 and ISO 100, hand held

◀ My idea in this portrait was to emphasize the model's striking eyes. I instructed her to whip her head around from right to left. When the hair fell in exactly the right position to complete the composition, I snapped the photo.

170mm, 1/125 of a second at f/5.6 and ISO 100, hand held

Casting Models

Sometimes I shoot models for a specific project with a planned and pre-visualized image in mind. At other times, I photograph models for fun. Either way, it is important that the model I cast is appropriate for the type of image I want to create. Good portraits show the inner person to at least some degree, and one thing that you cannot change—even with Photoshop—is the essential nature of the person posing for the camera.

For example, a brassy and busty blond might be very appropriate for a pinup shoot intending to echo the look of Marilyn Monroe. But this model would probably not work for an image that was intended to communicate contemplation. The model Maya shown below is pretty in an understated and un-made-up kind of way, but would never do for a shoot portraying a "vamp."

Fortunately, there are models with every possible characteristic you can imagine out there. If you haven't worked with a model before, study a model's online portfolios before you commit to working with them. Model web sites such as Model Mayhem, www.modelmayhem.com, provide a great way to find many different kinds of models. If you don't think you have the ability to evaluate a model based on an online profile and portfolio, then by all means get the input of a friend. I don't want to be sexist about this, but I find that women are often better than men at evaluating models for suitability to a task; so whenever possible, I get my wife's input before deciding to work with a particular model.

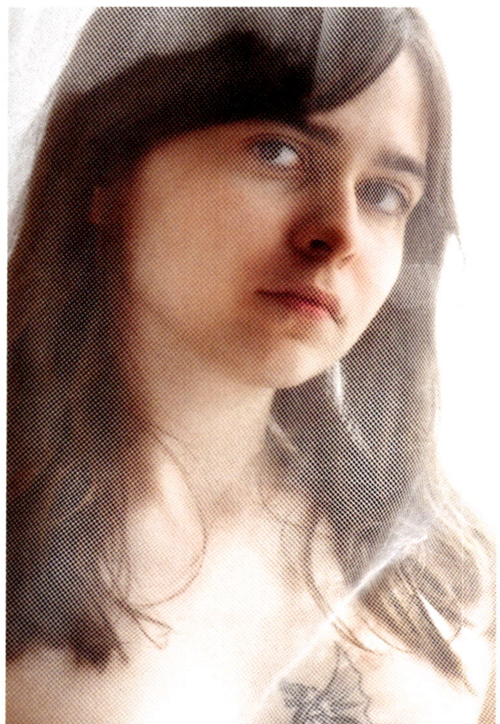

◄ I used a white gauze curtain to enhance this natural-light portrait. The primary source of light was a window to the right of the photo; a reflector on the left helped balance the lighting. (For more about lighting, turn to page 140.)

This model has a look with an ingénue appeal, so the gauze curtain was appealing. However, when creating a photo using models, one has to consider whether the look of the model fits with the photographic conception.

200mm, 1/125 of a second at f/7.1 and ISO 320, hand held

► I was struck by the simple and natural facial lines shown by this model, and strove to create a portrait that was apparently simple in lighting and concept—to echo the simple but elegant look the model favored.

200mm, 1/200 of a second at f/9 and ISO 100, hand held

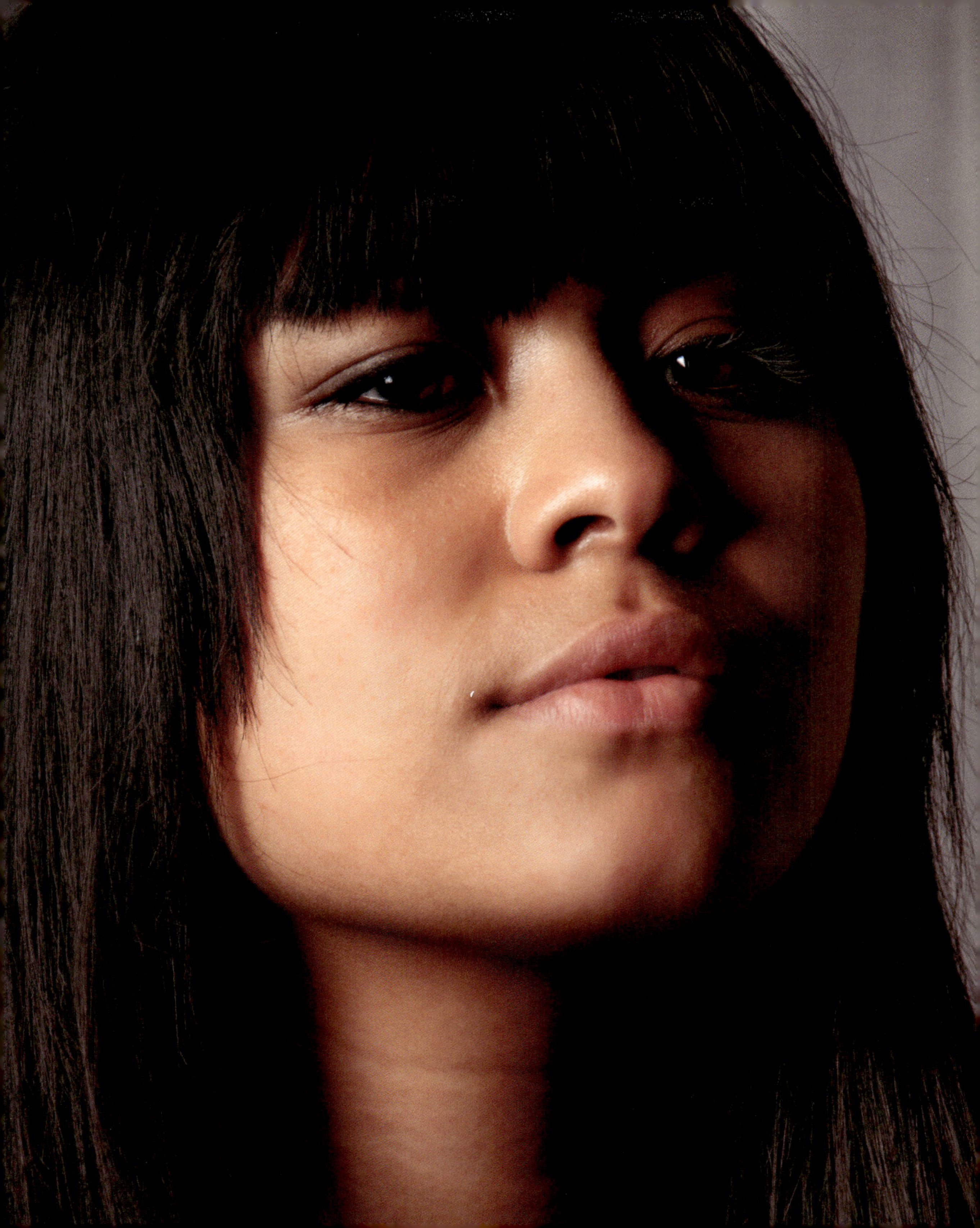

Propping

To prop a model or a portrait subject means to add an artifact to the photo, particularly one that is relevant to the subject. Effective propping has a great deal to do with the success of a portrait—and a prop that doesn't fit with the character of the subject or the context of the photo means almost guaranteed failure. In other words, propping is surprisingly important.

Some props work because they are significant to the subject and reveal information about the subject's character. For example, a particular old-fashioned pen that the portrait subject always uses might fall into this category. Eye glasses and pipes are other examples that might be used for this kind of prop.

Other props are more generic in nature, and work by changing the context of the portrait. For example, I was photographing a model in a fairly generic studio setup. Adding a western-style hat converted this model into a "cowgirl" (see page 99). The hat is a simple and basic thing, but it changes the entire context of the portrait.

Props don't have to be physically small. A ladder someone stands on is a prop, as is an overstuffed arm chair someone sits in. Props can be intimate, or large and dominating—and everywhere in between.

Whatever their size, it is extremely important to pay attention to props.

Effective use of props makes even mundane portraits seem to sizzle—and inappropriate and unattractive propping makes otherwise excellent character studies fail.

When is an article of clothing a prop? Can a special background be considered propping? What about over-the-top make-up?

There's no really clear dividing line, but props tend to be things the subject can handle—pipes, canes, umbrellas—or stand, sit, or recline upon.

If you are ever photographing someone and feel that you have come to a dead end, try adding or changing the props that are in use. It's amazing how a prop can change the entire nature of a shoot.

For large-sized props such as beds, ladders, and over-stuffed arm chairs, you may have to improvise based on what is available at your shooting location. I like to think about propping in advance, and to bring with me a box or two of smaller things that I think might be appropriate—and might act to stimulate the imaginations of portrait subject and photographer.

▶ I photographed this bride in a dark underpass, positioned so that a shaft of light illuminated her in contrast to the surrounding shadows. The wedding bouquet is an attractive prop in this photo. Try visualizing the image without the bouquet—you'll see that it wouldn't be nearly as effective.

50mm, 1/250 of a second at f/4.8 and ISO 200, hand held

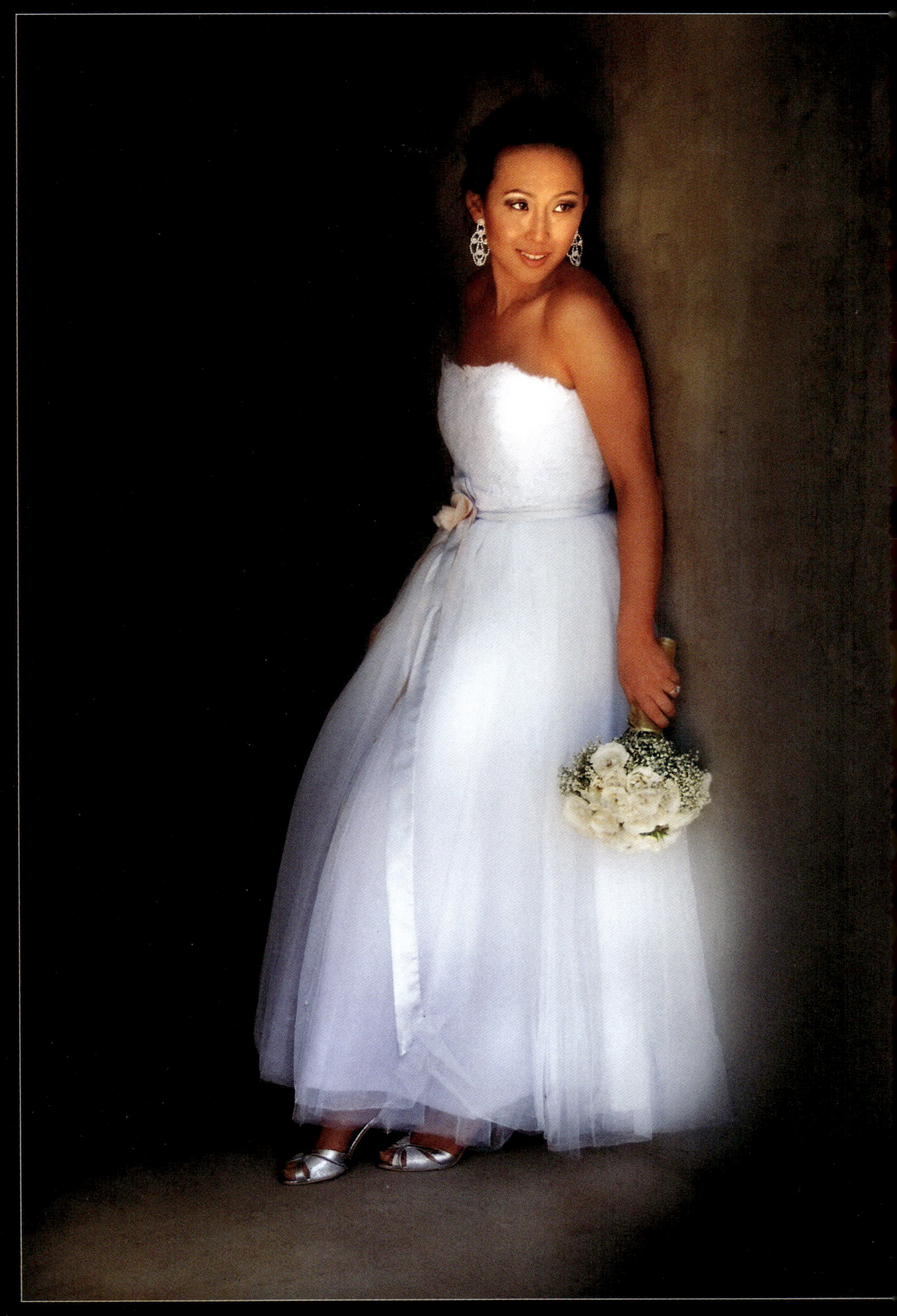

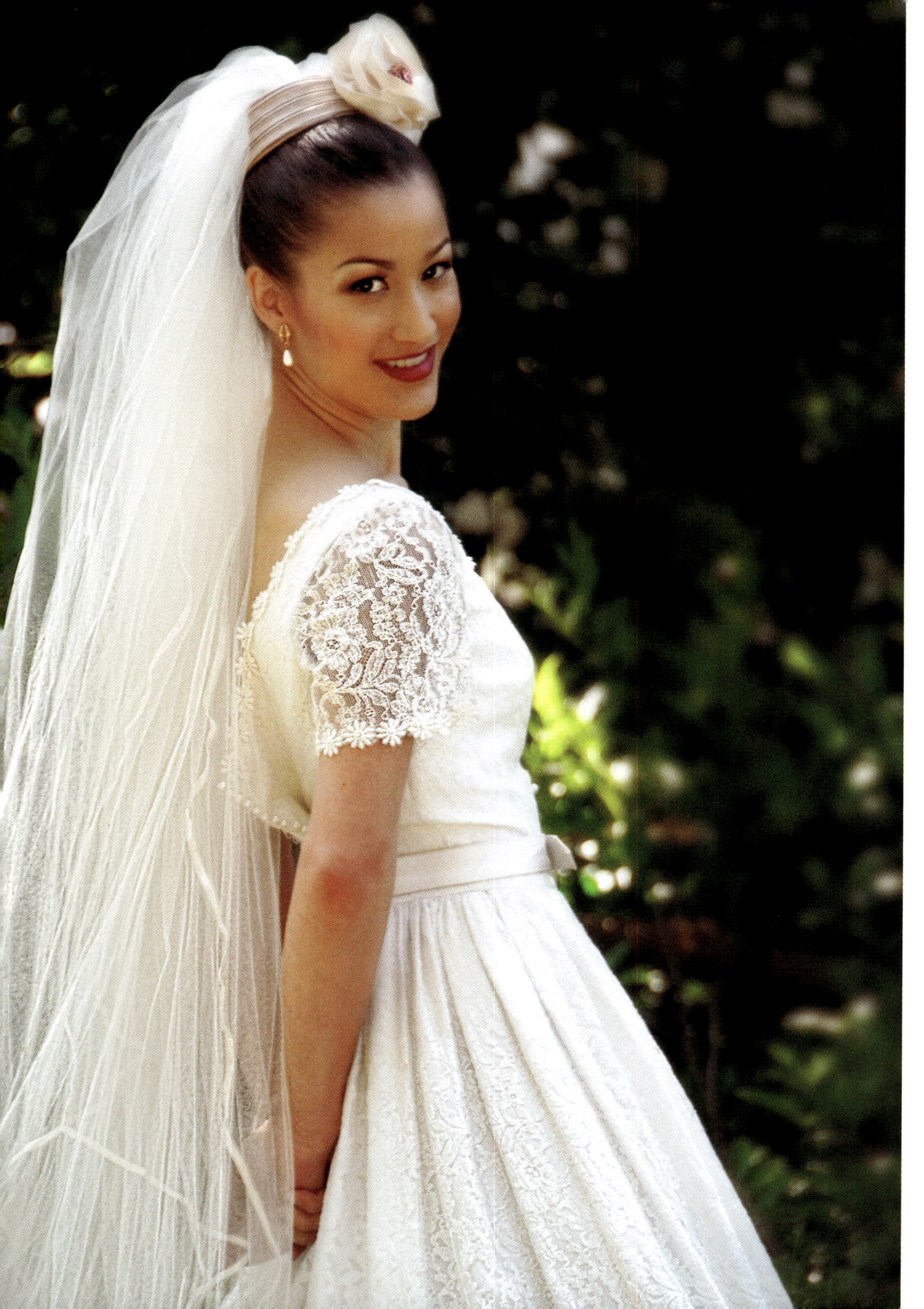

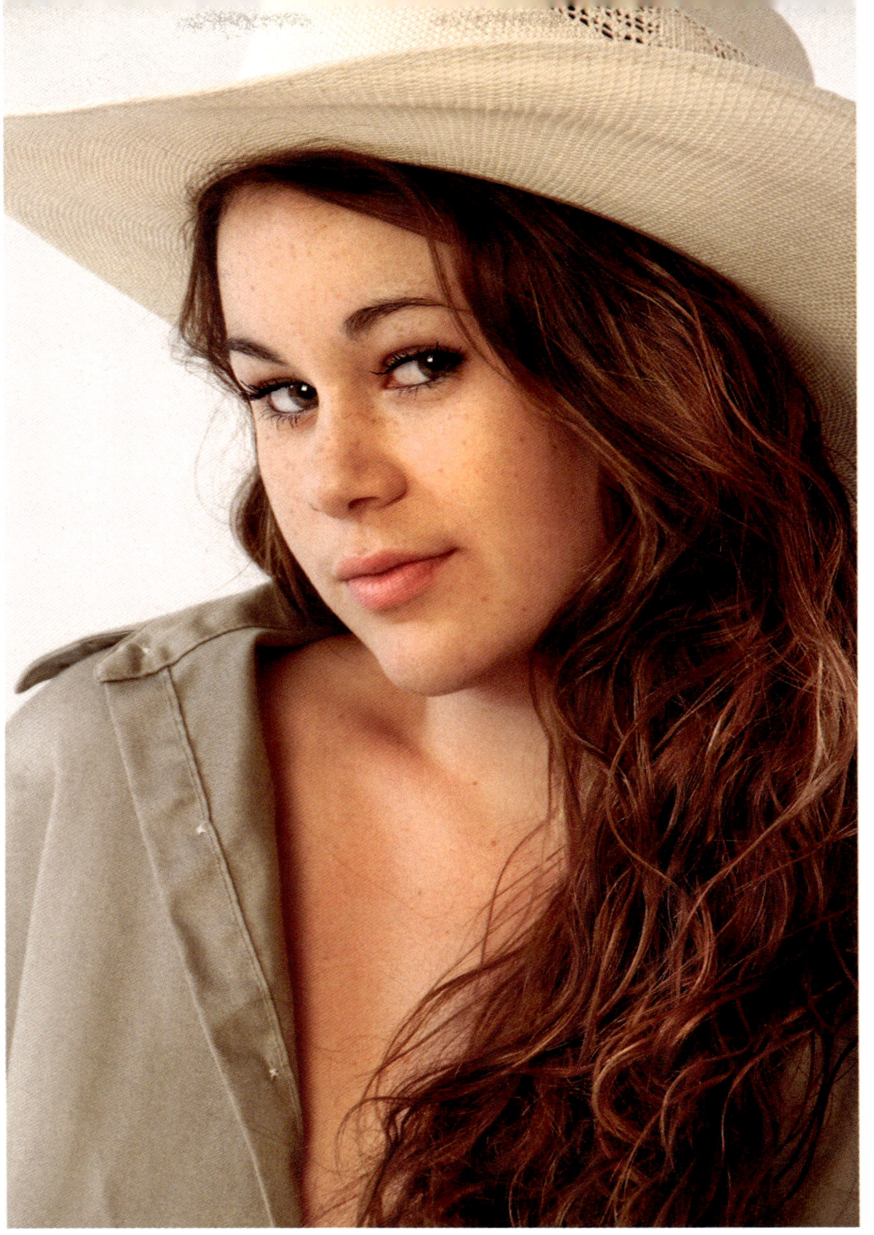

▲ The obvious prop here is the hat, which gives this model a very different look than when she was carrying a pink parasol (see page 47 for a look at the same model propped very differently). However, her magnificent and partially wild mane of hair should also be considered a photographic prop, with many different possible "uses" within a photo.

200mm, 1/160 of a second at f/9 and ISO 100, hand held

◄ To the eternal good fortune of wedding photographers, nowhere are attractive props more likely to be found than at weddings. The elaborate wedding dress shown here is as much a prop as it is a dress. Veils also make an attractive and romantic prop.

135mm, 1/125 of a second at f/5.6 and ISO 200, hand held

Clothing

In our society, clothing is vastly important. As Polonius famously and pompously noted in William Shakespeare's play *Hamlet,* "Clothes make the man." On the other hand, on either man or woman, clothing might be considered merely a prop. After all, we all came naked from the primordial ooze (or maybe it was the Garden of Eden?). But in fact, clothing is important in portraiture—and overlooked at one's peril.

In some cases—such as conceptual high-fashion photography or wedding portraits—elaborate clothing has its place.

But for the most part, when it comes to clothing, simple is better. Many shoots are wrecked when clothing clashes. In these cases, there's very little that the photographer can do to salvage the situation—except suggest that a simple, black turtleneck might work better.

Assuming that the point of the shoot is to create an attractive portrait, you should try to be careful that the clothing works well with the coloration of your subjects. Many people don't have a very good sense of this for themselves, so professional portrait photographers with studios often find themselves with an inventory of clothing.

You can take the same approach in a low-key way. If you are photographing in the studio, have some simple choices available. For women, some nice fabric can be used in a variety of ways as a wrap. For men, it's hard to go wrong with shirts that are basic black or basic white.

As a portrait photographer, you have a great deal to keep track of including lighting, the comfort and psyche of the portrait subject, along with your overall photographic composition. Clothing is one more element that can make or break an image.

On a commercial or advertising type of shoot, there is often a wardrobe stylist making sure the clothing is right. Having someone you know who is good with style and clothing can be beneficial to any portrait. This person can help you with the larger issue of finding the right clothing for the subject, or at least modifying an outfit to not ruin the shoot. An extra set of eyes can also help you spot the all important details such as buttons that are not straight, stained collars, and lint on dark clothing.

▶ This is an interesting photo of two models, partly because it shows that elaborate clothes do not always create an elegant look. The outfits shown here were carefully picked by a stylist, but they don't really work well with the way these gorgeous models are made up.

The intention of the shoot was to make up the model on the left to look like a "neo Geisha." This is an interesting concept and the make-up really works for this idea. However, the ruffled blue and yellow dress doesn't carry the Geisha idea.

The clothing on the model on the right works better because it is more simple.

1/160 of a second at f/8 and ISO 100, hand held

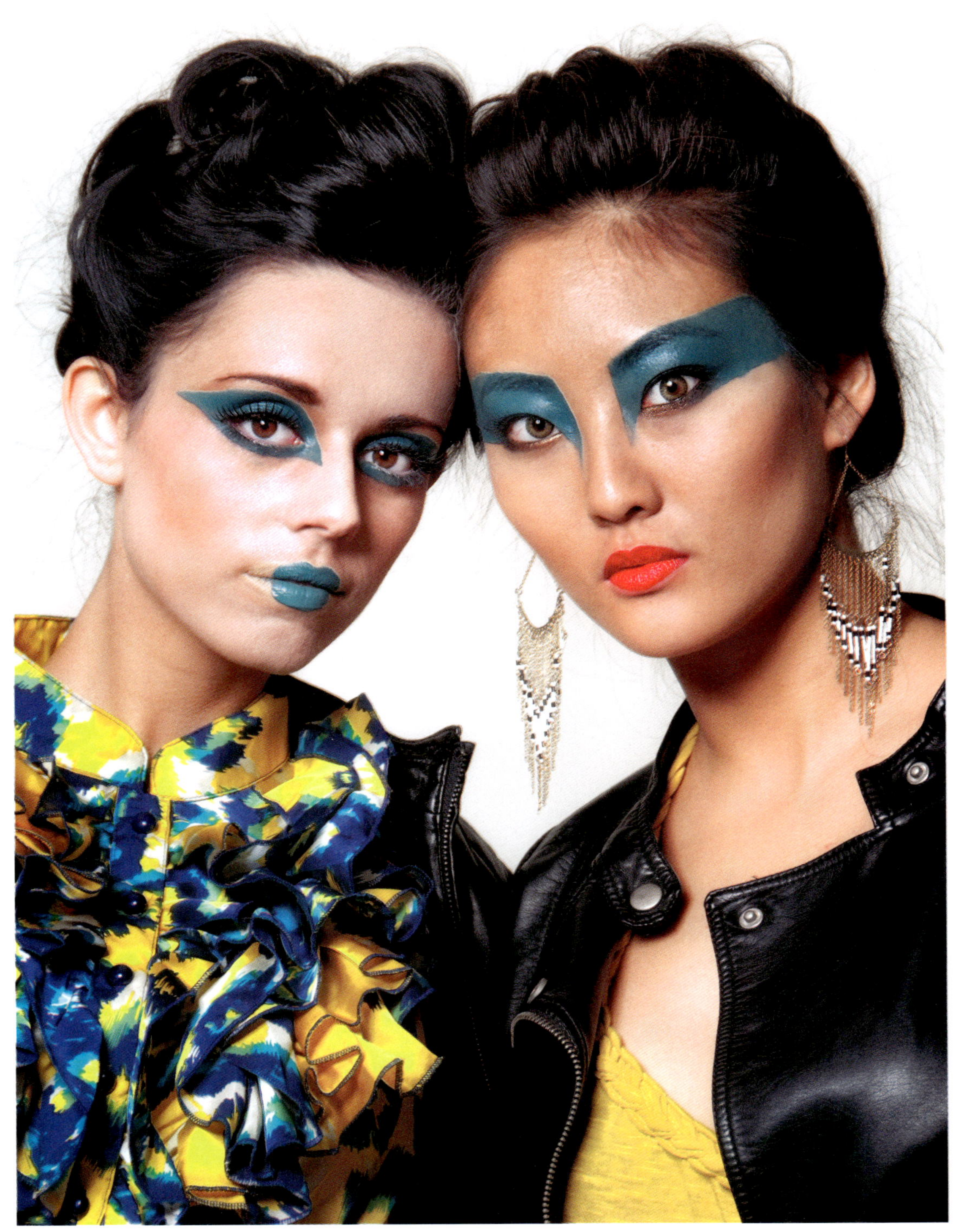

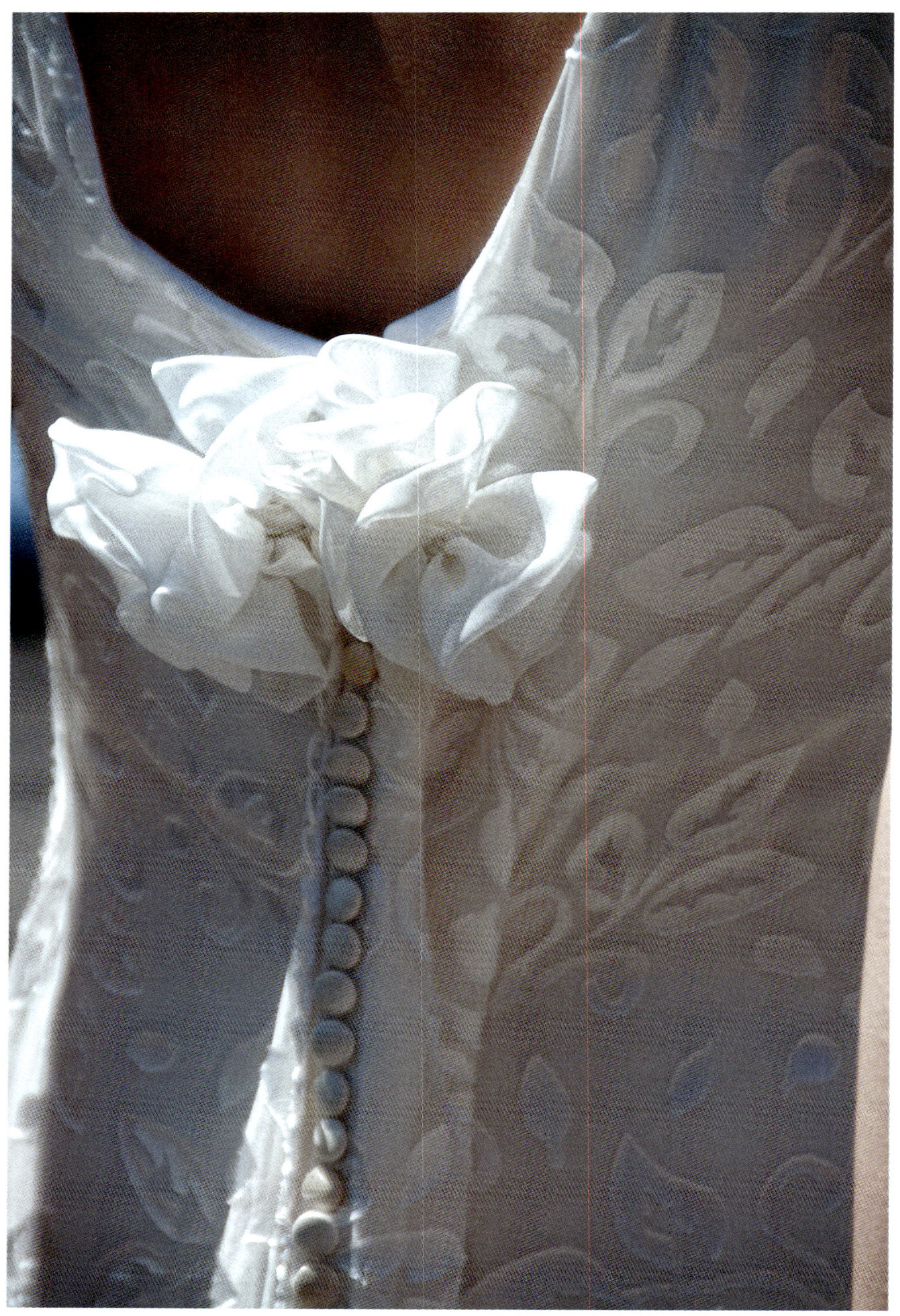

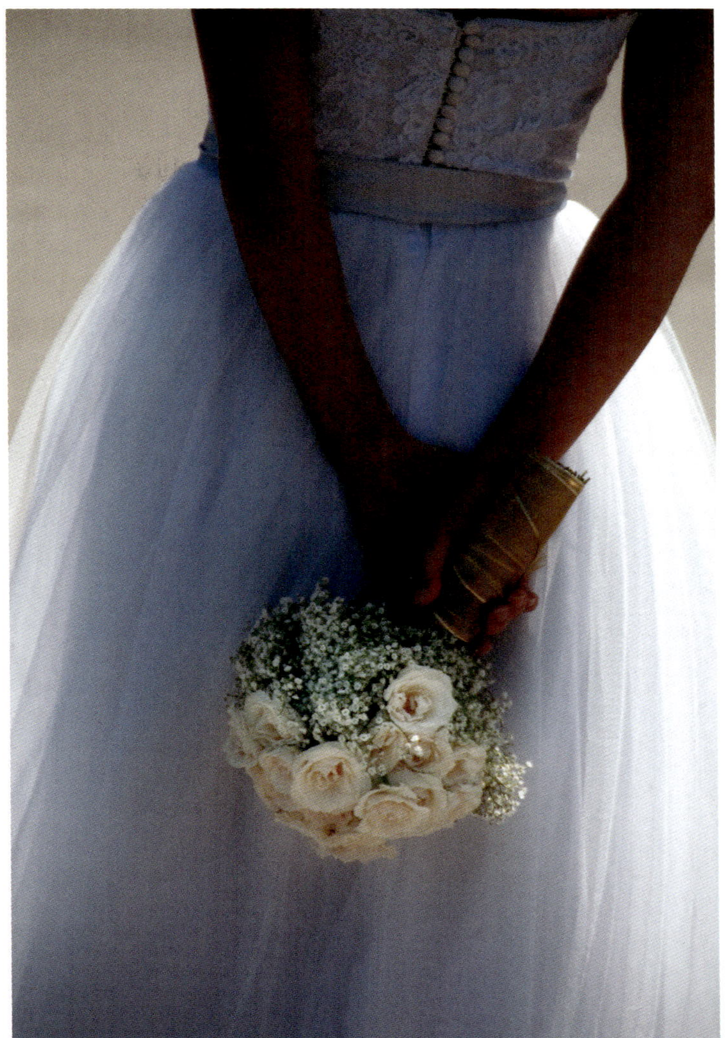

▲ Most wedding portraits are largely about the wedding dress. A photographer who doesn't pay attention to the dress and related items is missing a great deal—as the client will likely let him or her know. In this photo, the bridal bouquet—itself an important and beautiful prop—is featured and complements the wedding dress.

200mm, 1/1250 of a second at f/5.6 and ISO 200, hand held

◄ Even the small details of this handmade wedding dress are beautiful. Unless this bride is a high-fashion model, she is unlikely to often wear a garment so elegant and tailor made. It is therefore important to capture the back of the dress on this special day.

200mm, 1/1000 of a second at f/5.6 and ISO 200, hand held

Hair and Make-Up

If clothes make the man, then hair and make-up define the woman, particularly when it comes to models. Most professional models are sensitive to issues of hair and make-up, and have at least rudimentary skills with doing their own. However, for best results in a professional context, you are well advised to work with a professional hair stylist, and a make-up artist. Since these professionals need time to do their job, you'll need to plan your photography session accordingly.

In this society, we have almost a willful suspension of disbelief when it comes to make-up. Almost all models, male and female, have at least some make-up applied before they are photographed for a magazine, or appear on television or in a movie. We are often asked to believe that people who are wearing make-up are not.

Would the beautiful crash survivor in the Amazon still be wearing perfect mascara after seven days in the jungle? You tell me. Any kind of objective close inspection shows make-up—including subtle eye-liner on male actors—but we are in denial about this fact.

The result of this collective hypocrisy is that portraits without make-up, particularly of women, tend to look bare, naked, and neither as beautiful nor as glamorous as expected.

I'd welcome the day when the really natural look—and not a fake natural look that actually involves cosmetics—is fashionable. But until that day comes, I have to accept reality. It's far easier to create a nice portrait if the model is wearing appropriate make-up than to fix the ruins in Photoshop!

My preference is to work with a model who knows how to apply cosmetics that look good on camera, or with a make-up artist. It is important to communicate the look you want with whoever is doing the make-up and hair. For reasons of self-defense alone, I've had to learn a bit about make-up.

You, too, should learn to be able to tell when foundation has been applied too thickly, when mascara has not been well applied, when eye shadow is not even, and when eyebrows have not been shaped attractively. It's far easier to correct these problems before you've made the photos than to give the model a virtual make-up job in the digital darkroom.

Make-up can be more than trying to create a glamorous and pseudo-natural look. In my opinion, creative make-up artistry is a great thing and can lead to spectacular photography—although the results are seldom conventional portraits.

▶ This model also appears on page 6 and is the model on the left in the photo on page 101. In each photo, she has different make-up, hair, and propping. If you compare these images, you'll see what a great difference creative and effective make-up artistry and hair styling can make in the overall appearance of a photograph.

100mm, 1/160 of a second at f/5.6 and ISO 100, hand held

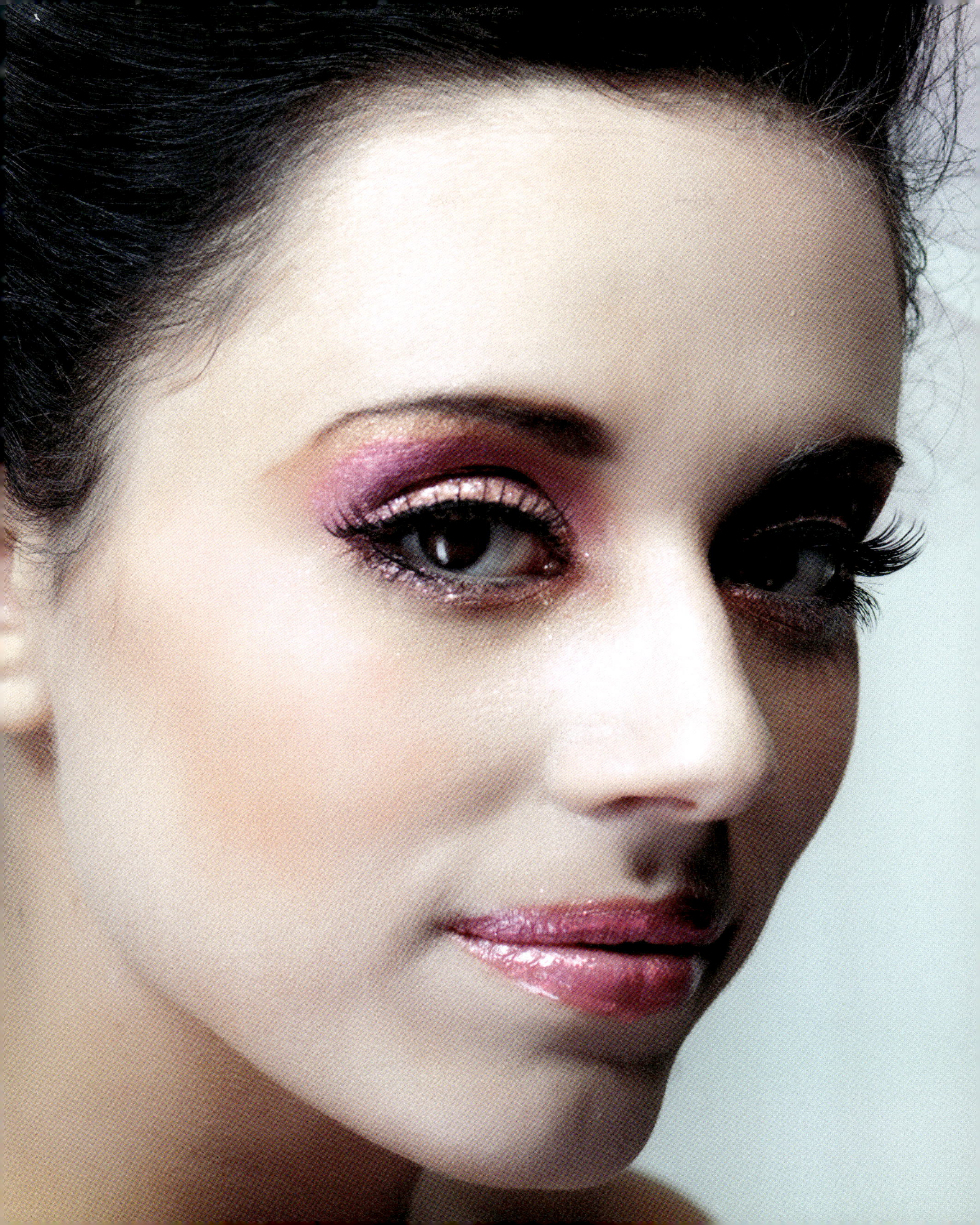

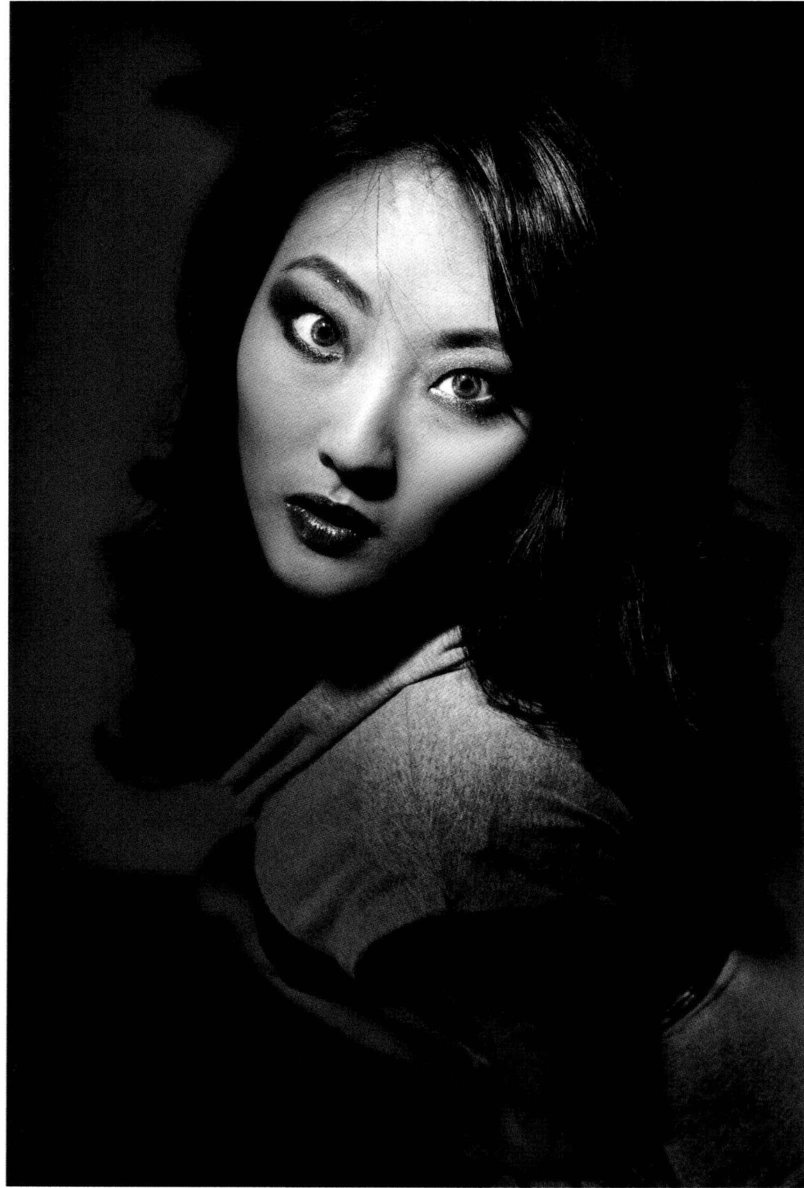

▲ The same person can look very different with and without make-up. In this monochromatic image, I used low-key lighting to accentuate the shape of the model's face and beautiful eyes.

24mm, 1/160 of a second at f/8 and ISO 100, hand held

▶ This is the same model again shot using low-key lighting to fully bring out the impact of the striking eyes and interesting, exotic make-up. With different make-up, you would never recognize her as the same person.

200mm, 1/160 of a second at f/6.3 and ISO 200, hand held

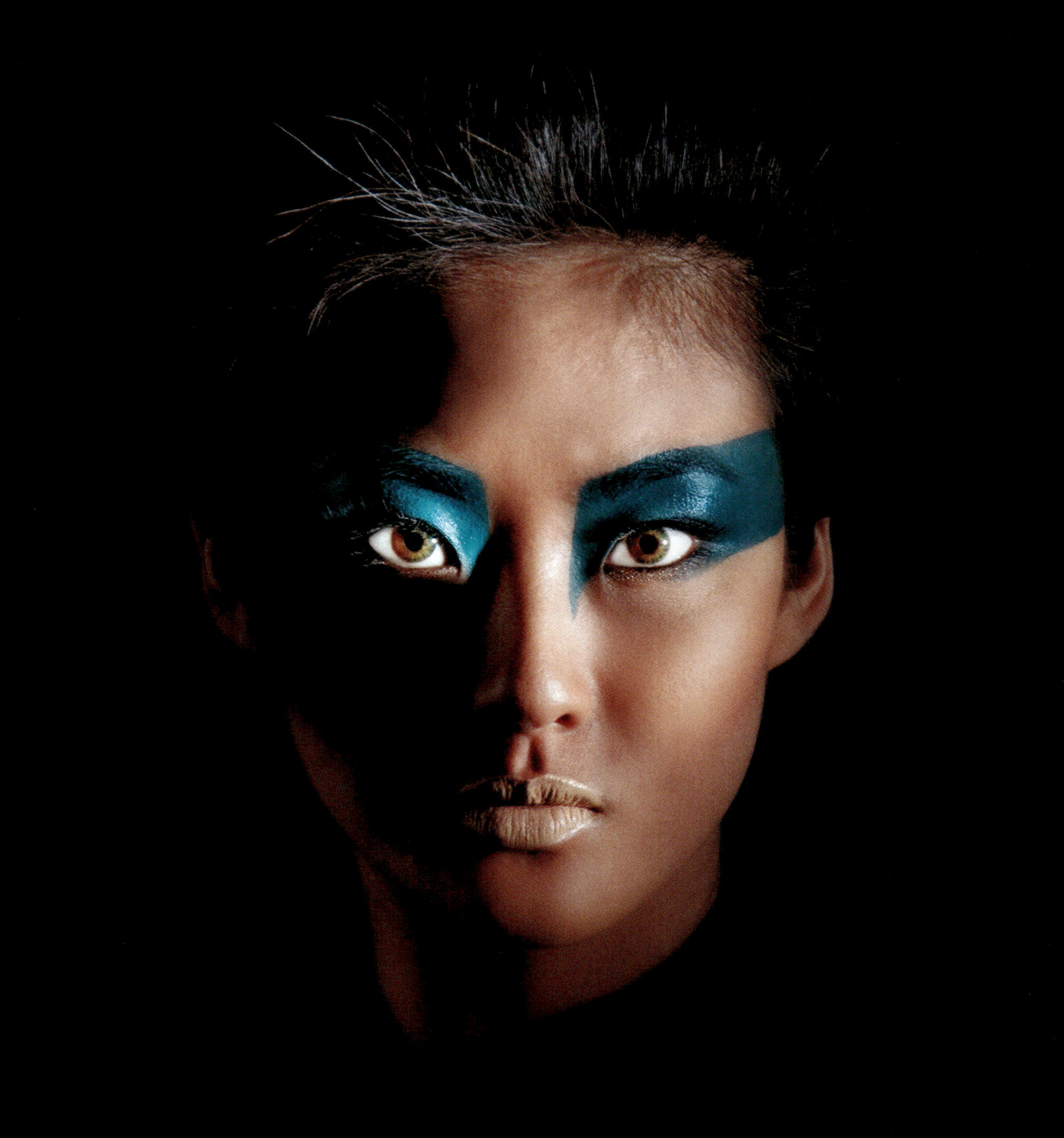

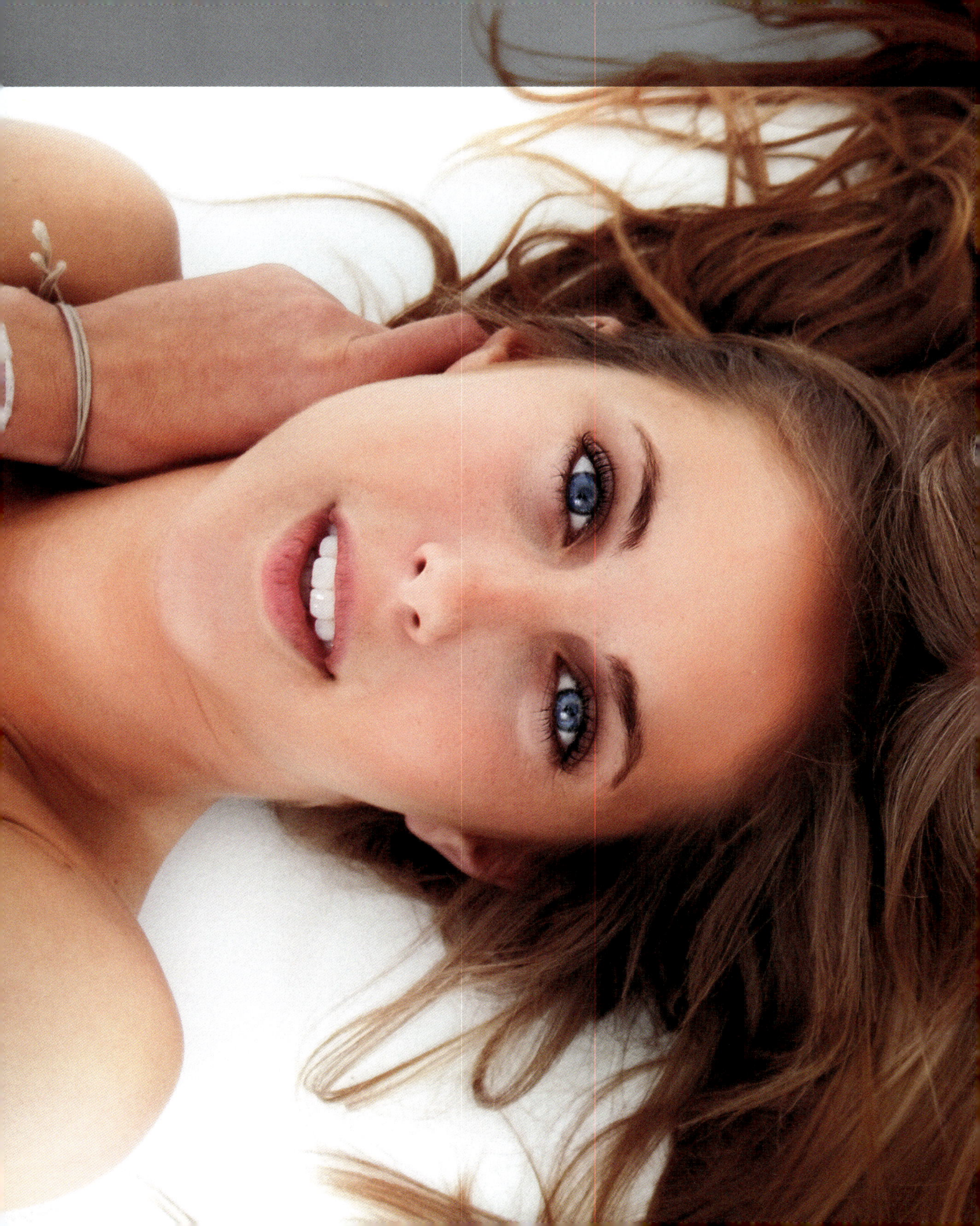

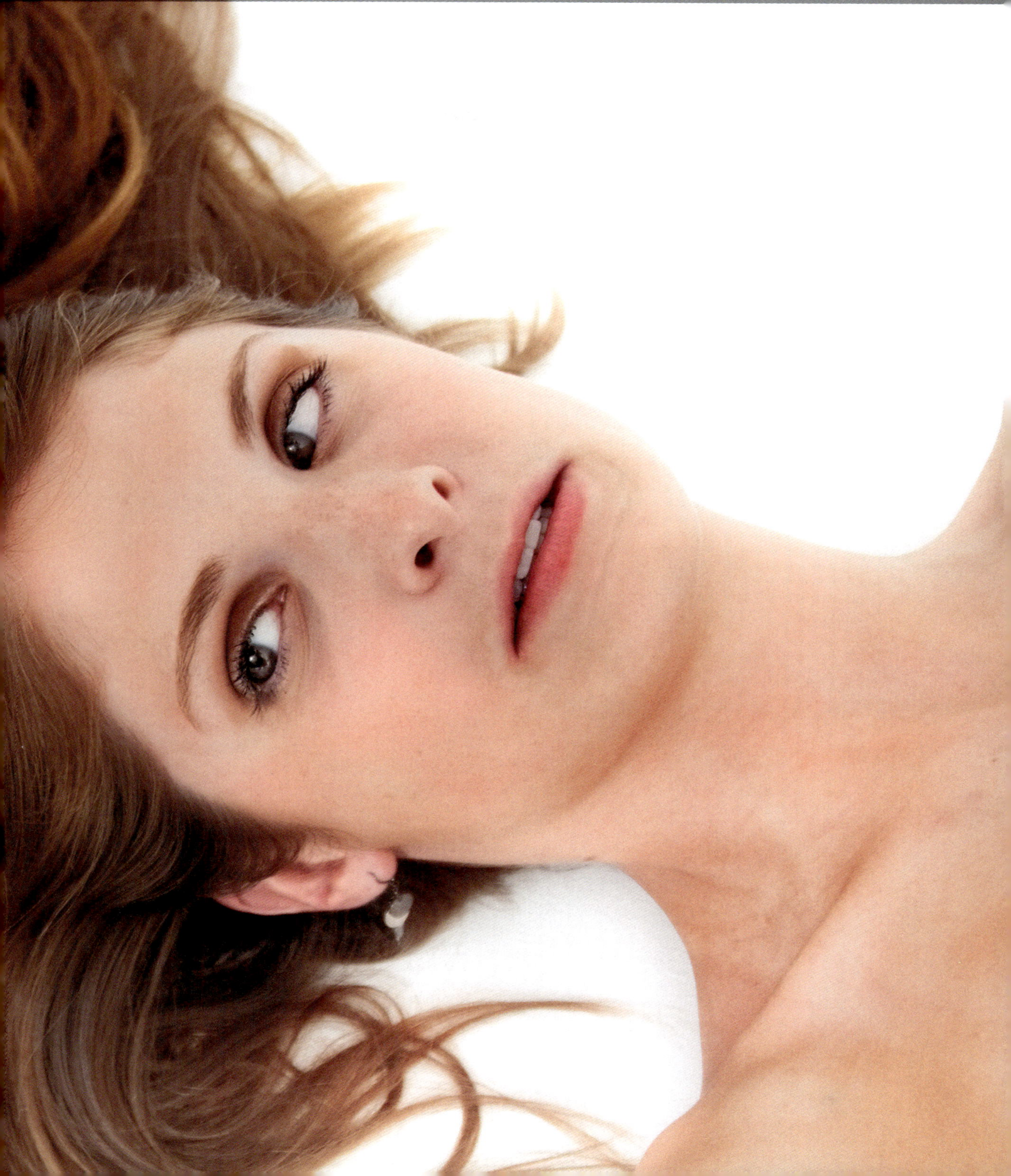

Posing

Posing refers to the arrangement or positioning of a model—or other subject of a photographic portrait.

To say that somebody is "positioned" suggests that they are passive, and completely being directed by the photographer. This is, in fact, sometimes the case. But usually when a photographer and model work together, the best poses are created through a collaborative process.

The photographer-subject relationship gets even more emotionally complex when the portrait is being taken of a subject who is not a professional model. Non-professionals are inexperienced and may be awkward in front of the camera. It may take considerable effort to help an amateur feel comfortable posing. A successful session depends upon the interaction of both players in the drama.

The more casual the photography, the less control over posing the photographer can expect. For example, in street photography, you very rarely get to tell your subjects how to pose. The best you can expect is to watch the movements your subjects make, and pick good moments to make your photographs. And as you might expect, making an unwilling kid hold a pose is nearly impossible!

The impact of posing made by the photographer and subject varies according to the many different kinds of portrait photography. But it's true overall from the photographer's viewpoint that posing involves both the visual skills of an art director and the inter-personal skills of a psychologist.

Taking the visual side of things, it's important to be able to look at bodies and faces abstractly, and as part of a composition. If the person in front of your camera were a landscape, how would you feel about the way things seem to fit together? There should be an apparent, organic wholeness to any portrait—the parts of the body should seem to relate to each other

▶ Quite rightly, a great many portraits emphasize faces. Faces do not exist in a vacuum, they are attached to bodies. Therefore, most portraits that are primarily about the face have to be posed to show the connection between the face and body. To highlight the interconnectivity of mind and body in this portrait, I asked the model to position her chin almost, but not quite, resting on her clasped arms.

150mm, 1/100 of a second at f/5.6 and ISO 100, hand held

▲ Pages 108–109: I photographed this pair looking straight down from above, using a white background.

The more people you add to a portrait, the more that can go wrong—or at least not quite right. It's difficult to catch a perfect expression on a single subject, and orders of magnitude more difficult when there are more than one. In this case, the woman on the left has an attractive and striking facial expression, and is looking right at the camera. I had just told a joke and the woman on the right started laughing, and then tried to restrain herself. This comes across as a quirky, rather than glamorous, look—but still makes for an interesting joint portrait.

56mm, 1/160 of a second at f/6.3 and ISO 100, hand held

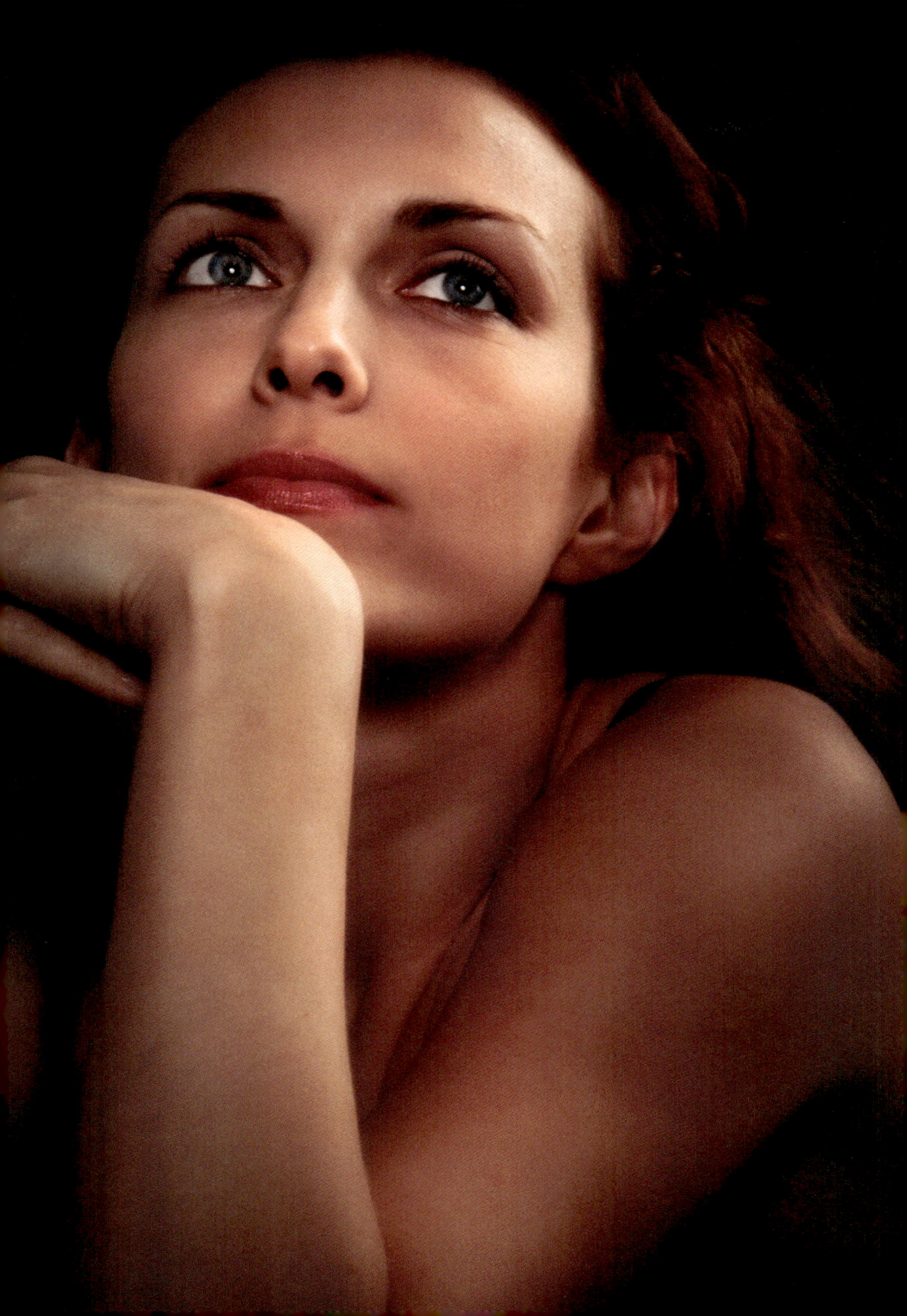

in a proportional way, and nothing should seem to be extraneous or out of place.

A particular area of concern when poses involve the full figure (rather than just the head) is the hands. Unless you are very careful, hands can seem awkward and not really part of the person they are attached to—almost as if the hands are separate animals with a life of their own. Since misplaced hands can ruin even the best poses, you should keep your eye on how hands are positioned and try to get your subjects to place their hands in a way that makes visual sense in relationship to the rest of their body.

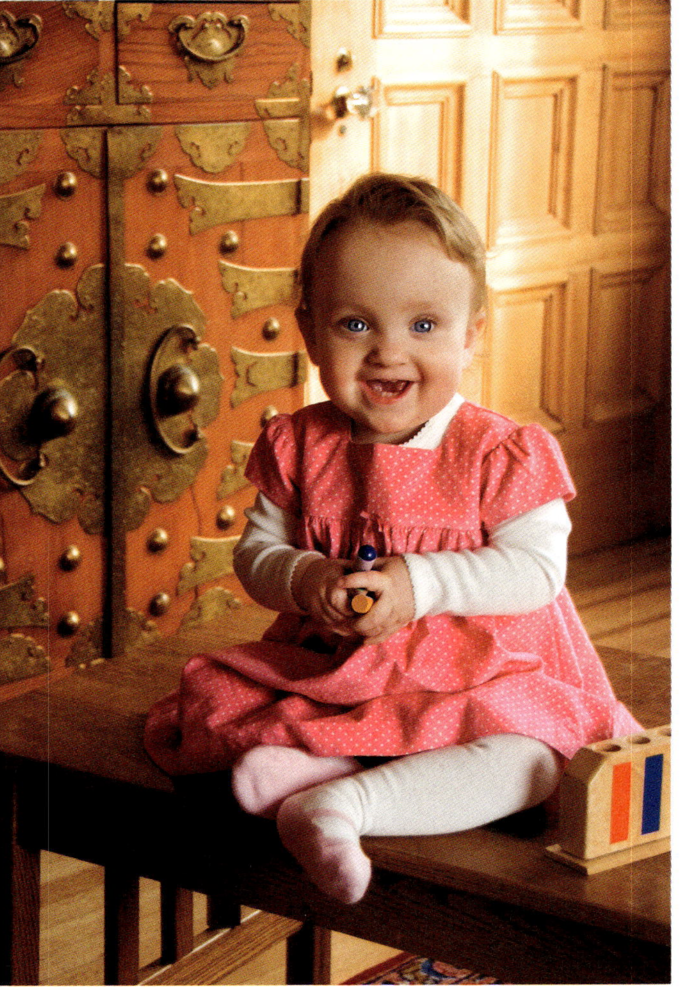

In portraits where faces loom large, be careful about the nose. An ugly view of the nose or nostrils can distract from even the most carefully planned head shot.

As I've mentioned before, the eyes are the most important visual element in many portraits. Therefore, you need to pay attention to the expression in and around the eyes—this is make or break for many portraits. A posing technique I often use is to ask my subjects to "smile with their eyes."

Tension doesn't look good. When someone is tense, lines appear on the face that are not normally present. It's a fact of life that many people get tense when they are photographed. Therefore, you should practice putting your subjects at ease by talking with them, and telling jokes. Music can help some subjects relax. Also, moving around or even jumping can help some models feel comfortable (see pages 116–119).

◀ In this environmental portrait of my daughter Katie Rose, the rich background of paneled wood and the Oriental chest adds to the viewer's appreciation of the context of the portrait. Children will not hold a pose for long, so it's important to snap these shots quickly when you see them.

48mm, 1/100 of a second at f/4.8 and ISO 500, hand held

▶ Dress-up occasions—such as Halloween—make for great natural posing of kids and family groups. Your subjects will be naturally proud of their costumes, and quite willing to "go the extra mile"—which for kids can simply mean following simple posing directions and holding relatively still when they look at the camera.

29mm, 1/13 of a second at f/4 and ISO 1000, hand held

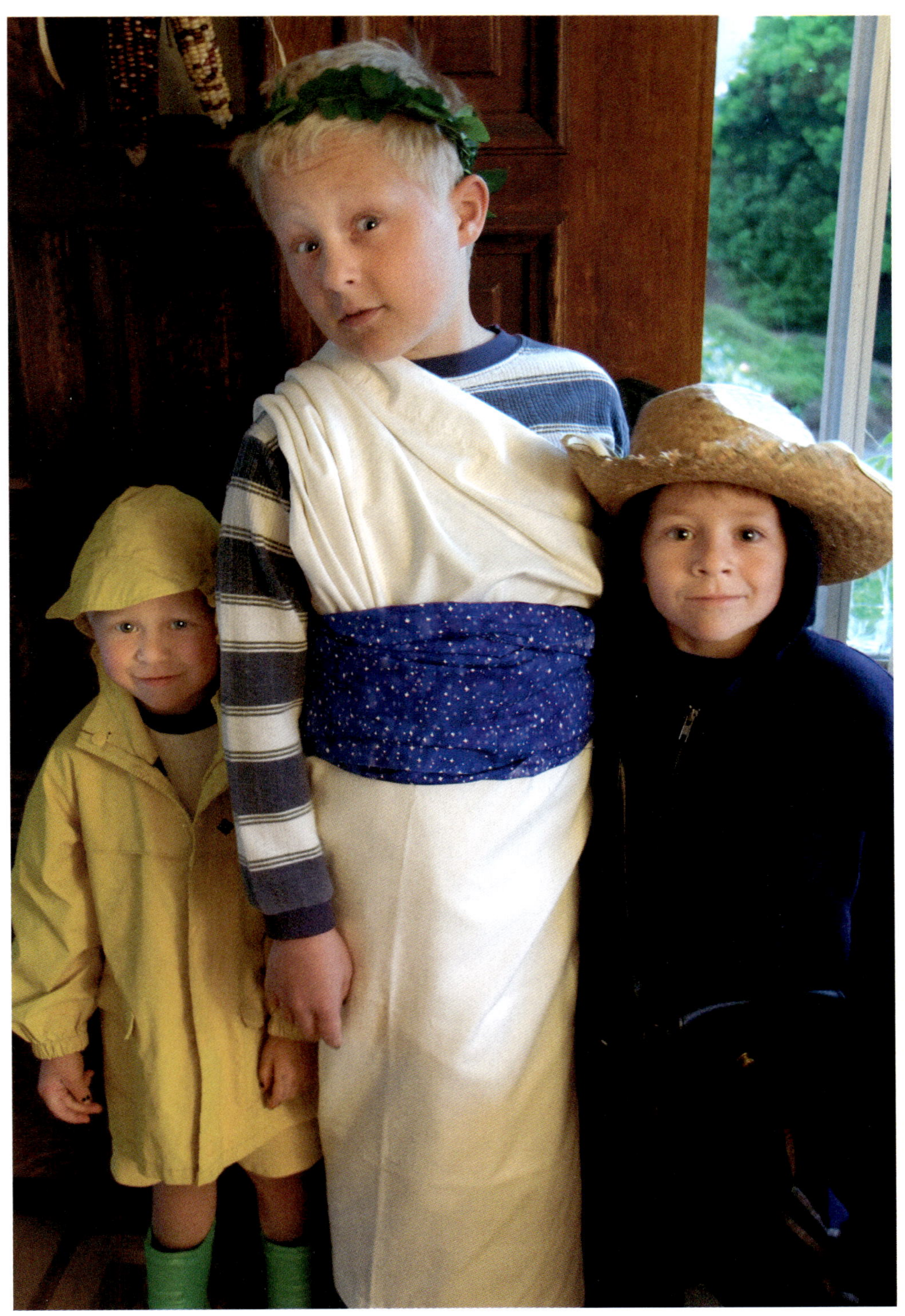

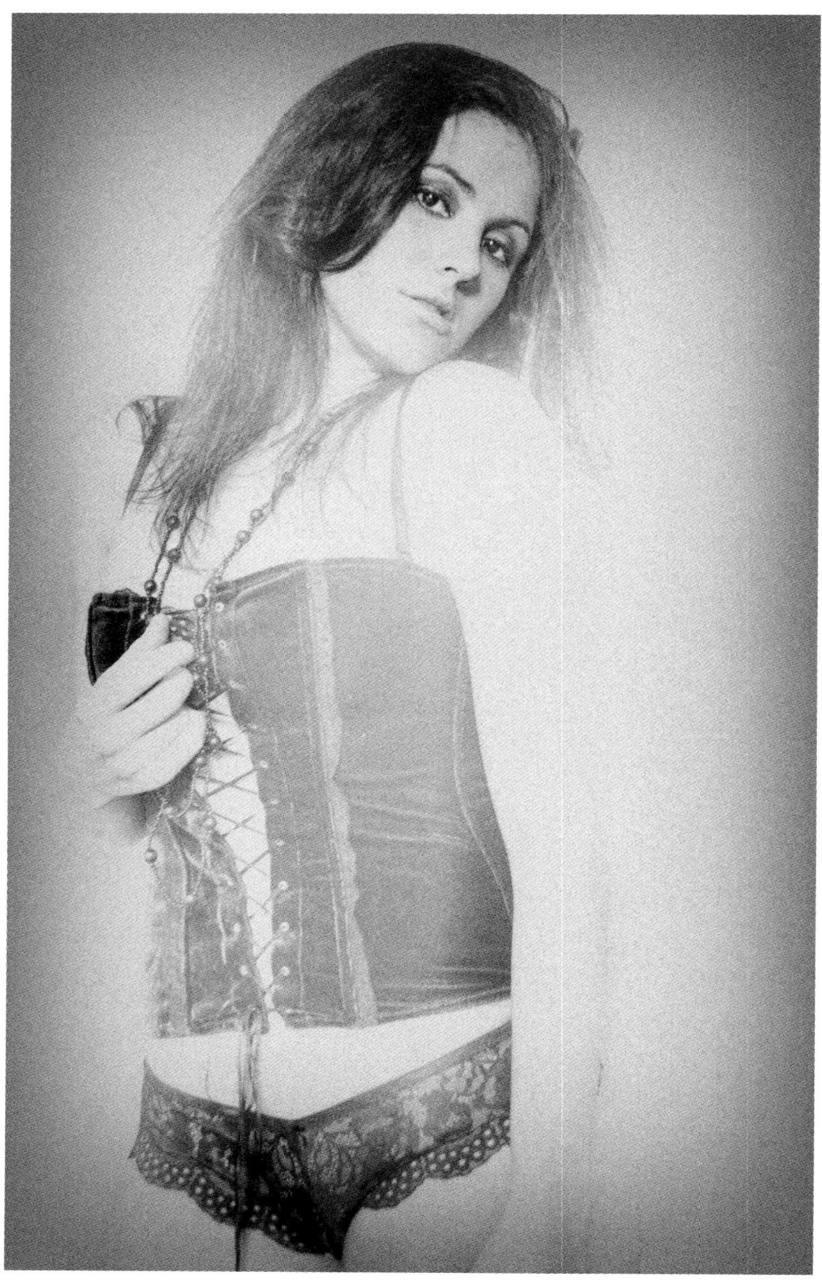

◀ You can see in this model shot that arms are often a significant issue in posing. This model wasn't entirely sure what to do with her right arm and hand. We worked out a pose where she was using her hand to hold on to her necklace. Touching or grabbing an item of clothing is a common solution to the issue of where hands should be placed.

Photoshop tintype simulation, 1/50 of a second at f/6.3 and ISO 1600, hand held

▶ What do you do with the arms? Most experienced models understand this problem, and have developed routines for positioning their arms and hands in ways that work well with their bodies. The danger is that you will end up with a pose that seems stale because the model has done it often before.

This classic model pose is one answer to arm placement, and in the context of this particular shot gives the model an unusual and dreamy look.

Infrared capture, 1/50 of a second at f/6.3 and ISO 1600, hand held

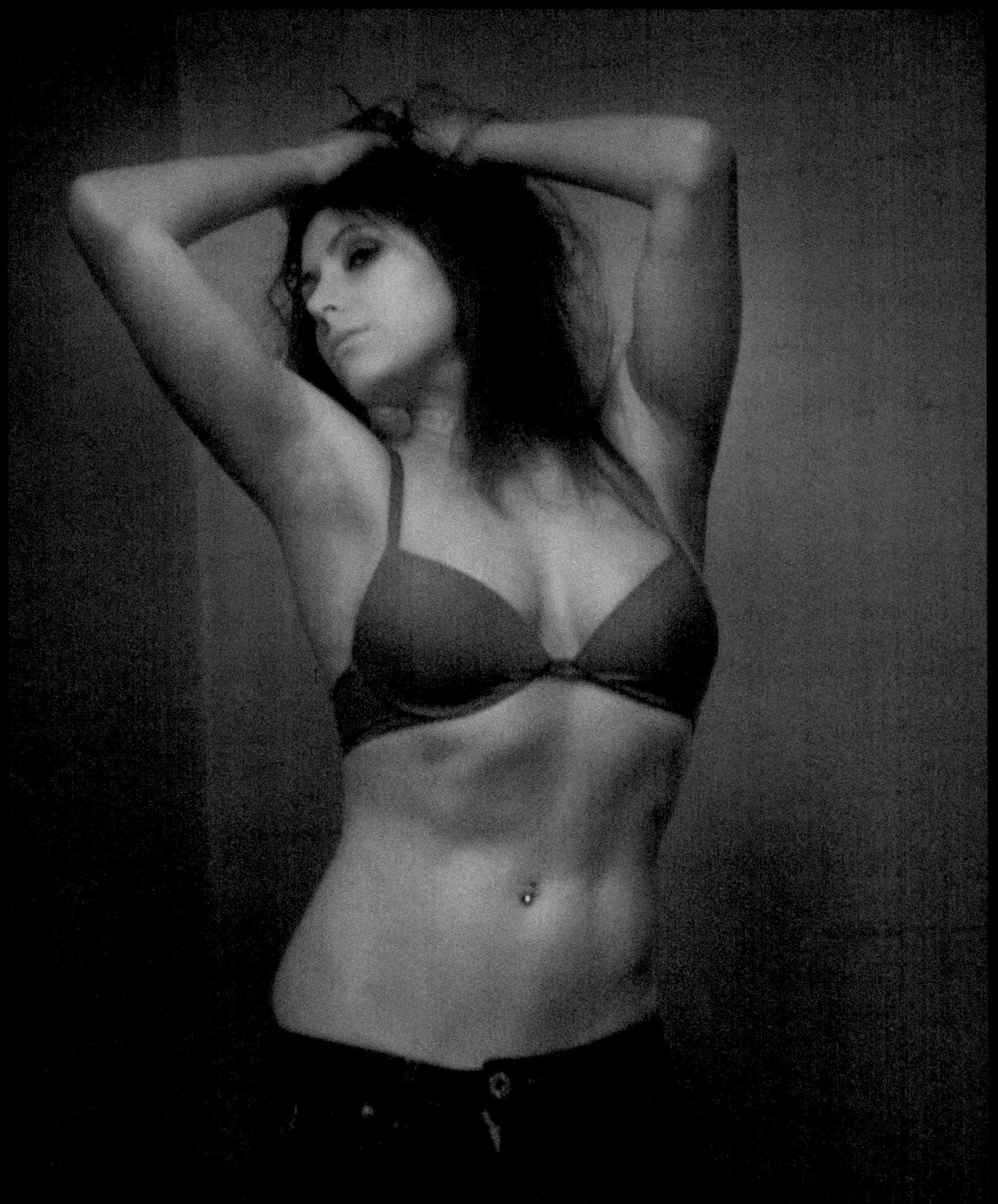

Jumping

Photographer Philippe Halsman said, "When you ask a person to jump, his attention is mostly directed toward the act of jumping, and the mask falls, so the real person appears." Halsman made a practice of photographing his portrait subjects, many of them famous celebrities, when they jump.

I've borrowed a leaf from Halsman's book, and when I encounter a subject who seems stiff, I often ask them to start jumping. I mostly use this as a warm-up, not for the photos that will get used. It's the rare portrait subject or model that doesn't find jumping amusing—and subsequent shots mostly show a more relaxed person.

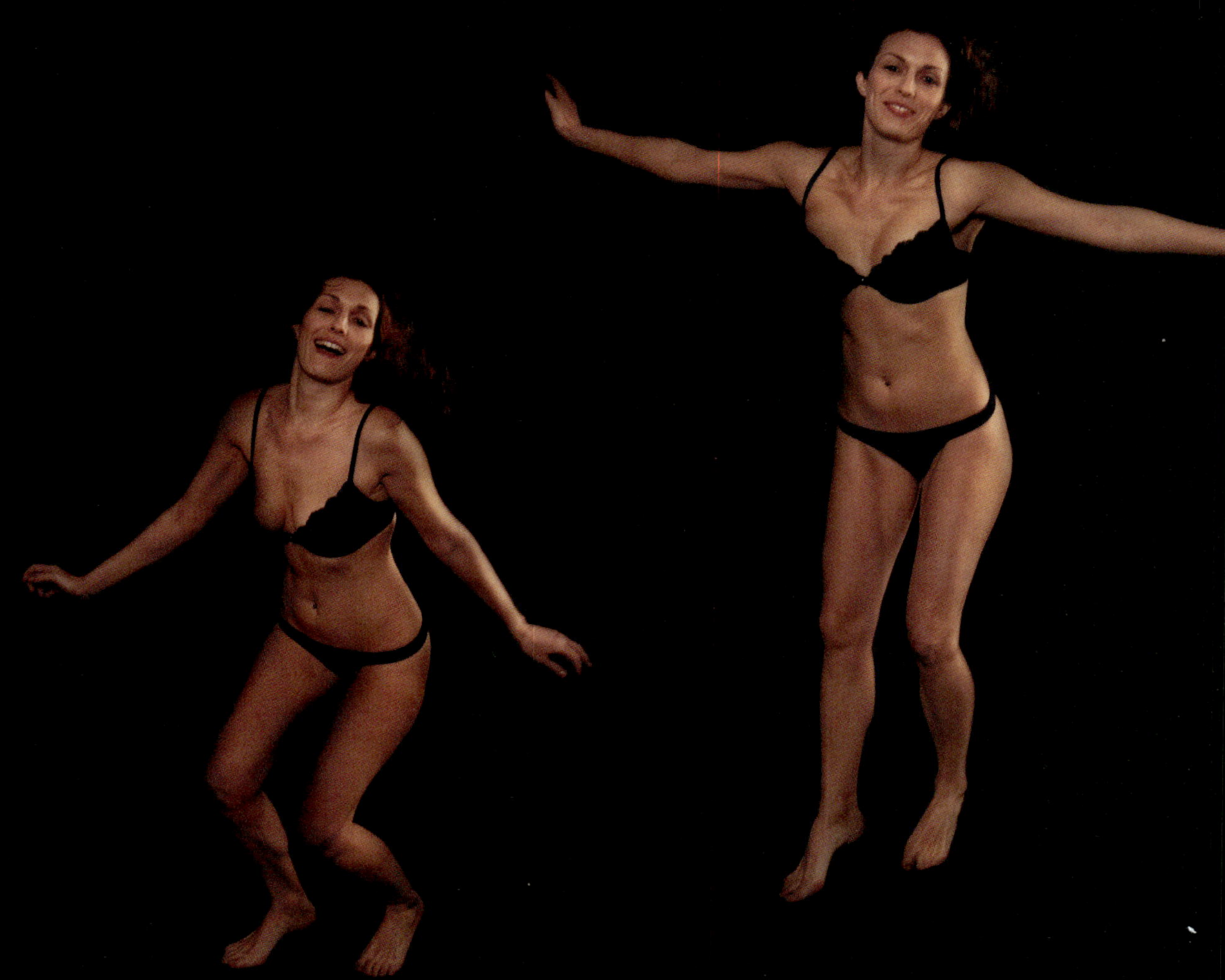

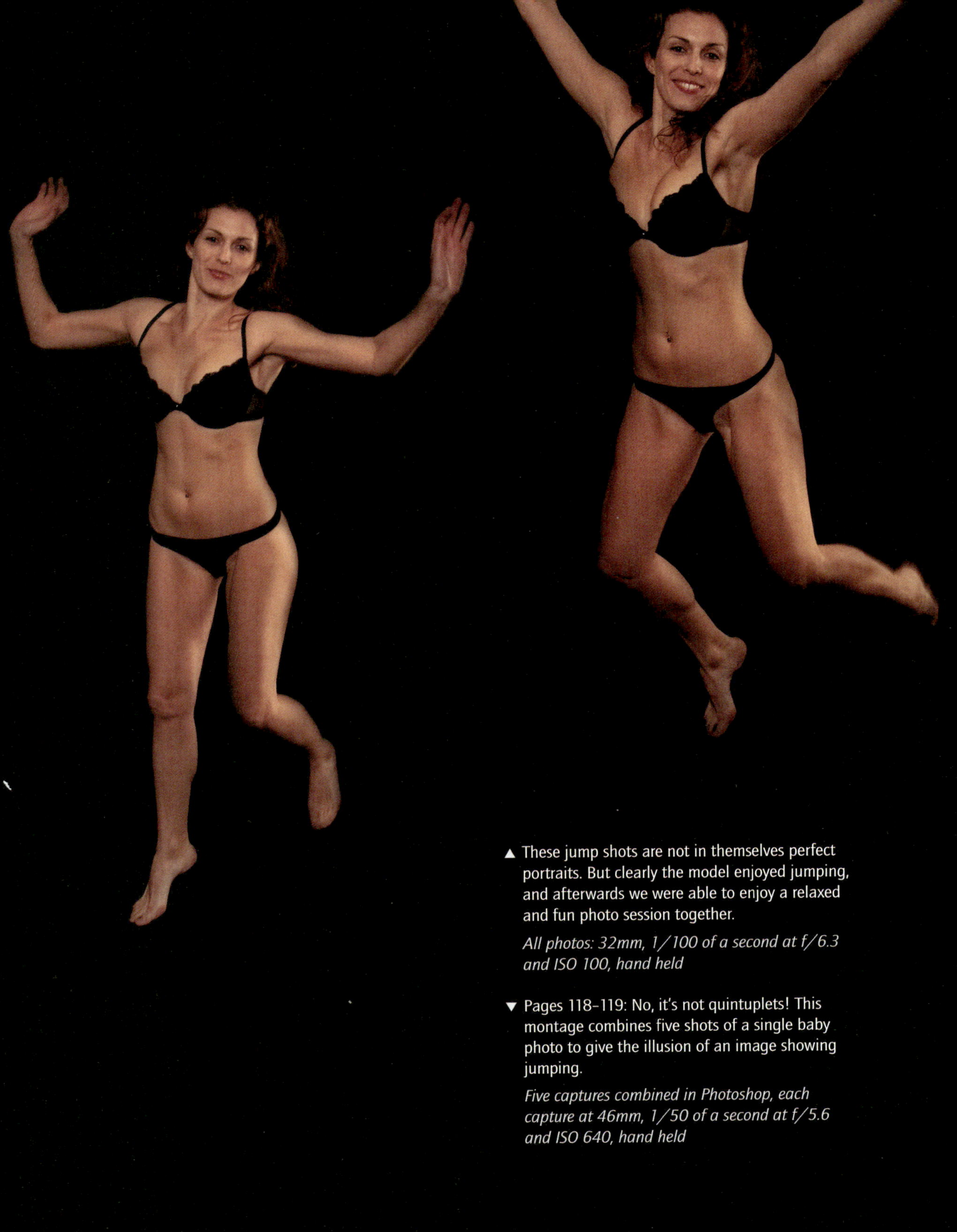

▲ These jump shots are not in themselves perfect portraits. But clearly the model enjoyed jumping, and afterwards we were able to enjoy a relaxed and fun photo session together.

All photos: 32mm, 1/100 of a second at f/6.3 and ISO 100, hand held

▼ Pages 118–119: No, it's not quintuplets! This montage combines five shots of a single baby photo to give the illusion of an image showing jumping.

Five captures combined in Photoshop, each capture at 46mm, 1/50 of a second at f/5.6 and ISO 640, hand held

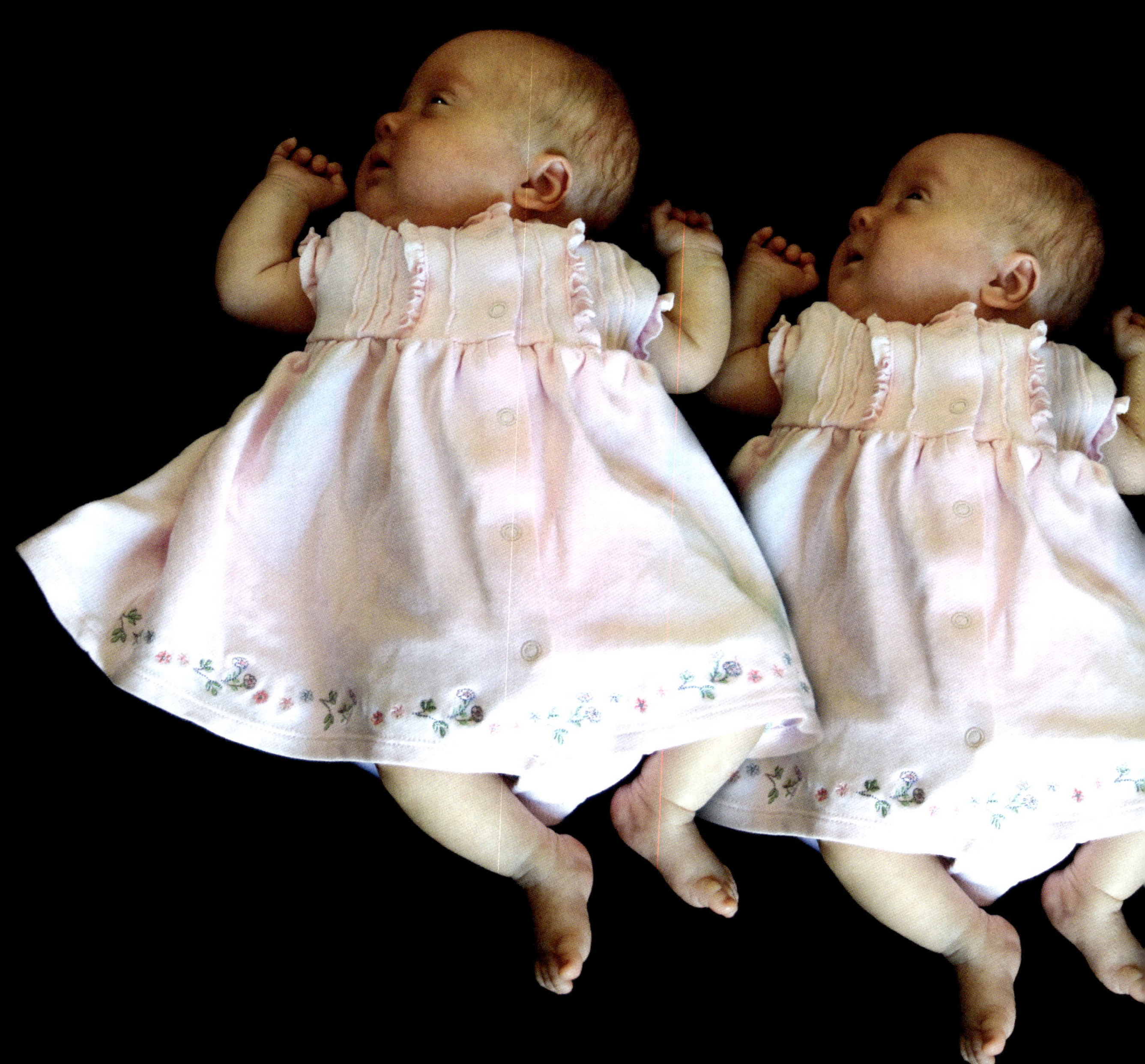

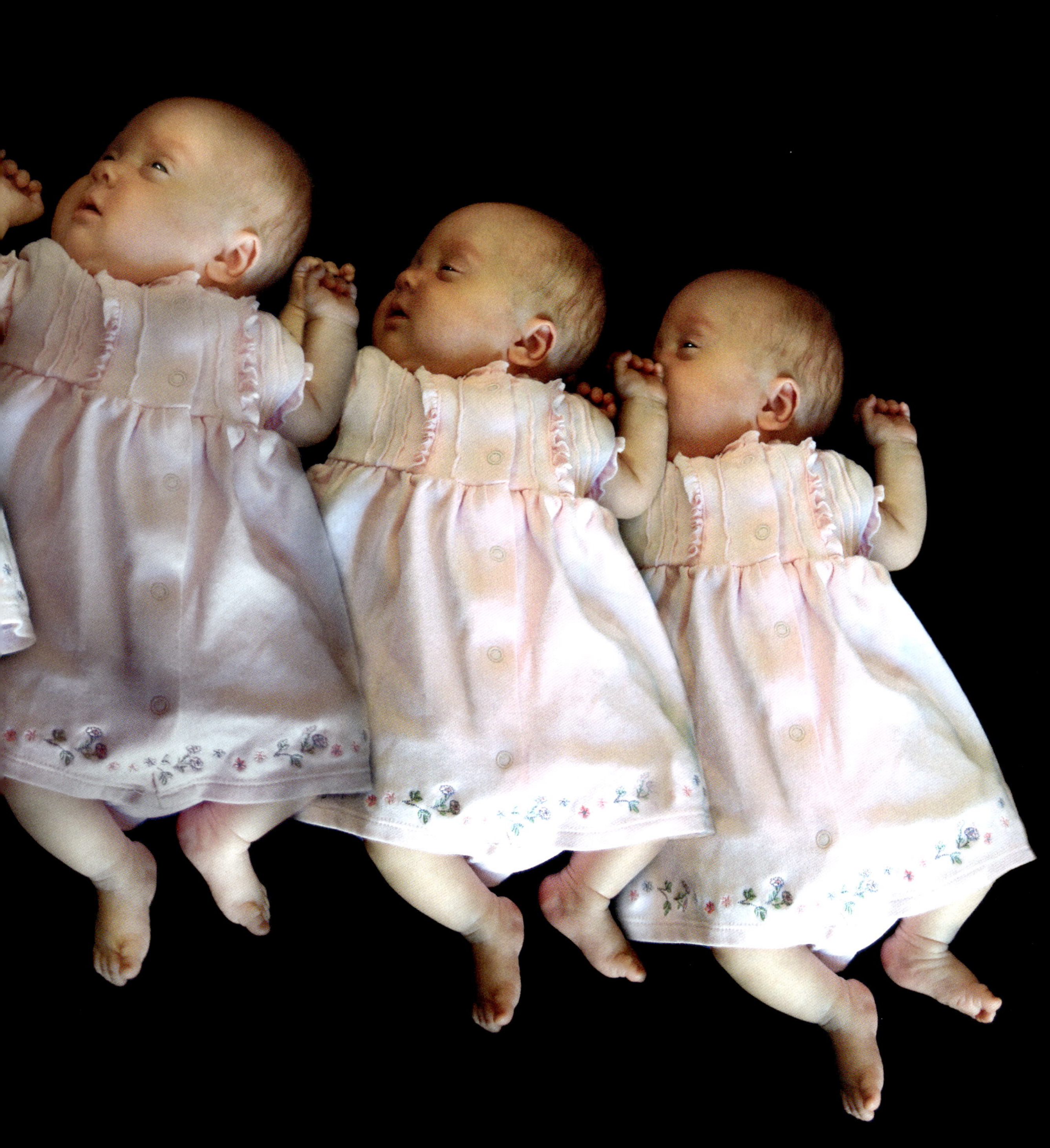

Backgrounds

Don't underestimate the importance of backgrounds in your portraits. You may think that a background does not matter in a photo dominated by a person, but it does.

It's very important to make sure that your background is chosen to work well with your portrait subject in the studio. It's hard to go wrong with a black background (for low-key, dark portraits) or a white background (for high-key, bright portraits), but do make sure your choice works well for both the skin tones of your subjects and for the image you have pre-visualized. It's worth bearing in mind that dark skin tones may not show up well on a black background.

If you do shoot with a colored background in the studio, you should keep the tone and attitude of the photograph in mind. For example, a light blue background can look good with a dark skinned subject (see page 93 for an example), and a red background can be used to present a blond subject as brassy and bold.

Don't neglect the possibility of improvising backgrounds. There's more to life in the studio than seamless paper on a roll. You might be amazed at what can be done with ordinary materials such as crumpled paper, corrugated cardboard, and bits of fabric.

Oil-painted backgrounds specifically designed for portraiture can work very well, especially when they are spot-lit. But I tend to be cautious with sets and painted backgrounds that are intended to appear to convert the studio into some other kind of environment, such as a countryside with fence, a bedroom, or an oak-paneled office. If you are not very careful, these kinds of backgrounds can look extremely "hokey."

When shooting outside, remember to keep in mind both the background and the portrait subject in the foreground. One classic amateur composition goof is to create an otherwise acceptable portrait with a tree coming out of the top of the person's head. This simply will not do.

Before, during, and after you make a casual portrait outdoors, or an environmental portrait in conditions that you don't entirely control, check your composition. If there's a visual flaw in the background, try to fix it—for example, by moving your camera position, or by asking your subject to move.

Another possibility with portraits, even those taken outdoors, is to bring your own background. It's easy to pop a black cloth into position, and all of a sudden have an uncluttered background that presents your subject with clarity.

While I often like to present my portrait subjects against relatively neutral backgrounds, it's also fun to use the magic of low depth-of-field. By focusing on your subject's eyes with the aperture of your camera wide open, you can make most backgrounds become soft and out-of-focus. See pages 132–135 for some tips related to this technique.

▶ A crumpled sheet of used seamless paper worked as an improvised background with a surprisingly exotic look.

75mm, 1/160 of a second at f/8 and ISO 100, hand held

▼ Pages 122–123: I chose to photograph this model in a yoga pose against a black background to emphasize the lines and tonality in this low-key image.

31mm, 1/125 of a second at f/6.3 and ISO 100, hand held

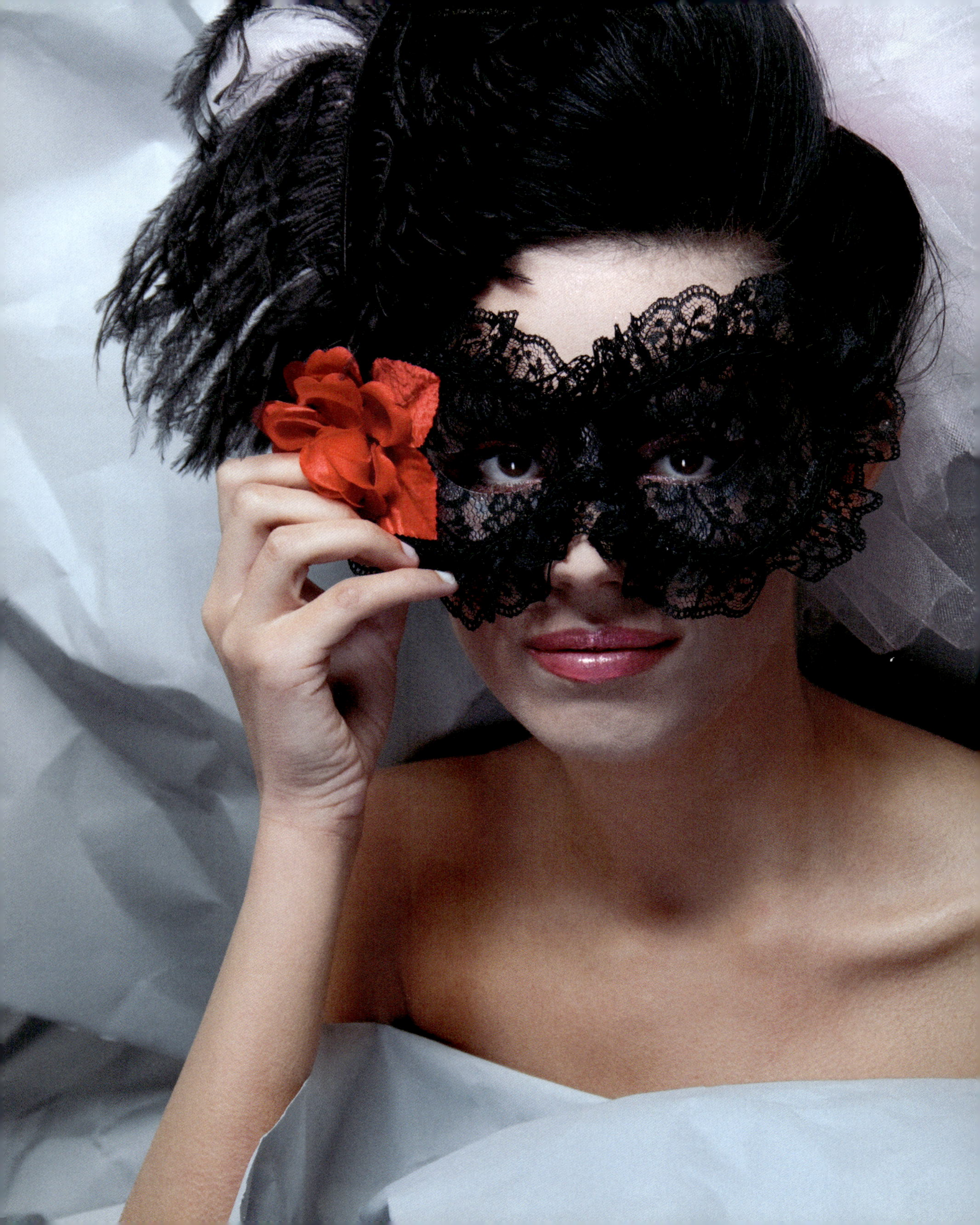

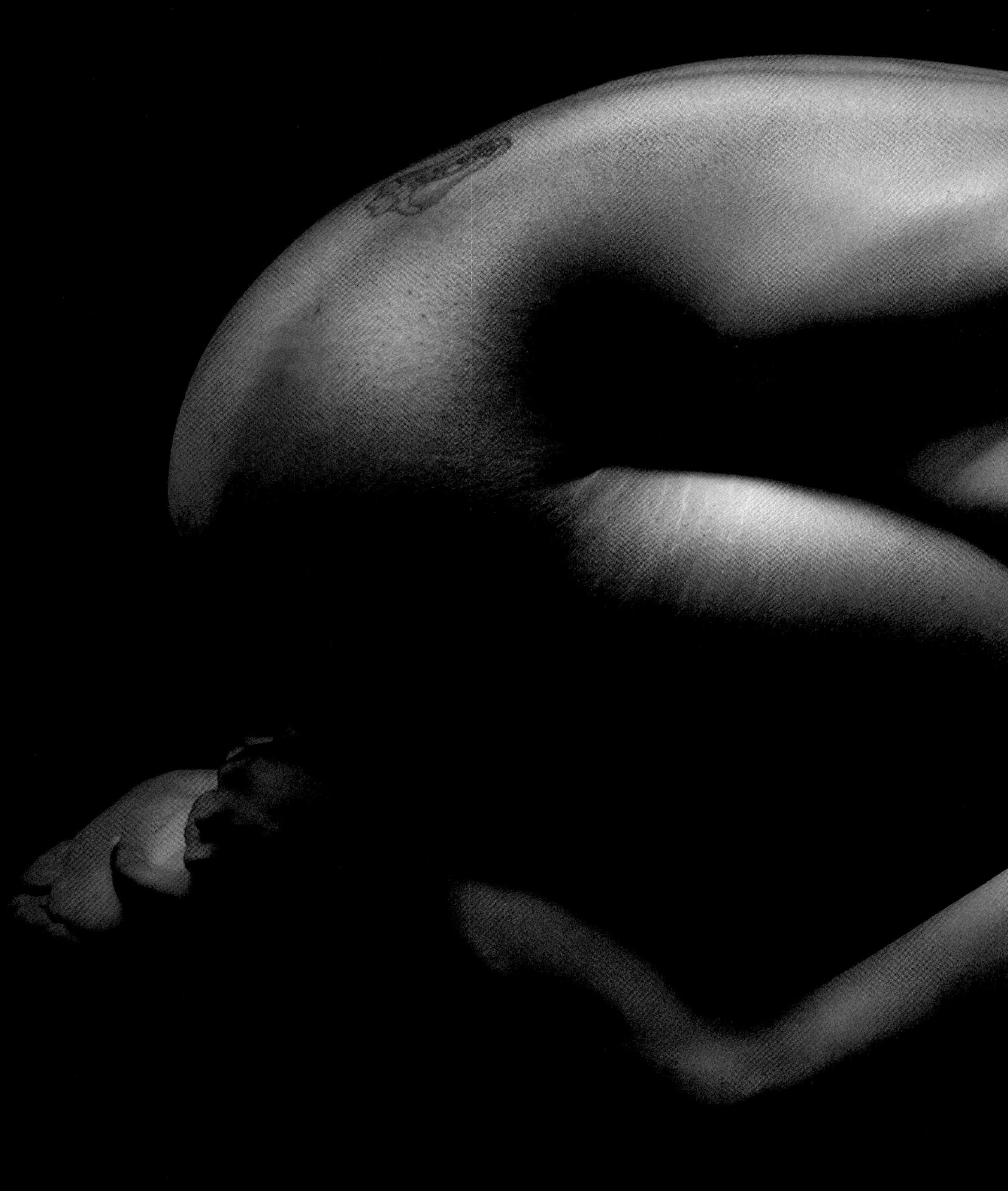

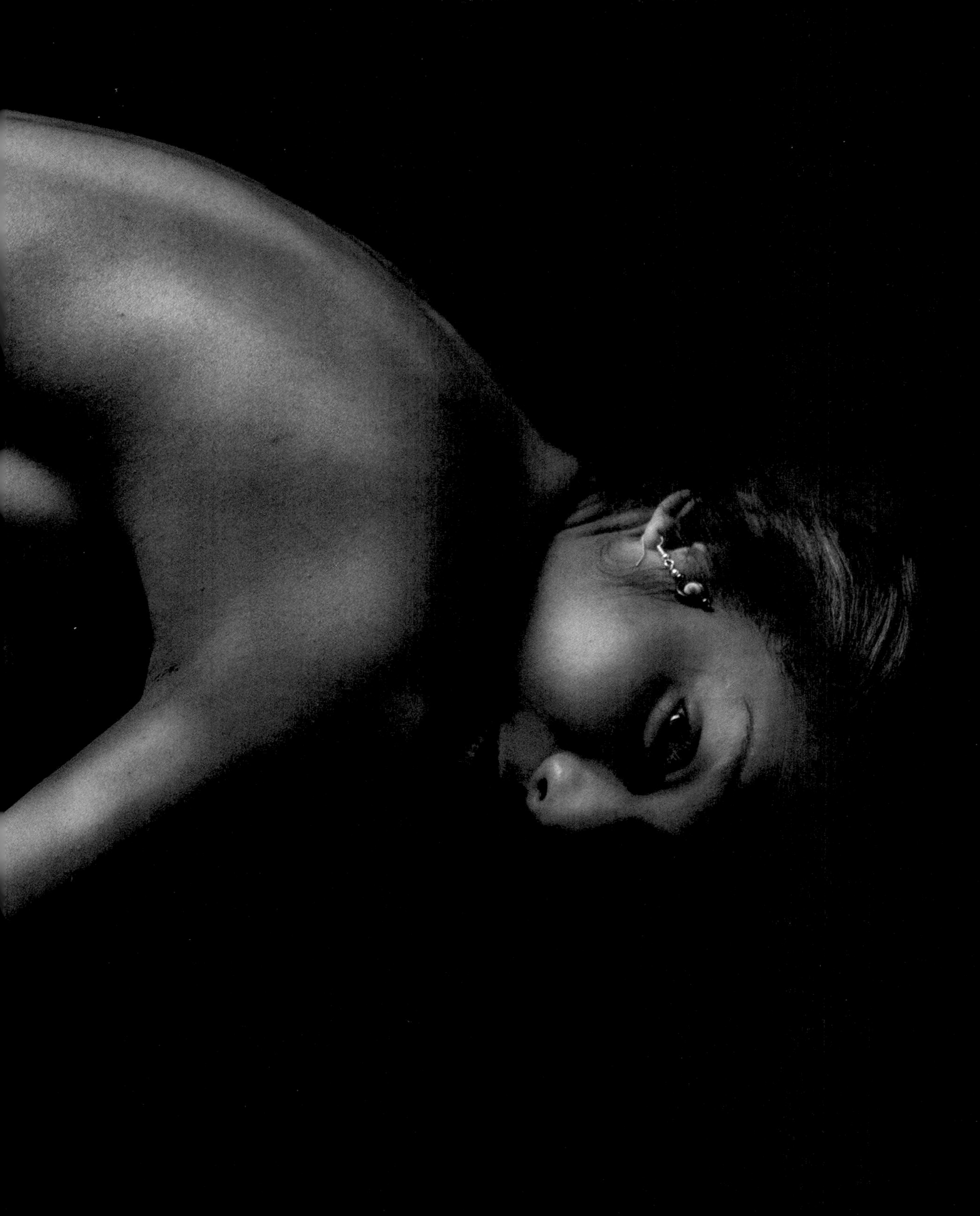

Positioning Your Camera

When considering the position of your camera in relationship to a portrait subject, the major factors to think about are:

- Are you looking up or down at the subject?
- Is the subject shown head-on, in profile, or at some angle in-between?
- How close are you to the subject?

Subliminally, a camera angle that points up conveys respect and that the subject is larger than life. This is an effect that should be used with moderation, and care needs to be taken not to show an unattractive view of the insides of the nostrils. But it is striking that we often tend to follow people we literally look up to. Case in point: studies have shown that the vast majority of Fortune 500 CEOs are much taller than the average person. It's quite rare to be a short CEO. So pointing the camera up at your subject is a way of visually indicating that the subject is worthy of respect—and this effect holds true even when the angle is quite slight.

Conversely, looking down on a subject is a covert indication that the viewer does not need to be in awe of the subject. You will not find Winston Churchill or Barack Obama often photographed from above! But children often are photographed from above—in part because we are simply used to seeing kids from that angle. Also, models are sometimes photographed from above using a ladder to convey a sense of intimacy because of the downward camera angle.

A variety of camera angles are important to consider because they can communicate important information about your subject. A straight-on camera angle can create portraits that seem to be an honest rendition of character—but it can also be predictable and boring. A profile view can convey the idea that the subject of the portrait is an interesting character, and unusual angles of view can be used to communicate quirkiness.

Being close to your subject can give you the opportunity to bond and create intimacy. If close means that the face dominates the portrait, then the image is likely to be more about character and less about shape and form. However, a telephoto lens from farther back can create the same relationship of the face to the size of the portrait frame—and usually creates a more flattering rendition of facial structure.

There's really nothing wrong with any camera position and angle you choose to experiment with in relationship to your subjects—but you should be aware of the possible visual impact of your choices that I've just described.

▶ When we interact with another adult, our expectation of whether we are looking up or down depends on our own height, as well as the height of the other person. But mostly, there isn't huge variation between adult heights—so it makes sense to position the camera so that it's almost straight-on towards adult subjects, or perhaps slightly looking up, as in this portrait of a Cuban farmer.

200mm, 1/160 of a second at f/6.3 and ISO 100, hand held

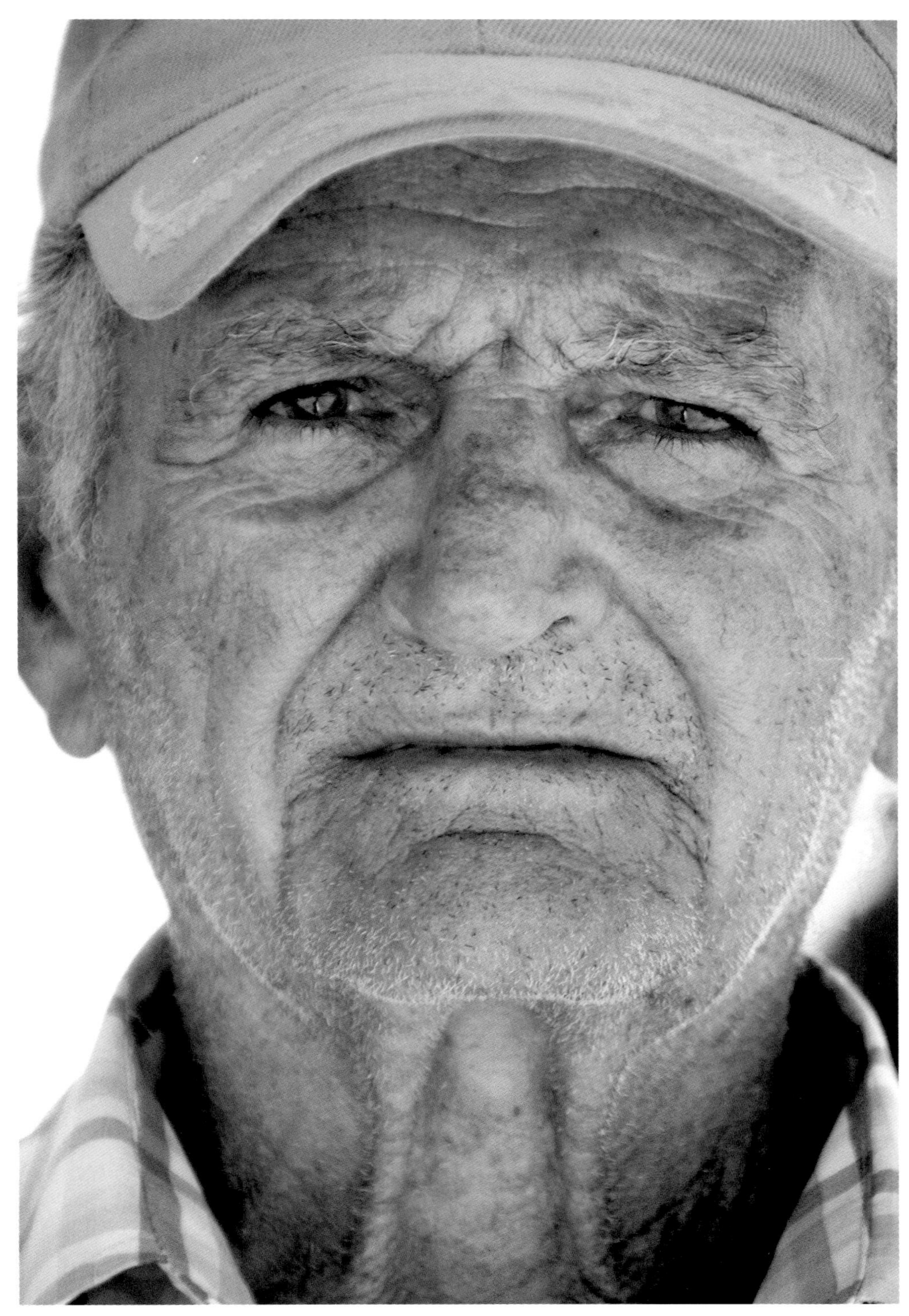

Making Camera-Eye Contact

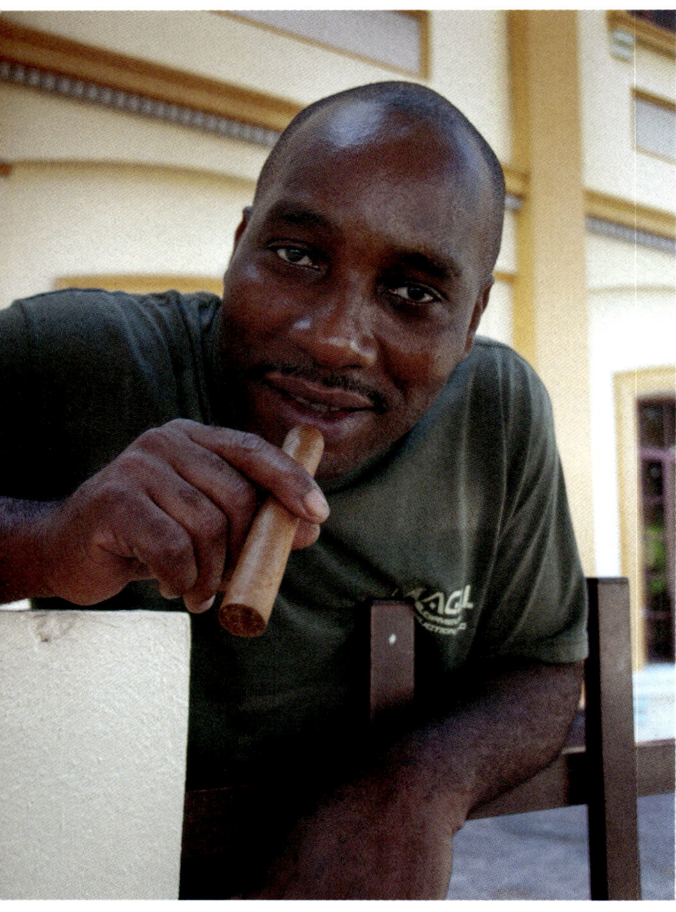

▲ Outside a cigar factory in Havana, Cuba, this man stopped me to talk. I used a wide-angle lens to increase the intimacy of the scene, at the same time taking care to center his eyes in the upper third of the composition.

24mm, 1/60 of a second at f/3.8 and ISO 100, hand held

▶ I shot a sequence of exposures of this plasterer. This one works best because his shy gaze is facing the camera, rather then averted as in the other captures. While he is not gazing 100% directly at the camera, there is something about his glance that is intriguing.

32mm, 1/320 of a second at f/9 and ISO 800, hand held

The eyes have it. When looking at a portrait, the viewer expects to gaze into the eyes of the subject. If you break this expectation, have a good reason for doing so.

On the other hand, if the eyes are included in a portrait, they are integral. Viewers will look first to the eyes, and then survey the rest of the scene. Plan to position eyes as an important element in your composition. If your depth-of-field is shallow and only one thing can be in focus, the eyes should be sharp. Selectively focusing on the eyes is crucial for many portraits.

It's important to capture a significant expression in the eyes. The portrait subject should usually be directed to look at the camera, not at you. At the same time, you should attempt to engage the subject so they look interested. As I've mentioned, jokes work well, as does the instruction to "smile with your eyes."

Pay attention to the direction of light hitting your subject's eyes, and also the reflections in the eyes. While these elements make up only a small area of a portrait, they can have a disproportionately large impact on the "feeling" of your portrait overall. Eyes are beautiful, without exception. If the light falling on the eyes does not emphasize this beauty, modify the light, or move your subject until you are satisfied.

For outdoor portraits, soft and indirect light often works best. I look for bright shade or overcast but bright days and try not to position my subjects in strong sunlight.

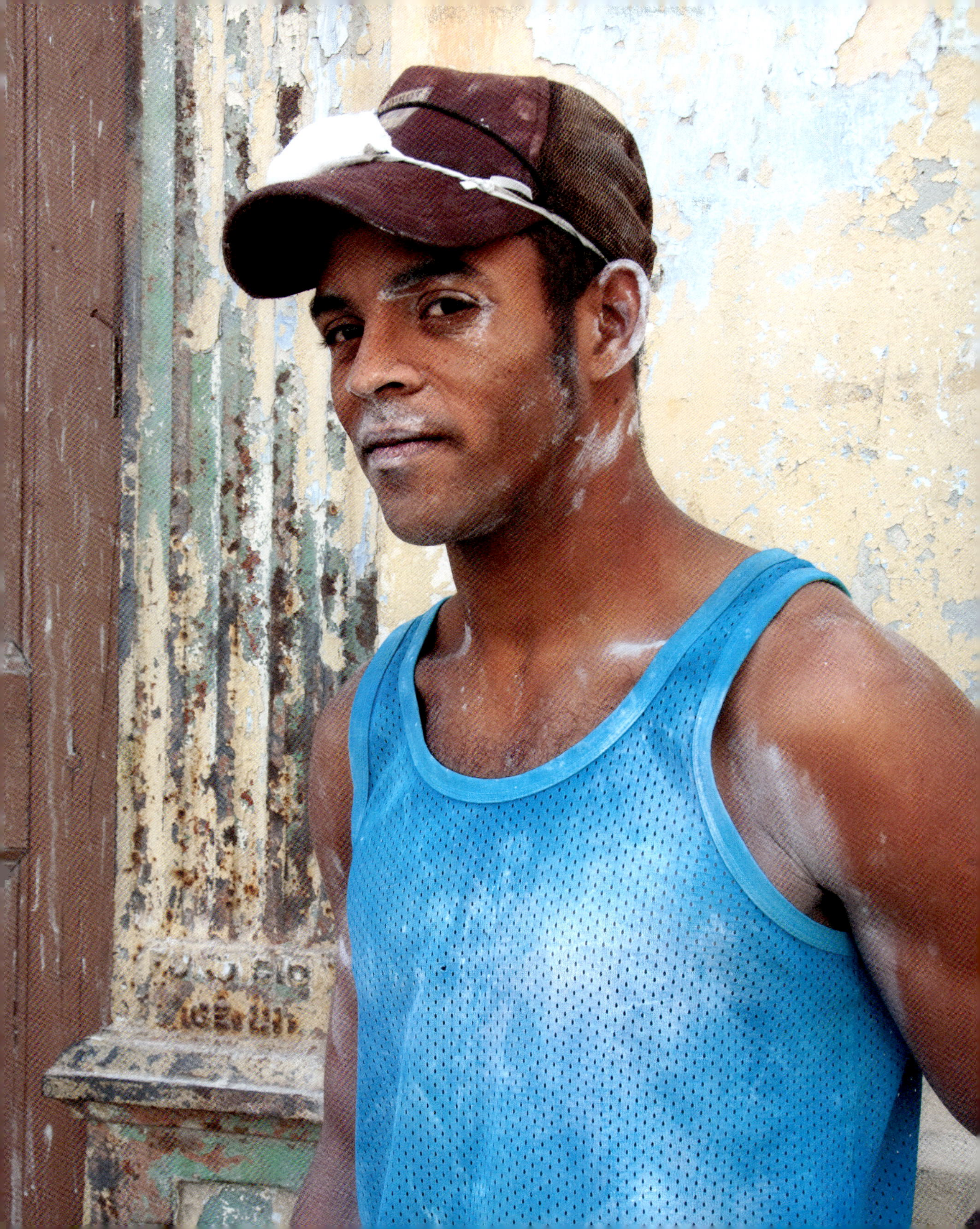

Movement and Shutter Speed

The shutter speed on your camera is set to a length of time, for example, 1/60 of a second. This duration controls how long the shutter is open to let light in to hit the sensor. Unless you are using a flash—for example, in the studio (see sidebar)—the shutter speed setting controls how motion is rendered.

Very fast shutter speeds (1/250 of a second and faster) freeze motion and render it crisply. Exposures of intermediate length (between 1/125 of a second and 1/15 of a second) mostly stop motion so people seem distinct, but there may be some blurring. Exposures that are longer than 1/15 of a second will usually show very distinctive (and sometimes creative) motion effects.

Portraiture is one area in photography in which stopping subject motion is usually one of the goals. To achieve this goal, you can ask your subjects to stay still (or glue them to the background!). More realistically, you can use a flash or plan to increase the shutter speed you use by some combination of adding light, opening the aperture of your camera to let more light in, or raising the ISO.

Shutter Speeds and Strobes

In the studio—or if you are using high-powered strobes in the field—your shutter speed setting usually doesn't matter that much. When you are lighting your exposure with studio strobes (powerful flash units), you should set your camera to the fastest shutter speed that it can use to synch with the flash units. It depends on the camera model, but usually this is between 1/60 and 1/250 of a second.

Whatever your camera's flash synch shutter speed, the actual length of the exposure is controlled by the duration of the flash—and not your camera's shutter speed. Usually, this is a very short amount of time—for example, 1/5000 or 1/10000 of a second—short enough to stop almost all motion.

Think of it this way: to make a given exposure you need a total amount of light, no matter where that light is coming from. When you are using flash units, a great deal of light is put out, but only for a short amount of time. This combination—a great deal of light in a short burst—equals out to be the equivalent of much less continuous light but an exposure for a longer amount of time.

By the way, if you are working with strobes in a studio, you'll need to trigger these units. One way to do this is with a wireless strobe transceiver attached to the flash hotshoe on your camera. You can also use a synch cord connected from the camera to the flash unit. Many strobes can be optically triggered which means that one flash—for example, the unit on the camera—triggers the other units.

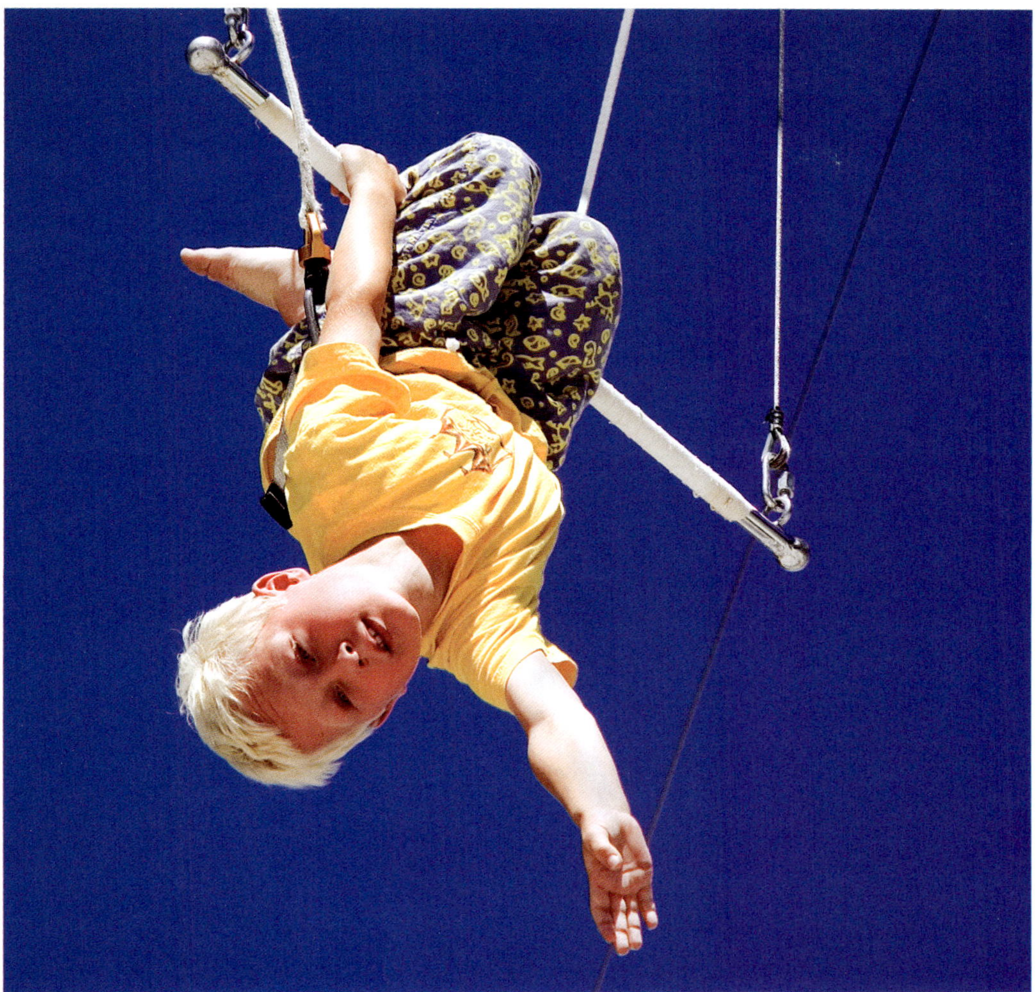

▲ The high trapeze was rigged outside on a bright, sunny day near Lake Tahoe, California. To crisply capture my son Julian as he flew through the air, I knew I needed to use as fast a shutter speed as possible. The 1/1250 of a second shutter speed used in this exposure stops the motion nicely.

70mm, 1/1250 of a second at f/4.5 and ISO 200, hand held

▼ Pages 130–131: In this two-minute exposure by moonlight, the motion of the clouds blown towards the camera gets rendered as lines in motion. The clouds that are further away from the camera look more like "normal" clouds. At the same time, the people in the foreground (exposed at 20 seconds) are only slightly blurred—and look almost like part of the landscape.

Two exposures combined in Photoshop, one exposure at 20 seconds (foreground) and one at two minutes (sky); both exposures 22mm at f/16 and ISO 100, tripod mounted

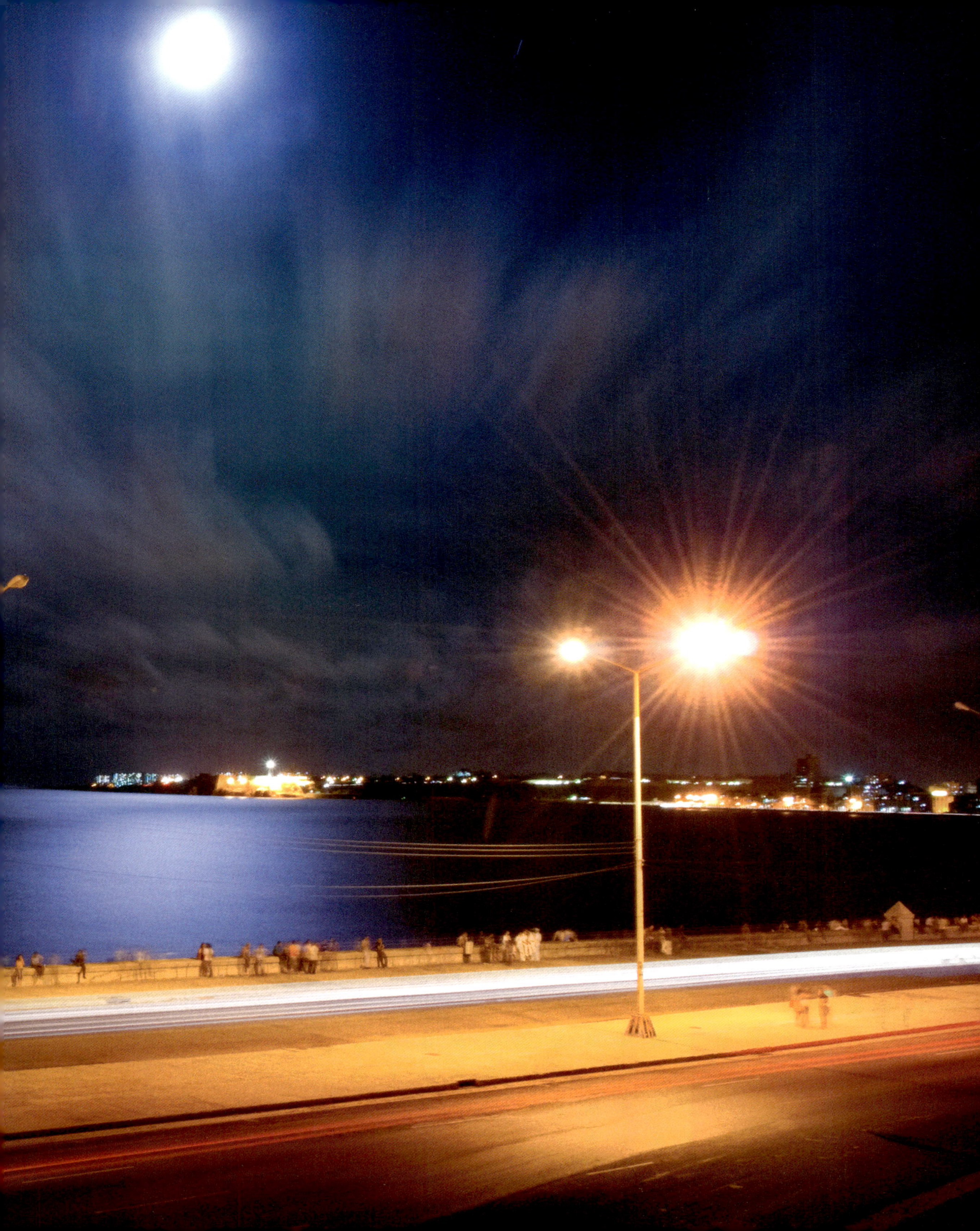

Aperture and Depth-of-Field

I confess: in much of my photography, I'm a tripod kind of guy. Furthermore, in my flower, water drop, and nature photography I tend to stop my lens down to as small an aperture as I can to get the most depth-of-field (or range in front and behind the subject that is in focus). Give me f/64 and I'll ask for more.

For the most part, this kind of approach does not work well with portraiture. You can leave your tripod at home when you are taking photos of people. Other than as a prop, you probably won't miss it.

As I've mentioned, in the studio the duration of the exposure is controlled by the length of the flash put out by the strobe units. This means that it doesn't matter what shutter speed setting you use on your camera (as long as you can synch with the flash units). It also means that you don't effectively make changes to the exposure with your shutter speed when you are using flash as your exposure. To change your depth-of-field, you need to make sure you have the appropriate amount of light coming from the flash. You can also change your ISO which can potentially allow you to change your f-stop and thus depth-of-field.

Both these approaches have their limits. Usually, it is not possible to endlessly crank the power on strobe units—and if you could do so you might get highlight blowouts. Although cameras can shoot at much higher ISOs than they used to, you don't want to shoot portraits at ISOs that are too high, unless you are trying for an intentionally noisy effect.

All this implies a fairly large lens opening and wide open aperture. F-stops from f/5.6 to f/11 are the norm in studio portraiture (bearing in mind that the smaller the f-number the bigger the opening in the lens). In turn, a large aperture means shallower depth-of-field—which is usually just fine for portraits.

A shallow depth-of-field portrait has the face, or even just the eyes, in focus with a blurred background and foreground. The viewer's eyes will go first to the sharper portion of an image, in this case the face.

The situation with location portraiture in terms of aperture and depth-of-field is pretty much the same as in the studio. Most likely, you'll want to freeze subject motion. This means that you can't go with too slow a shutter speed. Increasing the light is even less of an option in the field than in the studio. So increasing the ISO is your best bet to gain the leverage to close down your lens and get more depth-of-field, but who needs it?

In portraiture, moderate apertures are your friends. Just make sure the eyes are in focus. The name of the game is "f/8 and be there."

▶ A moderate aperture (f/8) ensured enough depth-of-field so that the entire plane of this model's face was in focus in this studio shot.

200mm, 1/160 of a second at f/8 and ISO 100, hand held

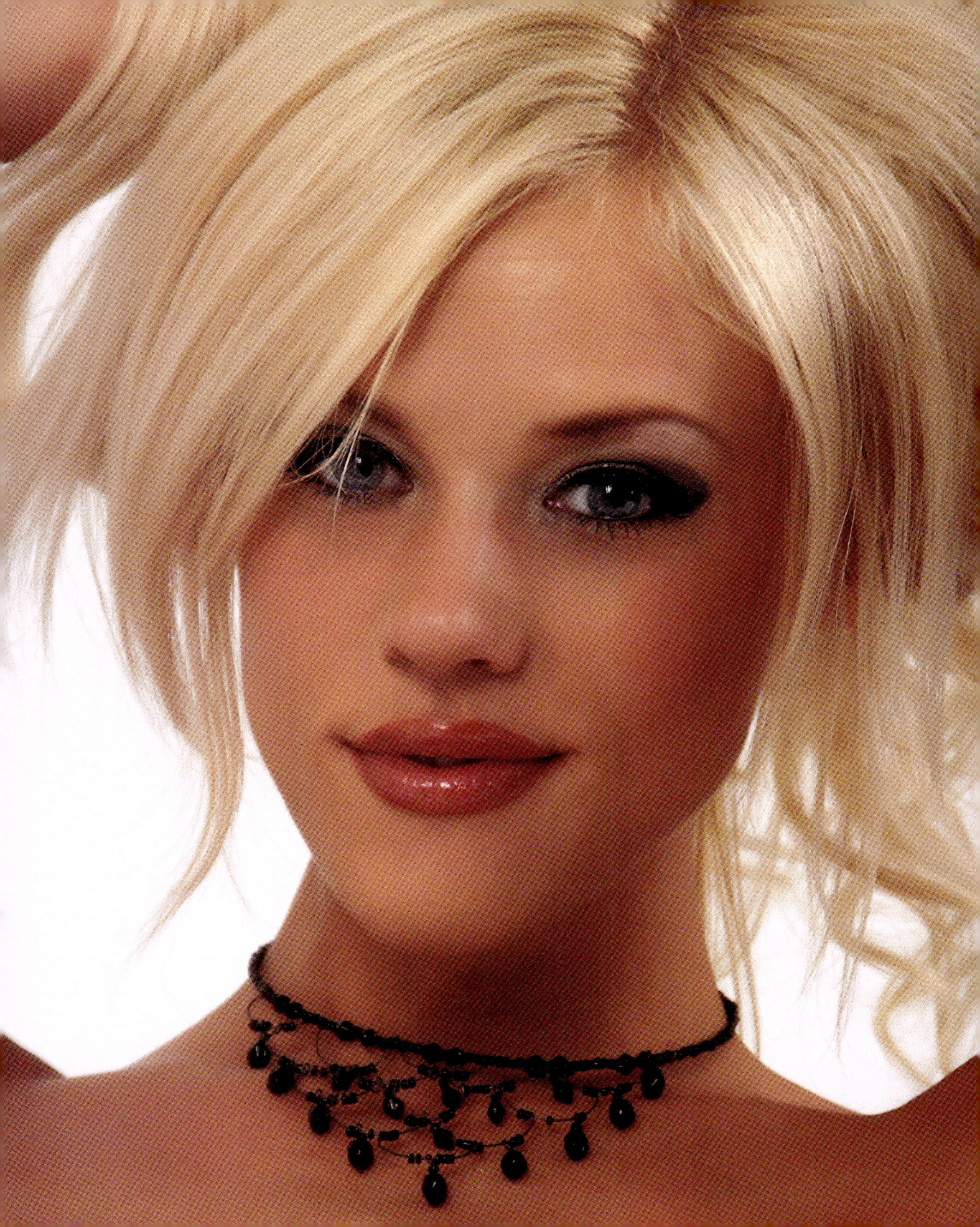

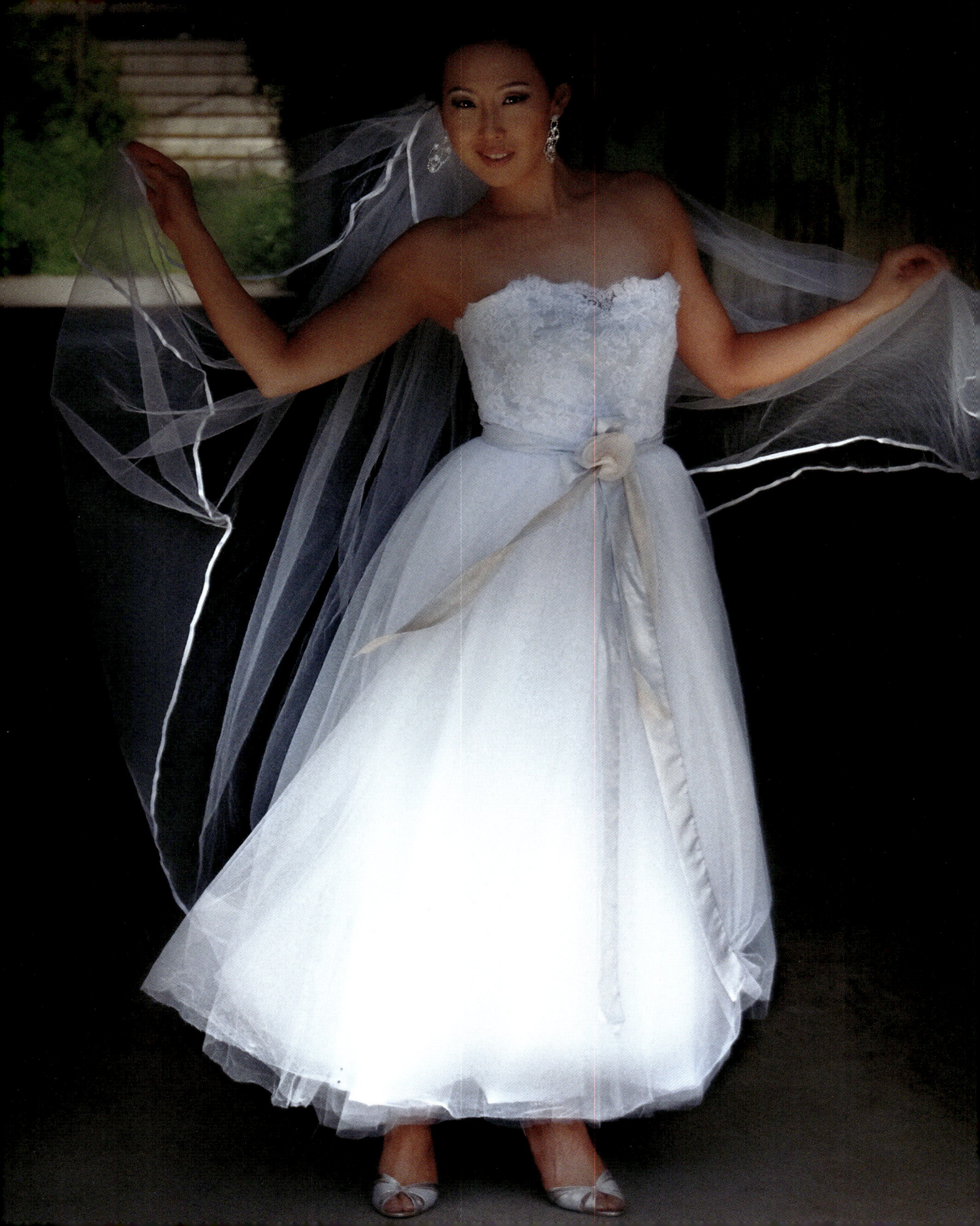

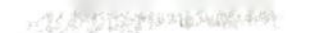

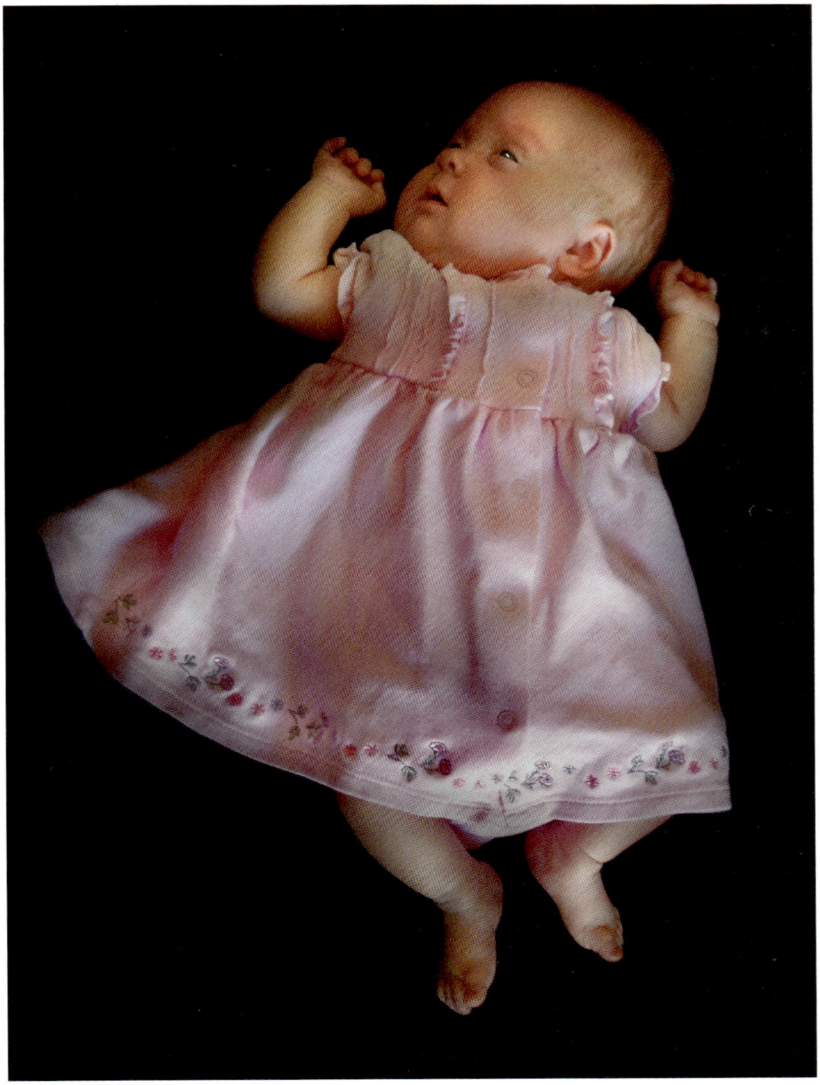

▲ We often look literally down on babies and small children—for example, in a crib. So this camera position, straight down in relationship to the child, seems much more natural than it would with an adult subject. From this elevated position, the baby appears close to flat, so you don't need any depth-of-field.

46mm, 1/50 of a second at f/5.6 and ISO 640, hand held

◀ In this photo, the wedding veil is the most important element (besides the bride) from a photographic standpoint. I shot the image with the aperture fairly wide open (f/4.8) to keep the focus on the veil while allowing the dark tunnel in the background to go out of focus.

55mm, 1/640 of a second at f/4.8 and ISO 200, hand held

Choosing the Right Lens

For the most part, portrait photography means using a lens in the 50-150mm range—in other words, normal angle of view to moderate telephoto. This is good news from one viewpoint: unlike many other kinds of photography, good portrait photography does not usually involve fancy specialized optics or expensive, unusual lenses. Most likely, the "kit" lens that shipped with your DSLR will do just fine for portraiture—as will the zoom lens that comes with a fixed-lens compact camera.

In many portrait situations, you don't want to use a lens that is much wider than normal because using a wide-angle lens makes facial features look distorted in a way that is not flattering.

On the other hand, using a moderate telephoto tends to compress the lines of perspective in the areas of the cheekbones and face in a flattering way. That's why a 85mm to 100mm lens is often considered ideal for close-in portraiture—particularly if the lens has a fast maximum aperture, and blurs the background attractively when it is used wide open.

For much of my portraiture, particularly in the studio, I like to use my 18-200mm zoom lens. All photographic hardware choices involve trade-offs, and this is not a perfect lens. But it does cover in one convenient and fairly lightweight package all the focal lengths I am likely to need in portraiture.

There are a few situations in which it makes sense to use untraditional focal lengths or lenses to make portraits. For example:

- If you want to bring a distant subject in closer for an intimate portrait, it makes sense to use a longer telephoto lens, perhaps around 200mm. I wouldn't suggest lenses longer than about 300mm for portraiture. Even if they are steady on a tripod—and these longer lenses cannot realistically be handheld—your subject will probably move at least slightly, creating unsharp looking images because of motion.
- Special soft-focus optics, such as the Lensbaby with its configurable "sweet spot"—area that is in focus—can be used to create memorable, unusual, and romantic soft-focus portraits.
- Extreme wide-angle portraits are almost never flattering, but they are certainly unusual and attention-getting. I've found that kids enjoy seeing themselves as captured using a fisheye lens, so in portrait sessions with kids I will often start by making a fisheye exposure. This loosens my subjects up so that they have fun with more conventional photos.

▶ Using a telephoto lens (200mm) brought this tobacco farmer closer, optically helped to "separate" him from his background, and emphasized the leathery lines on his face and neck.

200mm, 1/250 of a second at f/8 and ISO 100, hand held

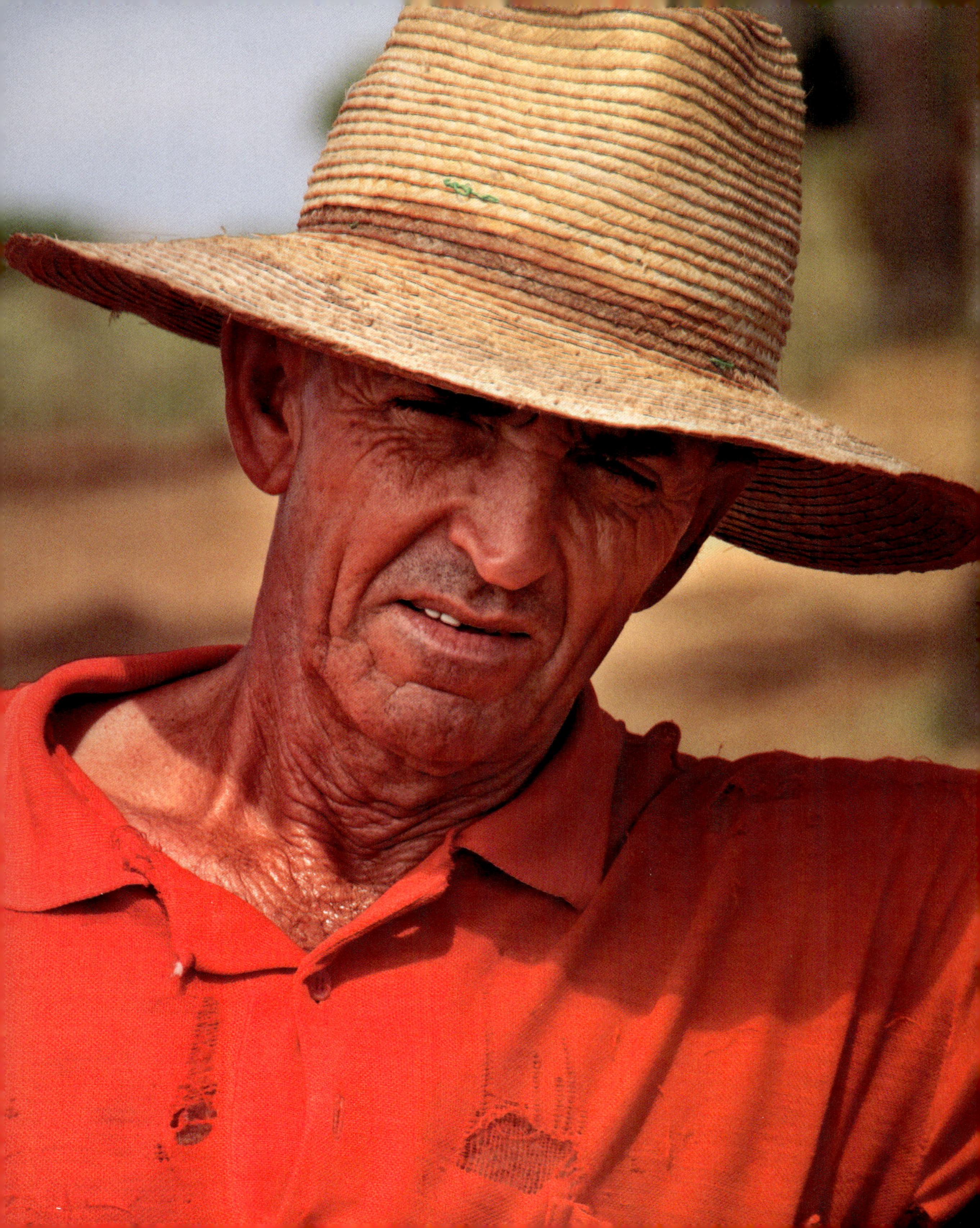

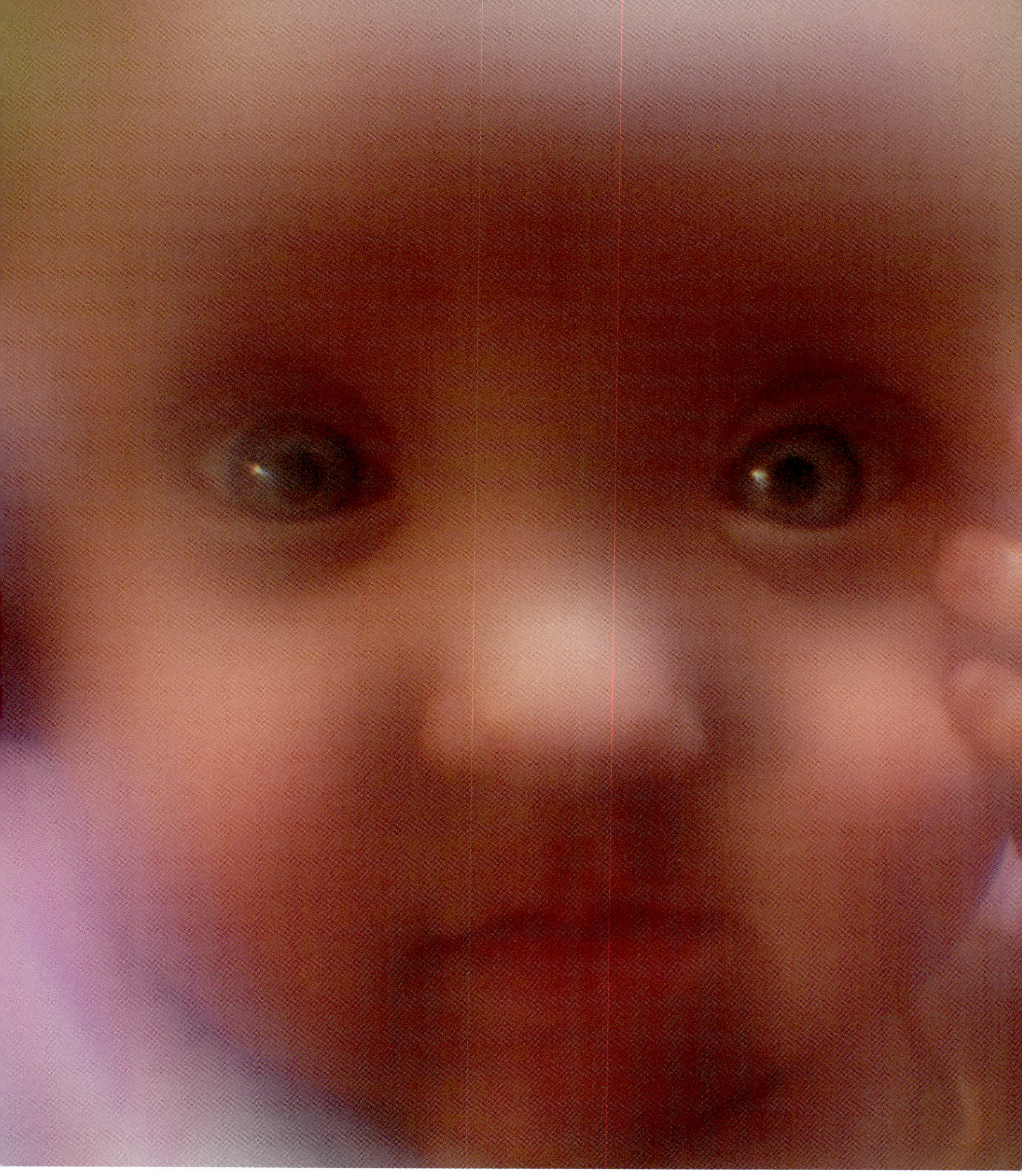

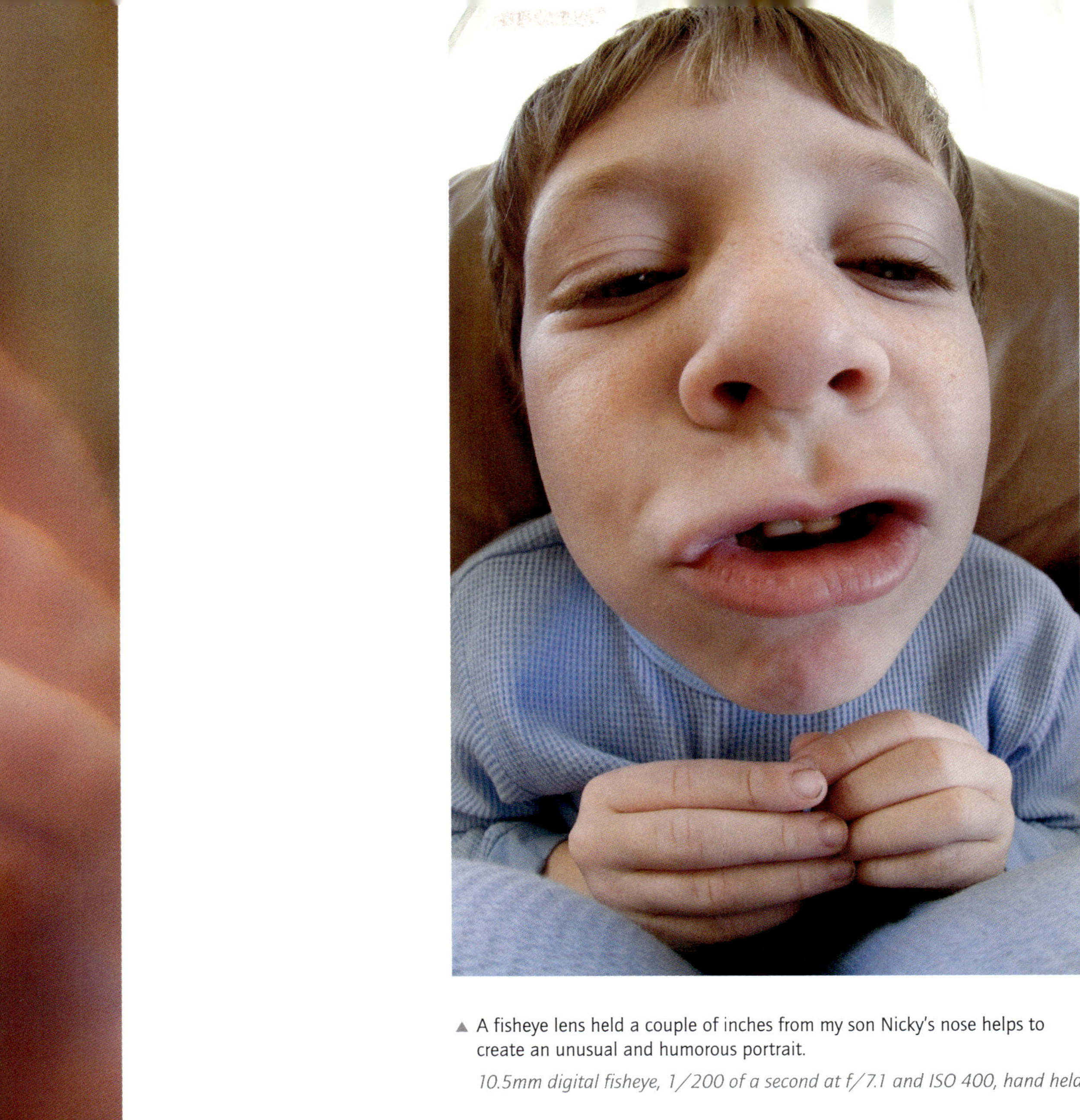

▲ A fisheye lens held a couple of inches from my son Nicky's nose helps to create an unusual and humorous portrait.

10.5mm digital fisheye, 1/200 of a second at f/7.1 and ISO 400, hand held

◀ Using a special purpose lens—the Lensbaby Composer with a plastic optic—I was able to create an intentionally out-of-focus image, with only the eyes relatively sharp. The Lensbaby allows you to move the lens around on a flexible base to position the "sweet spot"—the portion of the image that is in focus—where you'd like it. Normally, in Lensbaby portraits, the sweet spot should be positioned so the subject's eyes are in focus, relatively speaking.

Lensbaby Composer, plastic optic, 1/60 of a second using an f/4 aperture ring and ISO 320, hand held

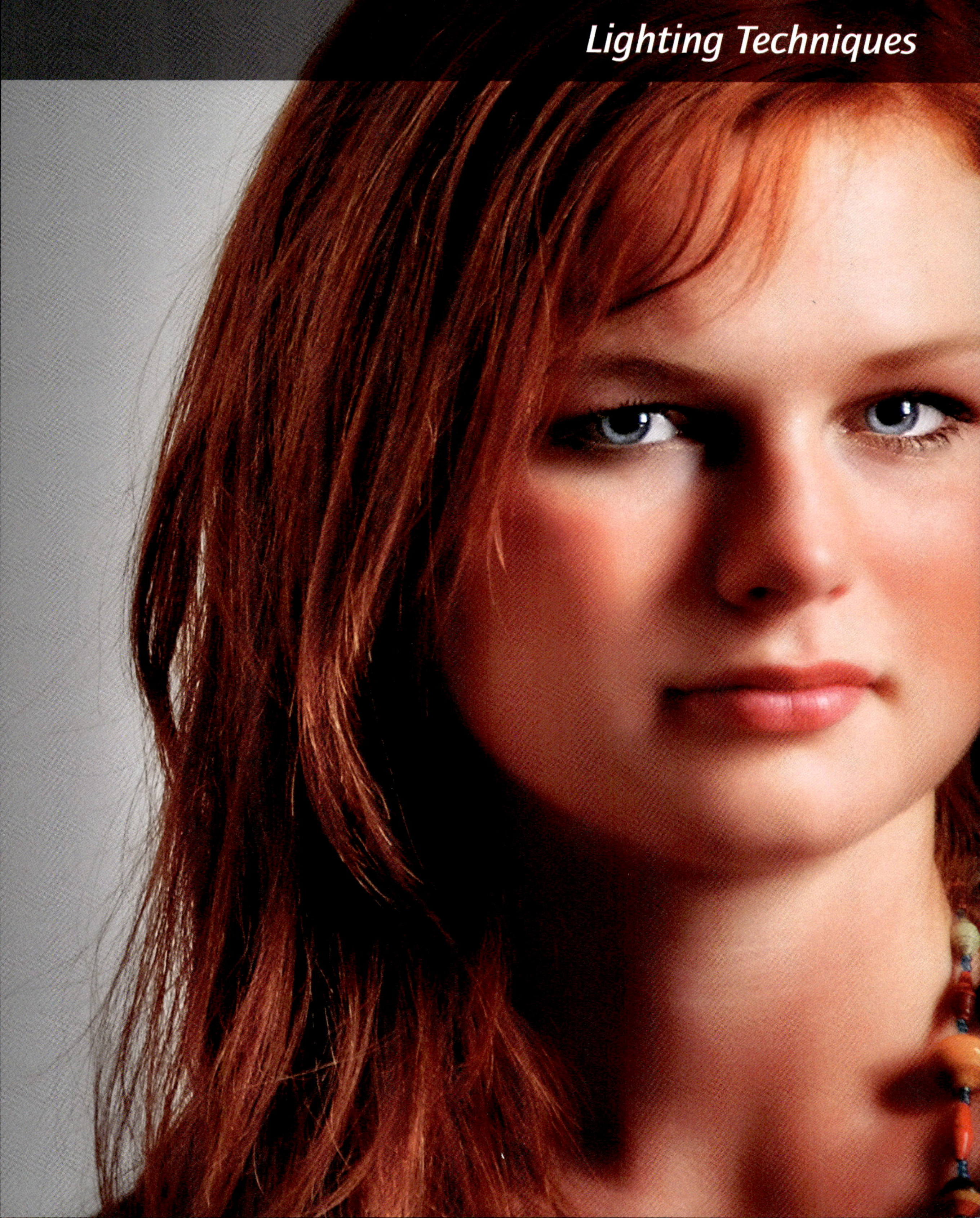

Working with Light

At a fundamental level, photography is about light—light reflected off surfaces, the ambient light in an environment, the way light makes things look. Without light there is no photograph. This is true no matter what the subject—you need light to illuminate a capture of a still life or mountain landscape just as surely as you need light to capture a portrait of a person.

And not just any old light! The difference between a just plain vanilla snapshot and a unique and wonderful portrait of someone is at least partially in the lighting.

Sure, it helps to have an interesting or attractive person to start with (pages 10–55), posed in a dynamic way (pages 110–119), and placed in front of a complementary background (pages 120–123). But without good lighting your portrait will not rise above the mundane.

A photographer can work with light actively or passively. In passive mode, the photographer observes the light, changes position relative to the subject, moves the subject if possible, waits—and when the moment is right makes the photo.

In active mode, the photographer sets up the lighting using a variety of possible light sources. But it's worth being clear that even when a photographer actively arranges the lighting, the passive skill of light observation is crucial. The usual procedure is to work by successive approximation: the light is arranged and then observed. Perhaps a test shot is made and inspected in the LCD. Depending upon the results, the light is adjusted, and the process iterated.

Therefore, in either active or passive mode, observation of light is a crucial skill. When planning a creative portrait you also

▶ I set this shot up with a large strobe-driven soft box to the left of Mathew the "flying dragon."

I asked Mathew to jump and my lighting assistant followed Mathew's movement with a second strobe. I used the magic of studio lighting—actually, the short duration of a studio strobe—to stop Mathew's motion in midair. It took quite a number of shots to get this effect right.

27mm, 1/160 of a second at f/11 and ISO 100, hand held

▲ Pages 140–141: In this shot, the red-haired model is lit using a single strobe-powered soft box, a diffused light source. The soft box diffuser is shaped as a rectangular light strip, positioned above the model and to her left.

The white circle to the model's right is created using an ellipsoidal spotlight aimed on a white wall. The ellipsoidal spotlight can vary both the size and focus of the spot, with the focus controlling whether the spot of light has sharp or soft edges. For a lighting diagram of this photo, see page 164.

Although the wall is white, it is comparatively darker than the model because the strobe doesn't reach the wall—which makes the light thrown by the ellipsoidal spot seem like a white circle in a black background.

200mm, 1/160 of a second at f/6.3 and ISO 200, hand held

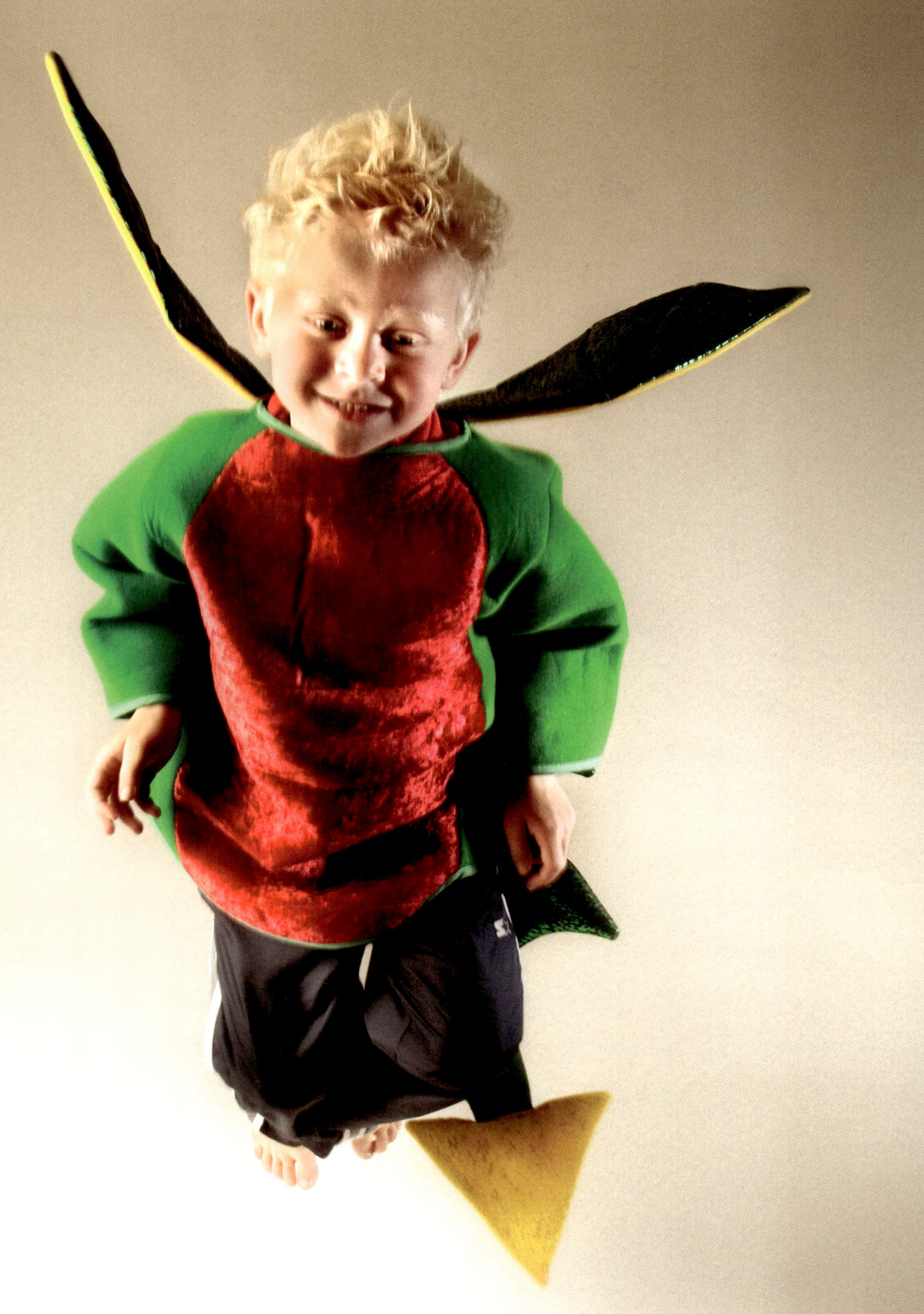

need to know the possible light sources available, as well as some basic ideas about lighting portraits.

To See the Light

Understanding light from the viewpoint of a pragmatic photographer means recognizing that light has three general characteristics:

- Intensity
- Direction
- Quality

Intensity of a light source simply means the strength of the light. Generally, care needs to be taken to make sure that a light source is strong enough to illuminate the areas you want to show, but not so strong as to cause highlight blowouts. In other words, overall light shouldn't be too high in contrast. However, this is not an absolute rule: sometimes—particularly in monochromatic portraiture—high contrast light makes a powerful and creative statement.

Direction refers to the direction from the light source to the subject that is illuminated. In this regard, it is worth keeping in mind the law of reflection, which states that the angle of incidence equals the angle of reflection.

Here's why the well-known law of reflection matters: when you are photographing someone you are not photographing the way the person is lit. Rather, you are photographing the light reflected off the surfaces the person presents. The law of reflection lets you know that the light coming off the person (the reflected light) does so at the same angle as the light directed onto the person (the incident light). This relationship is shown in Figure 1 below.

The law of reflection is important because you don't want light coming directly back at the camera. At best, this is unattractive

Figure 1: Fundamental law of reflection

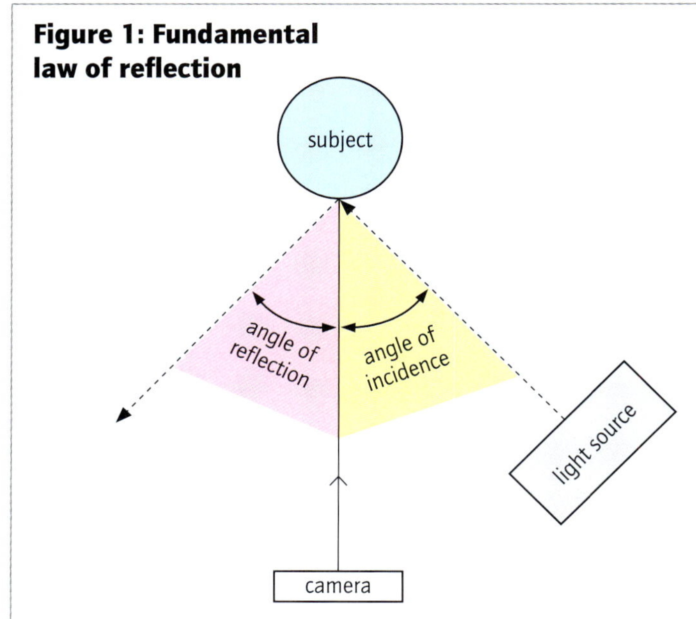

▶ My daughter Katie Rose is always in motion, as is typical for toddlers (unless they are asleep). Katie wandered around the studio, off and on the seamless paper background. I tracked her motion with my camera, and captured her in this high-key portrait, intentionally post-processing the image to make the background seem slightly overexposed.

This portrait was lit from two directions as you can see from the reflected highlights in Katie's eyes.

The primary lighting source was a large soft box to Katie's right, which helps give the lighting in the portrait a nice glowing feel.

52mm, 1/160 of a second at f/13 and ISO 100, hand held

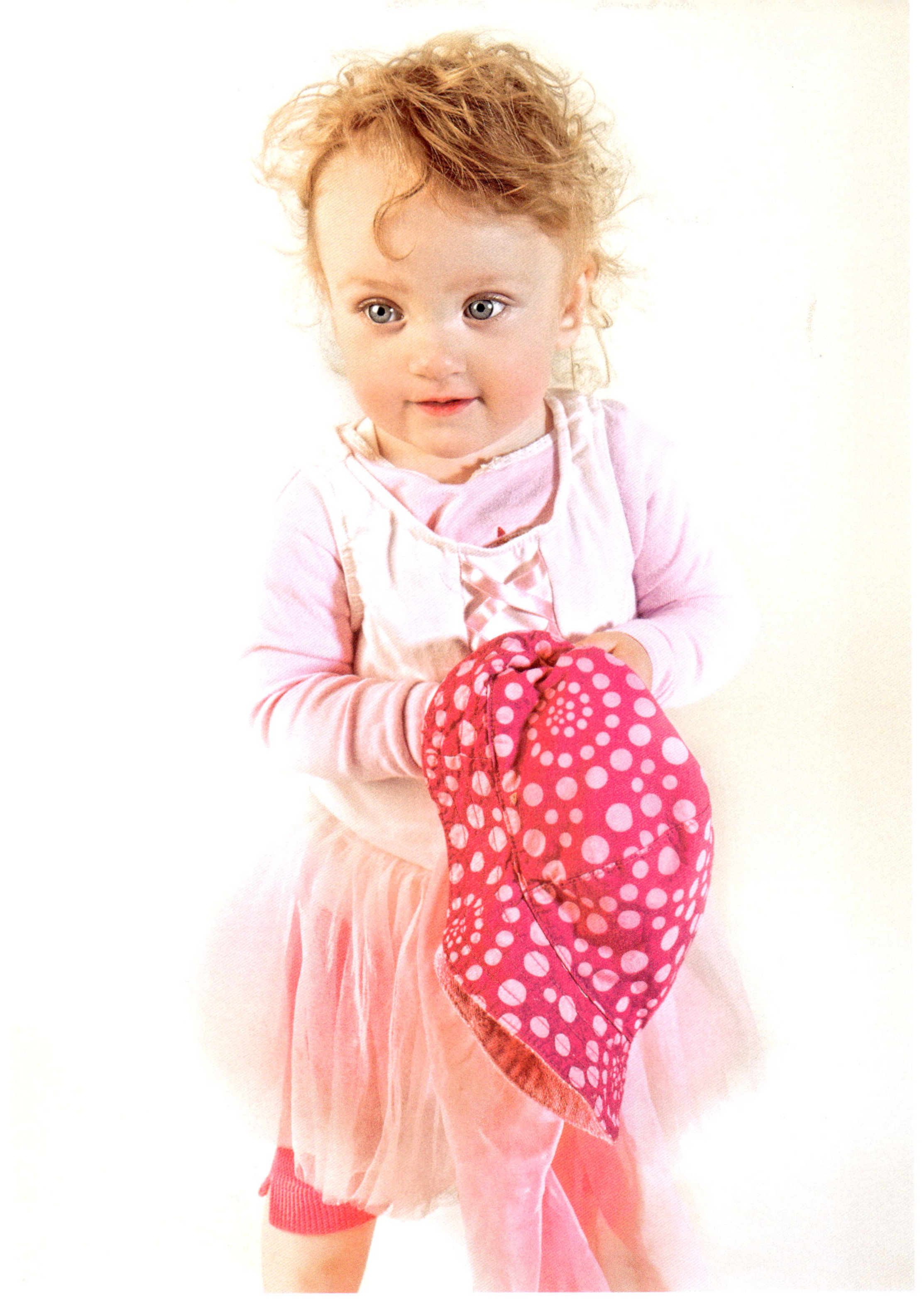

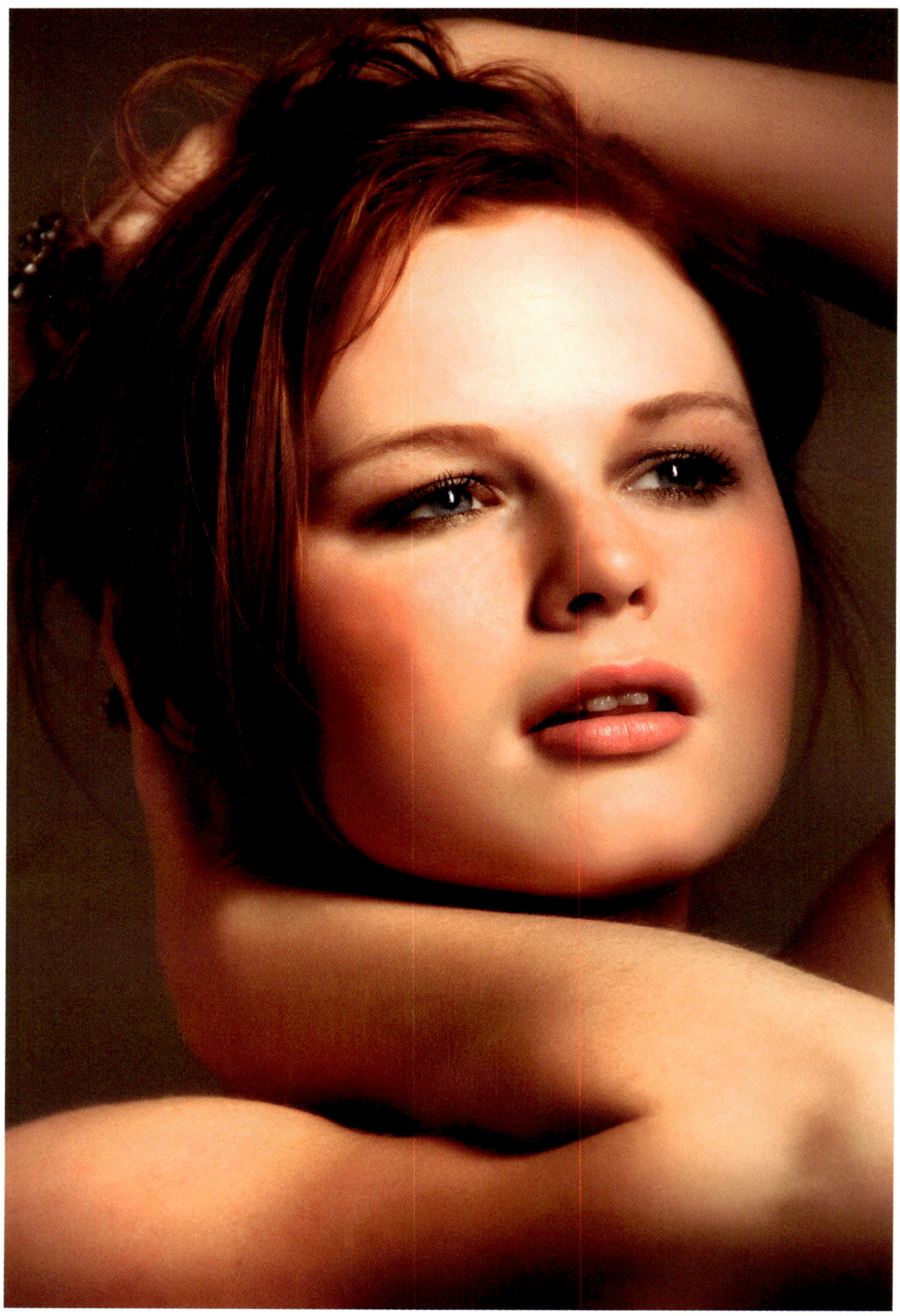

and at worst it leads to lens flares. That's why most portrait lighting sources are placed so that the light is reflected off the subject at an angle to the camera (the angle of reflection). Light that is captured at an angle tends to be softer and more attractive than direct lighting.

The ***quality*** of light is the hardest characteristic of light to pin down, and in practice is to some extent subjective and elusive. It's not at all obvious why natural sunlight has such a wonderful quality, or how one would go about describing that quality. But it's nonetheless true that often natural light has a quality that can't be beat. By the way, you likely know that there's no such thing as natural light in a vacuum. Daylight is constantly changing with characteristics that differ due to position, atmospheric conditions, time of day, and so on.

Many great photographers—for example, Ansel Adams and Edward Weston—have preferred to create portraits using only natural light, sometimes augmented by using devices such as fill cards and diffusers.

There are two important factors that help define the quality of light. One is color temperature. It can be measured. The other factor is where the light is on the scale from harsh to diffuse. This is a subjective matter but is still important to consider.

Harsh lighting is high contrast light, whereas diffuse light is soft and almost caresses. Both qualities of light have their place in portraiture, although soft lighting is probably used more often.

Color temperature just refers to the frequency of the light waves emitted by the light source. Usually, color temperature is expressed in degrees Kelvin, on a scale going from light we perceive as blue to light we perceive as red.

Your camera's rendering of color temperature is controlled by its white balance setting. Usually, Auto white balance works pretty well, although I prefer to set my camera to Flash white balance in the studio.

The advent of digital controls over white balance makes this light characteristic easier to manipulate than it used to be with film. In particular, if you are saving the RAW data provided by your camera rather than shooting JPEG (see pages 196–197), you can always adjust white balance after the fact.

Color temperature becomes a serious issue that is difficult to control in situations where there are multiple light sources, each putting out light with a different color temperature. When this happens, usually your best bet is to set your camera's white balance to the predominant (or most attractive) color temperature, and adjust the effect later in the digital darkroom.

◄ This lovely model is lit by a single strip light—you can see its reflection in her eyes. A large white board positioned to the left of the model provided "fill" lighting, so that the shadows on the left side weren't too deep.

200mm, 1/125 of a second at f/5.6 and ISO 200, hand held

Kinds of Light

There are many different kinds of light that can be used to make portraits; these different light sources can sometimes be mixed and matched with great effectiveness. It's important to be aware of the possibilities when you are thinking about a shot.

Many great portraits are made using natural daylight light. As I've explained, there are an infinite number of variations within the category of natural light. Natural light can be modified to create a more uniform light with a fill card that reflects light onto your subject—it can be intensified using a mirror, and it can be diffused. For example, by placing a gauze curtain over a window.

Besides natural light, probably the single most important source of light for portraits is flash. Flash units—also called strobes—come in many varieties, ranging from portable flash units designed to be mounted on your camera, or even built into your camera (see pages 154–157), to larger flash units that are primarily used in a studio (see pages 158–167).

As I've already explained, flash units put out a great deal of light but for a very short amount of time. This has a number of consequences. Generally, the duration of the flash controls the effective length of the exposure—and how motion is rendered—rather than the camera's shutter speed. It also can be hard to know in advance what a flash exposure will do, since you can't see the light until the flash is fired and you make an exposure. The duration of the flash is so brief that you can't really see what it does. In the studio, modeling lights help with this issue by giving a sense of at least the direction of the light before the flash is fired.

Besides flash, there are a number of different kinds of lights specifically designed for photography that do let you see what you are doing with the light. So-called "hot" lights—usually using tungsten incandescent or quartz halogen bulbs—do let you see what you are doing. However, they live up to their name (they get hot), and do not put out as much light as a strobe. LED lighting is a more recent fixed-light idea that has some real advantages over hot lights, but is currently fairly expensive in the sizes necessary to light portraits.

The ability of modern cameras to shoot at high ISOs without excessive noise means that these kinds of light sources have become practical for portraiture in a way that they didn't use to be. You can also use higher ISO settings with light sources around your home that you might not have considered for photography previously—like table lamps, skylights, and so on (see pages 150–153).

▶ This model is lit on the left using a strobe-driven soft box strip, and on the right by a *beauty dish* mounted on a second strobe unit. The beauty dish is a flash accessory that puts out an adjustable circle of attractively diffuse light with an opaque center—designed, as the name implies, to make people look beautiful.

150mm, 1/125 of a second at f/10 and ISO 100, hand held

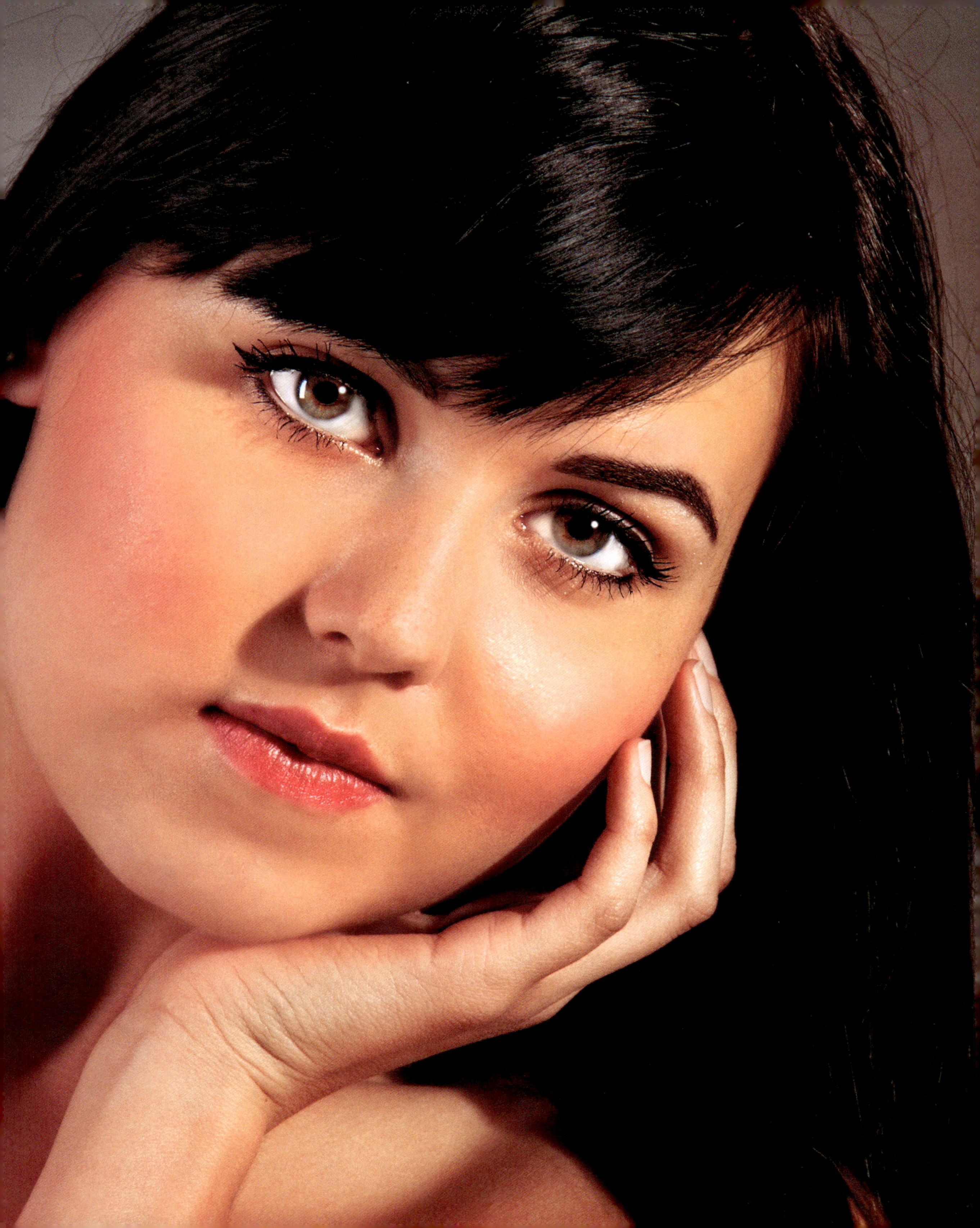

Lighting at Home

The general rule about lighting portraits at home is, try it! There's no penalty for failure, and you'd be amazed at how many great portraits can be made just using light sources you'll find around you.

The light coming through your windows is probably very nice at certain times of day. Take the time to watch its progression through the day so you can find out! If you don't quite like what you see, modify the window light with a piece of inexpensive gauzy fabric, or by opening or shutting curtains.

Need to make a portrait at night? Don't despair. It's amazing what you can do with low wattage incandescent bulbs.

Unlike some models, these work best when they are not naked. In other words, use a lamp shade when possible, or at least drape the lamp with fabric. Look closely at the quality of the light being cast on your subject, and adjust it to make the most attractive portraits.

Avoid fluorescent lighting. In my experience, all fluorescent tubes, including compact fluorescent bulbs—and even when you adjust for the white balance—tend to create very unattractive light. It's hard to overcome the flicker and color casts inherent in this kind of lighting.

Ceiling light fixtures also don't work very well because you can't move the position of the light, and it is always coming straight down—potentially resulting in odd shadows. It's much better to use table or standing lights. You can adjust the height or move around lights of this kind.

Don't hesitate to boost the ISO of your captures to make this kind of portrait. An ISO that would have been out of the question because of noise levels only a short time ago now produces quite acceptable results.

One other idea: if your subject is awake and in motion, and a good source of natural light is not available, you'll probably want to use flash as either a supplementary or primary source of lighting (see the example on page 153).

▶ Late at night, my young daughter slept peacefully, her face lit by the mottled light of a 15-watt light bulb. I didn't want to disturb her—all parents of young children will understand that it pays to let sleeping babies lie. So flash was out of the question, as was dragging more lights into the room. Instead, I chose to boost my ISO, and to create an intentionally noisy image that used to advantage the chiaroscuro effect of the low light.

105mm, 1/25 of a second at f/5.6 and ISO 1600, hand held

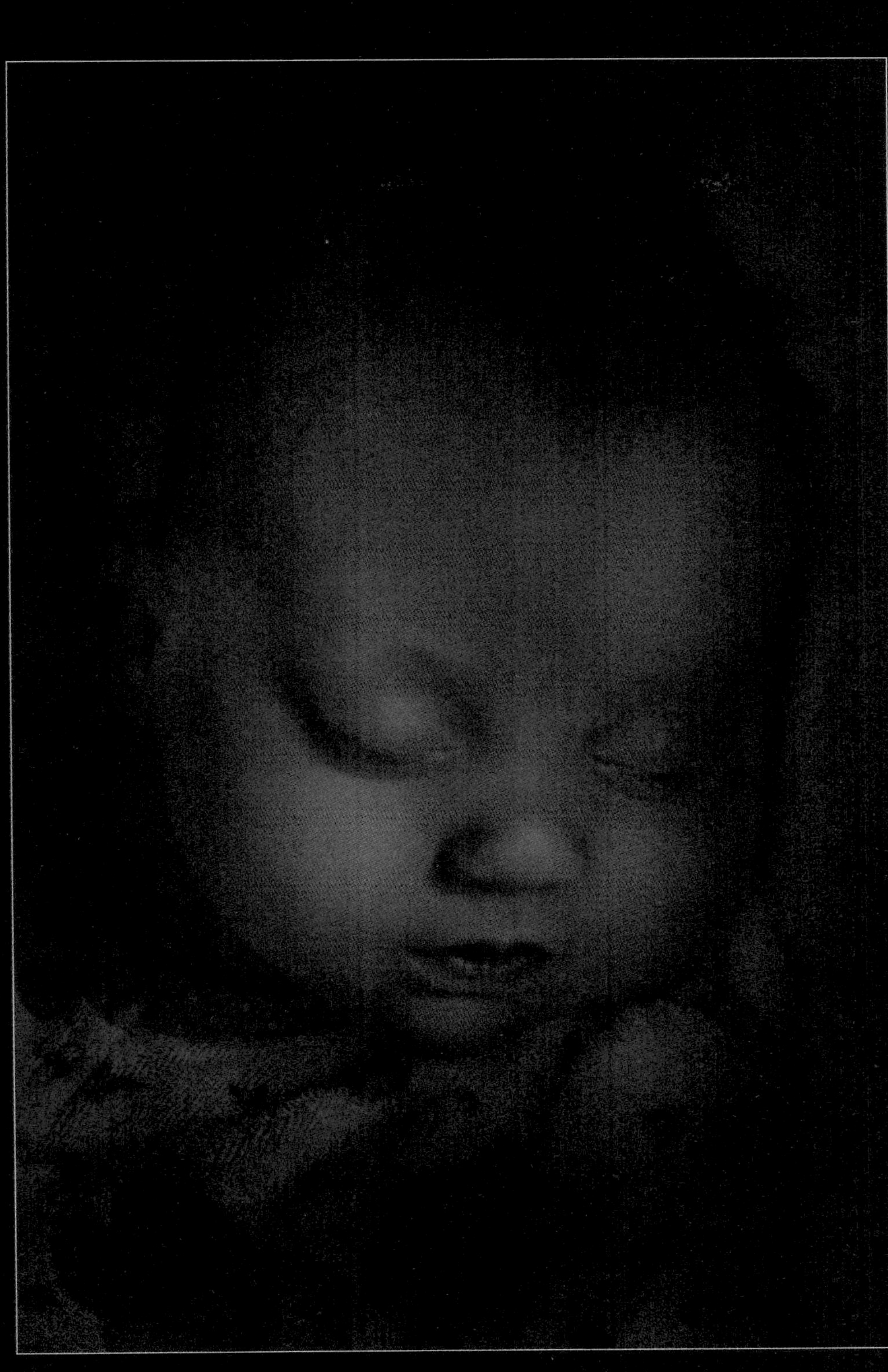

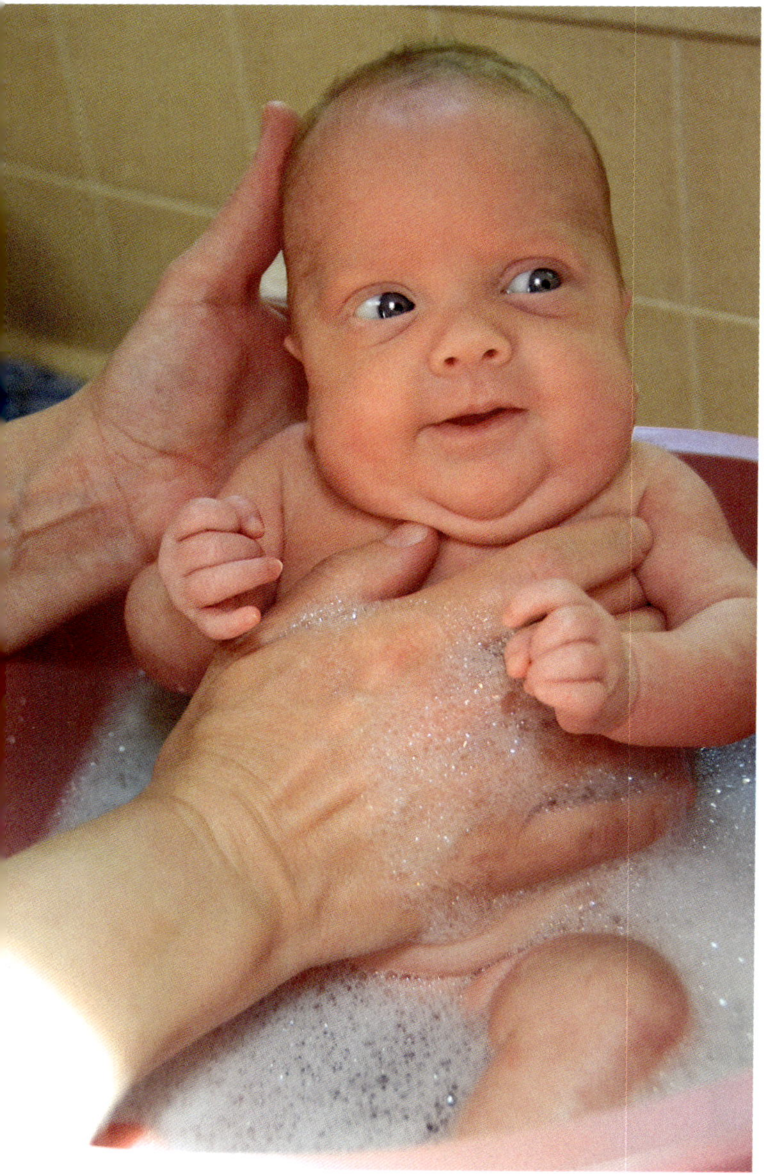

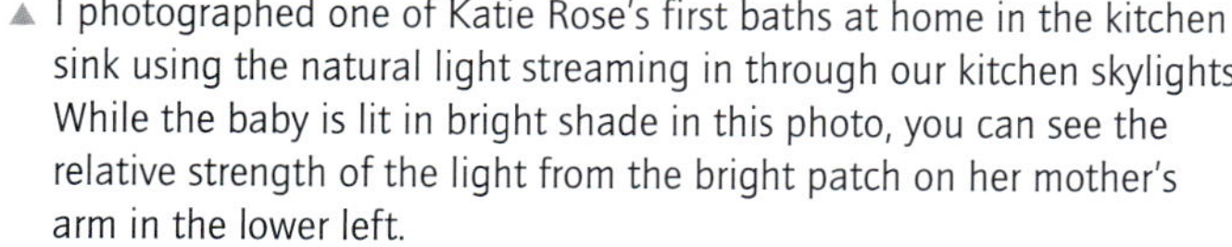

▲ I photographed one of Katie Rose's first baths at home in the kitchen sink using the natural light streaming in through our kitchen skylights. While the baby is lit in bright shade in this photo, you can see the relative strength of the light from the bright patch on her mother's arm in the lower left.

48mm, 1/100 of a second at f/5 and ISO 400, hand held

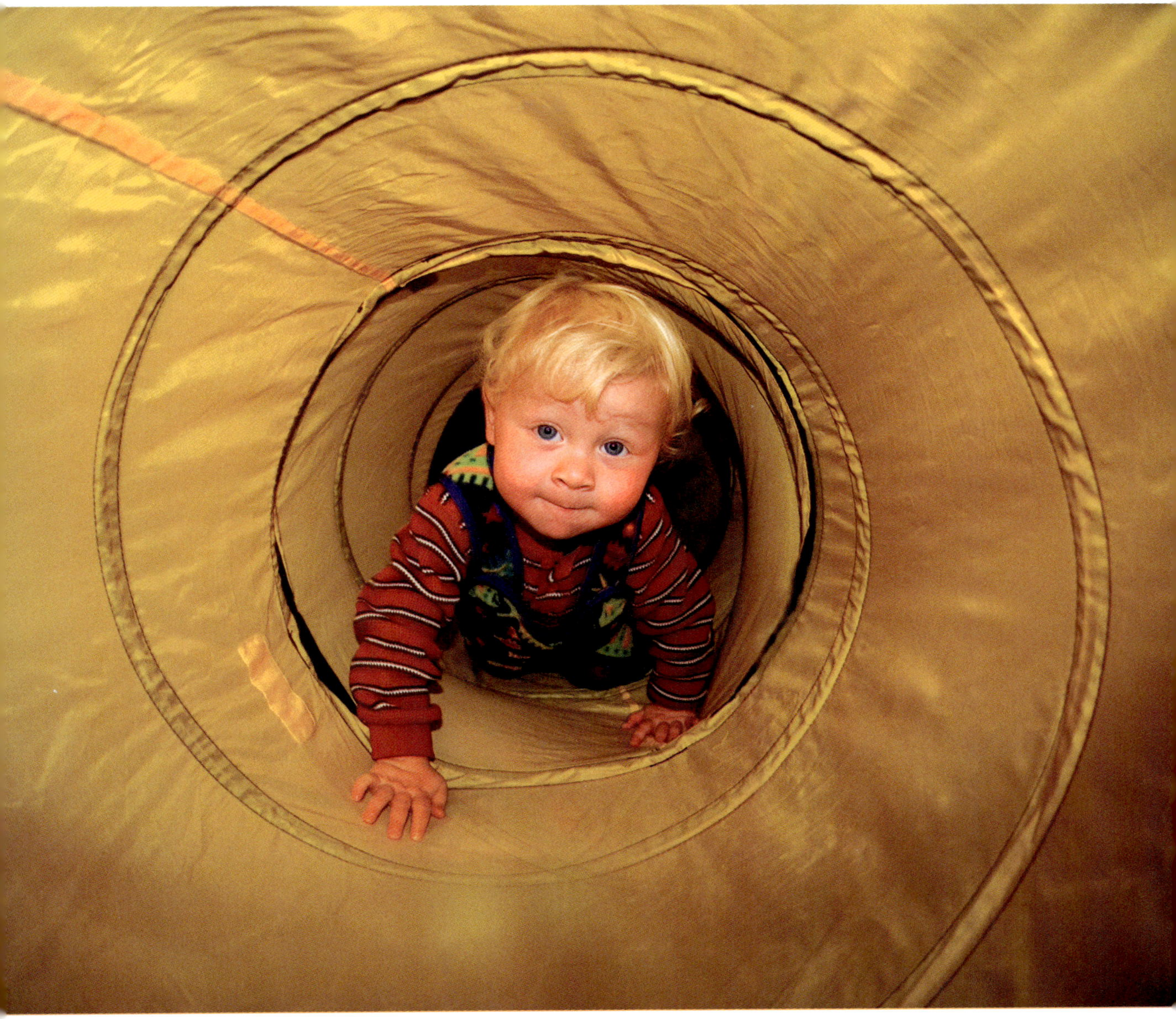

▲ To make this image of Mathew climbing through a tent, I placed the tent in our living room where it would pick up sunlight from the windows. Besides the natural light, the inside of the tent tunnel is lit using my DSLR's built-in flash unit.

I used a fisheye lens to exaggerate the length of the cloth tunnel entrance to the tent.

10.5mm digital fisheye, 1/60 of a second at f/2.8 and ISO 200, hand held

Direct Flash

I have to admit: I am not the greatest fan on earth of direct flash. But when you need it to get the shot, there's no substitute. Direct flash is convenient, fast, and capable of stopping motion in its tracks no matter what the ambient light conditions. Furthermore, lighting masters like Joe McNally are capable of linking many small flash units—sometimes hundreds of strobes, generally designed to be used on camera—to create incredibly sophisticated lighting effects (see the Resources section on 234 for further reading if you are interested in this topic).

My own opinion is that direct flash is less important than it used to be as a lighting source. These days it is possible to boost ISO into the thousands, and get quite good results. Therefore, available light works in many situations that would formerly have required a flash—and for digital photographers who know how to adjust their ISO outside of the studio, flash is swiftly becoming a special effect when you are affirmatively looking for the harsh light that direct flash provides.

The biggest downside of direct flash is that the quality of light can be incredibly harsh, with quick fall-off between areas that are illuminated and the background. For specific instructions on using flash units with your camera, check the documentation for your camera and the flash unit. Here are some tips that will help you get the best results when using a direct flash:

- Take off your lens shade. Normally, using a lens shade is a very good idea. However, with on-camera flash photography the lens shade itself can cast a very ugly shadow in front of the light emitted by the flash, especially if used with a wide angle lens.
- Get the flash unit as far off your camera as possible. A portable strobe mounted on the hot shoe on top of your camera is better than the built-in flash unit. If you can, move the flash unit even further off the camera using a bracket.
- Bounce the flash, don't point it directly at your subject. If you are using a flash unit that swivels and angles, point it at a surface that will reflect light back at your subject, or even at the ceiling. This will give you a measure of diffusion.

▶ I used a small flash unit mounted on top of my camera to make this portrait in the low-light conditions of the pizzeria where this portrait subject works. A diffuser placed on the flash head helped to make the light less harsh.

200mm, Nikon SB-800 Speedlight flash unit, 1/30 of a second at f/10 and ISO 200, hand held

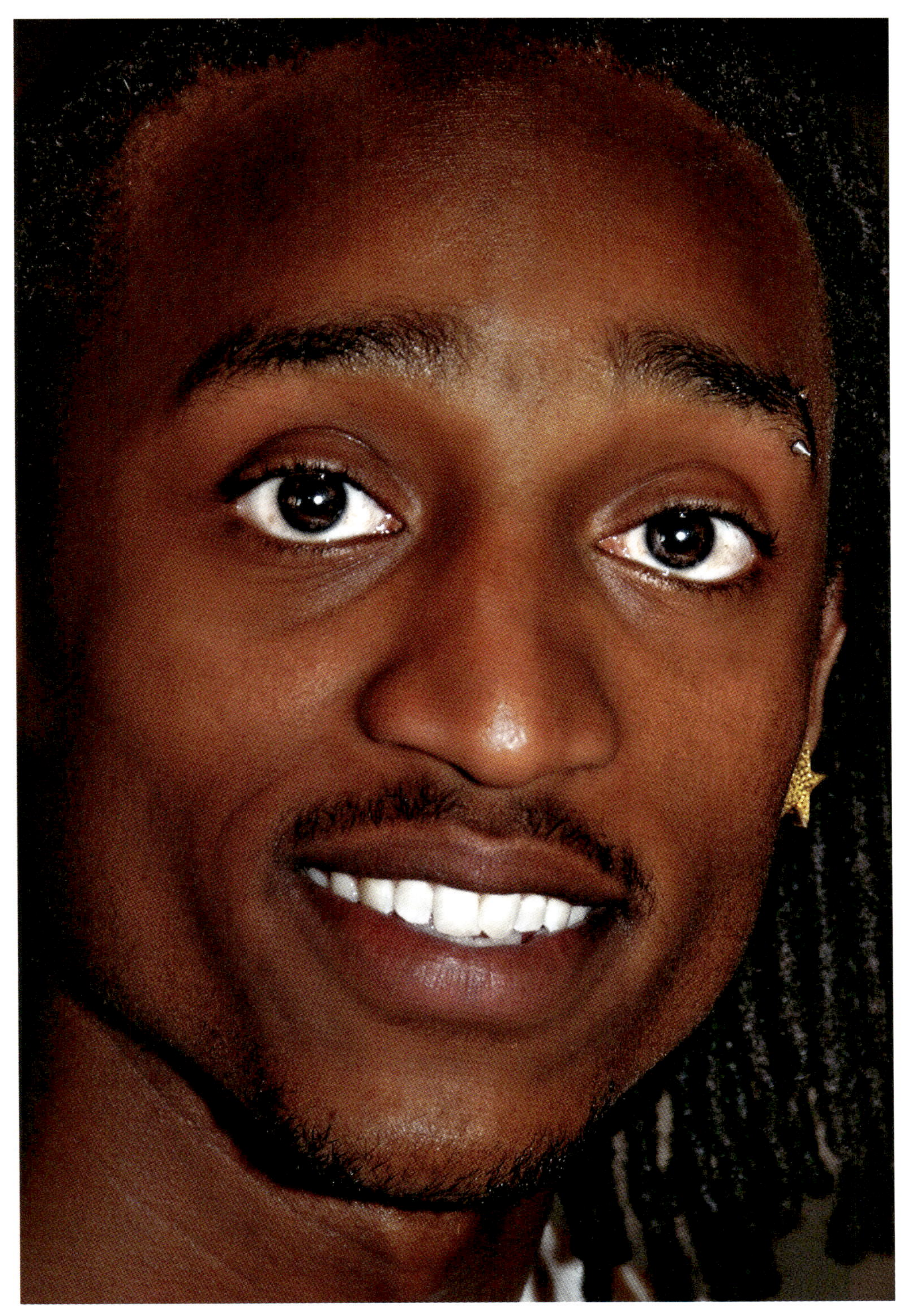

- Speaking of diffusion, there are many inexpensive diffusers you can add to small flash units. Usually, these diffusers are made of translucent plastic, and snap in place. Adding a diffuser will improve your direct flash result immeasurably by improving the quality of light you are lighting your subject with.

Of course, sometimes a scene is unfolding before you and you have to move quickly. In that case, sing praises for the flash that is built into your camera, grab the shots you can, and don't waste those never-to-be-repeated moments fumbling for exactly the right configuration of lighting equipment.

With these shots of Katie Rose blowing out the candles at her second birthday party I used the built-in on-camera flash, and a relatively long lens combined with a moderately high ISO to make sure I didn't miss this once-in-a-lifetime moment.

Below: 75mm, 1/60 of a second at f/5.0 and ISO 500, direct on-camera flash, hand held

Right: 105mm, 1/60 of a second at f/5.3 and ISO 500, direct on-camera flash, hand held

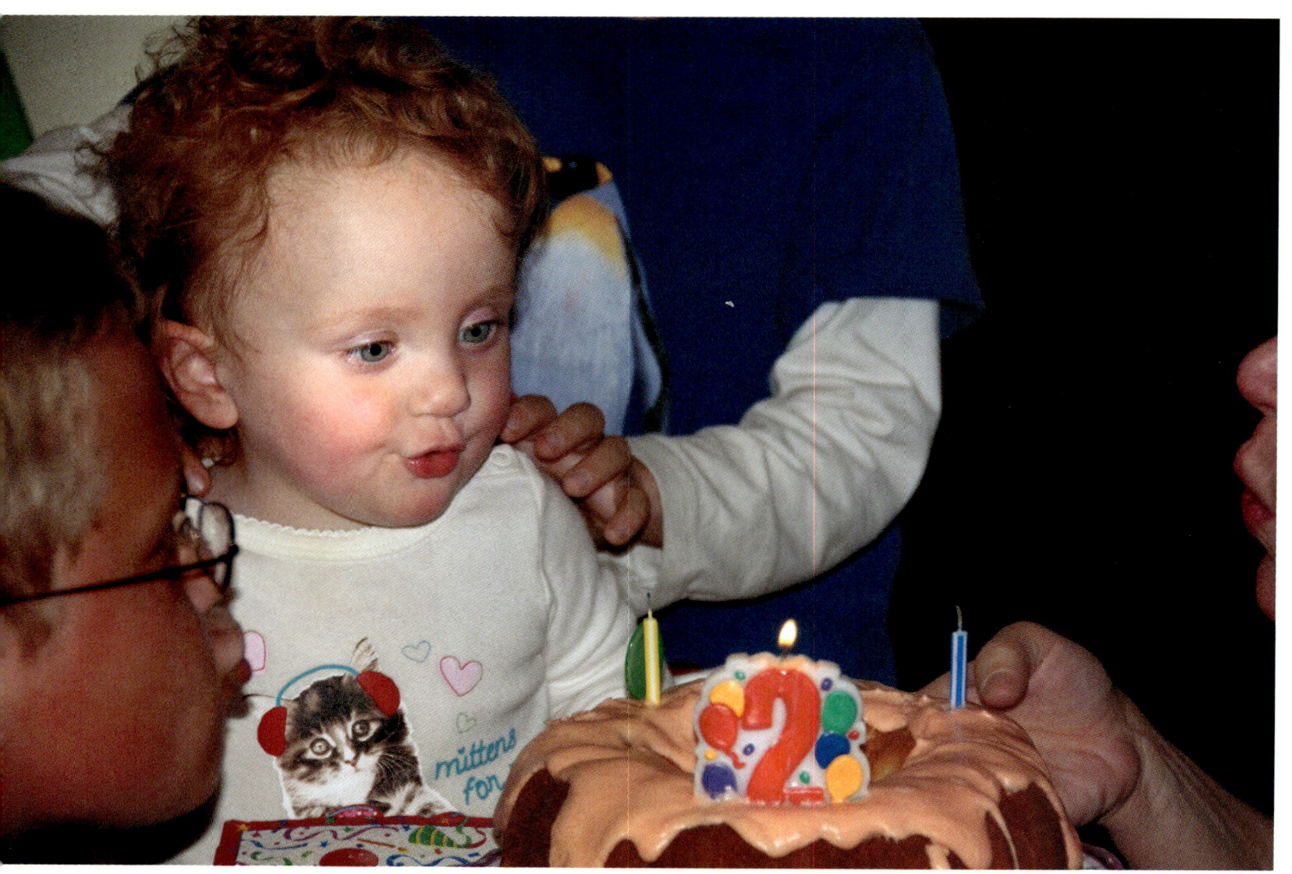

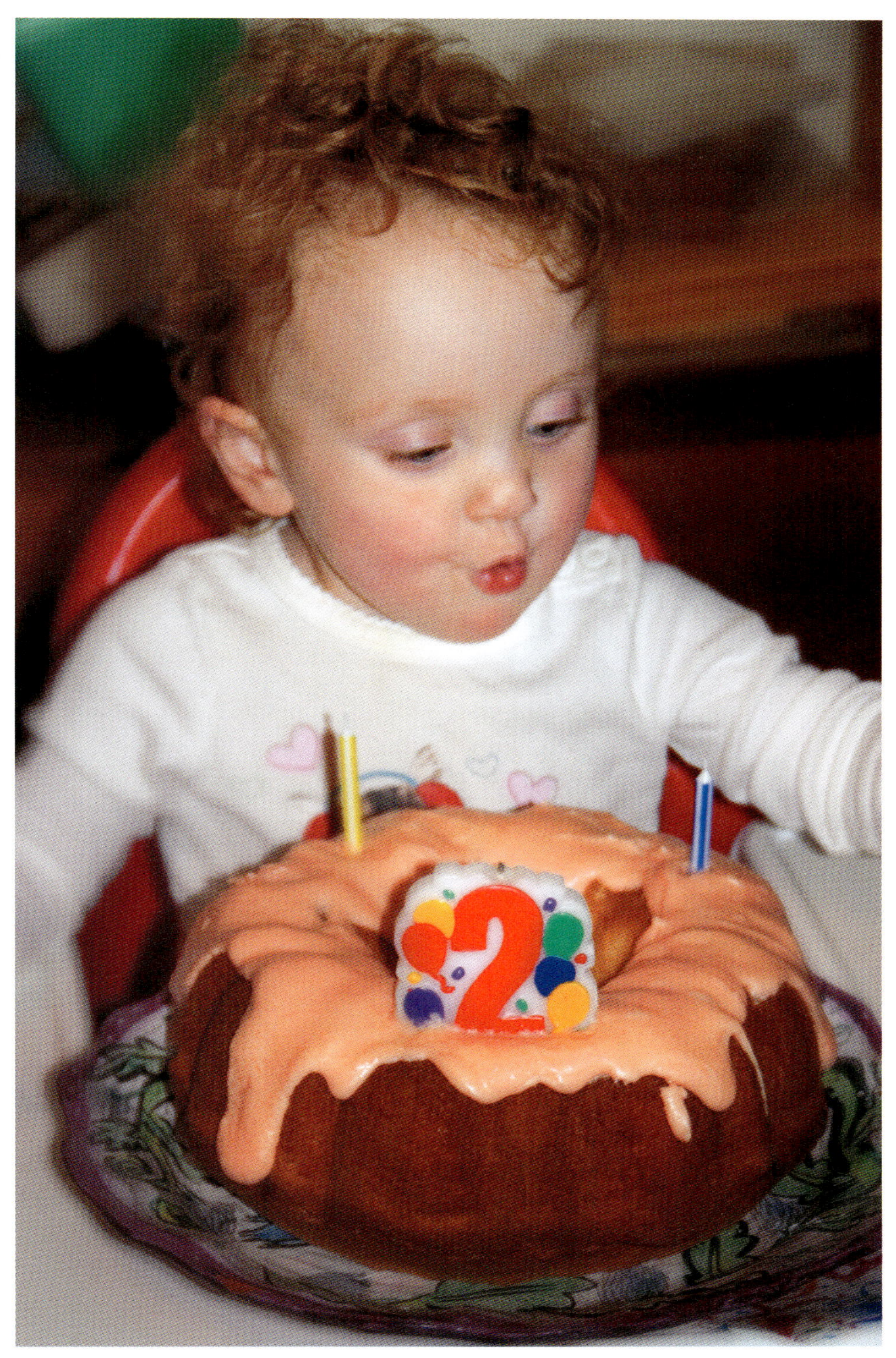

Studio Lighting

Studio portrait lighting is, of course, a huge topic and one that could fill many books—and I've listed some of the books about studio lighting that I've found helpful in the Resources section on page 234. If you don't have plans to shoot in the studio, you may think that you don't really need to know about this subject. But no knowledge is wasted, and understanding studio portrait lighting is important for even those photographers who have no immediate plans to get into the studio.

First, as I've already explained, studio strobes put out a great deal of light in short bursts. An advantage of this arrangement is that the burst of light stops the motion of your subject irrespective of the shutter speed setting in your camera. However, since you can't see the light (until you inspect your capture in your LCD) it can be hard to gauge the impact of your lighting choices—a situation helped in part with modeling lights on strobe units, which at least show the general direction of lighting if not the quality or real intensity.

The quality of studio lighting units range from very harsh—when a bare reflector is used—to diffuse and gentle through the use of units such as *soft boxes*. There are many possible ways to control, direct, and modify studio lights, including:

- *Snoots*, which block light into a tight circular area

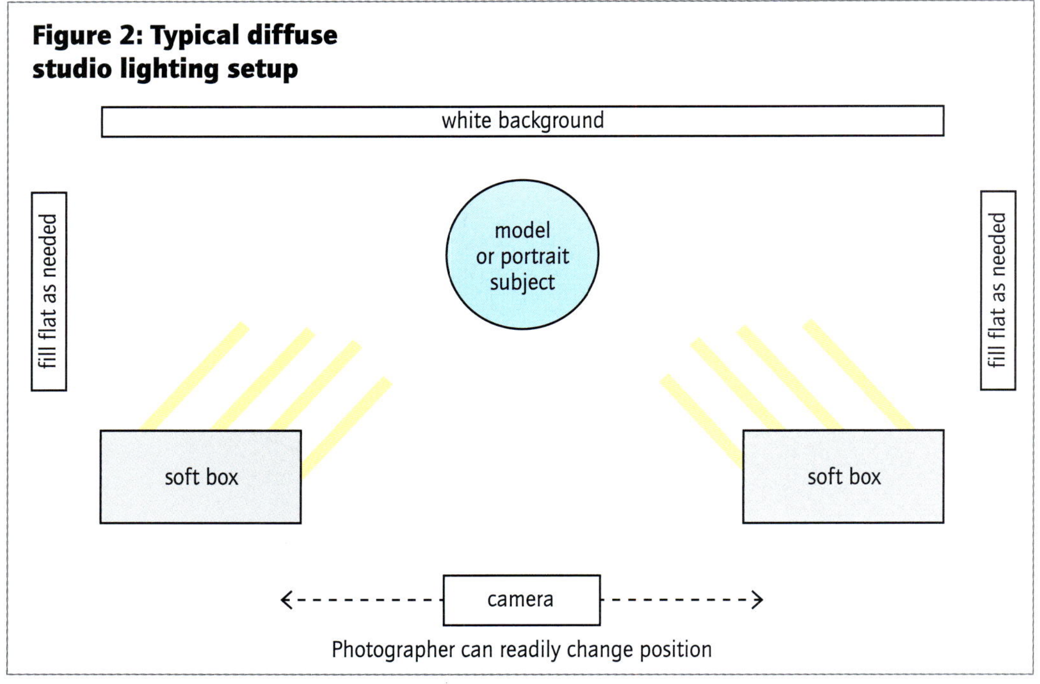

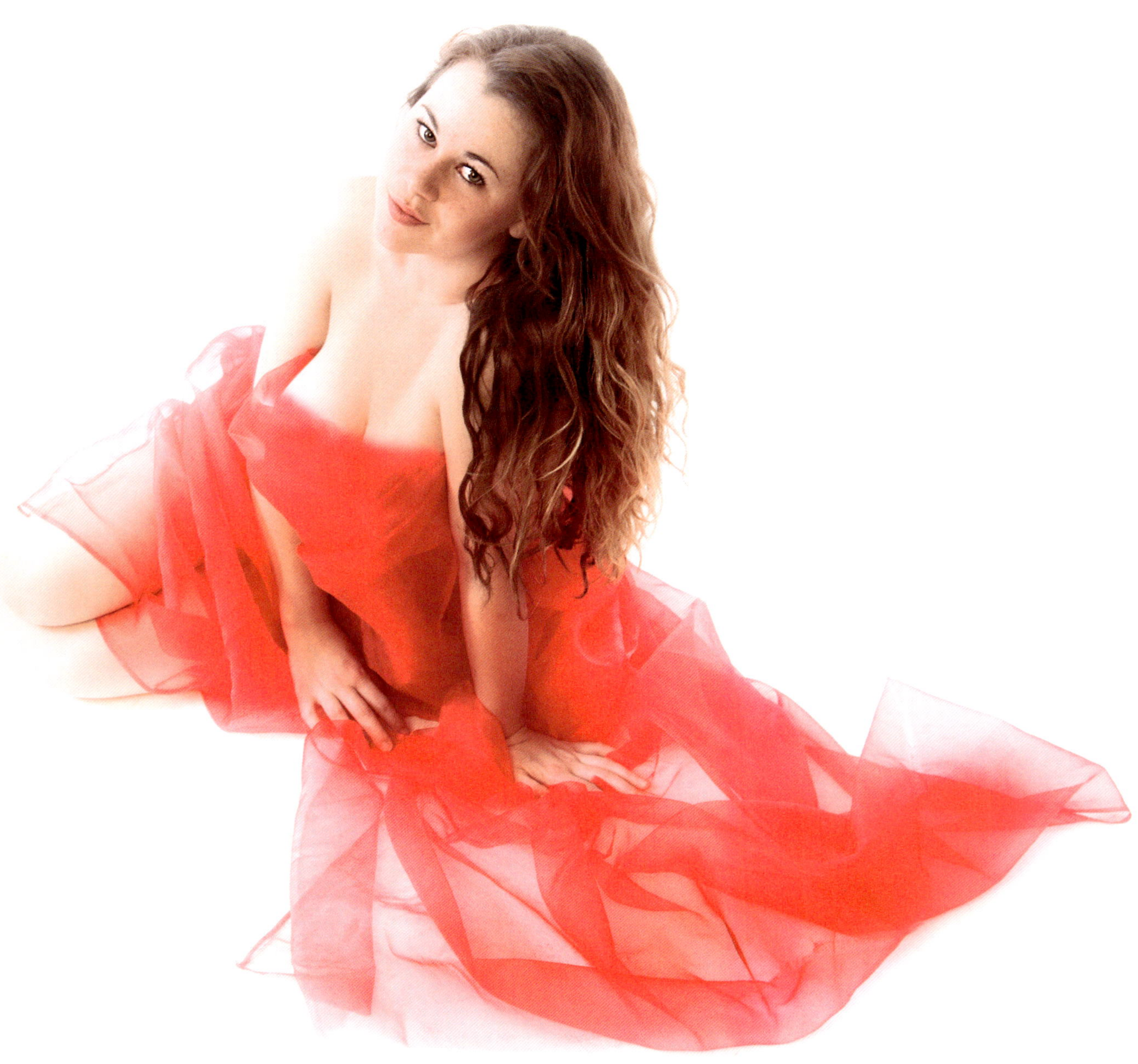

▲ A simple white background and diffuse lighting created with several soft boxes (using the setup shown in Figure 2 on page 158), as in this shot, makes everything look fairly good. This is the kind of lighting generally used for catalog photography. While most people will look attractive photographed with this setup, you won't get high contrast, moody lighting effects suggestive of strong characterizations.

34mm, 1/160 of a second at f/8 and ISO 100

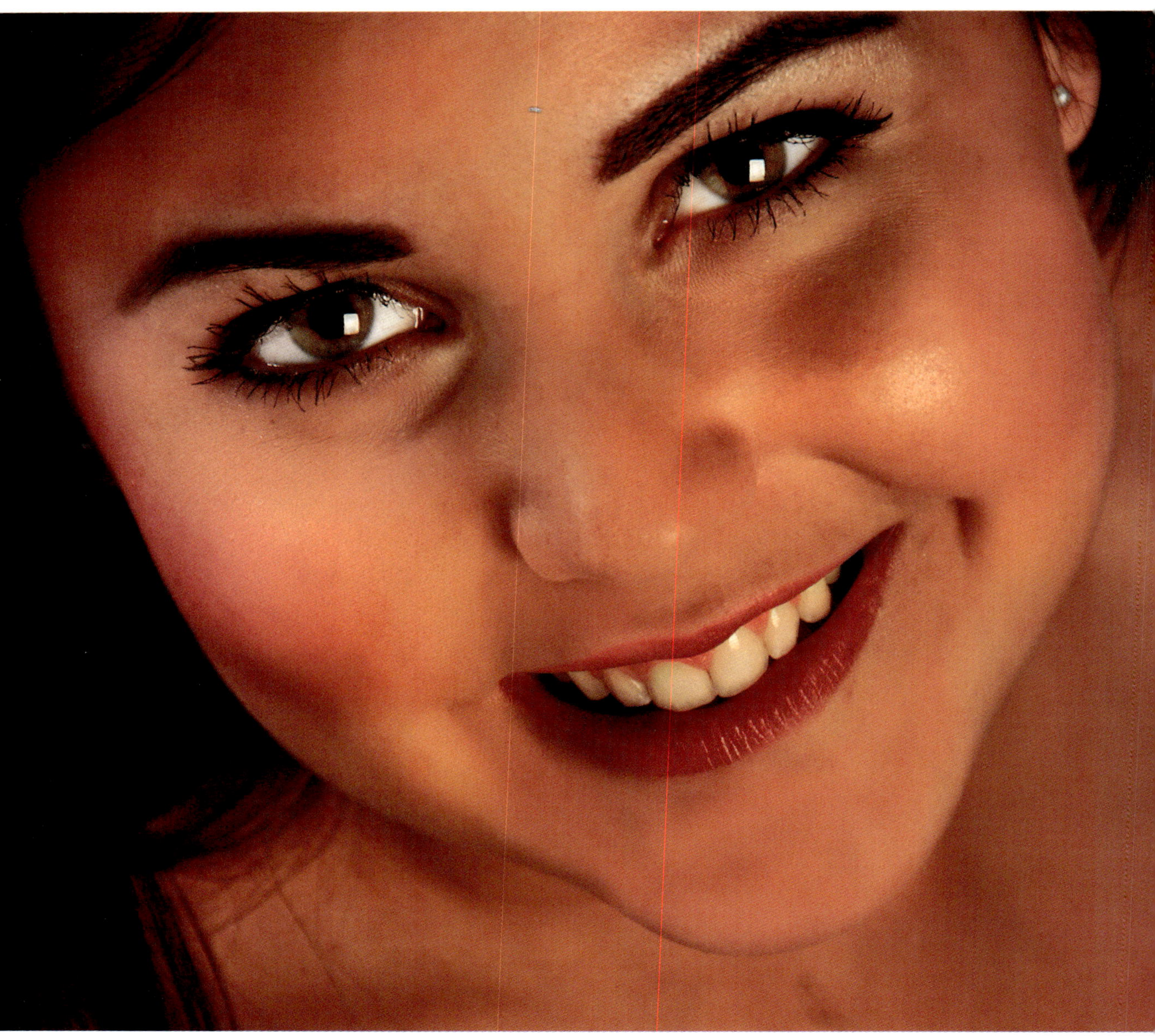

▲ Looking carefully at the catch lights in the eyes in this portrait, you can see the soft box strip light used to the model's right as the key light. I used a diffused light source (a rectangular "strip" soft box shown reflected in the model's eyes) to the model's left and a hair light above the model in a pretty typical portrait setup like the one shown in Figure 3 on page 161.

200mm, 1/160 of a second at f/10 and ISO 100, hand held

- *Barn doors*, which prevent light spill and allow you to control the precise area of illumination
- *Beauty dishes*, which are a circular light modifier with an opaque center, particularly useful in creating attractive portraits
- *Umbrellas*, which like soft boxes can be used to diffuse light sources
- *Grids, Cucoloris* ("cookies") and related modifiers, which are sheets with cut-outs that can be placed between a light source and the background to create mottled or patterned light

Depending upon the studio, one common arrangement is to use a white background and several diffuse light sources (such as soft box units) to create an overall diffuse light arrangement (see Figure 2 on page 158).

The arrangement shown in Figure 2 has very little in the way of shadows, makes most people or objects look almost as if they are floating in space, and is generally flattering light. Many catalogs are shot in this kind of light, as no great changes are required between shots.

This lighting arrangement is also very forgiving as to the positioning of camera and subject. You can stand almost anywhere and still get a good shot, although you do have to pay attention to the background to make sure your

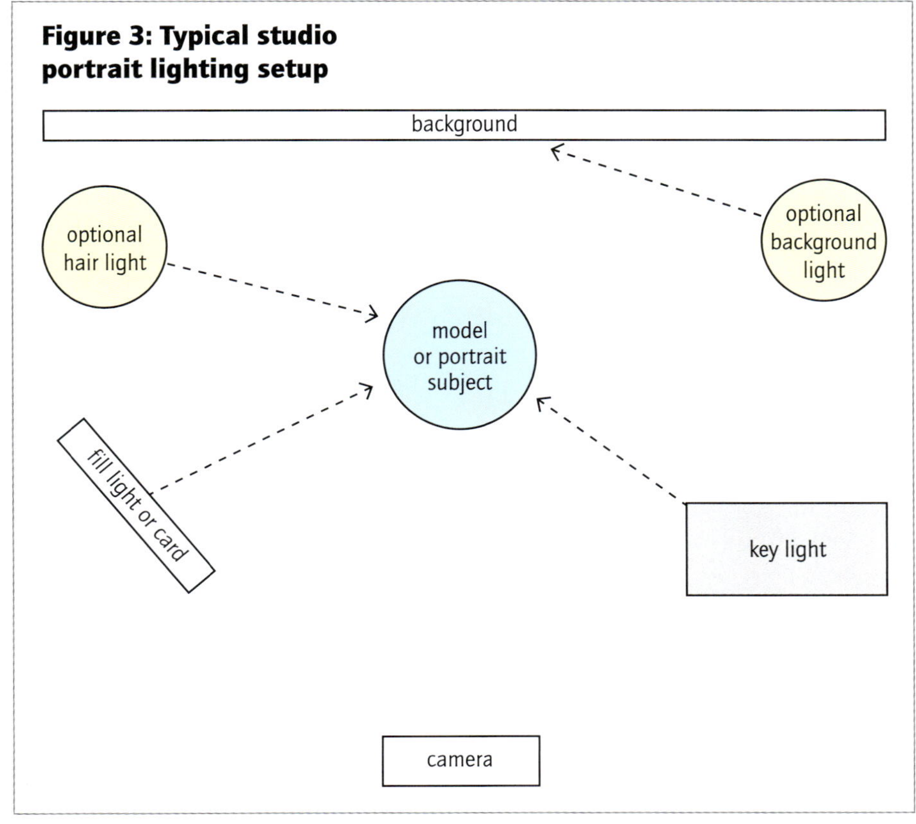

Figure 3: Typical studio portrait lighting setup

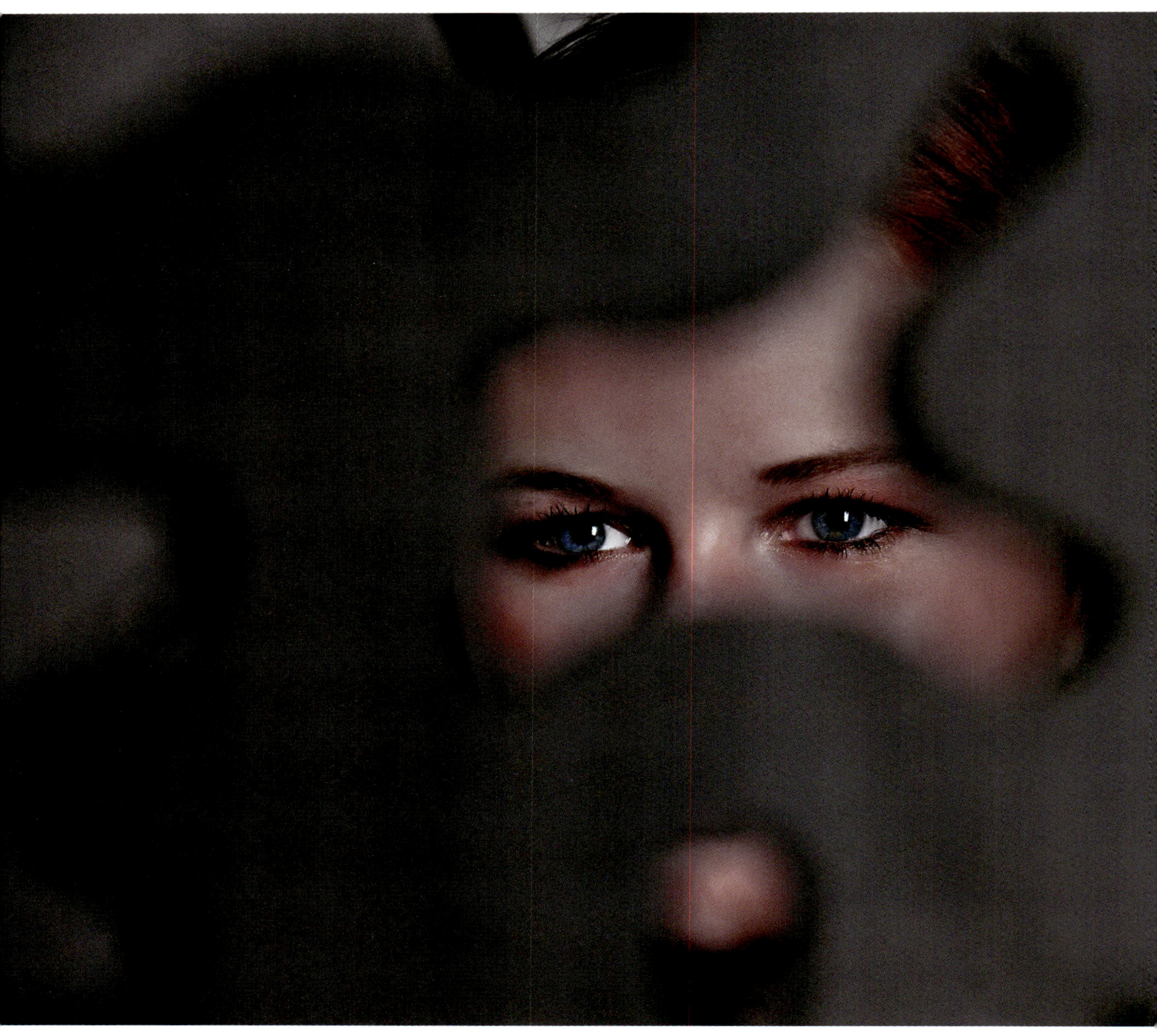

▲ In this photo, a model is seen looking through a cucoloris. A cucoloris—also called a *cookie*—is a sheet of cut-outs. The cut-outs are put in front of a light and used to project shadows. These shadows can be used to create a regular pattern for a background, or simulate motion or a leafy canopy.

Cookies have been constructed out of a number of different kinds of materials. The cucoloris shown here is a thin piece of wood with repeated versions of the same shape cut out of it.

You can see the results of using this cucoloris to project a background in the photos on pages 165–167.

200mm, 1/160 of a second at f/8 and ISO 200, hand held

framing hasn't ventured beyond its boundaries.

The downside to this kind of lighting is that it isn't very distinctive. One portrait will be pretty much lit like any other, and nothing about character is revealed. After a while, this can get pretty boring.

Figure 3 on page 161 shows a fairly typical lighting setup for portraiture. This lighting setup is a bit more complex than the catalog lighting arrangement I described earlier, but it also allows for a great deal more variation in the lighting.

A *key light* or primary light is shown in Figure 3 on page 161 to the right of the subject. (This light could be positioned either to the left or the right, of course.) The key light might be a diffused light source such as a soft box strip, light bounced off an umbrella, or a beauty dish.

It's a good idea to set the key light up before the other lighting is arranged. You'll want to make sure its height is appropriate for your subject: a standing portrait needs a higher light source than a seated or lying portrait. Put the light too high, and you'll get ugly nose shadows; place it too low and you risk "monster" lighting.

A rule of thumb is to position the key light so you just start seeing the *catch lights*—reflected light from the lighting source—in the subject's eyes.

A well positioned key light is, well, the key to good portrait lighting.

A second light—not as strong as the key light—balances the key light on the other side of the subject (sometimes a reflecting *fill card* rather than a light is used for this purpose), and a third light from above illuminates the subjects hair, and helps to separate the subject from a dark background if necessary. Sometimes a fourth light is used to light the background, if this effect is desired. Both the third and fourth lights are weaker than the key and fill lights.

With this general portrait setup, you can vary the pose and background, and generally create attractive lighting to suit most portrait subjects.

A variation on the typical studio portrait setup is shown in Figure 4 on page 164.

The arrangement in Figure 4 features a light or white background. As in the more typical portrait photography setup, a key light is set to one side and slightly above the subject. The shadows on the side that are not lit by the key light are ameliorated with fill, either using a second light or by reflecting light onto the subject.

In this setup, one light is specifically used to project onto the light background. The projection can be a circular spot, or a regular or irregular pattern—using either a dedicated spot light or a modifier such as a cucoloris.

In this arrangement, the position of the photographer in relationship to the subject and the light is crucial. There won't be that many options as to where you can stand, or in which direction you need to point your camera. You should monitor your results carefully as you go along, because slight variations in pose and position can make or break a photo made with this style of lighting.

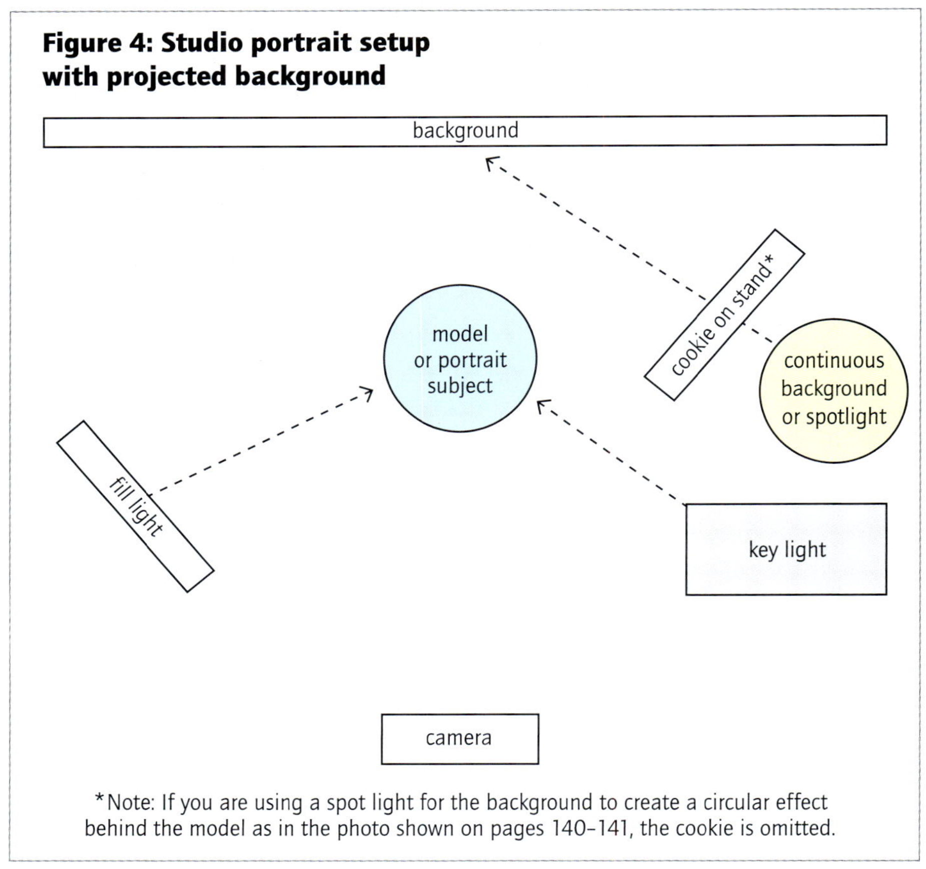

*Note: If you are using a spot light for the background to create a circular effect behind the model as in the photo shown on pages 140–141, the cookie is omitted.

▶ In this shot, a strip light provides glowing and attractive illumination of the model and her mane of hair, while a continuous spotlight behind a cookie adds dappled light.

Dragging the shutter at 1/30 of a second completes the picture by lightening the background relative to how it would be rendered at the faster flash synch shutter speed. At the slower shutter speed the pattern cast by the cucoloris on the white seamless paper creates an interesting background effect. The lighting setup for this shot is shown above in Figure 4.

105mm, 1/30 of a second at f/5.6 and ISO 200, hand held

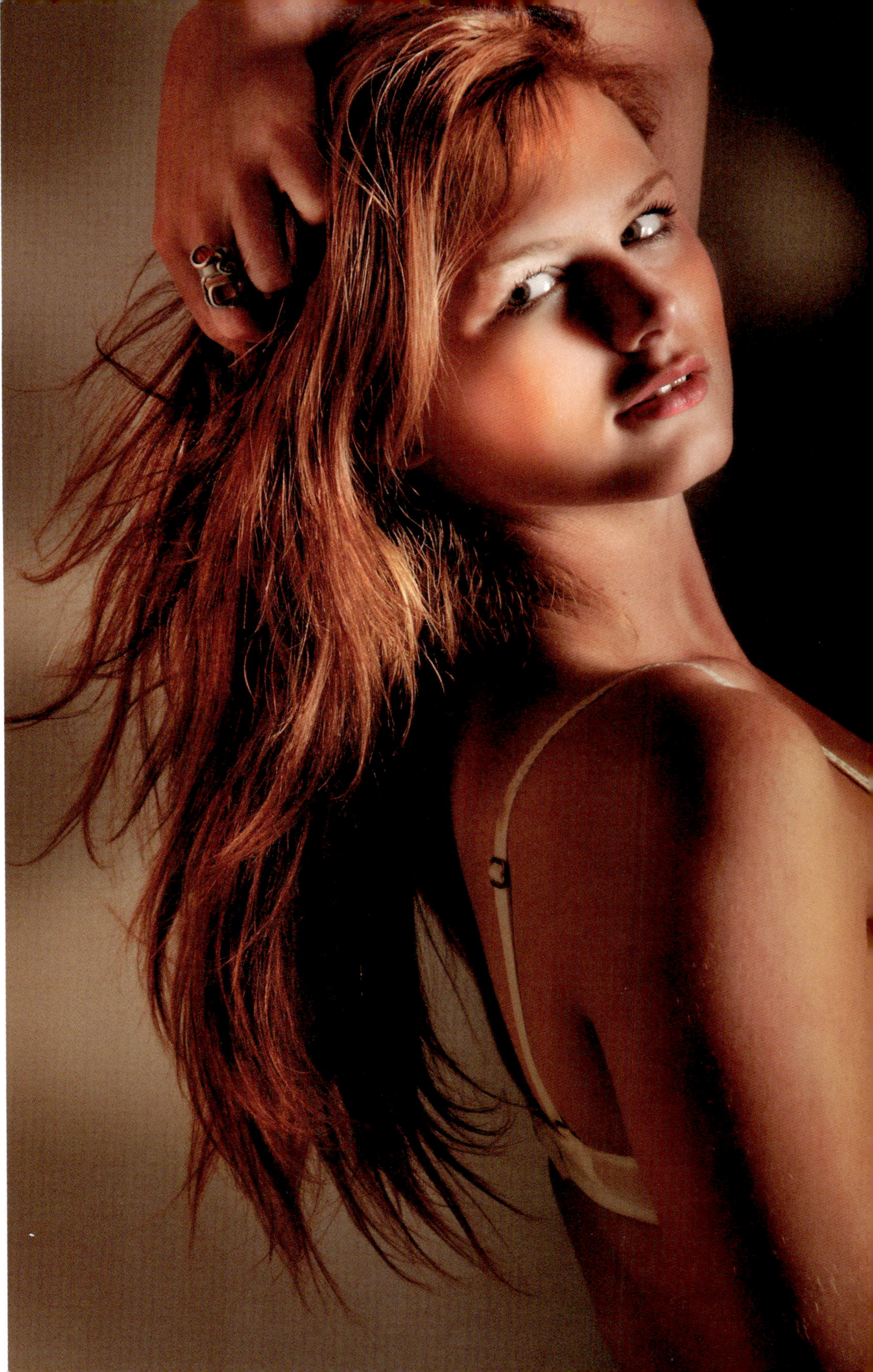

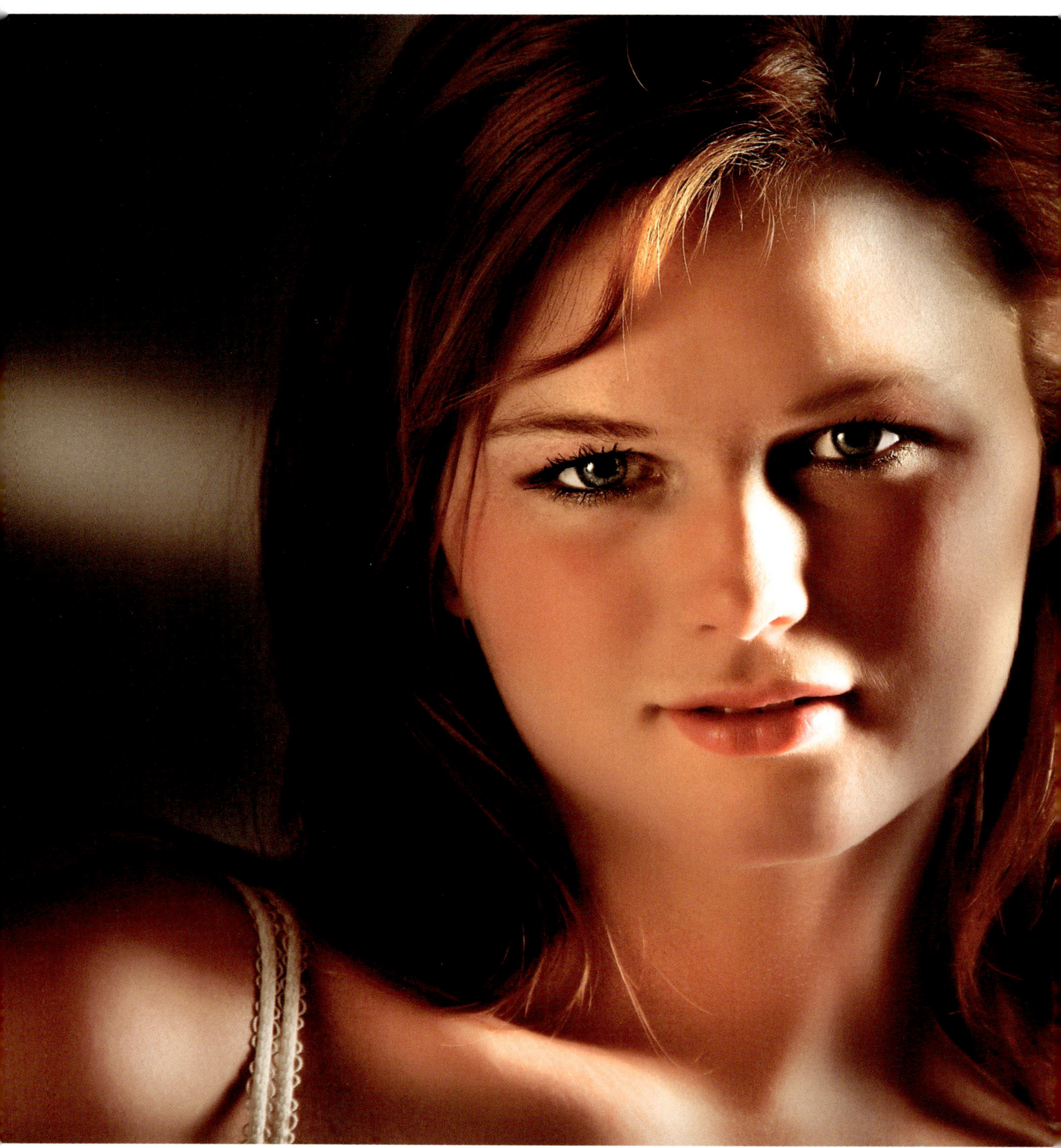

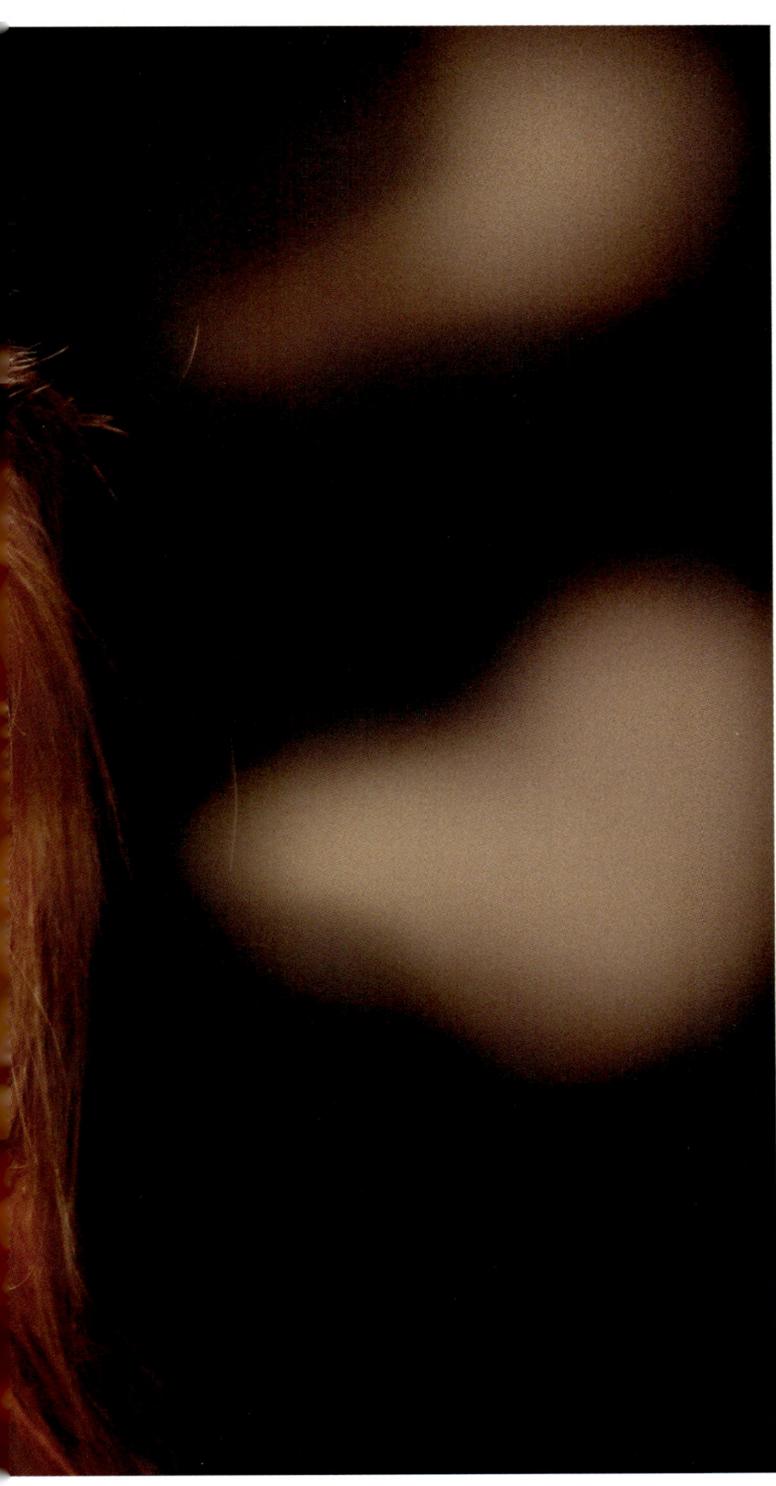

◀ I wanted to make sure that the shadow cast by a cookie was really visible in this photo. So I used *shutter drag* to expose so that the background had enough contrast.

Here's how this idea works: the studio lights are only illuminating the model. However, you can use any shutter speed you want as long as it is below the camera's flash-synch shutter speed, and it will not have an impact on the exposure of the model—which is controlled by the duration of the flash, not how long the shutter is open.

The background, however, is not illuminated by the flash. At my top flash synch speed (1/160 of a second) it would have been almost entirely dark, but at 1/30 of a second the shadow cast by the cucoloris is attractive with lights and darks. The lighting setup for this photo is shown in Figure 4 on page 164.

150mm, 1/30 of a second at f/5.6 and ISO 200, hand held

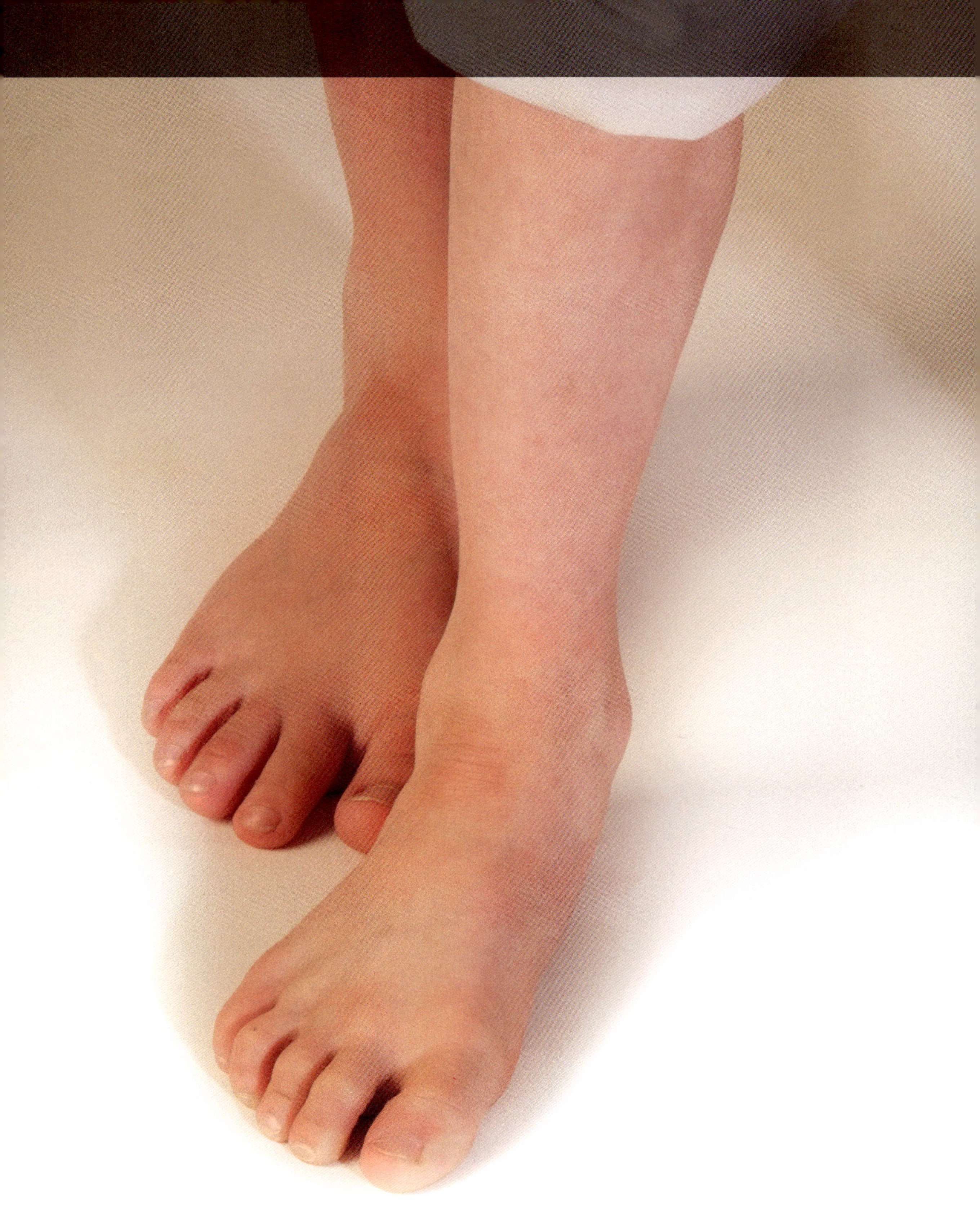

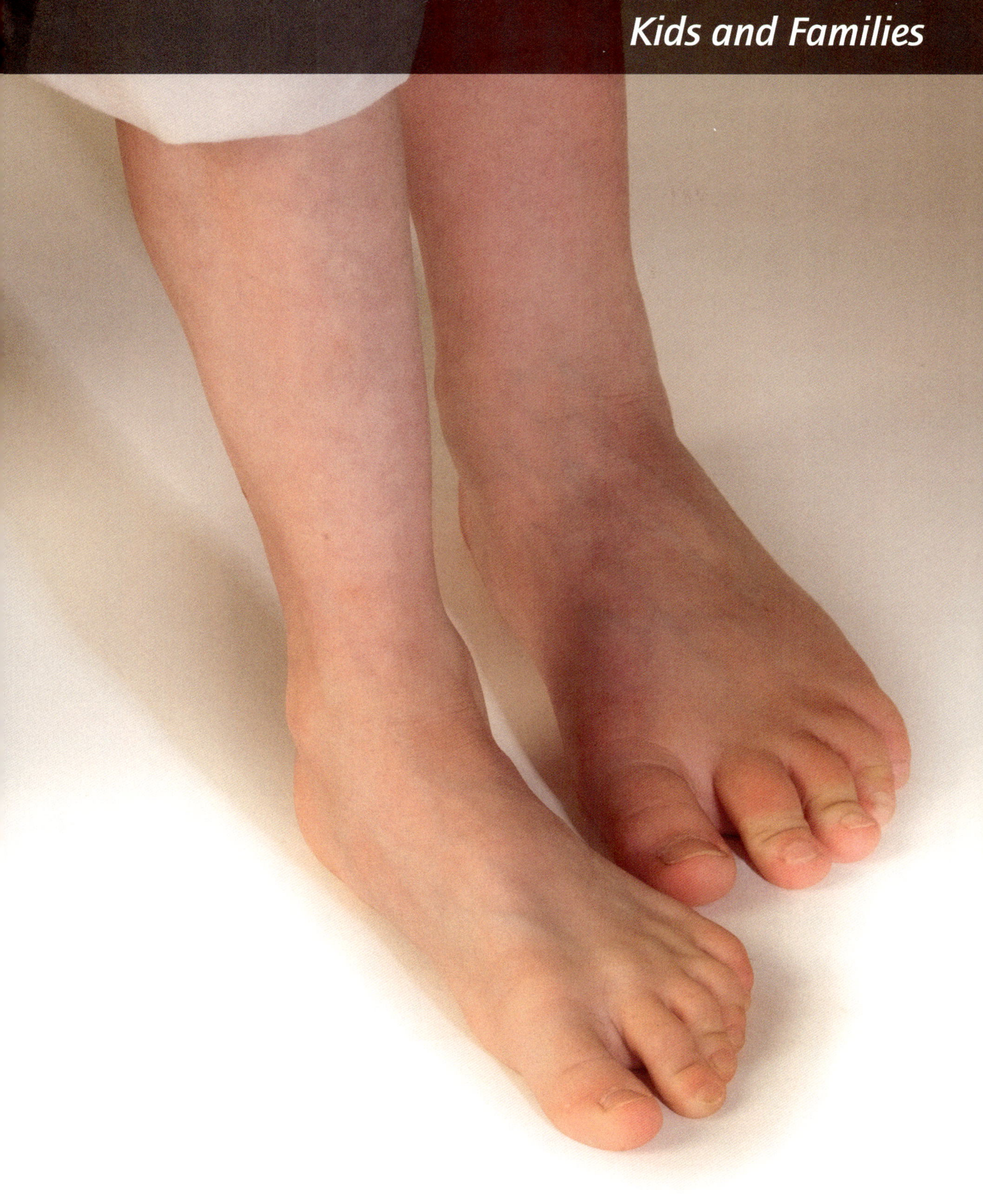

Photographing Kids

Life, as political philosopher Thomas Hobbes put it, may be "nasty, brutish, and short." On the other hand anyone who spends much time around young kids—who has a family, or who photographs children—might think that a better description is "dirty, chaotic, and surprise-filled."

Faced with the chaos that kids leave in their wake and all around them, the photographer—like the parent—has really only two options. You can attempt to control the kid energy and precisely position and pose kids as you would with adults. Alternatively, you can go with the flow and take advantage of the creative urges of your pint-sized subjects.

I strongly urge going with the flow. There's nothing to stop you from giving minor assists to the direction of the shoot, perhaps by setting up lighting in advance, providing appropriate props, or suggesting themes for playing. But you'll get photos that are more interesting, and truer to life if you give up the photographer's eternal quest for control—and just let kids be kids. Be ready to take advantage of the inevitable surprises with quick thinking and improvisation, but don't try to turn kids into little wooden statues in formal clothes. It just doesn't work.

The key thing when photographing children is to capture gesture, emotion, mood, facial expression, and fleeting fantasy.

I have to admit that my standards for a technically acceptable photo are relaxed when I photograph kids, partly because nobody who counts—the kids being photographed and their parents—really cares about technical perfection in this context. It's more important to get the image because as quickly as kids move, the opportunity will quickly be gone. I try my best to get eyes in focus, but if the photo shows the spirit of the child I'm not going to worry too much if my focus is off by a little bit.

To get a good portrait of a kid in action I'm perfectly prepared to boost my ISO like crazy (into the 800–2000 range). These are mostly photos taken with the lens wide open for maximum shutter speed and low depth-of-field. However, the maximum shutter speed possible, even with a boosted ISO, may not be very fast.

▶ With a sword in hand and a glint in his eye, Mathew makes it clear that he is a force to be reckoned with. Making fun costumes and appropriate props available tends to greatly enrich portrait sessions with children.

82mm, 1/160 of a second at f/11 and ISO 100, hand held

▲ Pages 168–169: Not all portraits are head shots. If you know anything about kids, you'll know they run around and play and spend a great deal of time on their feet. So consider shooting feet as in this image, or hands, when photographing kids. They can make a statement just "standing alone."

95mm, 1/160 of a second at f/13 and ISO 100, hand held

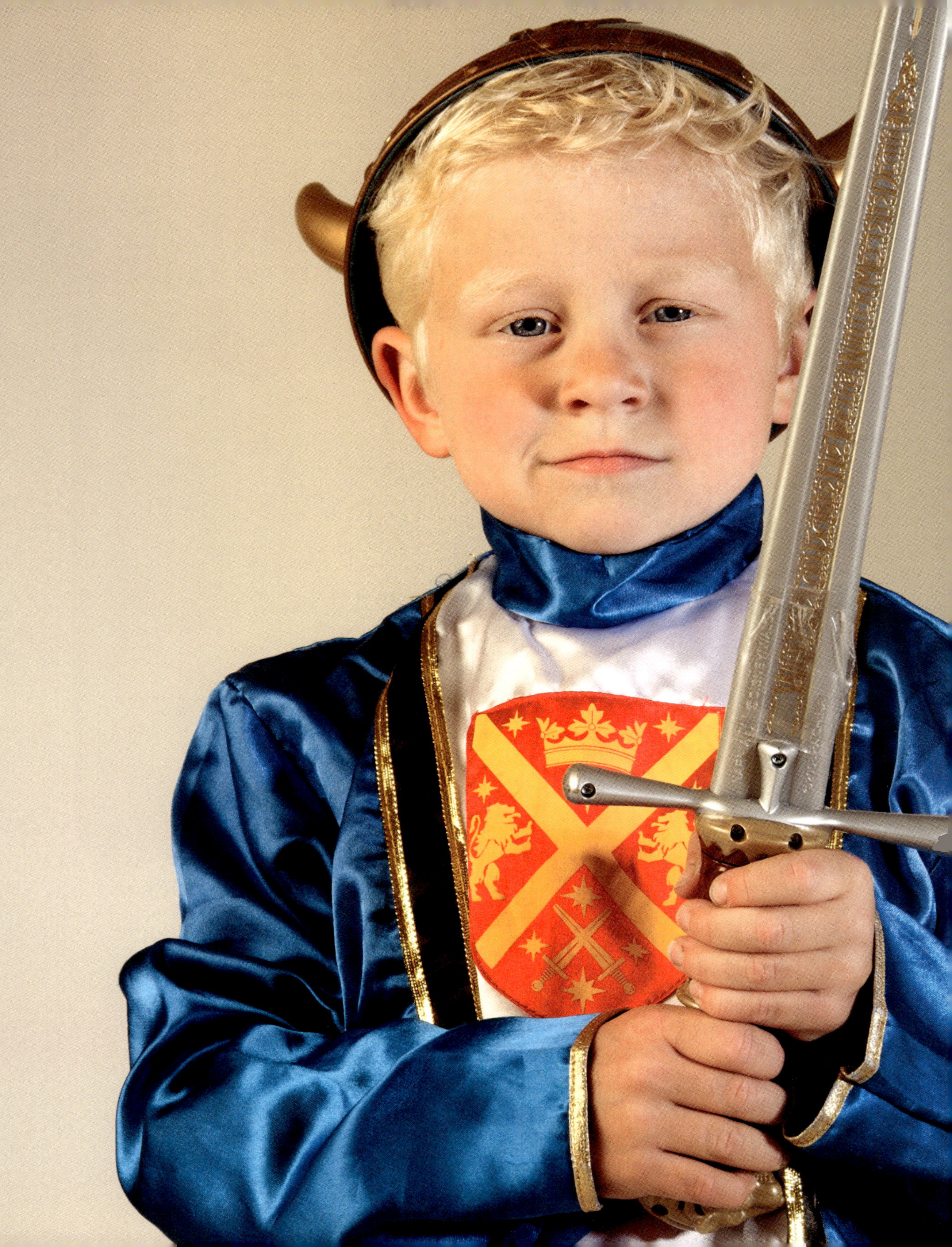

I'll hand hold shots of kids at slow shutter speeds that I wouldn't use normally without a tripod. This is a place where image stabilization (also called vibration reduction) is a really good idea because it does let you shoot hand held at slower shutter speeds than would otherwise be feasible.

My philosophy of photographing children is to be childlike: my camera is curious, active, and moves on with no regrets to the next shot. Don't try to stifle the inherent nature of your subjects: instead become more like them. Your photographs will become happier and more joyful, and better express the nature of your subjects.

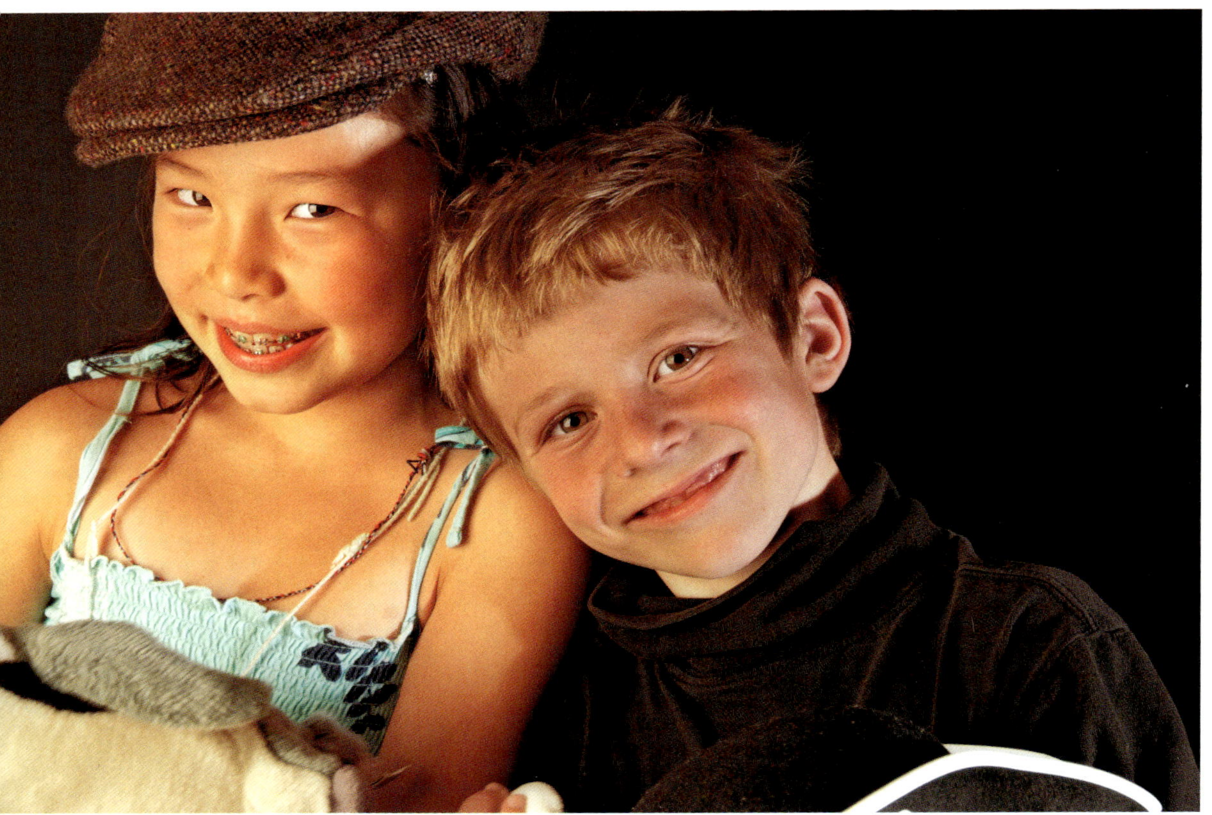

▲ You can see that Emily and Nicky are great buddies. They enjoy "mugging" for the camera, which can present photographic opportunities. However, the downside to this posturing is that they are always aware they are being photographed, and often do not look natural in photos. So it wasn't until well into this session that I began to be happy with the results.

75mm, 1/160 of a second at f/11 and ISO 100, hand held

▶ Letting kids choose their own props from among their animal friends helps kids achieve a sense of "ownership" over the photography session, and leads to better results. Emily is shown here with her teddy bear, and Nicky with his owl and pirate hat.

29mm, 1/160 of a second at f/11 and ISO 100, hand held

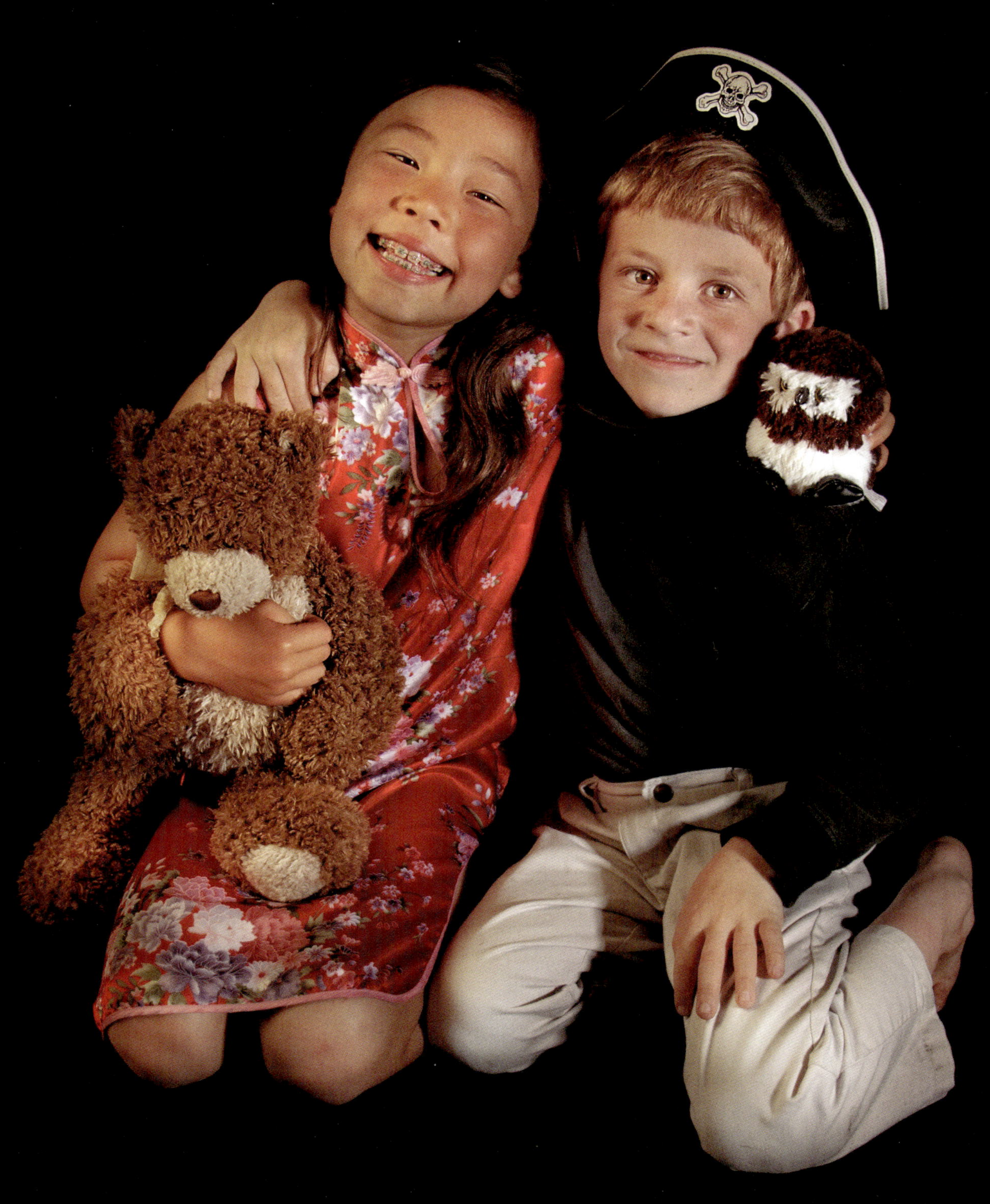

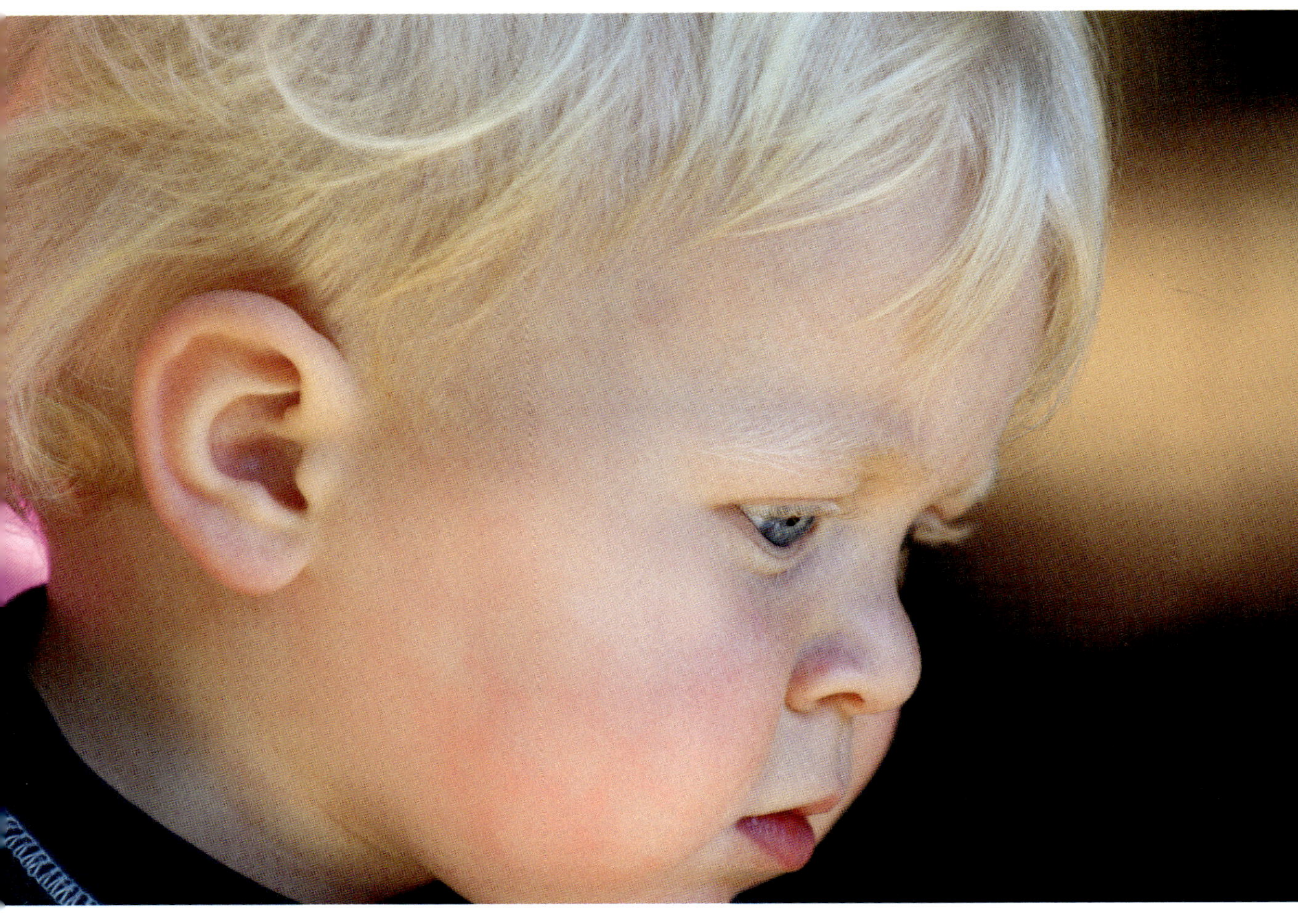

▲ In this low depth-of-field image, I intentionally let the background go out of focus to give the sense that Mathew is contemplative and thinking hard. You can almost see the neurons firing.

200mm, 1/320 of a second at f/4.5 and ISO 200, tripod mounted

▶ You get one chance at a shot like this one of Katie Rose in an outdoor bath, so it pays to be ready. The colors of the plastic rings are important to this composition; fortunately, most toys intended for small kids are attractively colored.

65mm, 1/60 of a second at f/5 and ISO 320, hand held

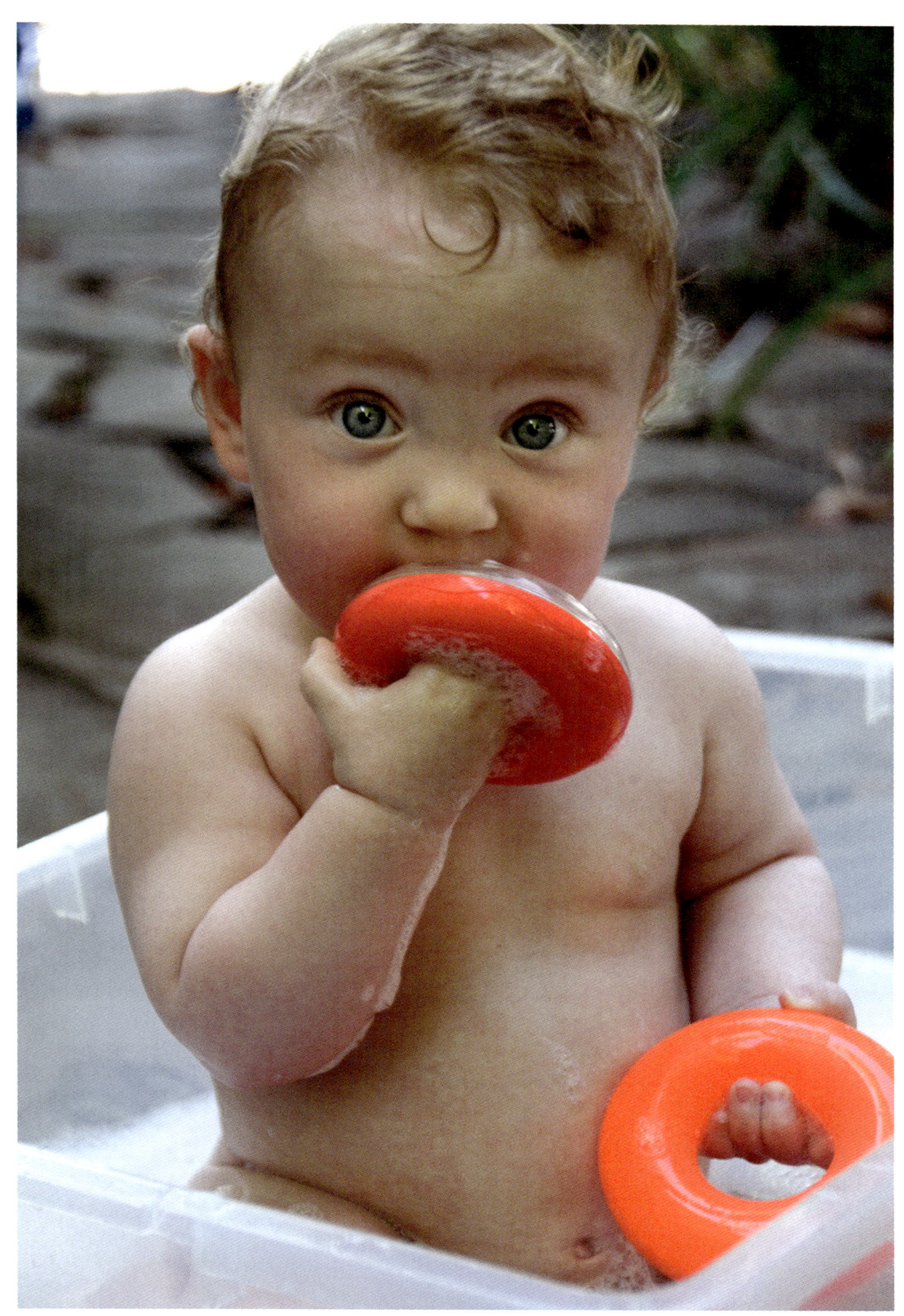

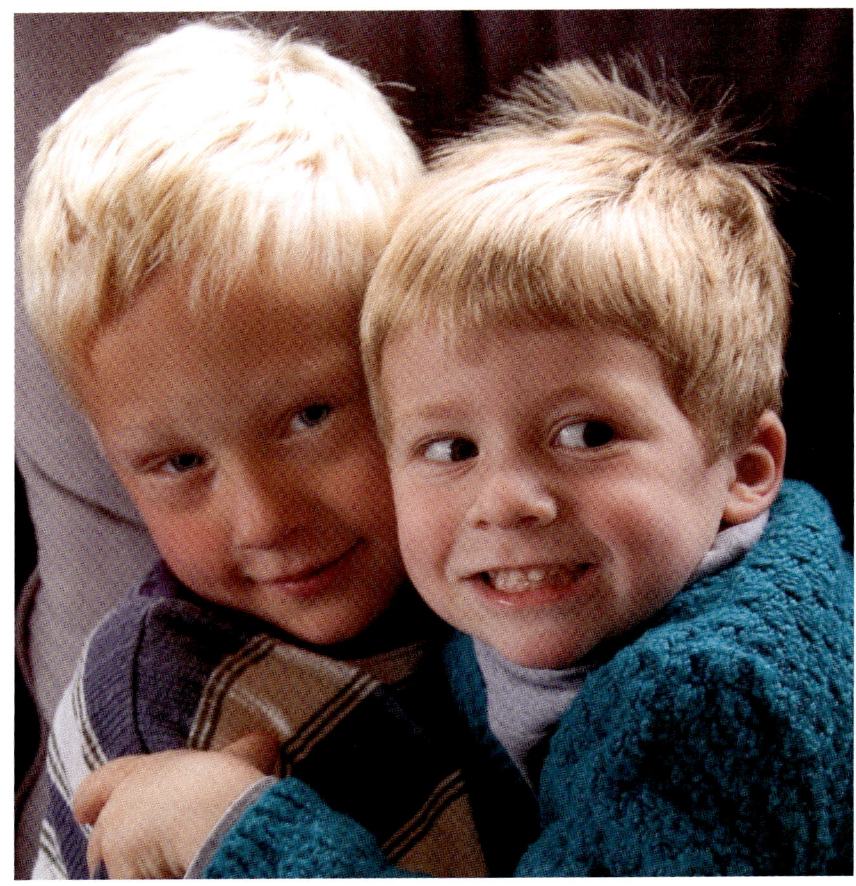

◄ Asking two brothers to pose together has some risks and is more difficult than a single portrait—because you need both boys to have interesting and acceptable expressions. However, when it works you get more character revealed. In this shot, you can see the quiet and loving nature of Julian on the left, and the comparatively mischievous expression worn by Nicky on the right.

70mm, 1/15 of a second at f/5 and ISO 200, hand held

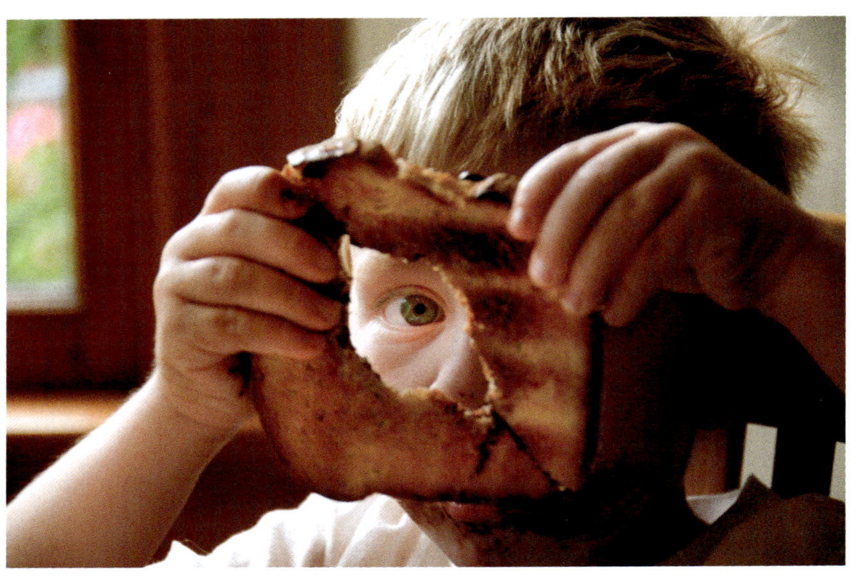

◄ A chocolate sandwich is a special treat, here used as a framing device for Nicky's eye.

95mm, 1/15 of a second at f/5.3 and ISO 100, hand held

► In the studio, Katie Rose, my two-year-old, kept wandering off and onto the seamless background with her tutu skirt on her head. The trick was to be ready for her with my camera—because no way she was going to hold a still pose for me.

36mm, 1/160 of a second at f/11 and ISO 100, hand held

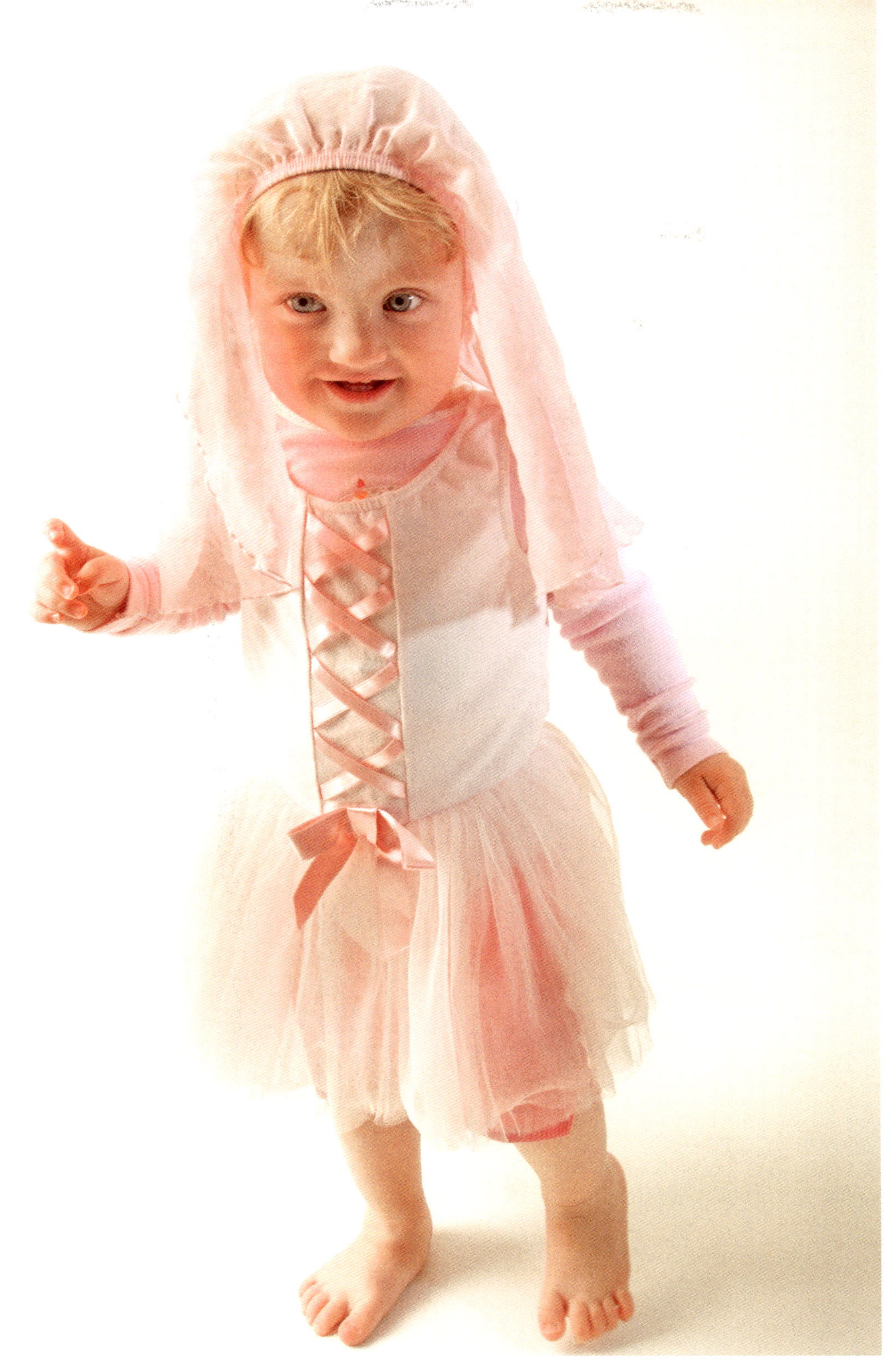

Working with Families

"Happy families are all alike," wrote Leo Tolstoy. When it comes to photographing children, families are a mixed—but necessary—blessing, although not necessarily all alike.

You need parents for there to be kids in the first place, and many parents will want to be present when you photograph their kids. Having parents present may make kids relax at first, but it will certainly skew the direction of the shoot, particularly when a parent feels inclined to start directing.

Things are different when it is your own family! While techniques do exist for including the photographer in a family photo—you can put the camera on a tripod, or use a mirror—the fact is that there are many more photos of my kids and family than there are of me.

If you are the photographer of your own family, keep a sense of perspective. No photograph is worth upsetting your spouse or kids. If your family has fun with photography, and enjoys the photos, they are likely to be much more supportive in the long run than if they are bullied into posing for your camera.

Photographing someone else's family for fun or profit presents other challenges. Once again you want your subjects to have fun, but you also want to show decent results commensurate with the time (and possibly money) set aside to create portraits. I recommend a clear discussion of goals and ground rules in advance. Many parents try to take over photo sessions of their kids with the best of intentions, but it doesn't usually work out well in terms of the quality of the photography—or the enjoyment of the kids in the process. Once again, it is worth noting that no photo is worth disturbing the peace of mind of a child.

As a practical matter, the more fun kids have the better your photos of families are likely to come out. Costumes and fun props are a great idea.

In less formal situations, think about the course of daily life. What really goes on in those happy families that are all alike? Try to capture these often unobserved events—they will make for interesting photos.

Norman Rockwell moments—preparing for Halloween, the first haircut, and so on—can make for great photos, and you should be ready. However, don't concentrate on photography so much that you are not fully present for the events themselves.

Family stories can sometimes be told through the details: hard working feet, hands being held across multiple generations, celebrations, and more. Don't neglect to watch for the trees when photographing the forest that is the family—sometimes a close-up can tell more of the whole story than a broader view.

▶ For this photo, Mathew chose to wear his dragon costume, and Nicky chose his own knightly attire. Once they were dressed in these outfits, I asked them to play "the dragon and the knight."

28mm, 1/160 of a second at f/13 and ISO 100, hand held

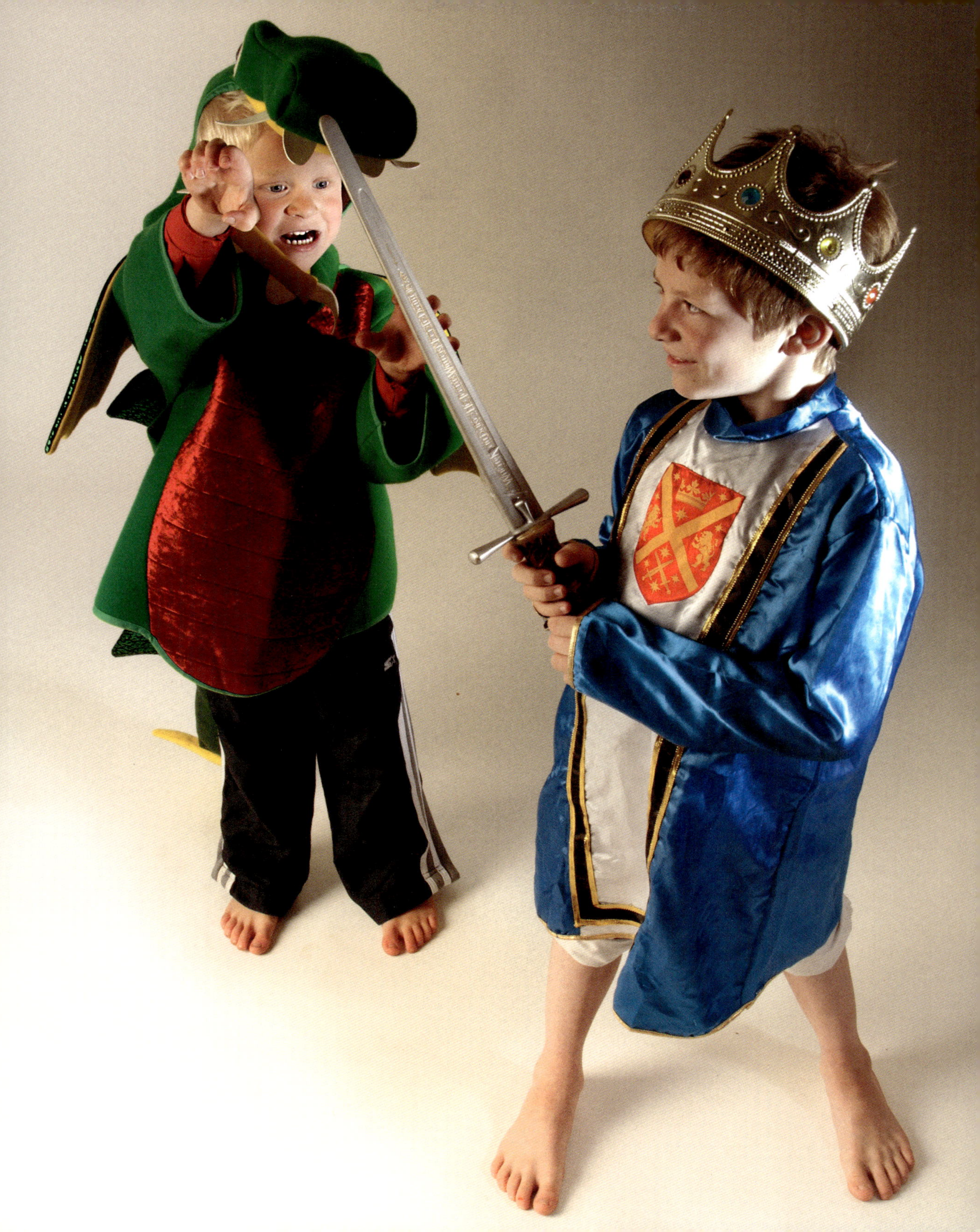

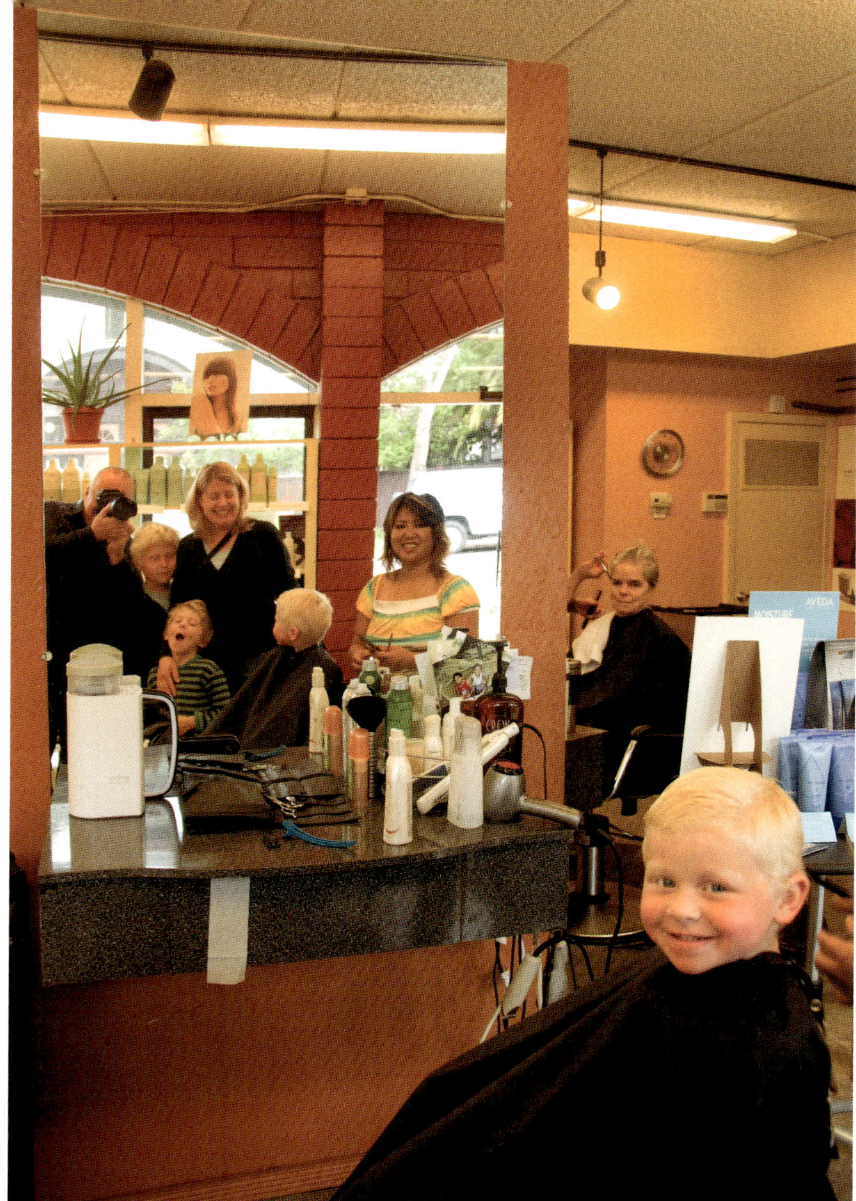

▲ Most of the family—including the photographer—can be seen in the mirror on the occasion of Mathew's first "real" haircut at a salon.

20mm, 1/80 of a second at f/4.5 and ISO 400, hand held

▶ The hands of Grandma Barbara are shown holding her granddaughter Katie Rose, with the comparative size of the hands across the generations being the point of this photo.

130mm, 1/25 of a second at f/5.6 and ISO 1250, hand held

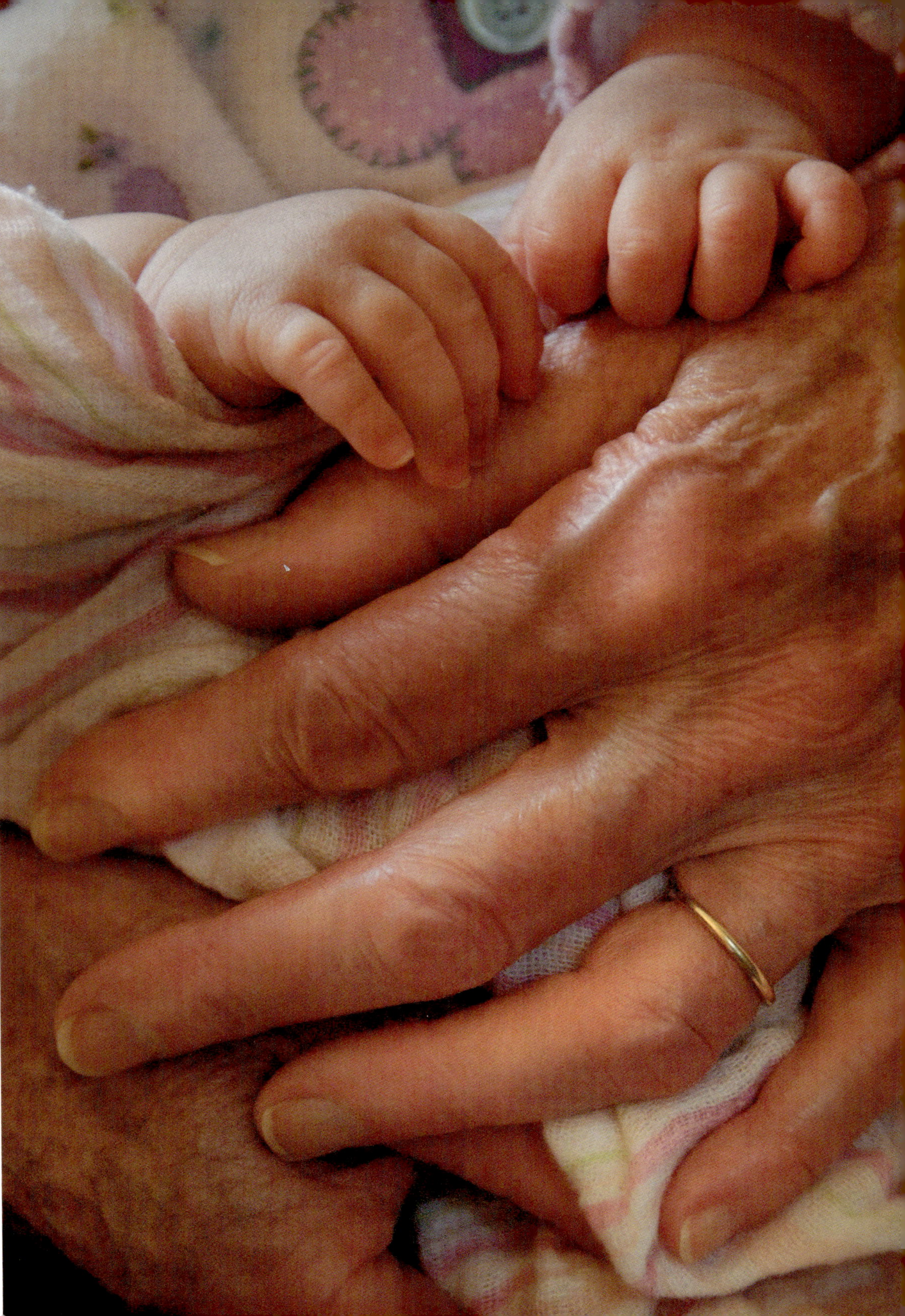

Portraits of Children

When I tell someone that I am making a "portrait," they often think of something formal—suitable for framing, dress-up clothes, and maybe as stiffly posed as a nineteenth century tintype. You probably won't be surprised to learn that I do not believe in formal portraiture of kids. My motto is to let kids be kids—and kids tear around, get holes in their clothes, and seldom stick in any pose long.

Still, it is sometimes nice to have some shots closer to formal portraiture—even when the subject is a child.

I find that the best strategy for achieving this result is to start by letting them do their thing, whatever that is, provided it doesn't result in the destruction of your studio or your living room. This kind of approach gets the nervous energy out of the way and lets the kids have some fun.

At some point down the line, you can start to think about generating portraits. To make this happen there are two general approaches. You can wait for it, and snap the portrait at the decisive moment. Alternatively, you can try to direct the kids into position, pose, and costume. Either approach can work, but is a little different than working with adults.

First, bear in mind that kids can be comfortable in small spaces that might not feel right to adults. A vast studio space or living room might seem cavernous to kids, so you are better off finding a more intimate shooting space.

If you are practicing watchful waiting, be sure to fire off photos from time to time. This will get the kids used to the idea that you are photographing so they won't suddenly change what they are doing when you start taking photos "for real."

Be prepared with the right exposure already set in your camera, and a background that works visually. Generally, as fast a shutter speed as possible is best—the side effect of having low depth-of-field helps isolate the subjects from the background, and no one is looking for f/64 end-to-end sharpness in this context.

When I am taking a more active role in planning a portrait, I'll often place my camera on a short tripod set at kids' height before I start directing. When I do get kids into costume I try not to be too fussy about minor details, and I phrase directions as gentle requests rather than commands.

Speaking of height, we're quite used to looking in a downward direction at

▶ I sat on the floor to make this portrait at a slight upward angle of Emily. A black background helps to make the portrait dramatic.

24mm, 1/160 of a second at f/11 and ISO 100, hand held

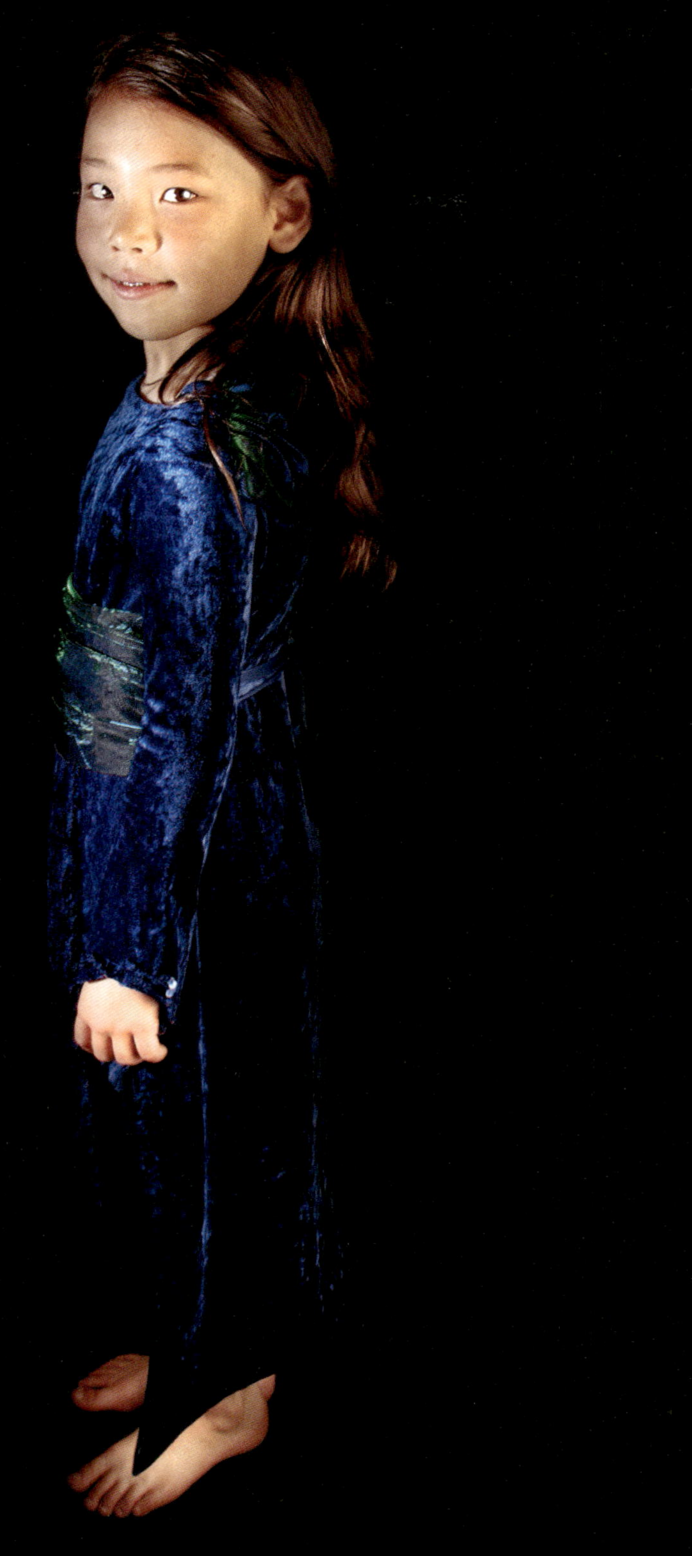

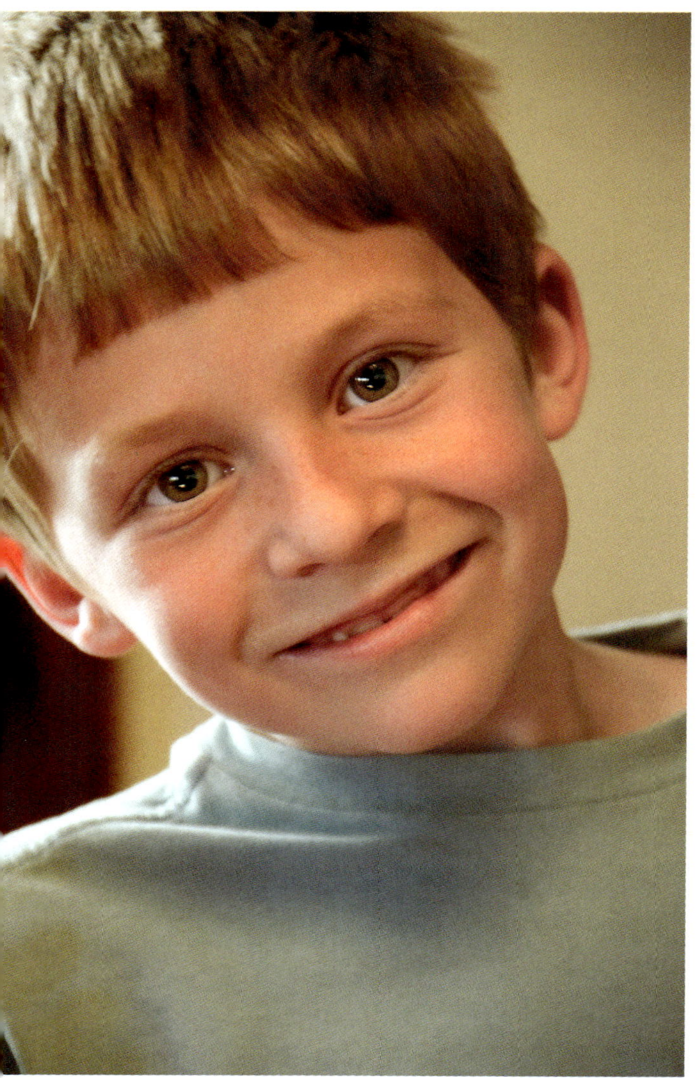

children—so, while head-on portraits of adults seem natural, head-on portraits of kids can look unusual. But personally I prefer to photograph kids as equals, and get down on their level so they seem to be my height—or even sometimes taller. I think this angle presents images of kids that have more dignity than the standard downward angle, and kids appreciate that I am not towering above them when I take their photo.

◀ While this portrait is a little soft focus because of the slow shutter speed I used, Nicky's charming character comes through loud and clear—a benefit that is more important than any technical considerations.

200mm, 1/15 of a second at f/5.6 and ISO 1250, hand held

▶ If a child is flexible and inclined to show off gymnastic poses like Nicky, by all means encourage this activity. Getting the chance to do something active will make natural poses more likely and keep your subject from getting bored. When you see a pose you like, you can say something like, "Stop there for a second, please."

46mm, 1/160 of a second at f/9 and ISO 100, hand held

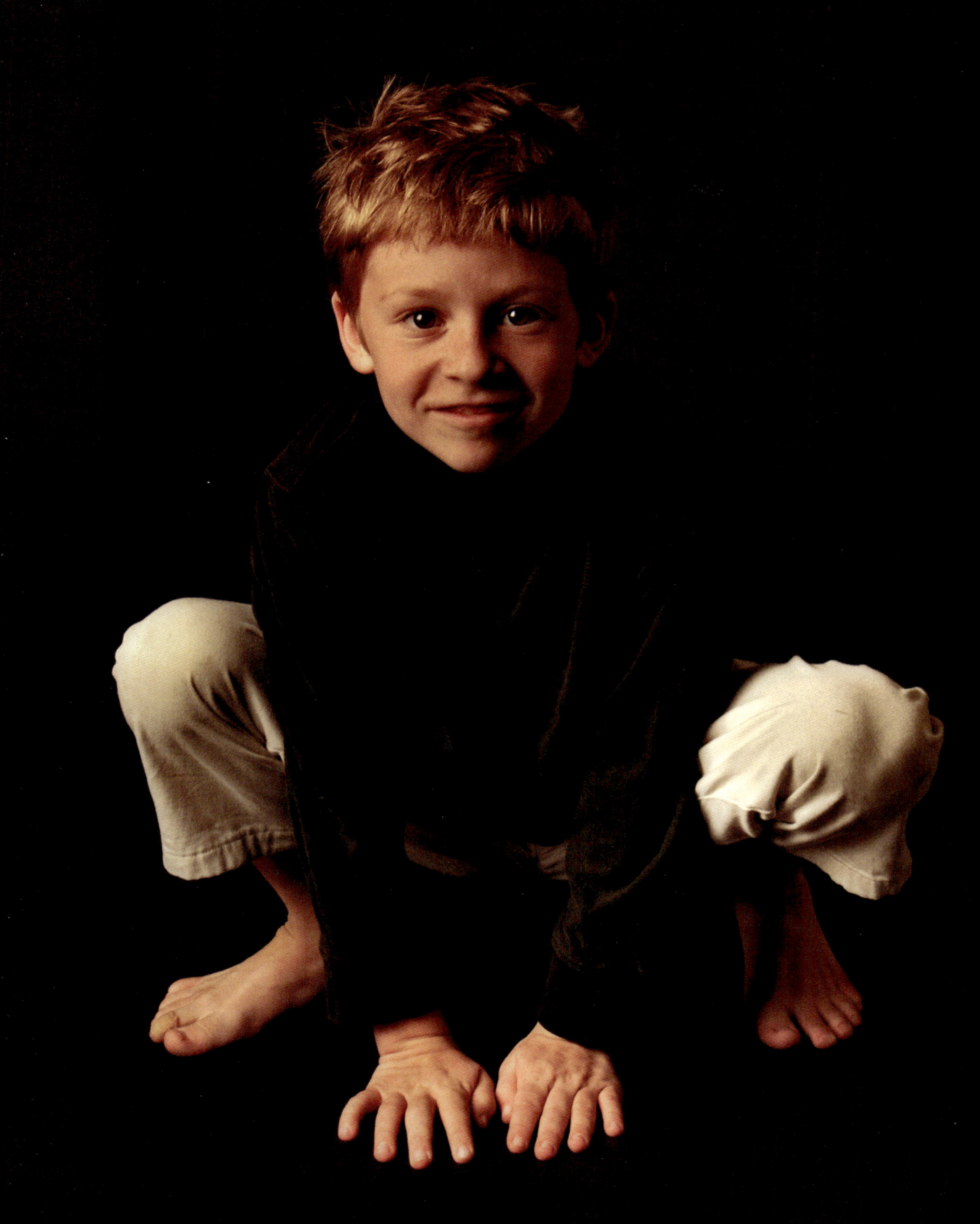

Casual Kid Photographs

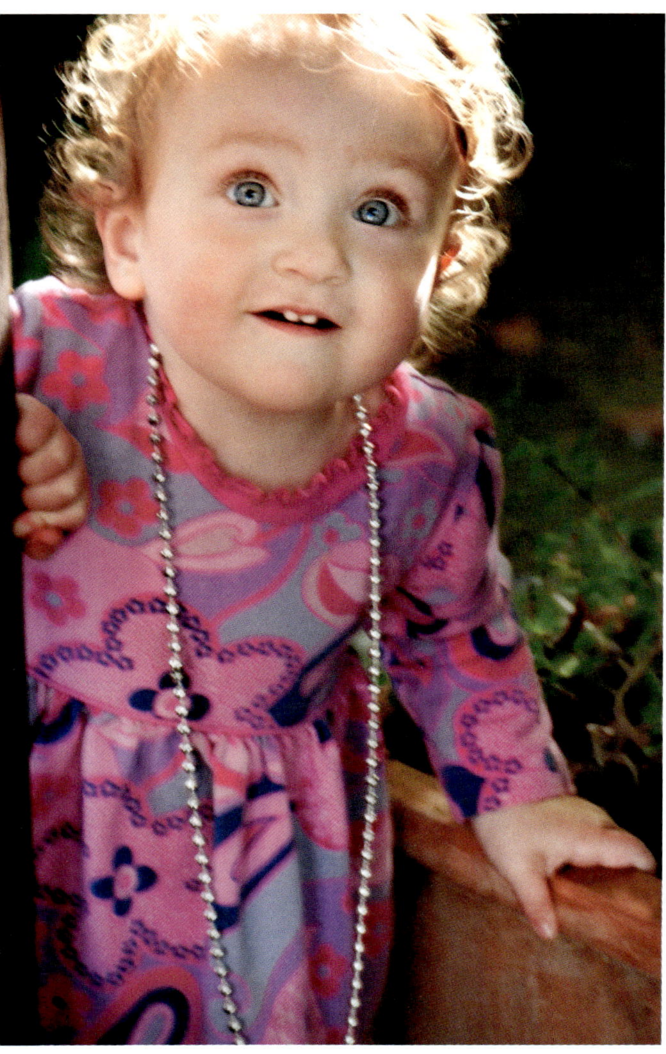

Even my formal portraits of kids don't have much in the way of formality. So how can you go even more casual?

The answer is by having kids doing things, or by capturing them in the process of engaging in activities. Try to find toys they like. Ask them to play at being a pirate. Have your camera ready at the face painting booth of a street fair. Look out for costumes, and for kids entering and exiting rooms. And always be aware of the light!

A quick trigger finger and a camera that is configured in advance is your friend when it comes to casual portraits of kids. Don't worry too much about exposure, just do the best you can. Pay more attention to what the kid is doing and the quality of light. Nobody will care if your exposure is dead-on and your focus is accurately centered on the eyes if the child has a dead expression and isn't doing anything interesting.

Casual kid photography is about the revelation of character—and having fun. It is not about documentation. To be perfectly honest, it is also about the "cuteness factor." Don't forget that kids are inherently cute—more so even than kittens and puppies. Capture that cuteness and your photos are winners.

▲ Backlighting can be very effective, as in this shot of Katie Rose coming through an open door. However, the problem with backlighting is that the face tends to go dark. Fortunately, with RAW digital captures this can often be corrected using multi-RAW processing in Adobe Camera RAW (ACR) or Lightroom (see pages 198–204).

170mm, 1/80 of a second at f/5.6 and ISO 400, hand held

▶ The quality of the light along with the natural attractiveness of Mathew helps make this an appealing portrait. But the really compelling feature is Mathew's big blue eyes—something the photographer doesn't have much to do with.

200mm, 1/30 of a second at f/5.6 and ISO 400, hand held

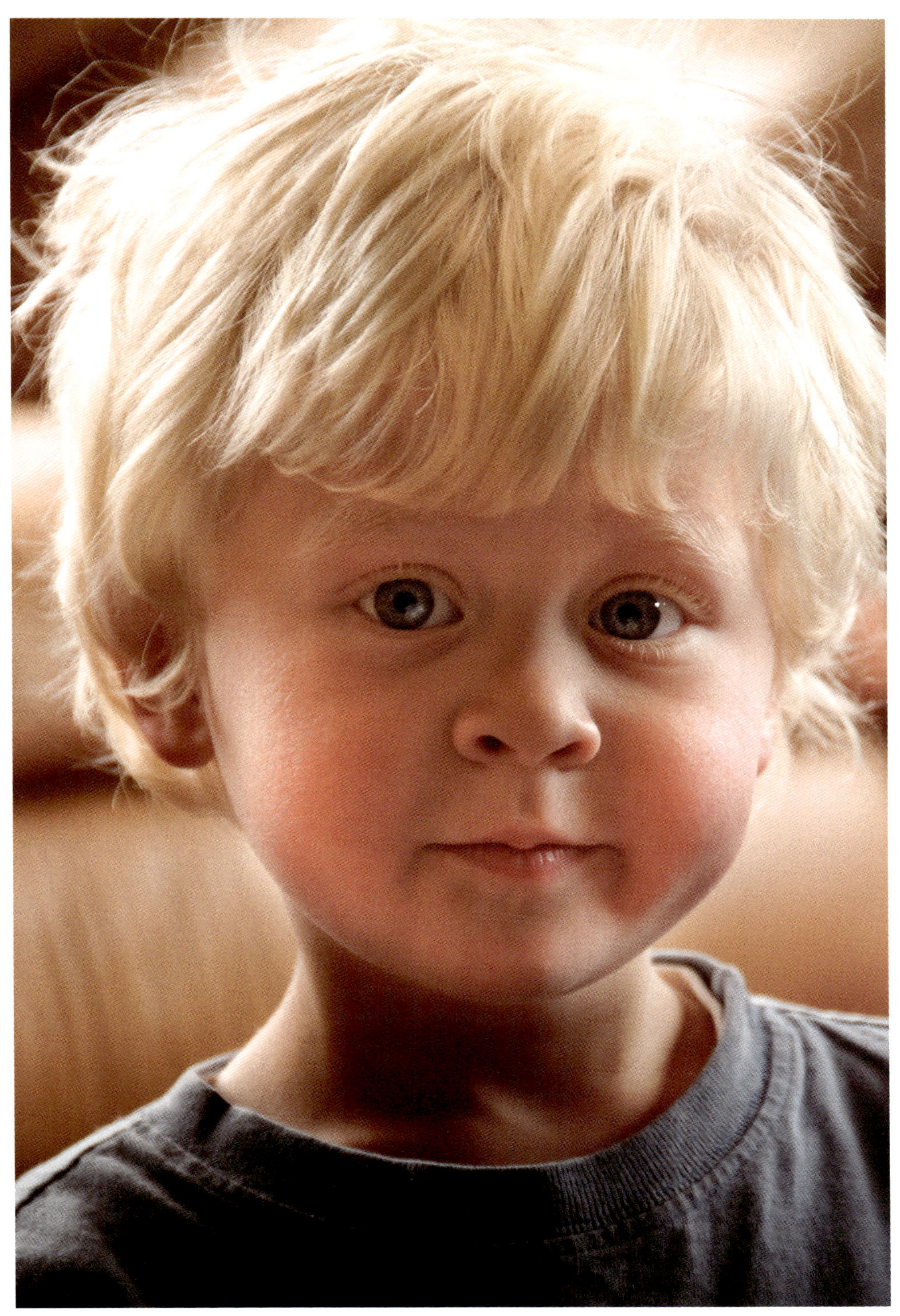

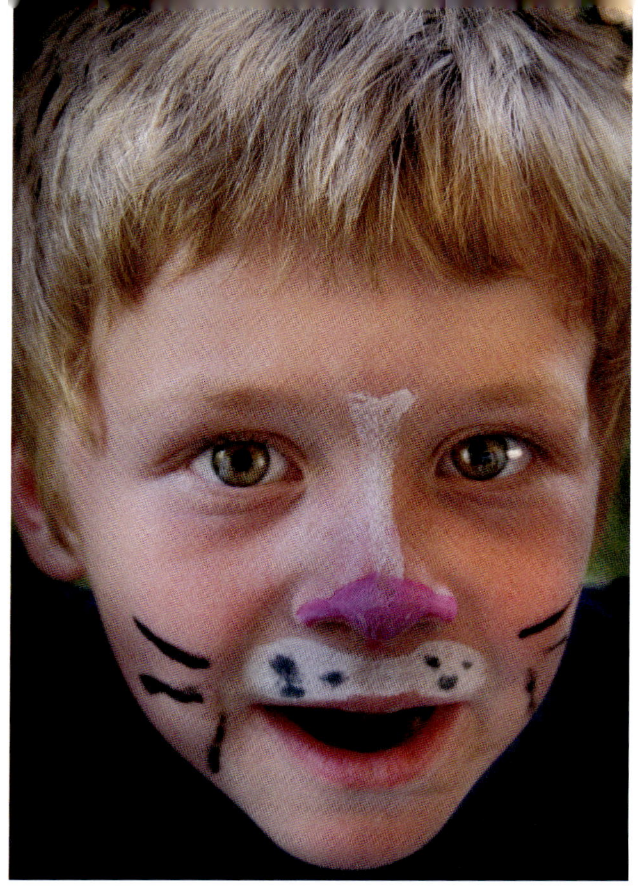

◀ Keep your eye out for opportunities like face painting in street fairs—always a worthy occasion to get striking portraits of your kids.

56mm, 1/100 of a second at f/7.1 and ISO 500, hand held

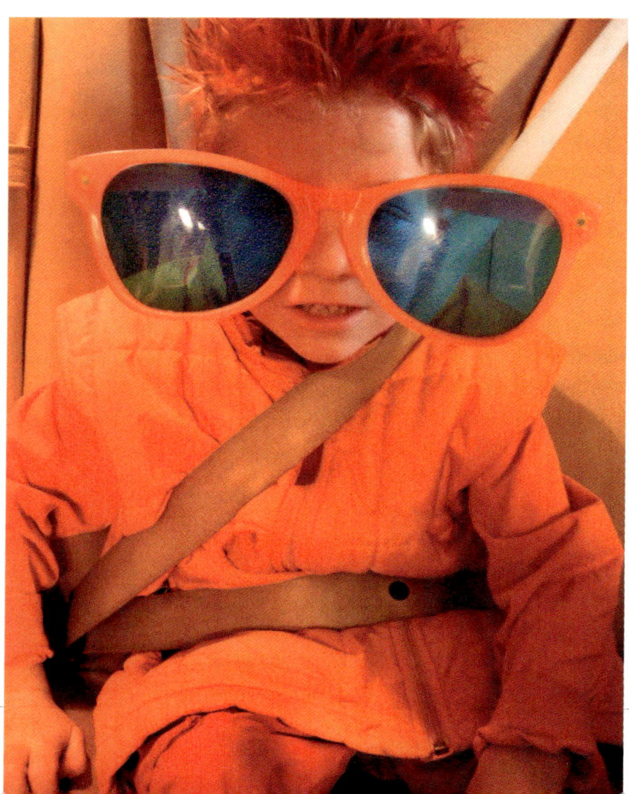

◀ The humor in this snapshot of a costumed child makes up for the hurried quality of the photography. In this kind of situation, a family photographer has to "use it or lose it"—you'll seldom get a second chance.

Canon Powershot G9, 7.4mm (about 35mm in 35mm terms), 1/13 of a second at f/2.8 and ISO 800, hand held

▶ Nicky was very eager to pose as a pirate, with his owl—rather than the traditional parrot—on his shoulder. I shot this image on an off-white background, then added the split orange-blue effect in Photoshop using the Nik Color Efex Pro filter pack.

26mm, 1/160 of a second at f/13 and ISO 100, hand held

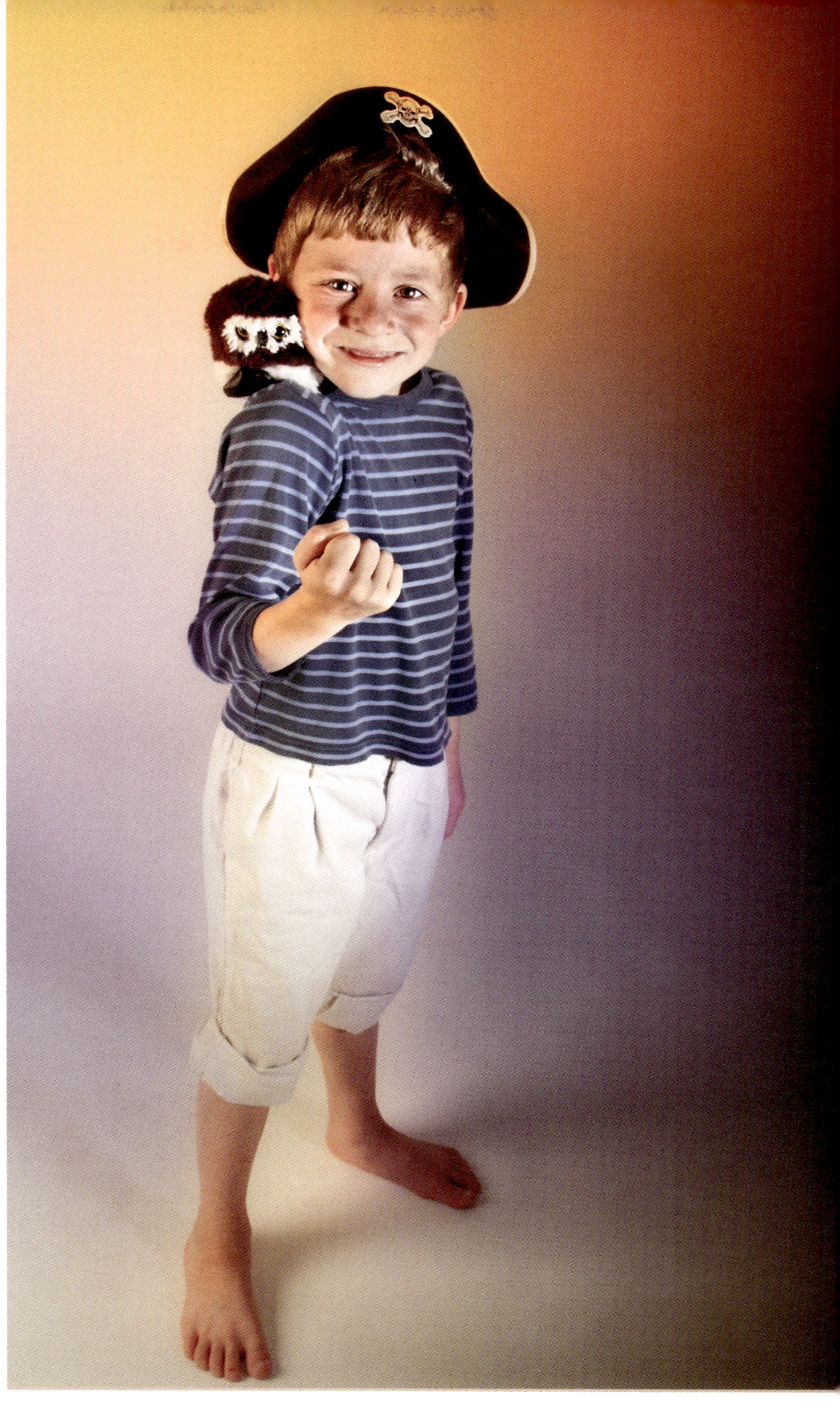

Environmental Portraits of Kids

A child should be the subject of his portrait. But sometimes the environment that a infant or small child finds themselves in says more than the child's face—or adds to the knowledge viewers get from looking at a conventional view.

Keep your eyes open for environmental details that shed additional light on the character of the child being photographed.

All photographs tell a story. Consider the narrative of your photos. How can this narrative be improved by stepping back in your viewpoint and including the details that surround your child—the toys, their friends, the context of their life?

Successful environmental portraiture of kids means including the context in the images you make. Adding these details will almost always make your photos more interesting—and tell a story that may go beyond portraiture.

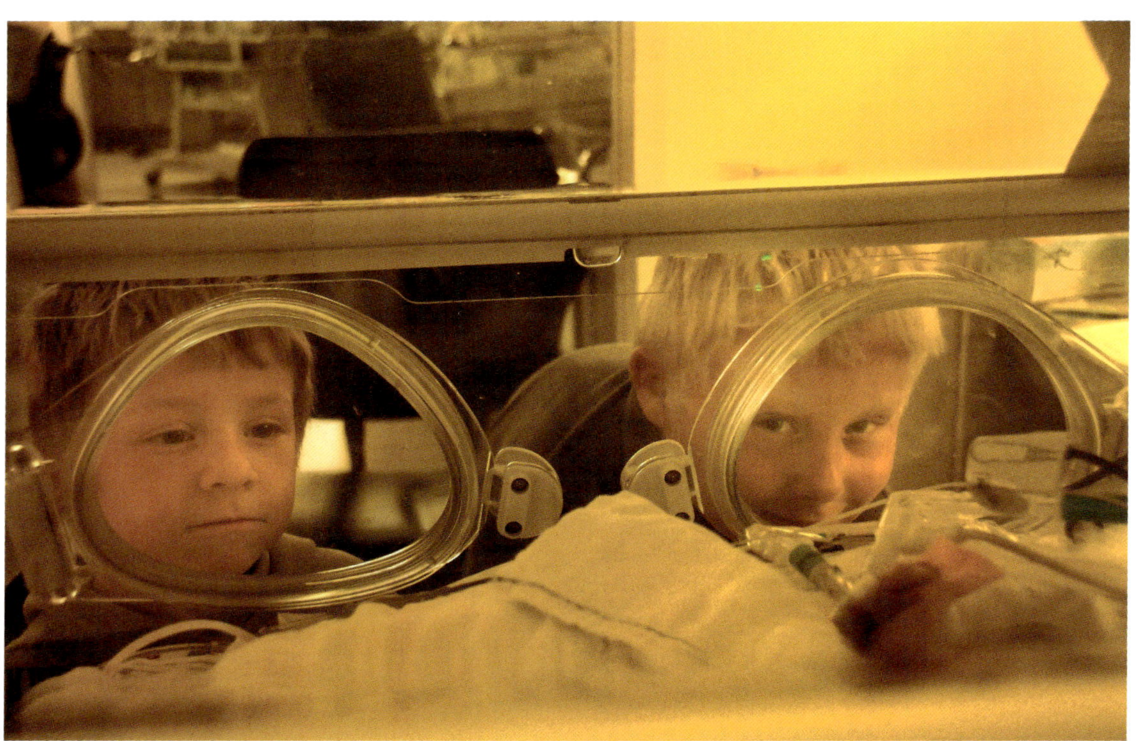

▲ Taken through the window of Katie Rose's incubator in the Newborn Intensive Care Unit (NICU), this portrait of her brothers says something both about them and the environment of the photo.

32mm, 1/40 of a second at f/4.2 and ISO 1600, hand held

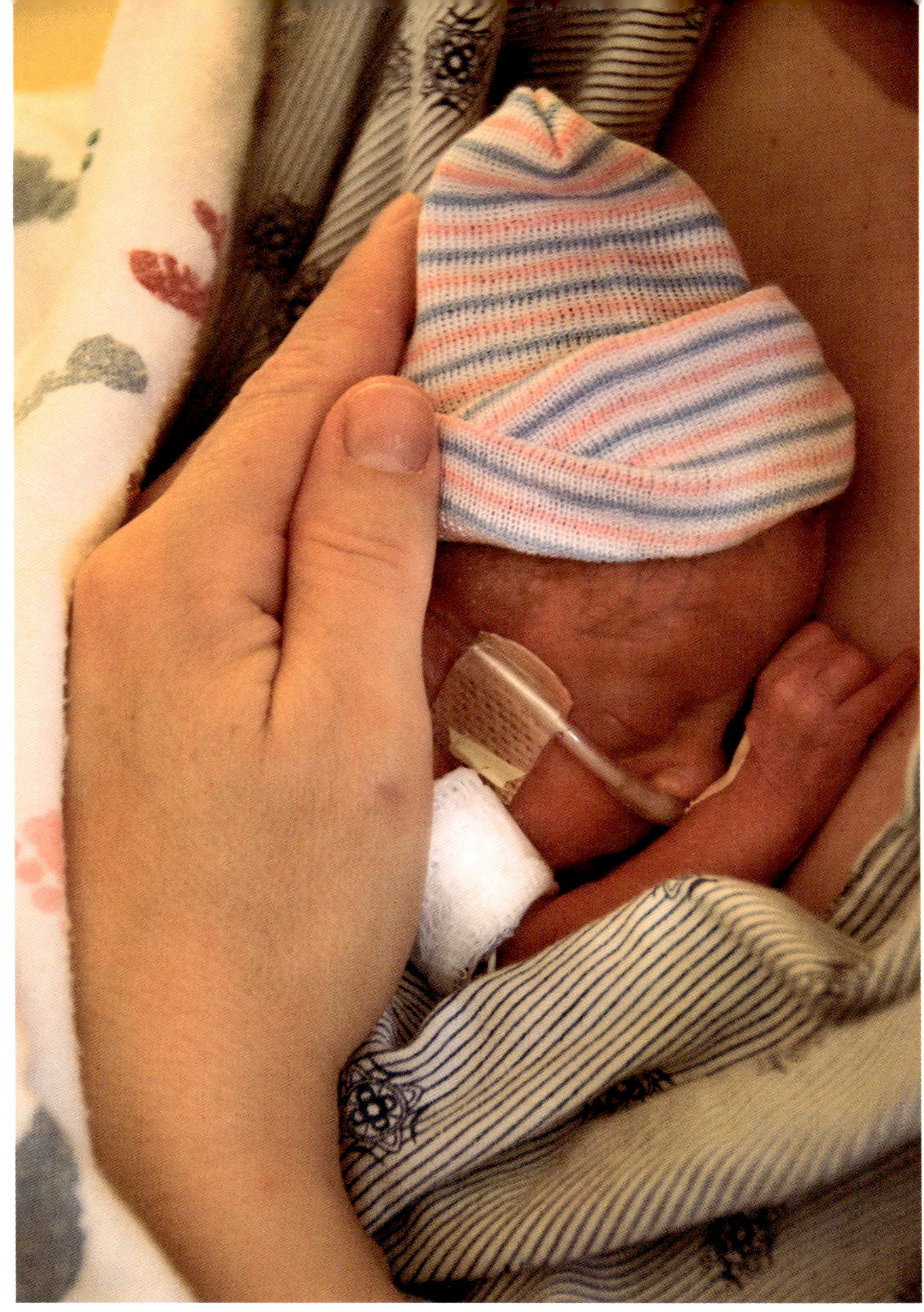

▲ Katie Rose was born prematurely at 24 weeks. She is shown here being "kangaroo" held by Mom. The environment—Mom's hand—shows the scale of what is going on, and exactly how tiny Katie Rose is in comparison.

80mm, 1/15 of a second at f/5 and ISO 2000, hand held

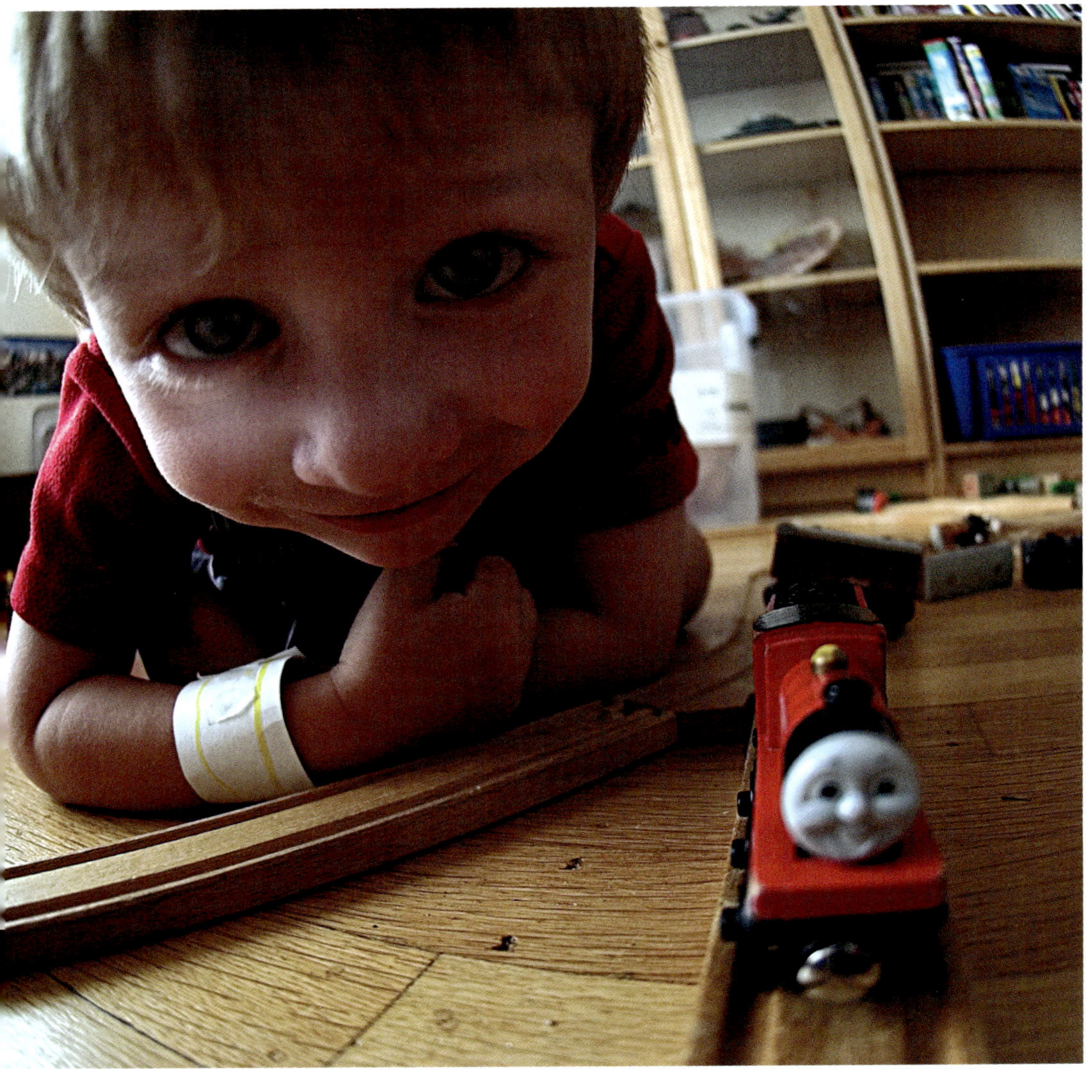

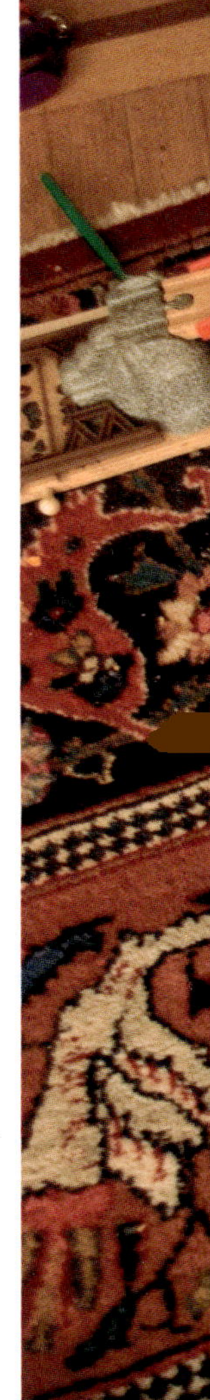

▲ I got down to the floor on my belly and photographed Nicky playing with his beloved trains using an extreme wide angle (fisheye) lens. The image is not technically perfect in a couple of ways—the point of focus could be chosen better for one thing—but the result is an unusual and humorous environmental portrait.

10.5mm digital fisheye, 1/30 of a second at f/2.8 and ISO 200, hand held

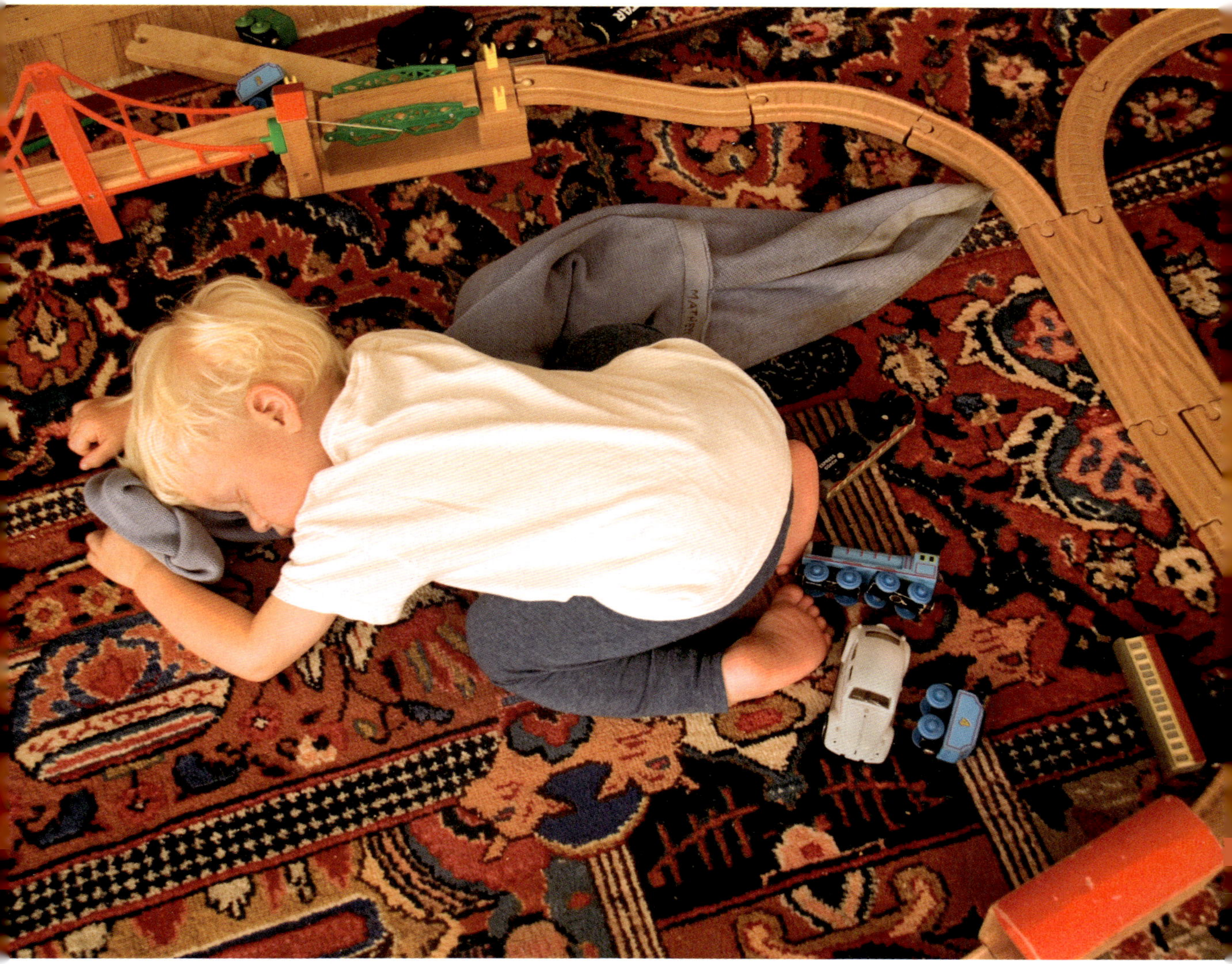

▲ In this portrait, the child's face is not really central, which is unusual. However, the environment—tracks, trains, comfort blanket—give a clue to the character of the child, and to what is going on: Mathew has played so hard that he dropped in his tracks.

27mm, 1/10 of a second at f/4 and ISO 100, hand held

Making Sure Your Kids Love Photography

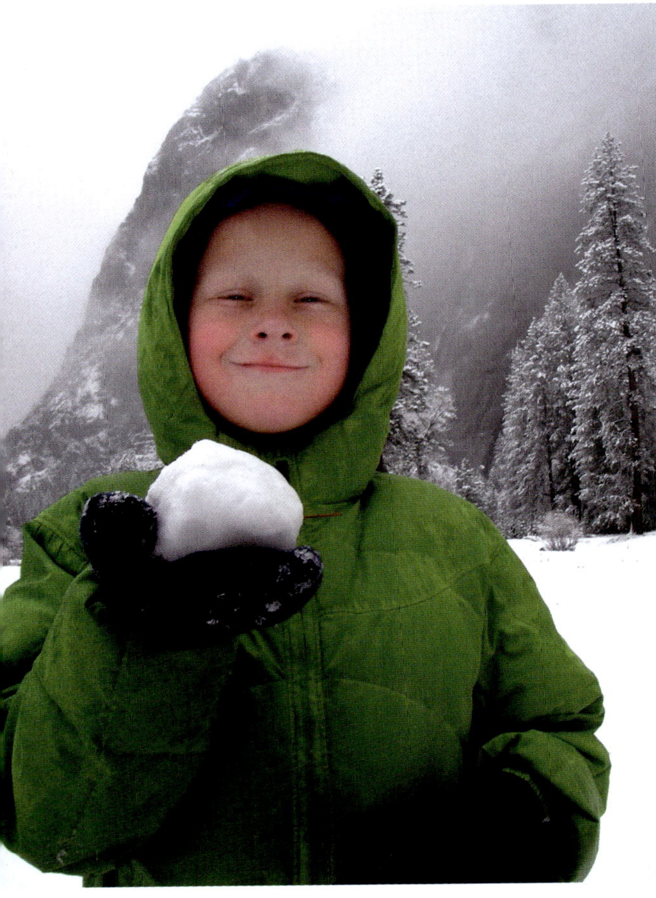

▲ Playing in the snow during winter in Yosemite Valley, California gives Julian something to do while his Dad photographs the scenery.

Pentax Optio WPi, 6.3mm (about 40mm in 35mm terms), 1/125 of a second at f/6.6 and ISO 80, hand held

Don't be a bore. Making sure your kids will love photography comes down to those four little words. They are important enough that I will say them again: Don't be a bore.

Kids get bored easily. When they are bored they are unhappy. There is no photograph on the planet that is worth making a child unhappy.

Parents and other photographers are guilty of boring kids in two different contexts. The first is insisting that their progeny pose when the progeny don't want to—and for longer amounts of time than anyone could reasonably be expected to endure. This problem is worst at traditional holidays. Please, don't make your kids pose in front of the Christmas tree if they aren't into it.

You'd think that the worst offenders would be photography pros—who "need" to get the photo, or may have their egos wrapped up in photography. Actually, enthusiastic amateurs tend to try the patience of their family and kids in this way far more than the pros. Any pro worth their salt knows they get better results by being low-key.

The second boredom hazard in relationship to your kids is a danger for avid photographers. If you are going to spend a great deal of time photographing something, and your kids are along, make sure they have something to do. This can be as simple as a snowfield to play in, or a book to read. But don't expect kids to wait patiently while you line up your tripod if they are bored—and don't expect them to appreciate your photos if you bored them to tears making the images.

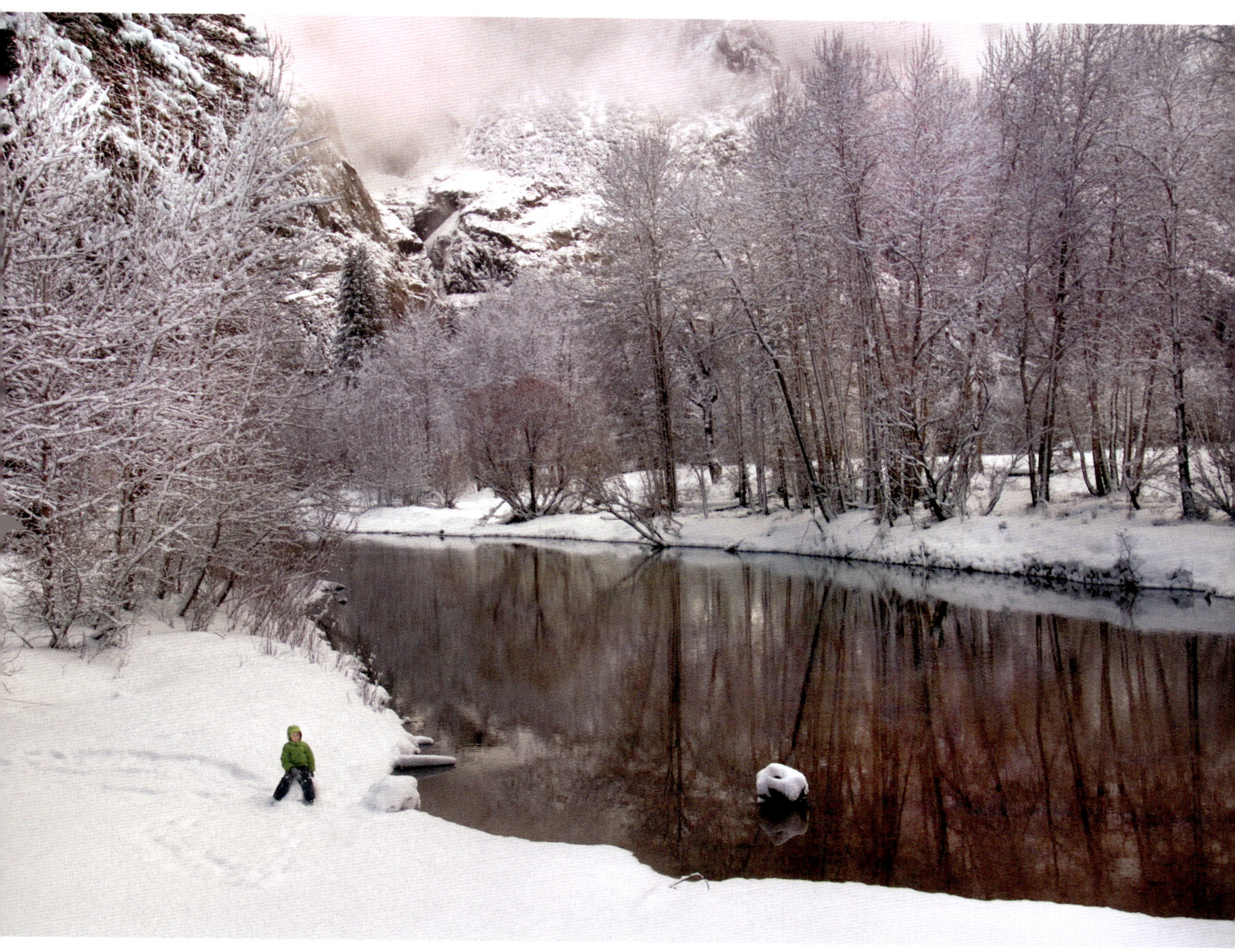

▲ Along the Merced River in snowy Yosemite Valley, California, Julian plays in the snow while his Dad photographs the impressive landscape made famous by Ansel Adams and others. For Julian, his trips to Yosemite and the high desert of the Eastern Sierras with his photographer Dad have become some of his fondest memories.

29mm, 1/125 of a second at f/7.1 and ISO 100, tripod mounted

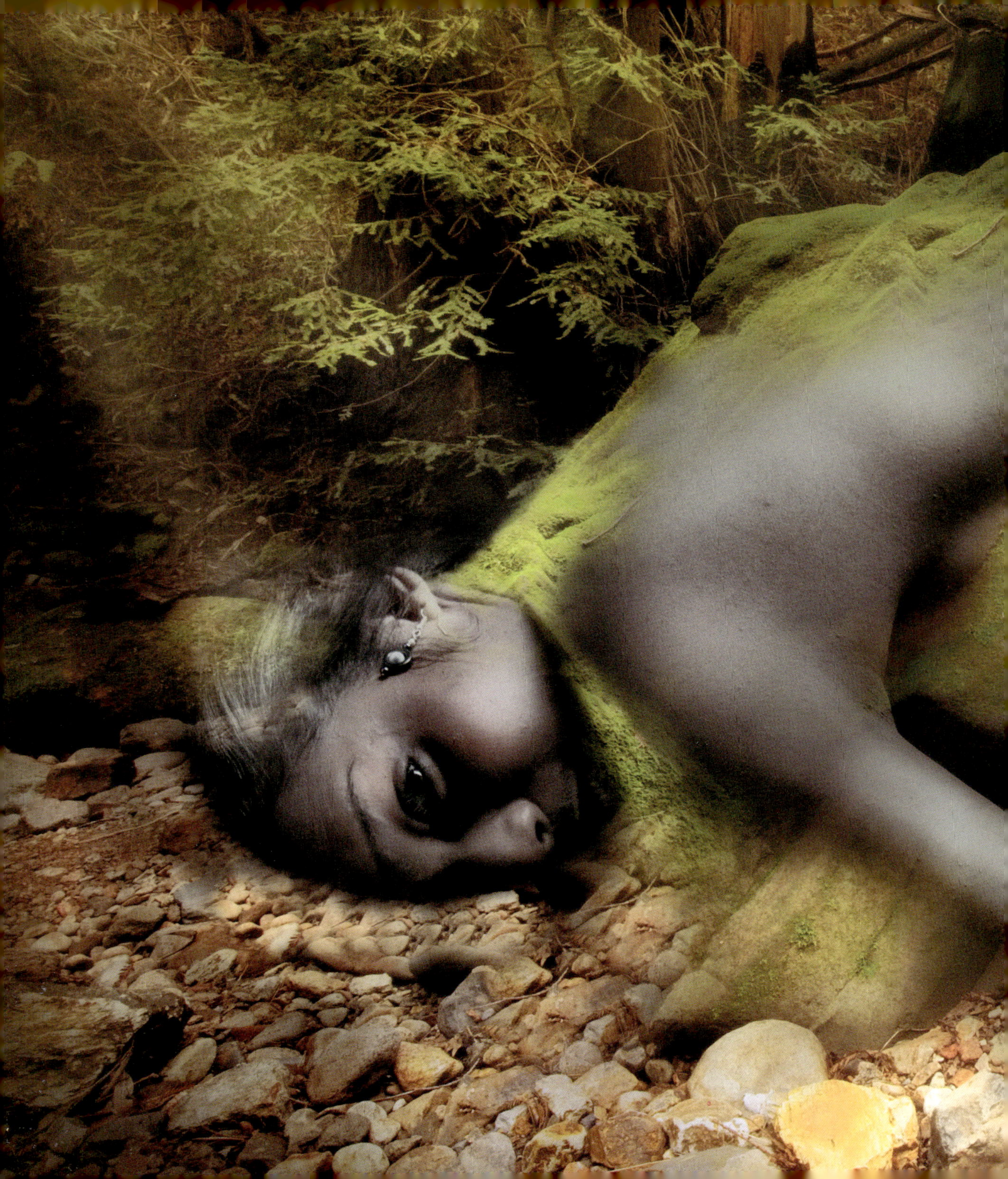

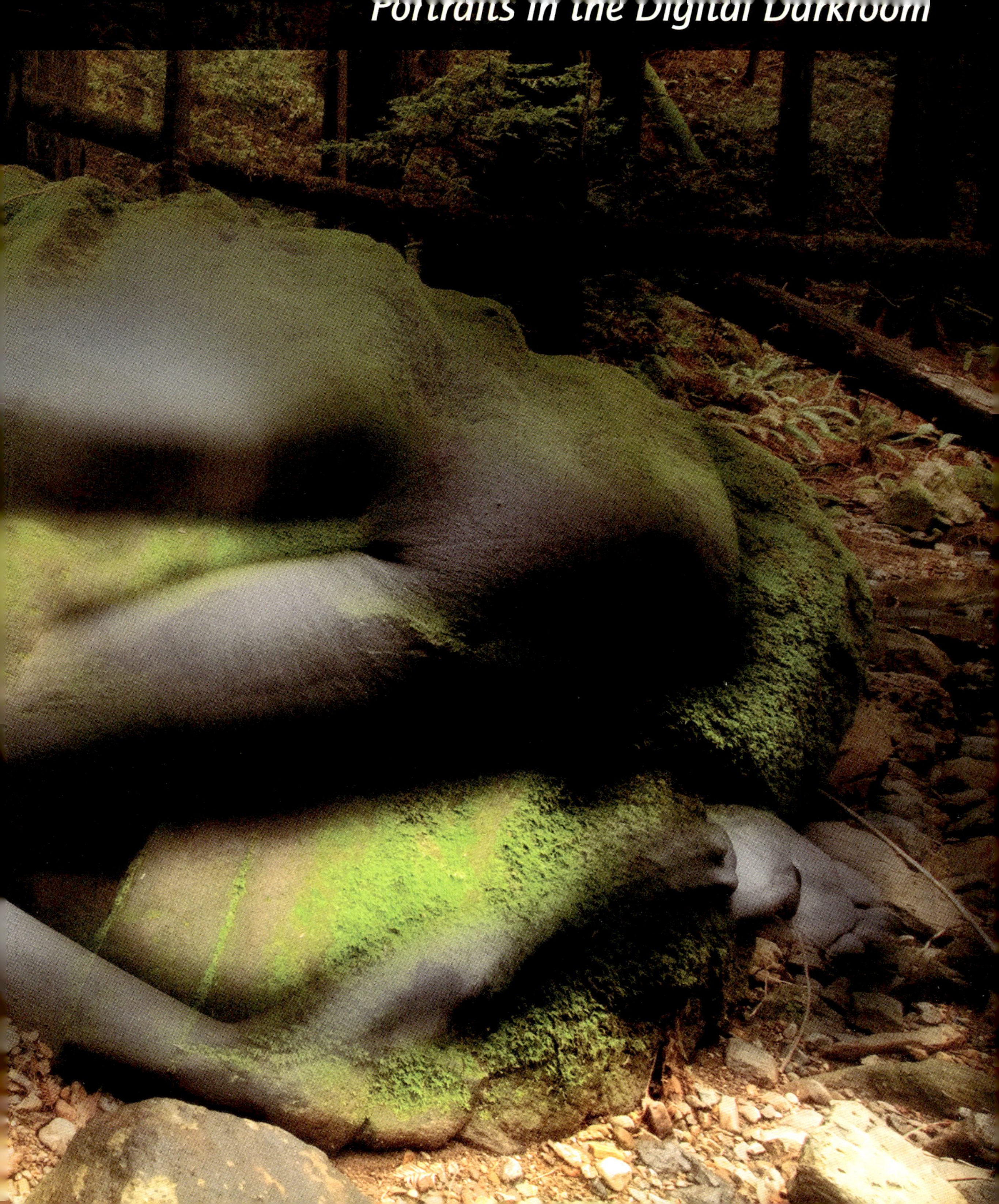
Portraits in the Digital Darkroom

Workflow and File Formats

Workflow means the process of creating a digital photograph from the moment the shutter is pressed to the final use for your image. It also includes the important topic—beyond the scope of this book—of how you store and preserve your images.

One thing that's clear to anyone who creates many portraits using digital cameras is that a great deal of the artistry is in the digital darkroom, which mostly means Adobe Photoshop. Furthermore, to get the best advantage of digital photography you need to save your captures as RAW files.

Most cameras will save photos as JPEGs or in RAW. While camera manufacturers have their own versions of RAW, they all have in common the idea of preserving all the data obtained by your camera when you made the capture. This is in distinction to saving your files as JPEGs, in which most of the data is thrown away—with the camera and not you choosing a single interpretation of the information that your camera's sensor captured.

Ansel Adams said that his negative was the score and his print was the performance. To bring the Ansel Adams metaphor into modern times, the RAW file is the score, and what you do with it in Lightroom, Photoshop, or some other software program is the performance. A great deal of the artistry in digital photography has to do with rendering an image after the capture.

How much retouching is too much?

When it comes to portraits, how much retouching should you do? This is a good question, and the answer largely depends upon the context.

For example, I rarely perform extensive retouching on portraits of children. Sure, sometimes I'll clean up messy faces—but only if the mess doesn't help tell my story. As far as that goes, children's skin—unlike most adults—usually doesn't need work in the first place.

On the other hand, glamour portraits of models almost always require extensive retouching, and leaving anything that is perceived as a flaw is inappropriate.

Sometimes our flaws *are* our characters, and to remove the flaw is to water down the character. Yes, with four kids and a life in photography I've earned my wrinkles.

So the upshot of the question of how much you should retouch is that it depends—upon whom you are photographing, the point of the photo, and how it will be used.

▲ Pages 196–197: To create this photo composite, I flipped the black and white shot of the model shown on pages 122–123 horizontally and combined it with a forest landscape. My idea was to show a portrait of a woman rising—or waking up in kind of a birth ritual—from the forest floor. So I worked in Photoshop to add an interesting lighting effect that conveyed my intention.

Model shot: 31mm, 1/125 of a second at f/6.3 and ISO 100, hand held; Forest landscape: 12mm, 8 seconds at f/22 and ISO 100, tripod mounted. Images combined as layers in Photoshop with lighting effects added using the Mystical Lighting plugin from Auto FX software.

Multi-RAW Processing

One of the most important reasons for shooting in RAW as opposed (or in addition) to JPEG is because you can alter the exposure and white balance of the image after the fact when converting the RAW file. While there are some practical limits how far over and under the "as shot" exposure you can take an image using multi-RAW, there's a great deal of exposure latitude after the photo has been taken because you have access to all the data made at the time of exposure.

This story keeps getting better. You can also process different portions of the image individually, in a process known as *multi-RAW processing*. Using multi-RAW processing techniques, you don't have to process an image uniformly. If part of your image is too bright, part too dark, and part just right, you can keep the "just right" part, and adjust for both over and under exposure as I'll show you in a moment.

The example I'll show you uses a portrait that is apparently too bright on the right and too dark on the left. The technique shown for adjusting these issues uses Adobe Camera RAW (ACR) and Photoshop. It's equally effective to multi-process photos in Adobe Lightroom, followed by Photoshop. For more details about both multi-RAW processing techniques, see my *Photoshop Darkroom* books (listed in the Resources section on page 234).

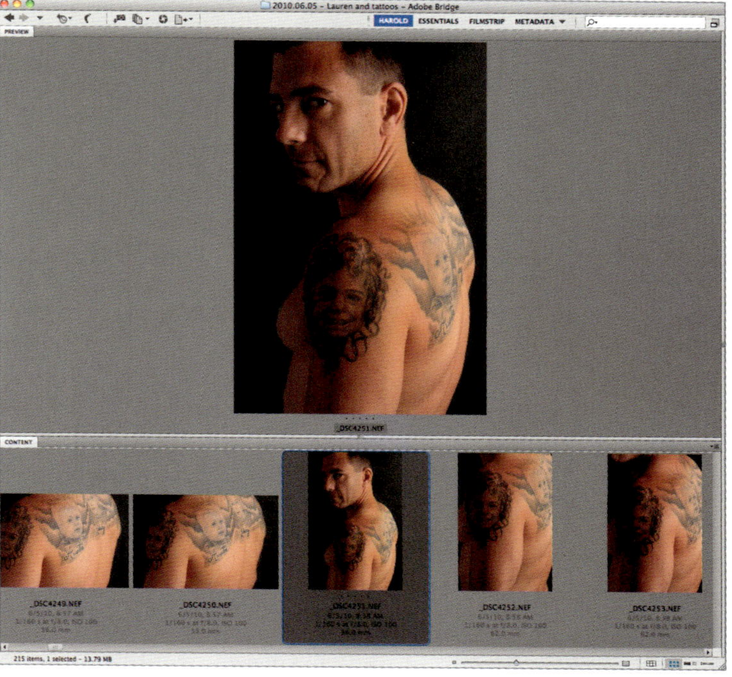

▶ Looking at the captures in Adobe Bridge, I could see right away that the right side of the portrait of Scott with his tattoos was too bright, and the left side was too dark.

I knew I would need to process a lighter version to get the detail on the left side of the image—parts of Scott's face, chest, and his left arm. I would also need a darker version to tone down the brighter areas on Scott's back.

▶ Step 1: Open the RAW capture in ACR.

Leaving the default "As Shot" settings, hold down the Alt key and click Open Copy to open this "As Shot" version in Photoshop.

It will appear in the layers palette as a "Background" layer. This version will be used as the basis for a multi-processed layer stack in Photoshop.

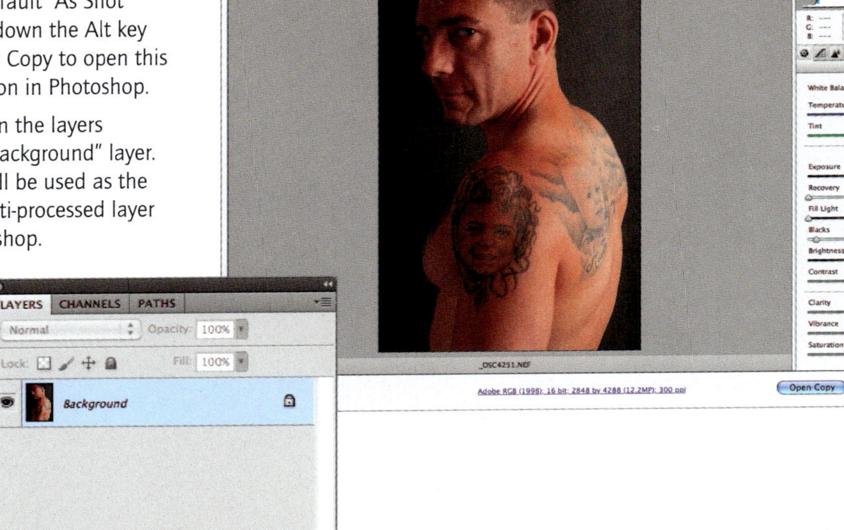

▶ Step 2: Open the RAW capture *again* in ACR. Move the Exposure slider to the left, the Black slider to the right, and the Brightness slider to the left to make this version of the image darker and expose Scott's back correctly.

Hold down the Alt key and click Open Copy to open this darker version in Photoshop. It will appear in the Layers palette as a "Background" layer.

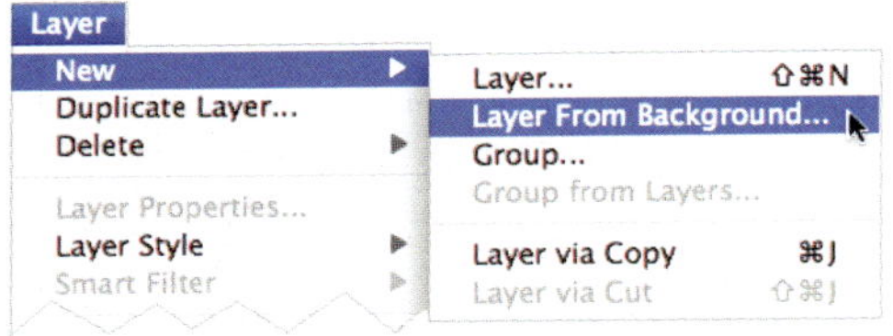

▶ Step 3: Choose Layer ▸ New ▸ Layer from Background and rename this darker version "Darker."

You now have two versions—the Background version and the darker version—of the same image open in Photoshop.

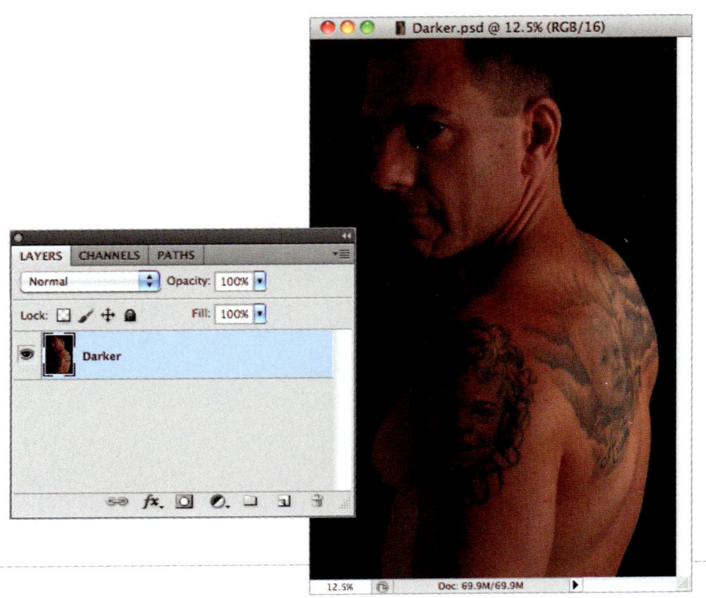

▶ Step 4: Hold down the Shift key and use the Move Tool to drag the darker version from its window onto the Background version's window. Release the mouse before you release the Shift key. This will perfectly align the layers on top of each other.

There are now two layers in the Layers palette: "Darker" and "Background."

▶ Step 5: With the "Darker" layer selected in the Layers palette, choose Layer ▸ Layer Mask ▸ Hide All to add a layer mask to that layer.

The Hide All layer mask hides the layer it is associated with (in this case the "Darker" layer). So all you will see in the image window right now is the "Background" layer. The layer mask appears as a black thumbnail in the Layers palette.

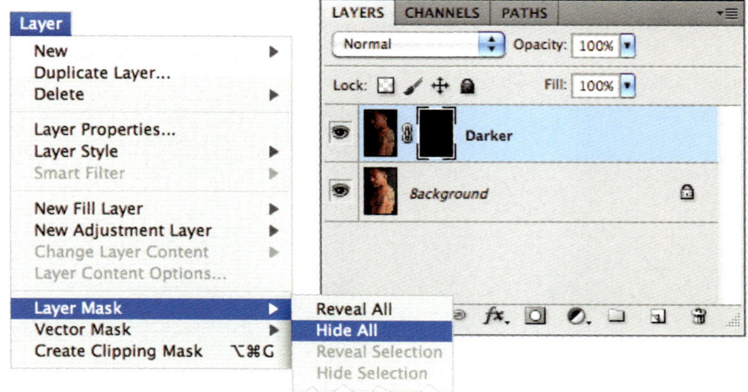

▶ Step 6: In the Layers palette, make sure the layer mask on the "Darker" layer is selected.

Select the Gradient Tool from the Toolbox and drag a white-to-black gradient from the right-hand side of the window to the left-hand side of the window. This darkens the area across Scott's back.

You can see the gradient on the layer mask thumbnail in the Layers palette.

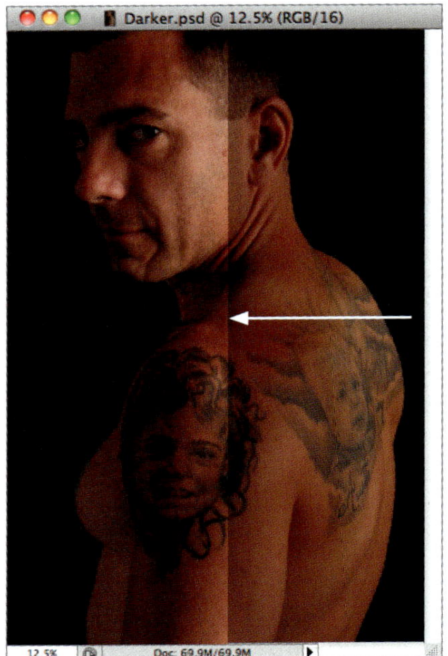

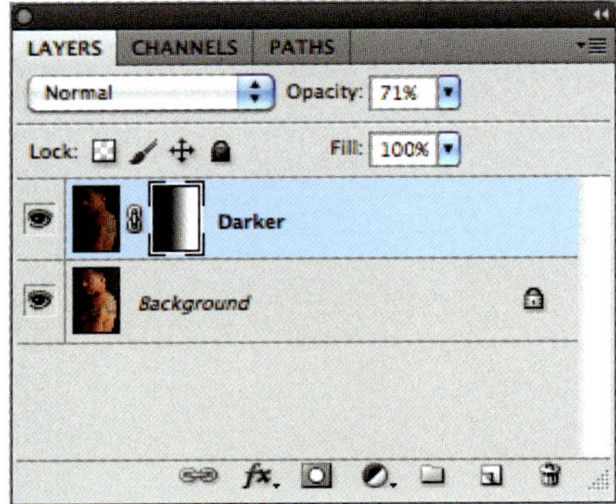

▶ Step 7: Go back to the original RAW capture and open it *again* in ACR. This time, you are going to create a lighter version that is exposed correctly for Scott's face, chest, and left arm.

Move the Exposure slider to the right, the Black slider to the left, the Fill slider to the right, and the Brightness slider to the right.

Hold down the Alt key and click Open Copy to open this lighter version in Photoshop. It will appear in the Layers palette as a "Background" layer.

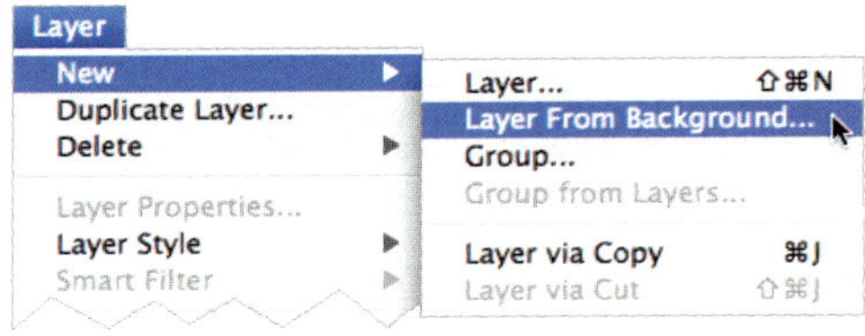

▶ Step 8: Choose Layer ► New ► Layer from Background and rename this lighter version "Lighter."

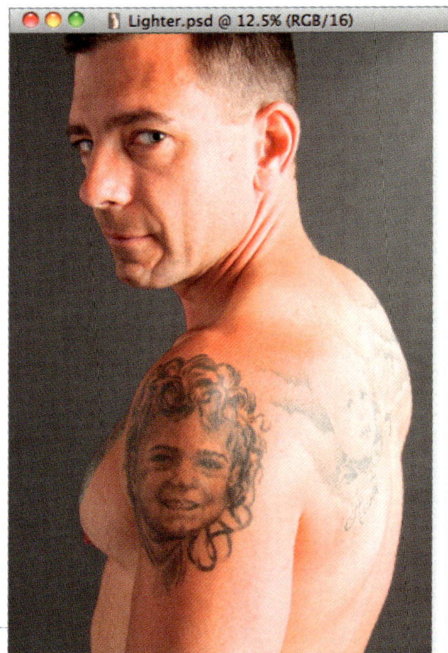

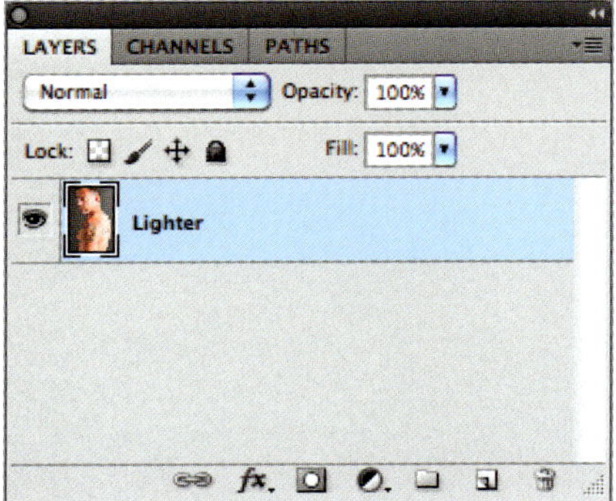

▶ Step 9: Hold down the Shift key and use the Move Tool to drag the lighter version from its window onto the window you've been working on that contains the two layers—"Background" and "Darker"—and the gradient on the layer mask. Release the mouse before you release the Shift key. This will perfectly align the layers on top of each other.

There are now three layers in the Layers palette: "Lighter," "Darker," and "Background."

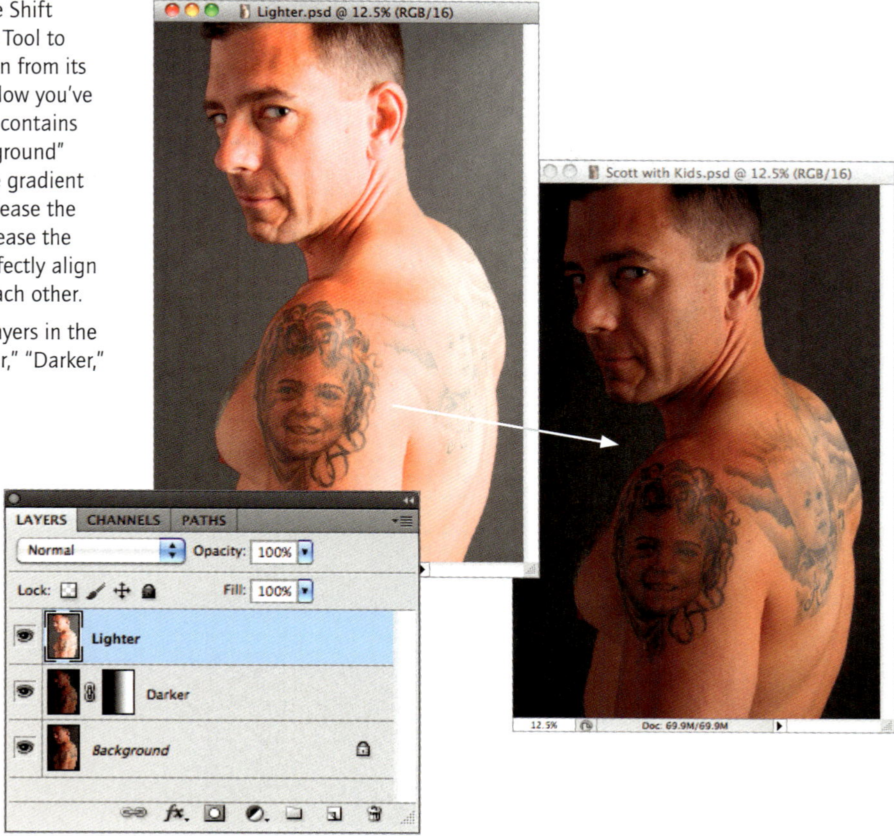

▶ Step 10: With the "Lighter" layer selected in the Layers palette, choose Layer ▸ Layer Mask ▸ Hide All to add a layer mask to that layer.

The Hide All layer mask will hide the "Lighter" layer. So all you will see in the image window right now are the combined "Darker" and "Background" layers. The layer mask will appear as a black thumbnail in the Layers palette.

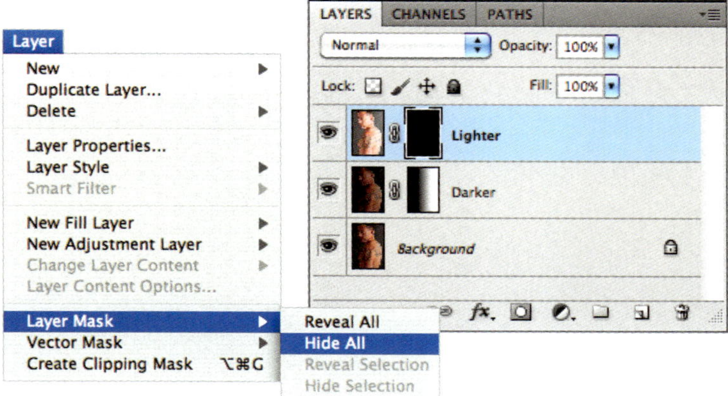

▶ Step 11: The final step for this image is to lighten the left side.

The Gradient Tool won't work to blend the "Lighter" layer into the other layers in this situation because you don't want the lightness extending all the way to the left edge of the image. You only want to make some areas of Scott's body lighter.

So for this step, make sure the layer mask on the "Lighter" layer is selected in the Layers palette and then select the Brush Tool from the Toolbox. Set the Foreground color to white, and set the Brush Tool to an Opacity of 50% and a Hardness of 0%.

Selectively paint in parts of Scott's face, chest, and arm. As you paint, the layer mask thumbnail in the Layers palette shows you the areas you've painted.

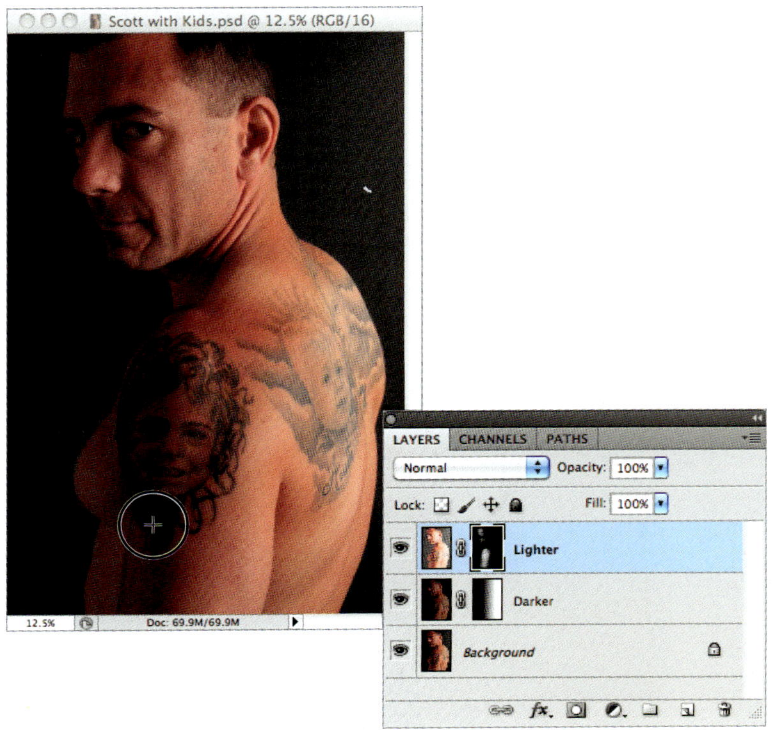

Saving Your Work

Some of the techniques that I explain in *Creative Portraits* are inherently pixel destructive. For example, cloning pixels, painting on a layer and then merging layers down both destroy pixels.

This means that as part of your workflow, it is very important to save copies of your work before you apply these techniques. For the details of archiving and workflow in Photoshop, see *The Photoshop Darkroom* books mentioned in the Resources section on page 234.

And don't say I didn't warn you! Always have an organized workflow, and archive a copy before doing anything that destroys pixels.

▶ Scott works as an intensive care nurse. He wears his heart on his skin—a tattoo of each of his four kids as they looked when they were two years old. These wonderful portraits cannot have been easy to make.

I photographed Scott on a black seamless background with a soft box to his right. A large fill card to Scott's left helped bounce some light into the deep shadow areas. However, as seen on the computer monitor Scott's back was still too bright, and his left-hand side was too dark—so I'm happy that I was able to adjust the image using multi-RAW processing.

36mm, 1/160 of a second at f/8 and ISO 100, hand held

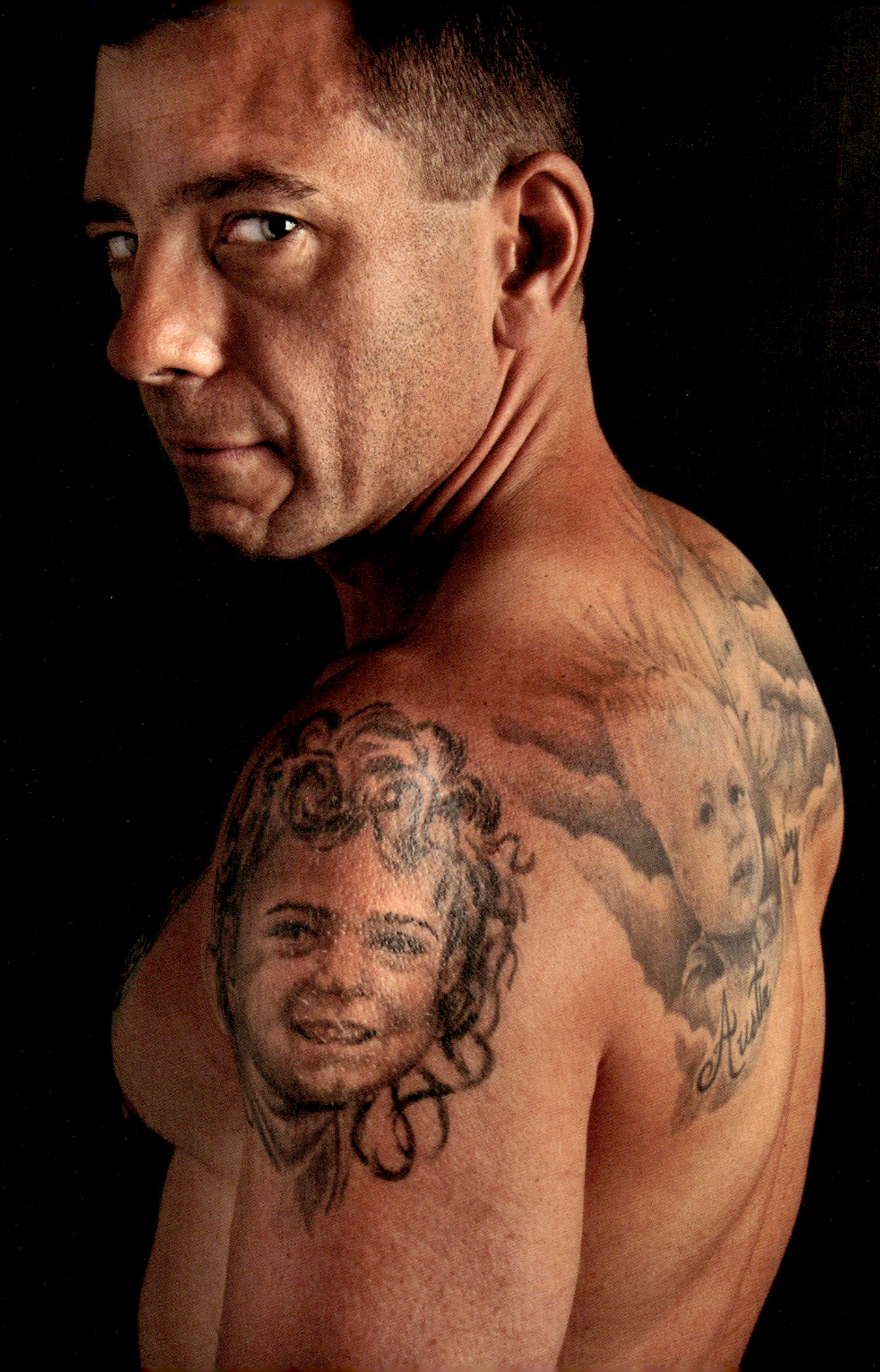

Fixing Flaws

As I've previously noted, you don't always want to fix flaws. The amount of retouching I am prepared to undertake depends upon the character of my portrait subject and the context of the portrait. But some portraits, and some flaws, cry out for fixing. And in some cases, the vanity of your portrait subject makes them insist on a "digital makeover."

For example, you seldom want reality to intrude on a glamorous portrait of a beautiful woman. After all, that's why cosmetics and make-up are used in our physical world—and digital make-up isn't so different conceptually. By the way, makeovers don't only apply to faces. I've spent a great deal of time on occasion providing virtual manicures and pedicures, among other things.

The first line of defense when it comes to fixing flaws is the destructive—but fantastically useful—Clone Stamp Tool.

The Clone Stamp Tool uses the colors from a sampled area from an image as "paint." When you use the Clone Stamp Tool, the pixels in the area you are working on are replaced with those from the sampled area.

The Healing Brush Tool and Patch Tool are very useful variations on the Clone Stamp Tool. They also take a sample from an area that you choose and let you apply that color and texture to areas that need work, automatically blending and smoothing the colors from the surrounding area.

But before I pull out the tools in my quiver, the first step I take is to do a close scrutiny of the image so I know what needs fixing. As I find the areas that need work, I figure out my game plan. In other words, I make an inventory of problems—and in glamour shots there are always some.

For example, take the natural light headshot shown to the right. There are a number of skin flaws—these are inevitable in anyone, even a gorgeous model—and I've circled a couple of them in the close-up below. In addition, there are some issues with the lip lines, the smile lines above the lips, and a few areas with slightly blown-out highlights. Also, the model's hair is casting a somewhat awkward shadow on her cheek at the middle right of the image.

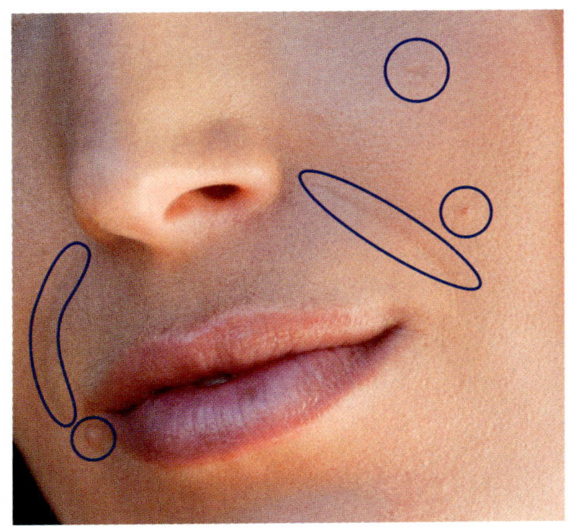

▲ Even beautiful models need some help with their skin. In the areas that I've circled, you can see the lines and bumps that need work.

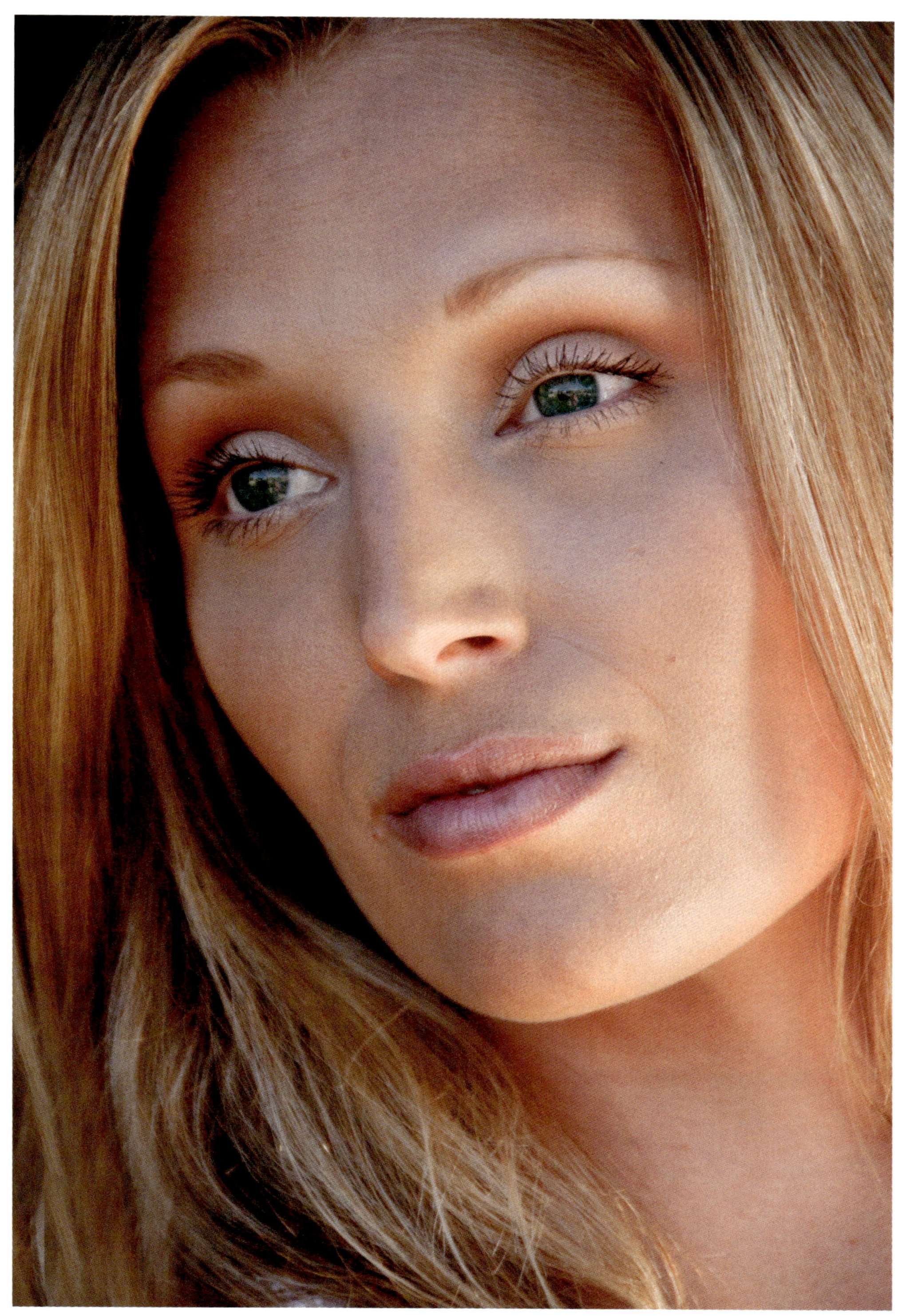

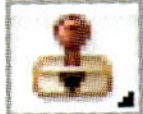

Use the Clone Stamp Tool to remove blemishes

Step 1: Select Layer ► Duplicate Layer so you are working on a duplicate layer, not the original.

Step 2: Zoom in so you can really see what you are doing.

Step 3: Choose the Clone Stamp Tool from the Toolbox.

Step 4: On the Options Bar set the Clone Stamp Tool to sample all layers at 100% opacity and 0% Hardness. Set the size of the tool slightly larger than the size of the blemish you need to fix.

Step 5: Hold down the Alt key and click over the area you want to use as a sample to replace the blemish. Take care to click on an area that is similar in color and tone to the area you want to replace.

Step 6: Click and/or stroke with the tool to remove the blemish.

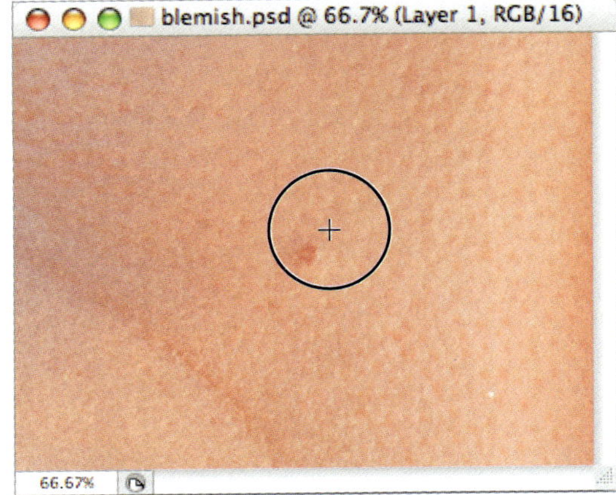

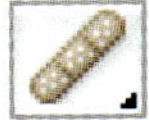

Use the Healing Brush Tool to remove lines

Step 1: Make sure you are working on a duplicate layer and zoom in so you can see what you are doing.

Step 2: Choose the Healing Brush Tool from the Toolbox.

Step 3: On the Options Bar set the Source to Sampled and select Sample All Layers. Set the Hardness to 0% and set the size of the tool slightly wider than the line you are going to conceal.

Step 4: Hold down the Alt key and click over the area you want to use as the sample. Take care to click on an area of pixels that is similar in color and tone to the area you want to replace.

Step 5: Stroke on the line with the tool. Photoshop will automatically blend in the tone and texture of the area.

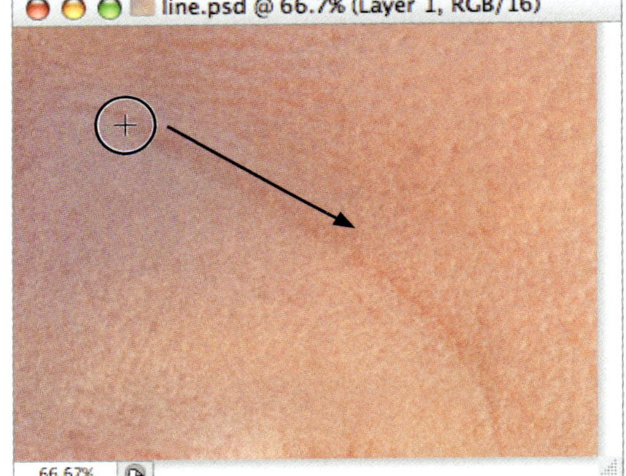

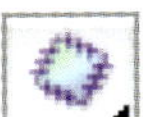

Use the Patch Tool to hide shadows

Step 1: Work on a duplicate layer and zoom in so you can see what you are doing.

Step 2: Choose the Patch Tool from the Toolbox.

Step 3: On the Options Bar set the Patch to Destination.

Step 4: Hold down the mouse and marquee select the area that you want to use to conceal the shadow. Be careful to sample from an area that is similar in color and tone to the area you want to replace.

Step 5: Drag the selected area over to the shadow you want to remove. Photoshop automatically uses the surrounding pixels to blend in tone and texture.

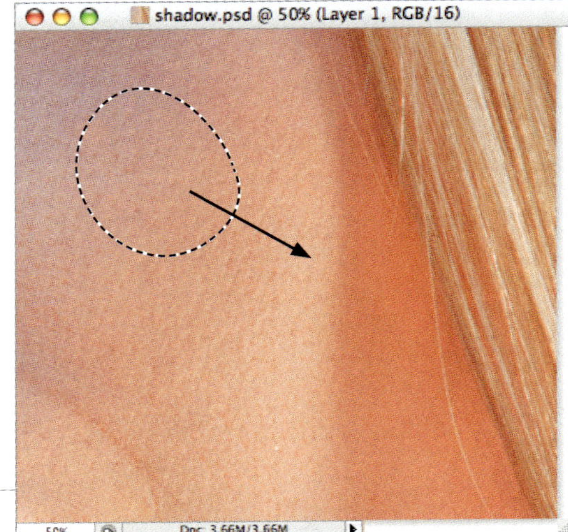

Working with Skin

You can enhance skin by painting at partial opacity over areas that have problems, first getting a good sample of the color of skin tones from a surrounding area. Used carefully, this is a technique that can be very effective. However, it can be a tedious and time consuming process, particularly when there are a number of Photoshop plugin filters that essentially "fix" skin—and sometimes creatively enhance skin—as a kind of batch process.

Before you apply one of these filters, you should fix all the obvious flaws that can easily be repaired. If there's a red mark—for example, a blemish—the best that a filter will do is show you a smooth, creatively enhanced blemish. You want to remove it before you apply overall filters.

Be sure to work on a duplicate layer when you apply an overall filter to modify the appearance of skin. This has two benefits. First, if you like the effect but think it is a bit too strong you can dial it back by taking down the opacity of the layer it is on. Second—and this is a very significant extension to the concept of applying an overall filter—once the filter has been applied to a layer you can use a mask to selectively use the filter. This means that some areas can have the filter applied while others do not. For example, you might wish to apply a skin filter to a model's cheeks, but not to her hair. Furthermore, the application doesn't have to be the same strength in all areas.

There are a great many possible filters and third-party products you can use to enhance skin—and not all of them are labeled specifically for that usage. In this section, I'll show you the impact of some of my top choices for enhancing skin tones and the overall look of a glamour portrait. Don't kid yourself: in digital portrait photography with a dramatic or glamorous look, a great deal of the craft and art comes from how you process the image after the photo has been taken. Being good in the digital darkroom is every bit as important as being good behind the camera.

It's worth experimenting with as many of these as you can get your hands on—and realize that you can mix and match, apply one filter treatment to one part of an image, and another to other portions of the image—and combine filters in an endless array of settings and possibilities. Essentially, this is a matter of your vision. There is no right, and no wrong—only the choices you make in the context of the way the final portrait comes out.

You'll find web addresses for the software tools I show in this section on page 235. In almost all cases, a working trial version is available for free download.

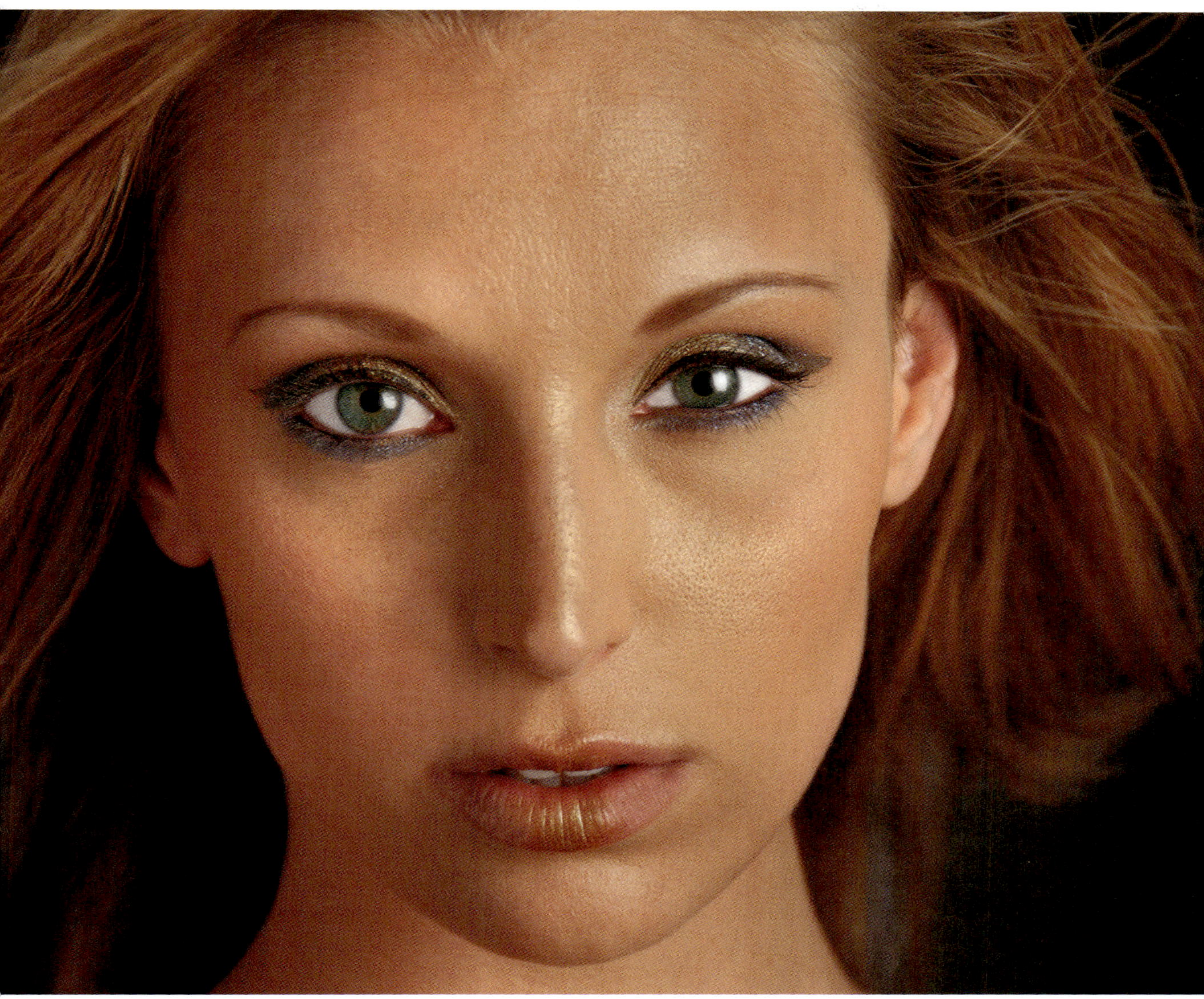

▲ At this stage, major flaws have been corrected, but no filters or special effects have been added. The two eyes are shaped somewhat differently, but that's part of what makes this portrait human, and I decided not to make them the same size.

The examples on pages 212–217 will show you a few tools and plugins you can use to enhance portraits.

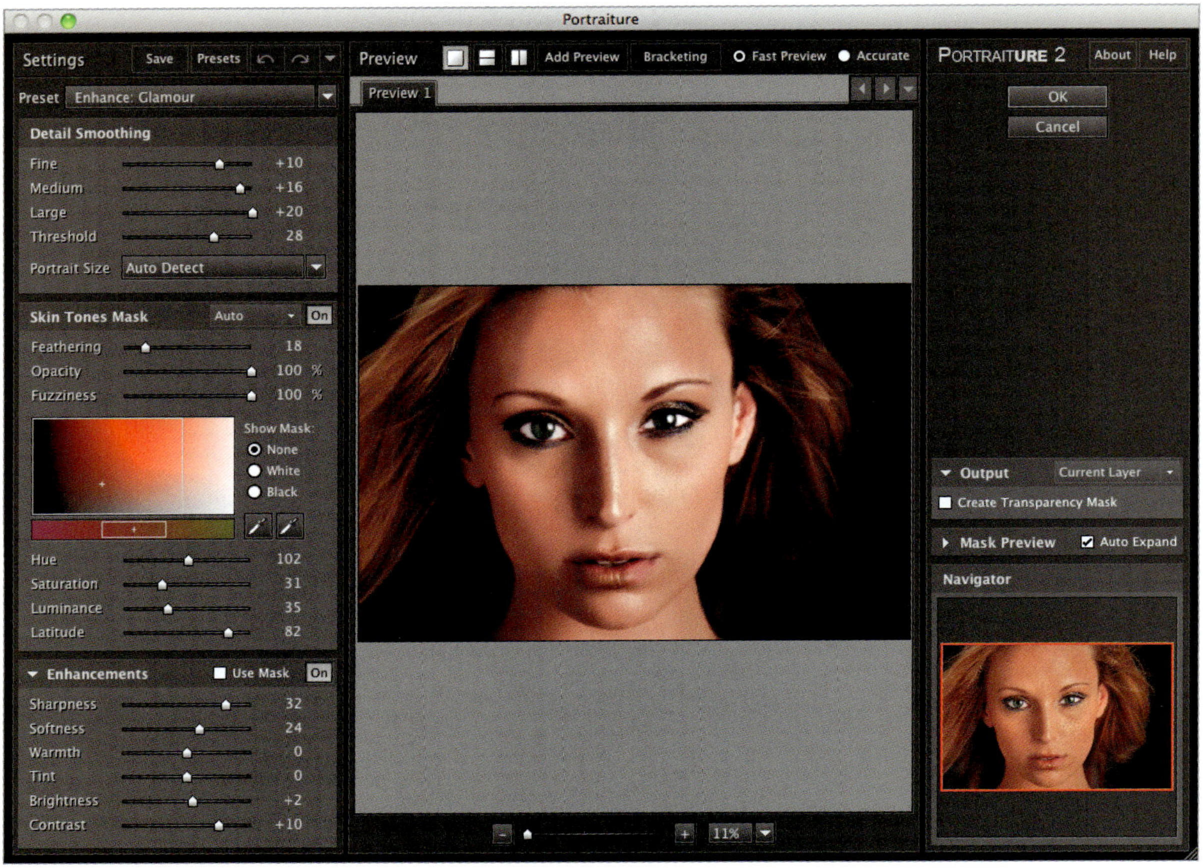

Imagenomic's Portraiture Photoshop plugin contains a number of presets that you can use to adjust an image. These presets are intended specifically for use with portraits. The filters range from those that add glamour and lighting effects (above) to those that smooth and enhance skin (right).

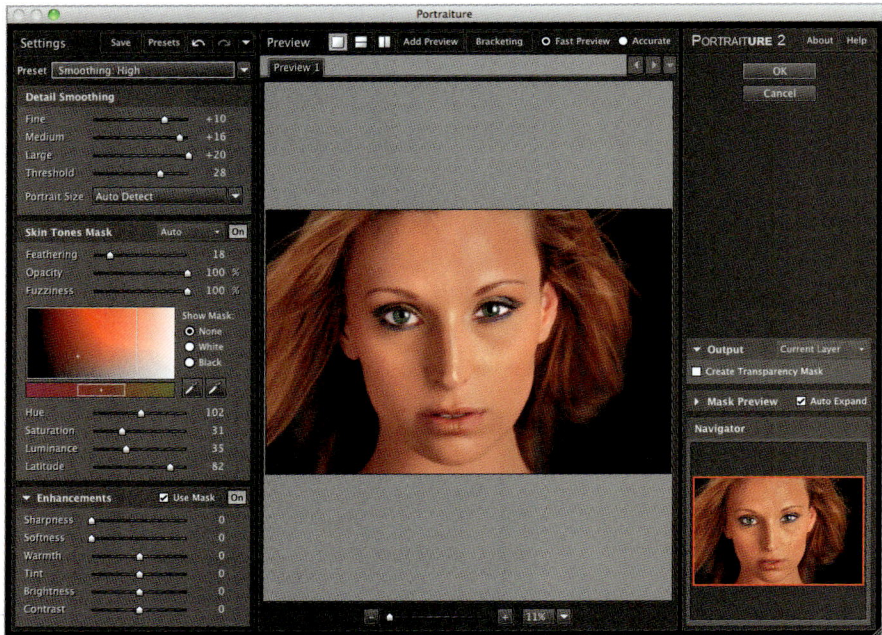

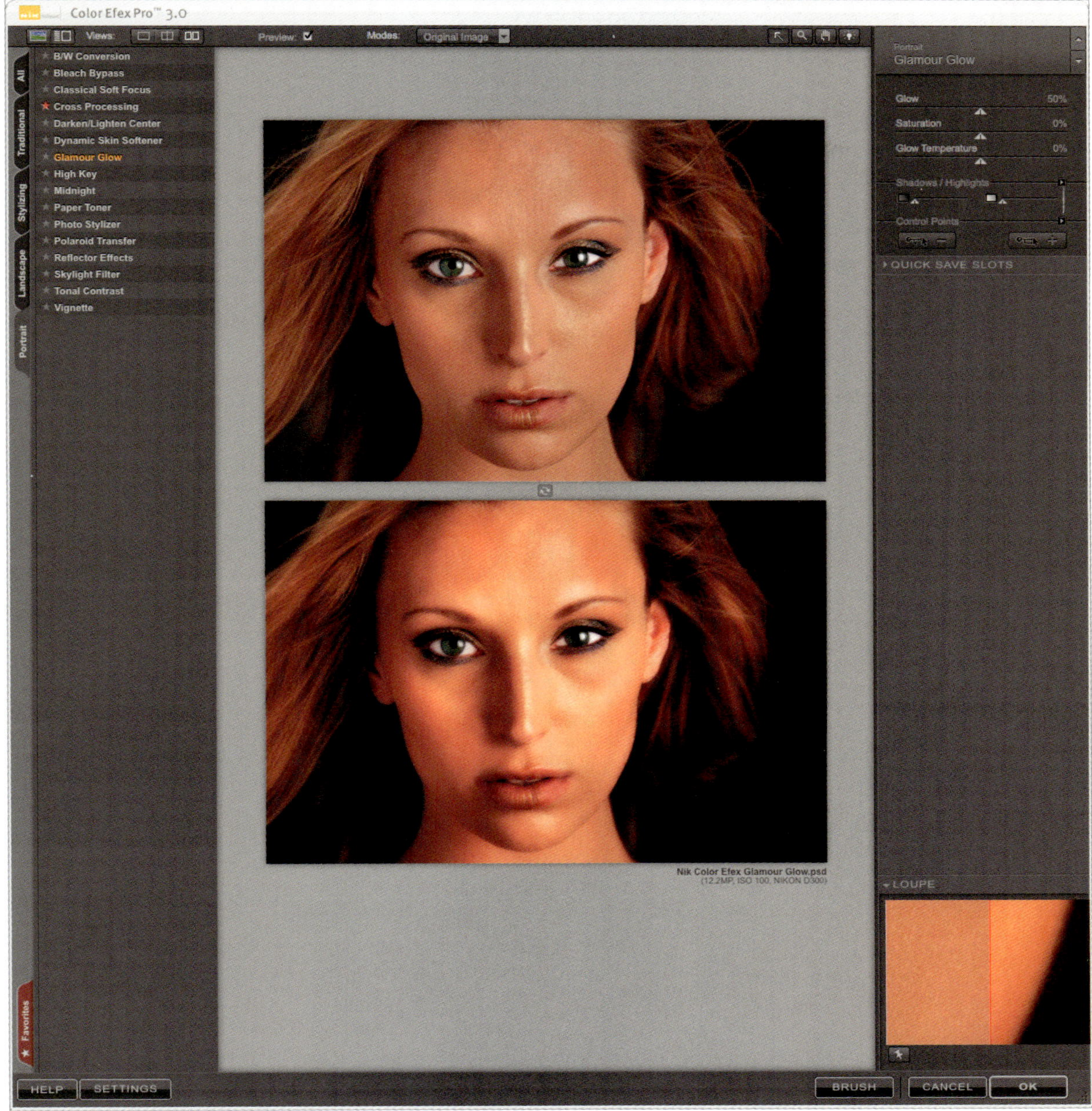

▲ Nik's Color Efex Pro 3.0 filter pack is one of the most extensive third-party filter add-ons for Photoshop. This product also works with Lightroom and Nikon Capture NX. I use Color Efex almost every day in my creative Photoshop work. While this collection of filters is designed for a great deal more than portraiture, there are a number of filters included that work well with portraits—for example, the Glamour Glow filter shown here.

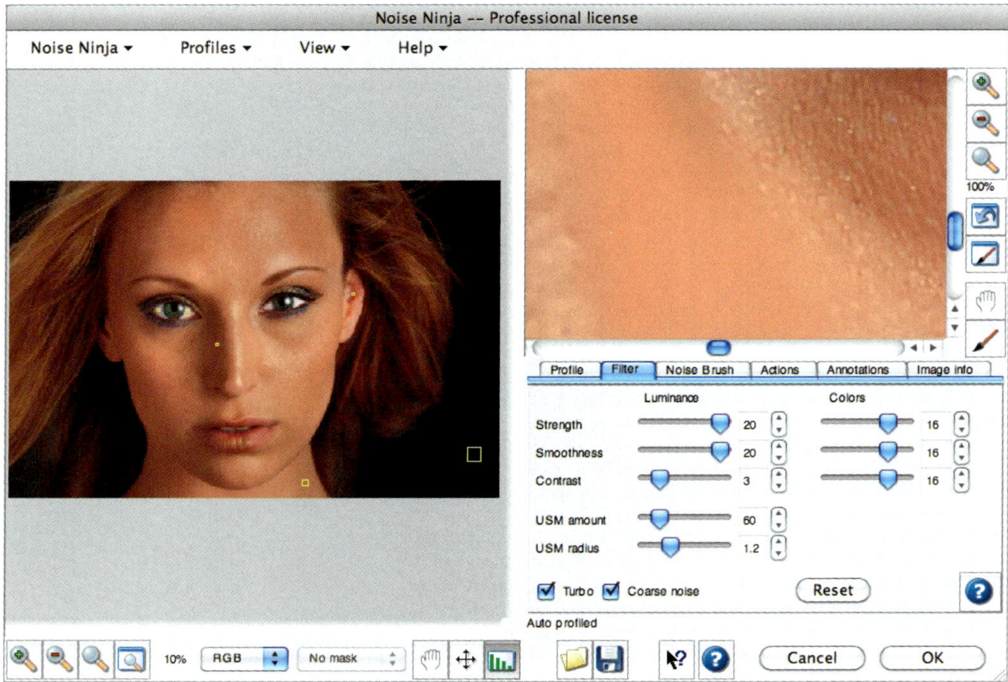

▲ PictureCode's Noise Ninja can be used at extreme settings (like the ones shown here) to remove noise in order to smooth skin, though you don't want to apply the smoothing to an entire image because details such as eyes and eyebrows will lose sharpness. There's an attractive naturalness to smoothing with Noise Ninja that is hard to get with other options.

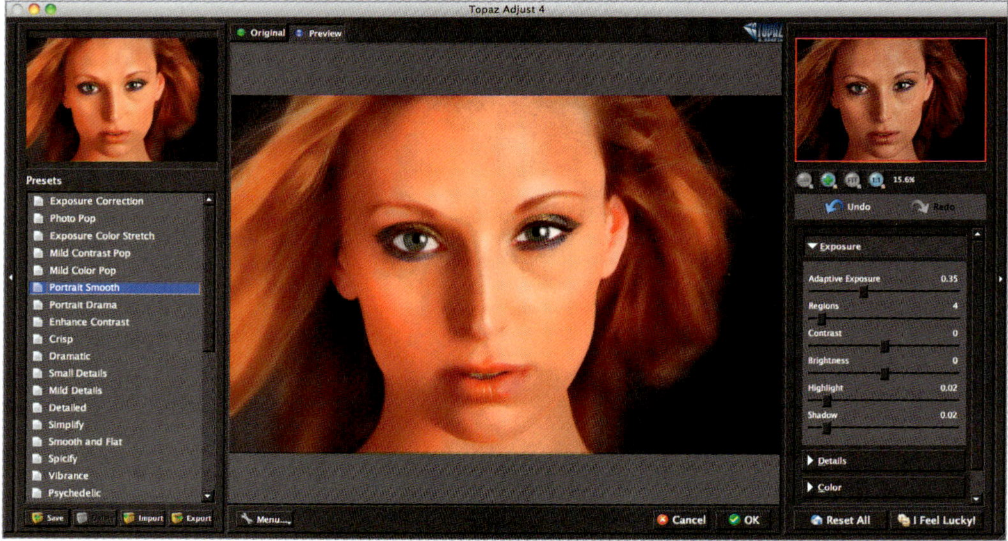

▲ The Adjust 4 Photoshop plugin by Topaz includes many useful filters and presets that you can customize and save, including several intended specifically for use with portraits.

- Adding a blur can be an effective way of rendering soft skin without a great deal of effort. I chose Filter ► Blur ► Gaussian Blur in Photoshop to apply the Gaussian Blur shown here, using a radius setting of 9 pixels.

  Usually, I use layers, masking, and the Brush Tool to paint in areas to create a selective focus effect rather than treating an entire image with Gaussian Blur.

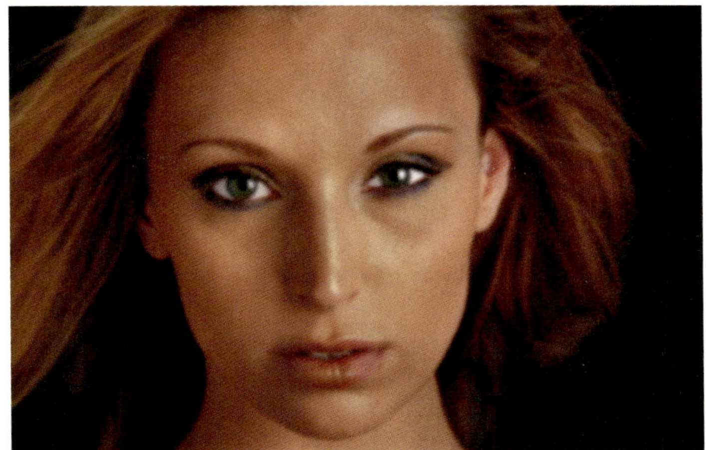

- It sometimes surprises people to learn that adding noise can improve some portraits by increasing definition in areas such as cheeks. To add the noise shown in this example, I chose Noise ► Add Noise in Photoshop and set the Amount to 26%.

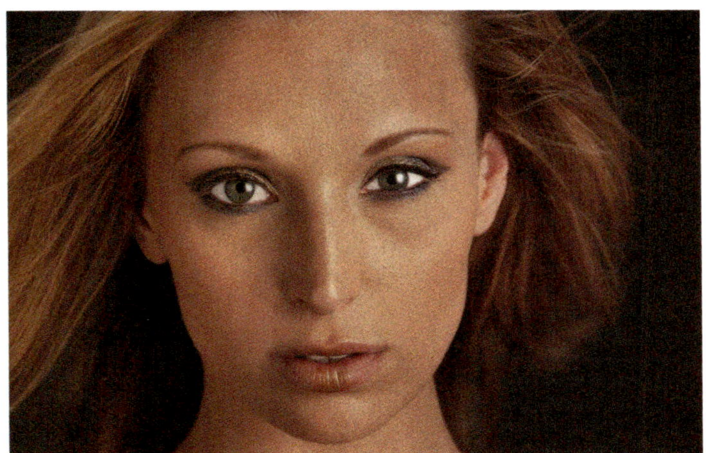

- This example shows Imagenomic's Photoshop Portraiture plugin at work using the Smoothing High preset. You can see that it does indeed smooth the entire portrait, including the skin and hair.

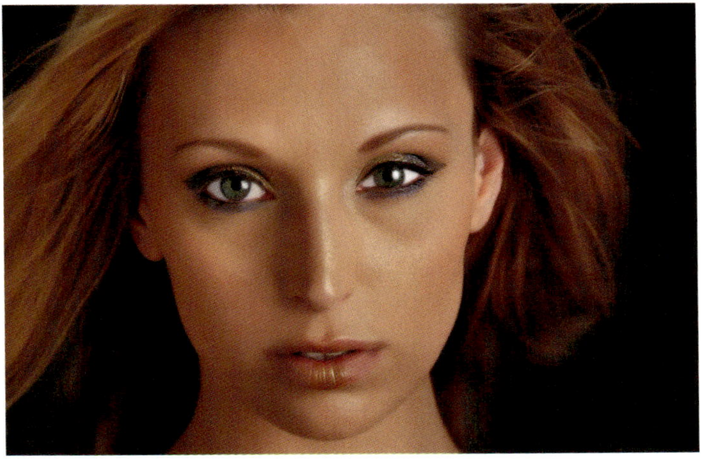

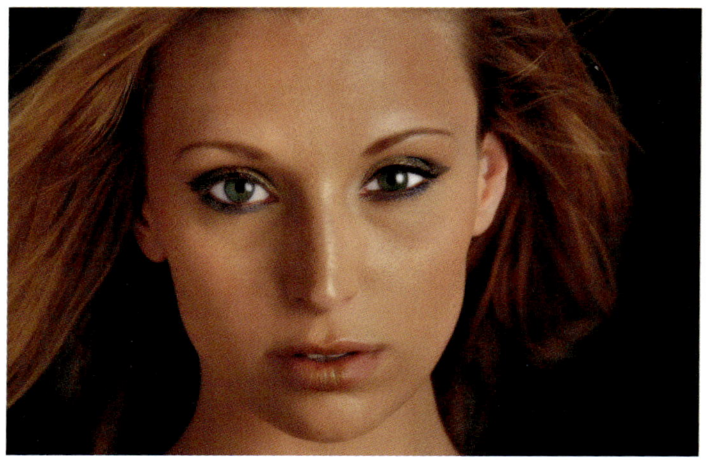

This example shows the Enhance Glamour preset from Imagenomic's Photoshop Portraiture plugin. This preset smooths while evening out skin tones to create a more uniform look.

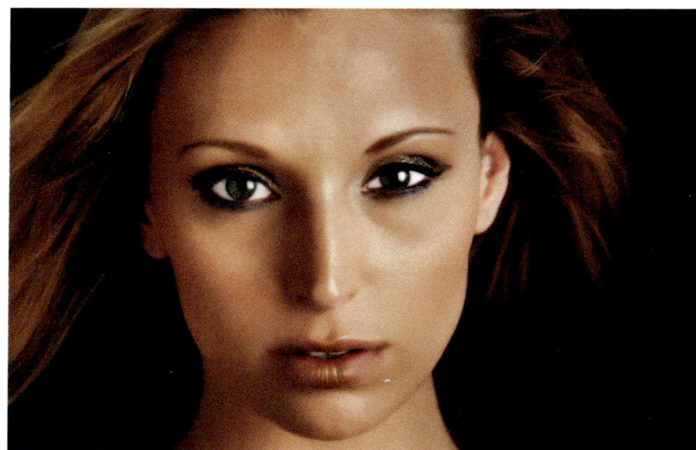

The Glamour Glow filter in Nik's Color Efex Pro 3.0 filter pack is one of my favorite portrait enhancements, but it needs to be used in moderation, usually at about 25% opacity. This filter smooths while also increasing the contrast between lights and darks in the portrait.

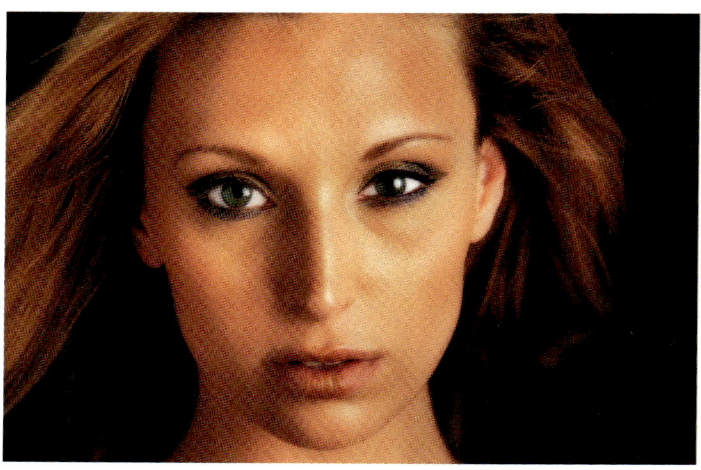

Removing noise often serves to smooth flesh areas in a portrait as shown here using PictureCode's Noise Ninja. However, this is generally not a good effect to apply uniformly to a photo, because you'll lose sharpness and details. So when I use noise removal for smoothing, I always apply it selectively using layer masks and the Brush Tool.

- The Topaz Labs Adjust plugin provides a number of useful filters and presets, including the Portrait Smooth filter shown here. This filter adds softening around the edges, picks up the highlights, and adds a warmer tone to the entire image.

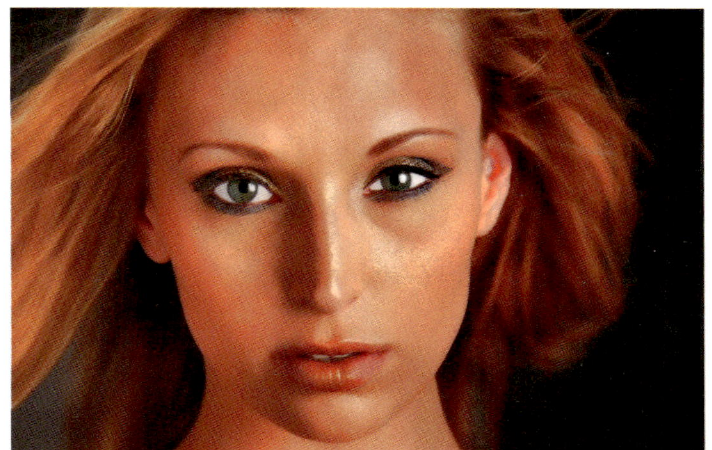

- The Portrait Drama filter from Topaz Labs adds an edgy quality to an image. Highlights and shine are increased while the overall image is slightly desaturated.

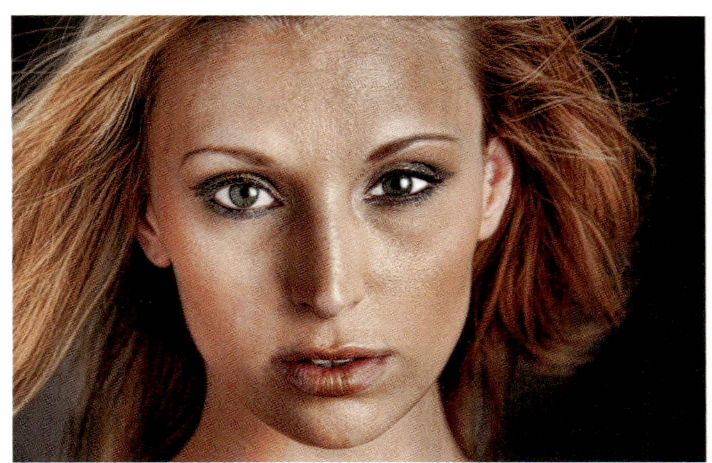

- The Smooth and Flat filter from Topaz Labs softens the area around the face with blurring, smooths out skin tones, and reduces highlights.

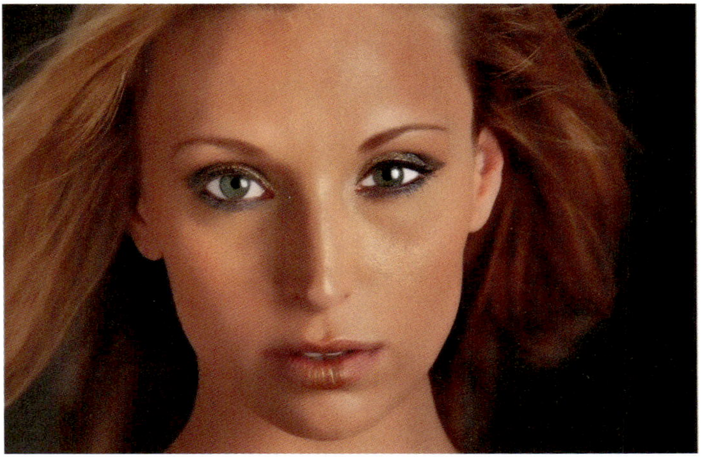

Enhancing Eyes

From the very beginning of this book I've made it clear that eyes have a special place in portraiture. If you get the eyes right, probably everything else will fall into place. Therefore, you need to pay special attention to eyes when you are post-processing your photos, particularly in images where the primary impact is glamorous.

Here's the checklist of things to observe for possible work, along with some suggestions about how to proceed.

- Make sure the iris of the eye appears colorful and translucent—however, the pupil can stay black and opaque. You can lighten the iris by blending a Photoshop layer with itself in Screen blending mode, adding a layer mask, then carefully partially painting in the areas that should be brighter.
- Beware of eye whites that show too much red. This can be highly unattractive. The best approach to fixing this problem is to paint over the eye whites with your color set to white and a partly opaque brush. There's a balancing act here: some red veins are normal and you don't want to remove them all, but eyes that are too red seem tired and unattractive.
- Even the most well applied make-up can show flaws up close. Pay particular attention to mascara and eye-liner. Correct these cosmetic problems using cloning.
- Contact lenses are fine, but you don't want them to show in your portrait. Contact lenses often leave a small circular line in the eye whites around the iris. You may have to look hard to see this line in the eyes on top to the right. Paint out this line with a white brush, or use the Clone Tool.

One other point: the catch lights, or highlight reflections, in an eye are often what gives an eye sparkle and interest. I sometimes use a white paint brush to add a little more life to a catch light. While this effect can be overdone, in moderation it can enhance portraits a great deal.

▼ Lauren's right eye after retouching but before the catch light has been adjusted.

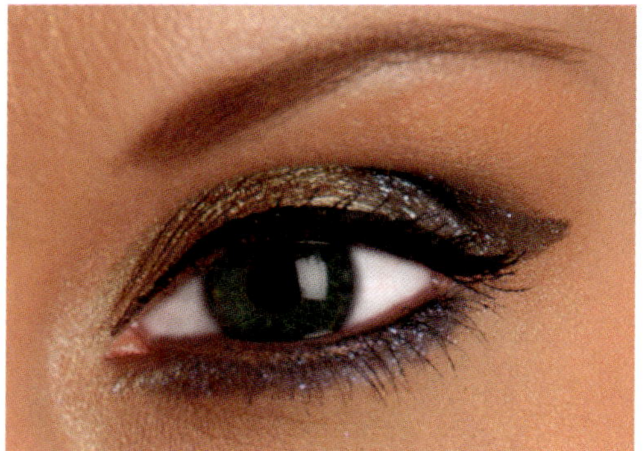

▼ The eye after the catch light has been painted using white with a brush at a low opacity setting.

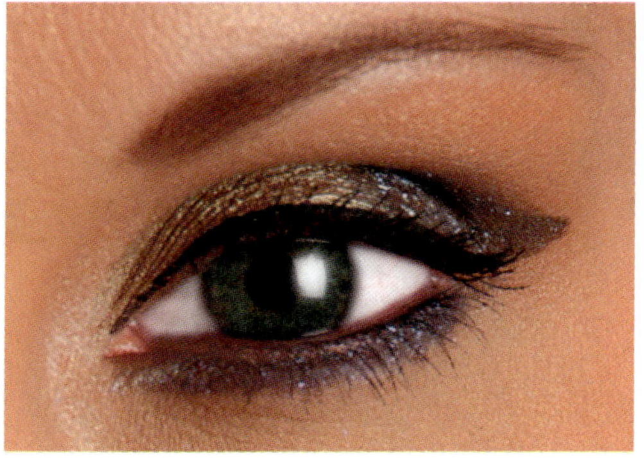

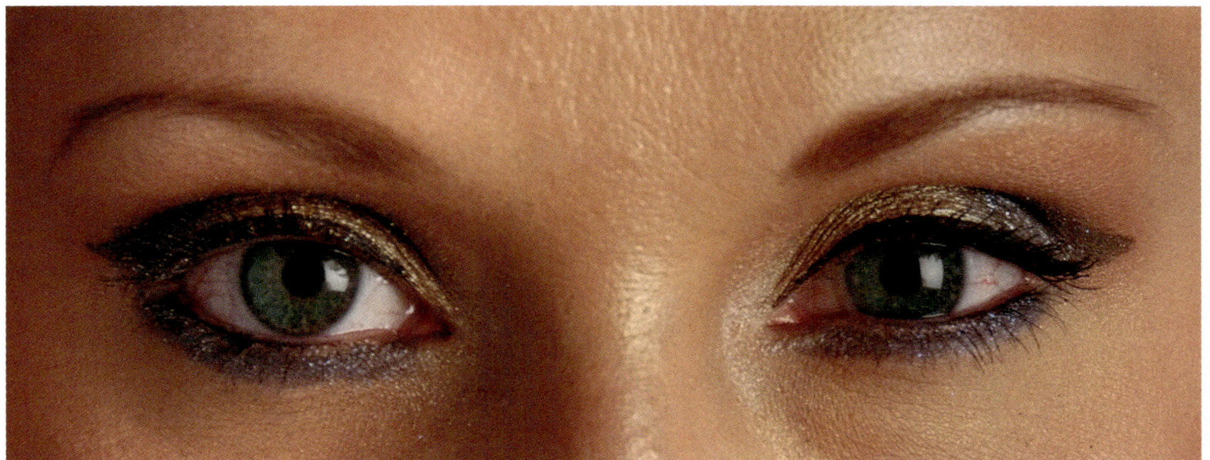

▲ Before starting work on Lauren's eyes, the whites were bloodshot and the edges of her contact lenses showed. Also, the eyes lacked a sparkly luster.

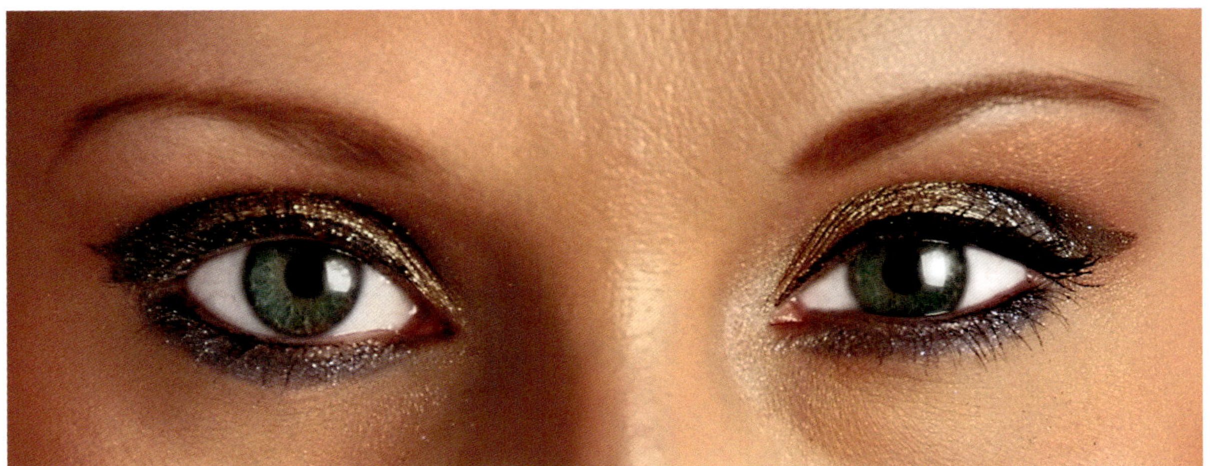

▲ After working on Lauren's eyes, the whites are clear, the contact lens edges are gone, and the catch light from the studio soft box in each eye has been brightened by painting in with additional white at about 20% opacity.

▼ Pages 220–221: To enhance this studio shot, I first removed flaws as explained on pages 206–209. Next, I enhanced the model's eyes. Finally, I applied a variety of effects to help improve the skin and the drama of the image. I used Noise Ninja applied selectively to smooth the skin in a flattering way. Nik Color Efex Pro's Glamour Glow at about 20% and Topaz Adjust's Portrait Smooth filter at about 30% were the finishing touches.

120mm, 1/160 of a second at f/7.1 and ISO 100, hand held

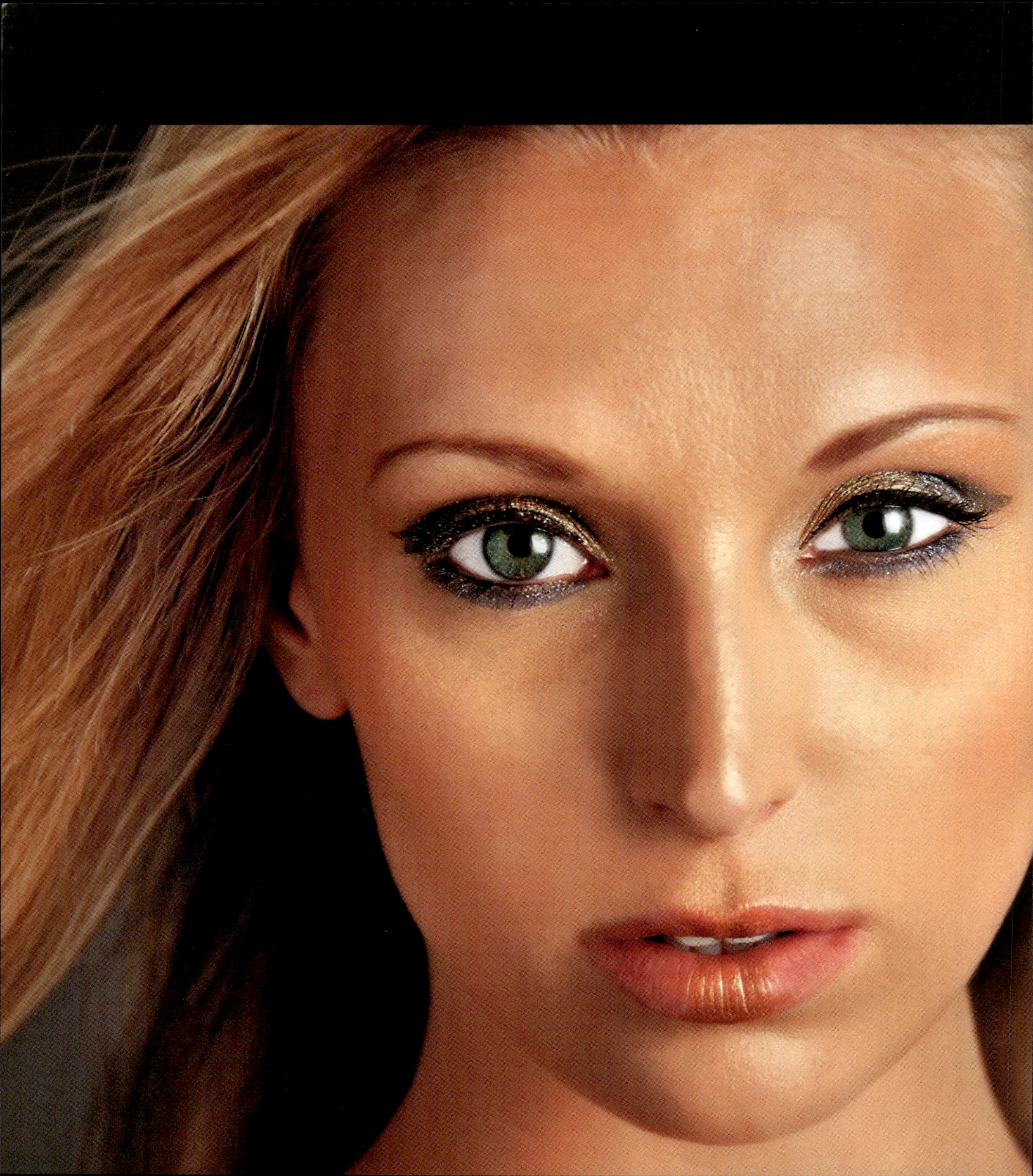

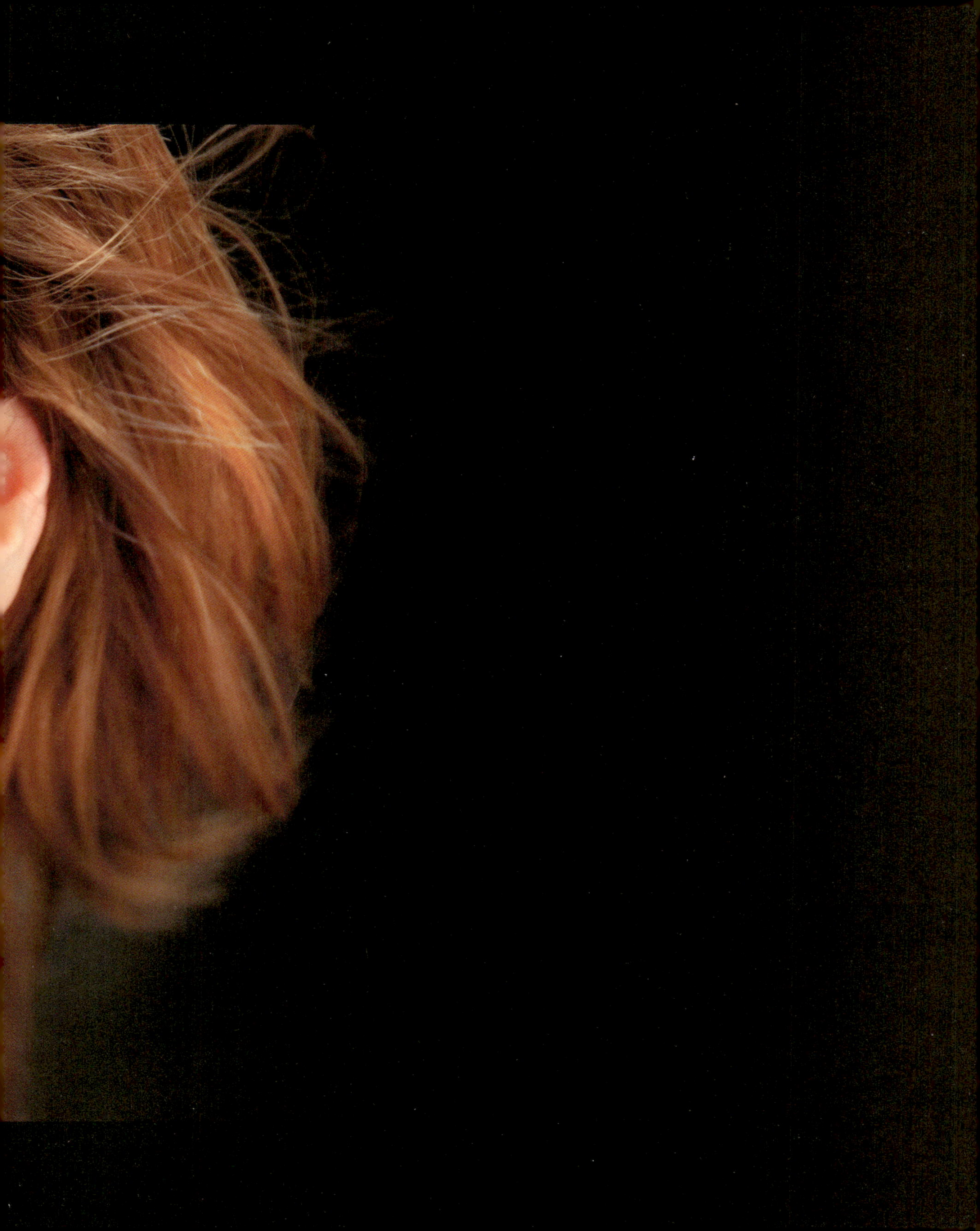

Selective Sharpening

There are many techniques for sharpening photos that work quite well. For example, you'll find five different sharpening filters on the Photoshop Filter menu alone. In addition, recent versions of Adobe Camera RAW (ACR) provide very effective sharpening.

However, when it comes to portraiture, I like to do sharpening a little differently. Before I explain, let me note that there are two kinds of sharpening, done either:

- To appropriately prepare an image for a specific output device or printer so that the photo will look its best.
- To enhance the visual appeal of an image without regard to output devices.

This discussion applies to the second of these goals, enhancing the visual appeal of a photo, and not sharpening for output.

Whatever method of sharpening you use—and Photoshop's Smart Sharpen is not bad—the most important thing is to apply the sharpening selectively. This means applying the sharpening effect to a duplicate layer, adding a layer mask, and painting in the areas you want to sharpen. When it comes to portraits, I suggest sharpening the eyes and maybe a few strands of hair—and leaving the rest of the portrait alone.

My preferred sharpening method that I'll show you here is to use the LAB color space to only sharpen monochromatic information. I believe that leaving the color information alone leads to sharpening that seems pleasing—and doesn't look artificially over-sharpened. Here's how it works.

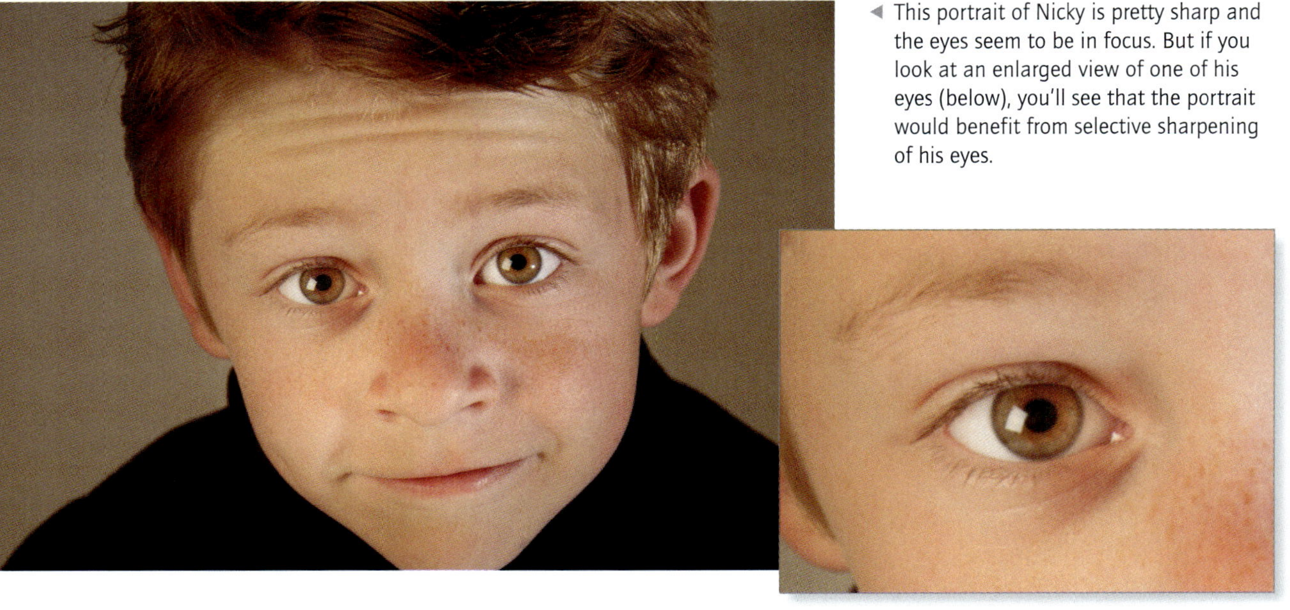

◄ This portrait of Nicky is pretty sharp and the eyes seem to be in focus. But if you look at an enlarged view of one of his eyes (below), you'll see that the portrait would benefit from selective sharpening of his eyes.

▶ Step 1: Convert the image to LAB color by selecting Edit ► Convert to Profile.

In the Convert to Profile dialog choose LAB Color as the Destination Space. Make sure the Engine is set to Adobe (ACE), the Intent is set to Relative Colormetric, and Use Black Point Compensation is checked. Then, click OK.

Note: Once you have selected the conversion settings in this dialog box, you won't need to set them again. In the future you'll be able to quickly convert to LAB by choosing Image ► Mode ► Lab Color.

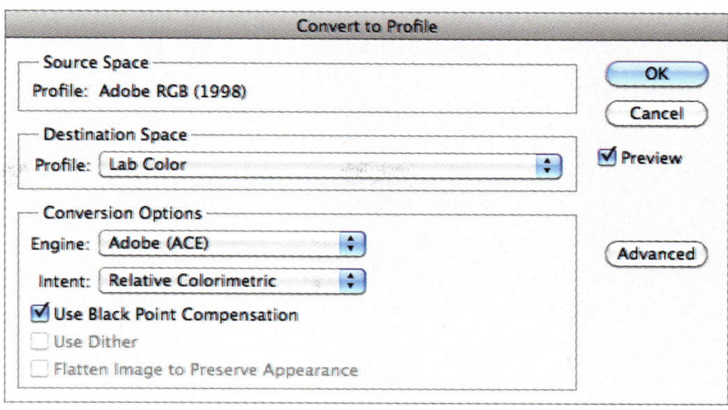

▶ Step 2: Choose Layer ► Duplicate Layer to duplicate the Background layer. Name the new layer "Sharpening."

▶ Step 3: In the Channels palette, click the Lightness channel to select it.

The Lightness channel contains the monochromatic information in the image, and no color information. All the channels should be visible (as shown by the eyeball icons in the left-hand column), but only the Lightness channel should be selected.

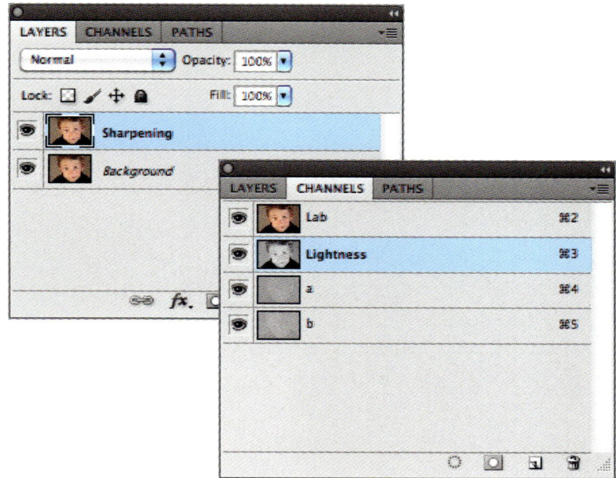

▶ Step 4: Make sure the "Sharpening" layer in the Layers palette is selected, and then choose Filter ► Sharpen ► Unsharp Mask. The Unsharp Mask dialog box will open.

For eyes in portraits, I suggest starting by first setting the Threshold to 9 levels and the Radius to 4.2 pixels. Then, play with the Amount slider; I usually set it between 50% and 100%.

Trial and error will show you what works best. The Unsharp Mask is a relatively old sharpening technique that primarily works on the lines that are at the edges of shapes, and creates very attractive sharpening when applied—not too heavily—to the Lightness channel.

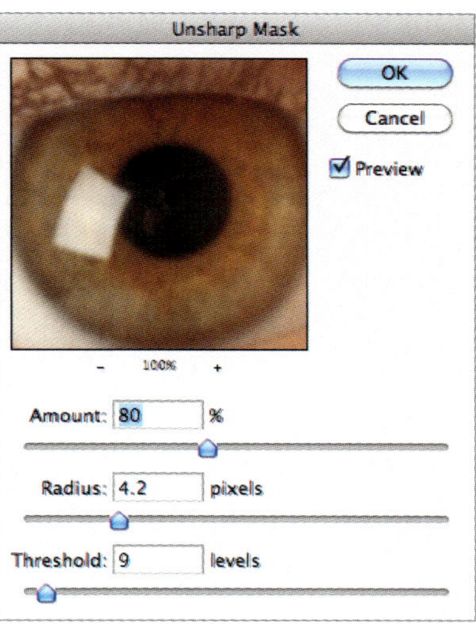

▶ Step 5: Choose Layer ▸ Layer Mask ▸ Hide All to add a black Hide All layer mask to the "Sharpening" layer.

The Hide All layer mask will hide the "Sharpening" layer. The layer mask will appear as a black thumbnail in the Layers palette.

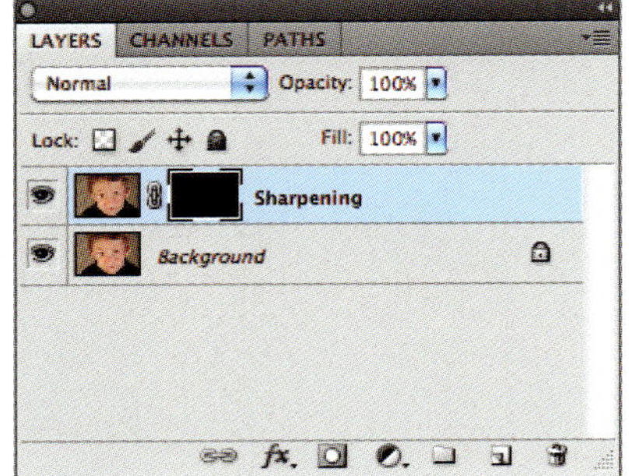

▶ Step 6: Select the Brush Tool from the Toolbox and use the Options Bar to set the brush to 100% Opacity and 100% Flow. Then set the Foreground color to white.

▶ Step 7: With the layer mask selected in the Layers palette, use the Brush Tool to paint in the eyes. As you paint, the thumbnail on the Layers palette will show what you have painted.

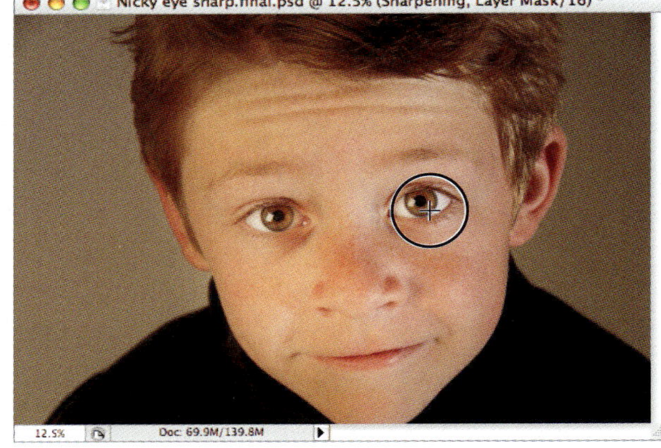

▼ Step 8: Choose Layer ▸ Flatten Image to merge the two layers together.

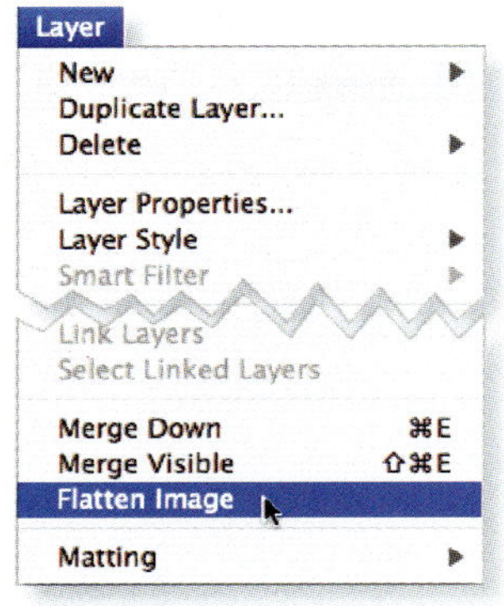

▼ Step 9: Select Image ▸ Mode ▸ RGB Color to return the image to the RGB color space.

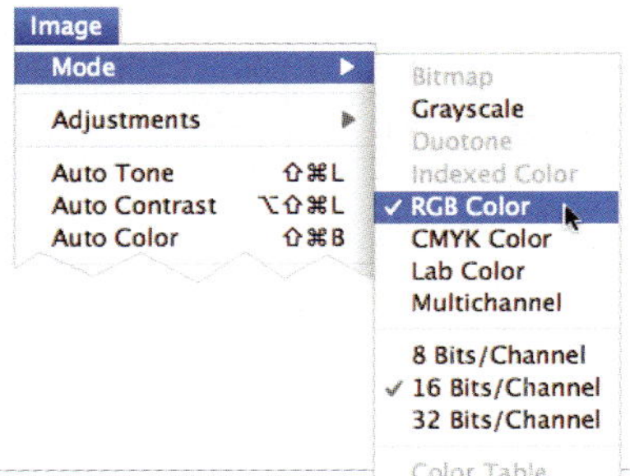

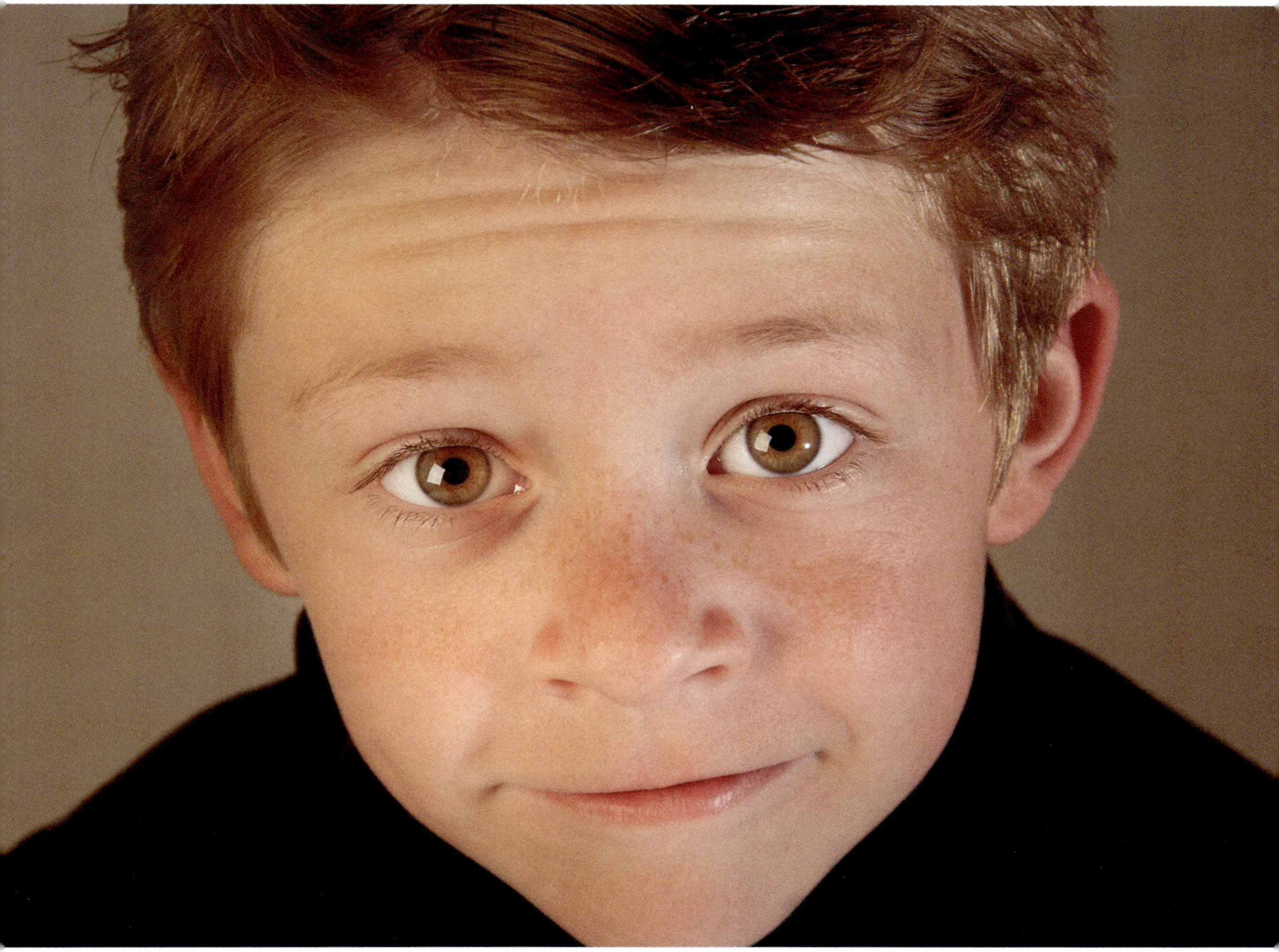

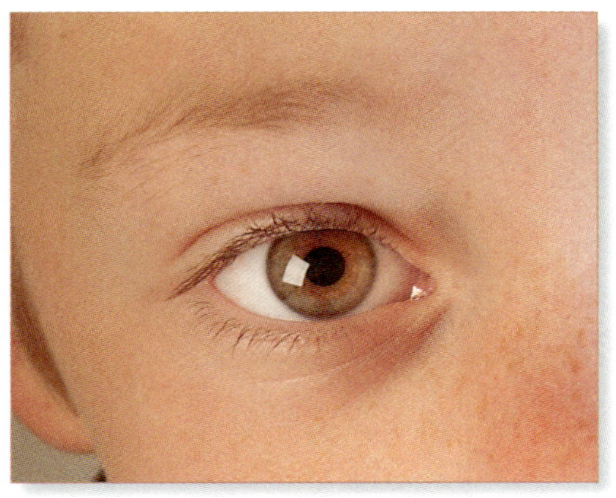

▲ The most prominent feature in this studio portrait of Nicky is his eyes. Therefore, I used selective sharpening of the Lightness channel to emphasize the visual appeal and impact of Nicky's eyes.

If you compare the enlarged view of Nicky's sharpened eye (left) with the enlarged view shown on page 222, you'll see that the LAB sharpening has really made his eye look crisp.

95mm, 1/160 of a second at f/11 and ISO 100, hand held

Black and White

Black and white photography is a great art form that is intertwined with the history of photography, dating from a time in which monochrome was all there was. Today, the situation is different. Photographers choose digital black and white as a matter of conviction and for artistic reasons, not because they have to.

There are a number of consequences of the changing role of monochromatic photography. No longer do you have to shoot solely in black and white. But you do need to know how to see in monochrome, when to use monochrome as a creative expression, and how to use the software that is available to convert color images to monochrome. High-quality digital monochromatic photos start as RAW files, are processed using the full color information in the files, and then converted with energy and subtlety to monochrome.

Each of these topics is important, and covered extensively in my book *Creative Black & White: Digital Photography Tips & Techniques* (Wiley, 2010).

When thinking about monochrome in the context of portraiture bear in mind that black and white imparts a certain gravitas. The intentional choice of a medium associated with the history of photography and art carries some weight. In an age of point-and-shoot digital cameras, not all photos work well with this treatment. For example, it doesn't make sense in most cases to present family snapshots monochromatically.

For the most part, monochromatic photos are simulations, being actually RGB or CMYK files that have been made to look as if they were monochrome. This is an exciting state of affairs—but one with some risk. If you are presenting a number of monochromatic images, many of the treatments that can easily be applied, such as simulating toning, can clash with other monochromatic treatments. You may have better results applying the same finishing touches to all monochromatic photos in a group.

Ultimately, black and white can be very satisfying, because it reduces compositions to the basic elements of lines, and the spectrum from light to dark. In portraiture, without color you see the facial planes clearly and are not distracted by color. Even so, there should be an aesthetic justification for the choice of monochrome—since in today's digital world it is an intentional choice.

▶ To create this monochromatic portrait, I started with the RAW file. Prior to converting the image, I adjusted the exposure, fixed the flaws, and worked on the skin. To convert the photo to black and white, in Photoshop I used two Black & White adjustment layers. The bottom half of the image was converted using the High Contrast Red Filter preset, and the top half using the Green Filter preset. The two layers were combined using a layer mask and a gradient.

150mm, 1/160 of a second at f/7.1 and ISO 100, tripod mounted

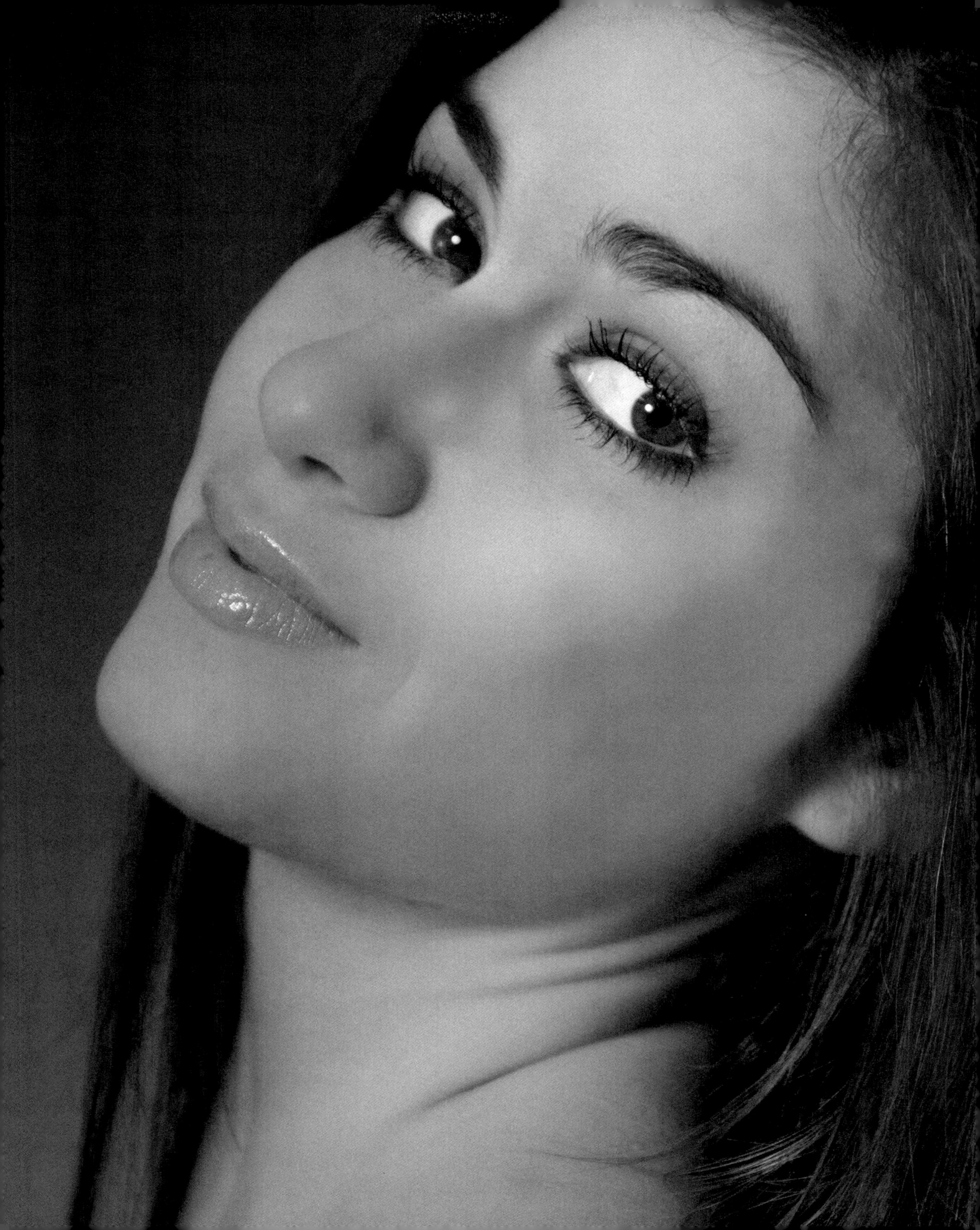

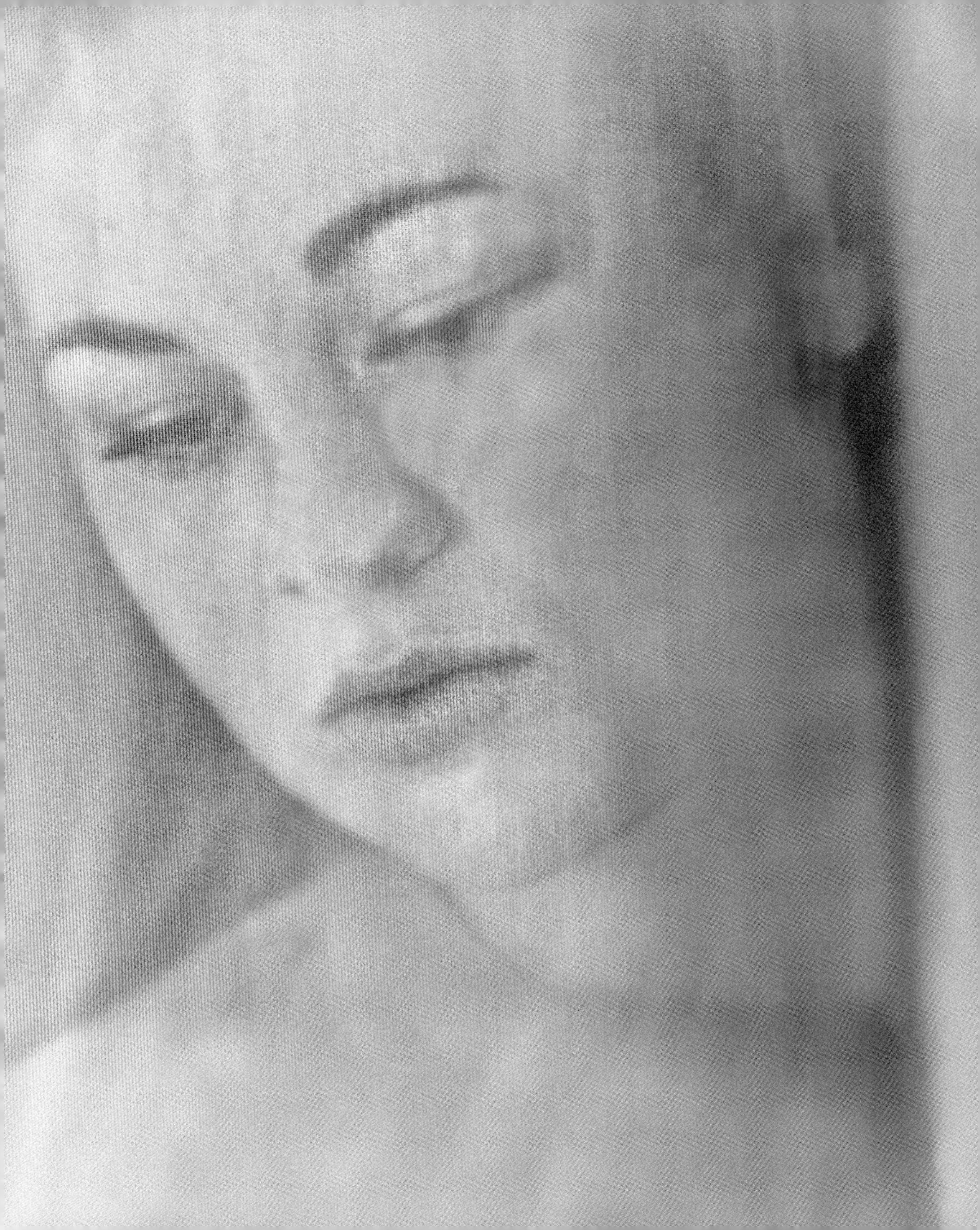

◀ The color version of this shot is on page 13. Since the version on page 13 doesn't have much color range in any case, and because I planned to soften the image in a monochromatic conversion, I thought this image was a great candidate for monochrome. It's a very cool thing about digital photography that you can process a single image in multiple ways. There's no longer a choice of either color or monochrome because you can have it both ways.

200mm, 1/160 of a second at f/11 and ISO 100, hand held

▶ When I processed this photo, my goal was to create a monochromatic image that showed the contrast between the highly textured rope on the right and the portrait on the left. My strategy was both to smooth out the portrait and increase the contrast in the rope.

To start with, while still working in color I added a selectively applied layer using Imagenomic's Portraiture set to Smoothing High. This created a more even texture in the facial structure. Next, I applied the Psychedelic filter from Topaz Adjust to the rope area of the photo at about 35% opacity.

To convert to monochrome I used a layered approach by combining the filters within Nik Silver Efex. The bottom layer is Antique Plate; next Soft Skin is applied selectively to flesh areas; next the Neutral filter is applied at about 40% opacity; and finally, on the top of the layer stack, I applied High Structure to the rope (but not the face).

As a final step, I used Silver Efex to add some virtual selenium toning and a small amount of pseudo film grain.

200mm, 1/125 of a second at f/8 and ISO 100, hand held

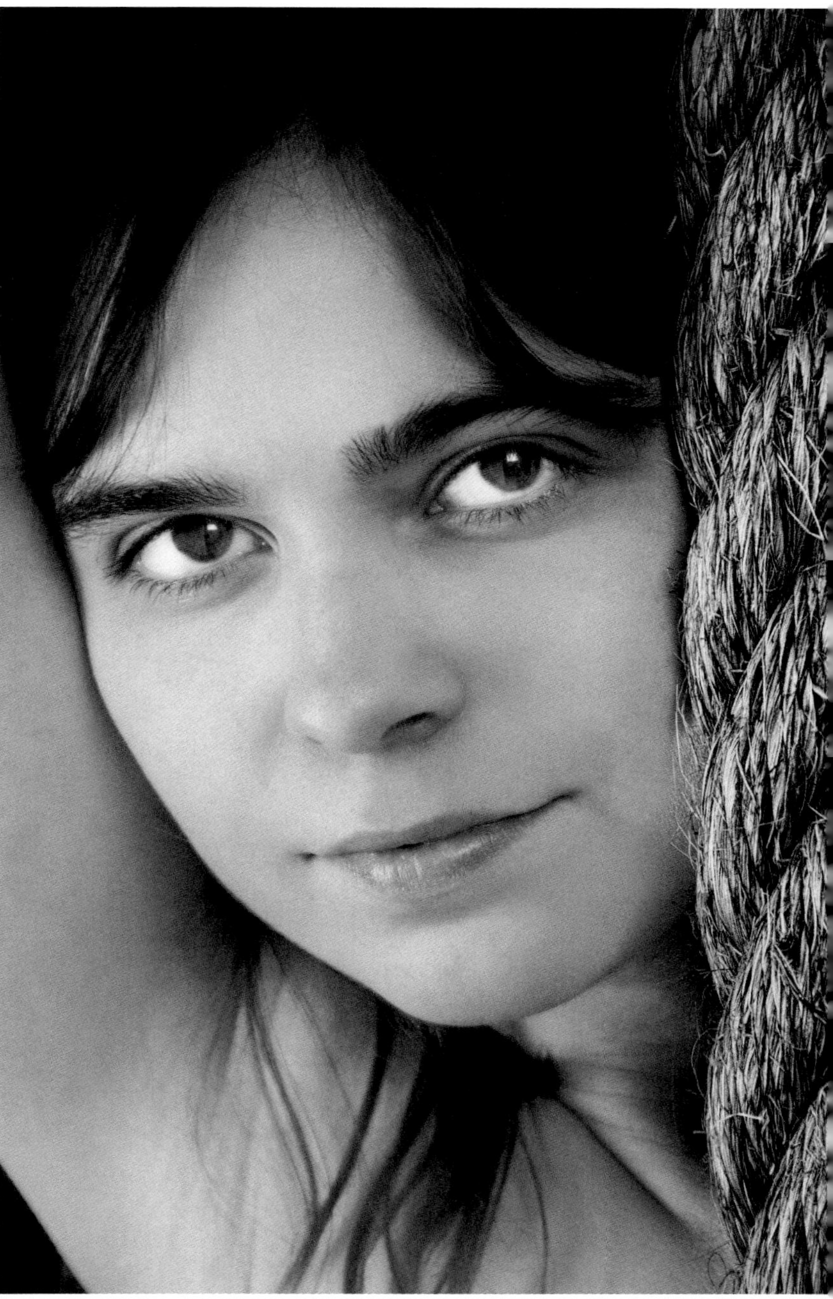

LAB Color Inversions

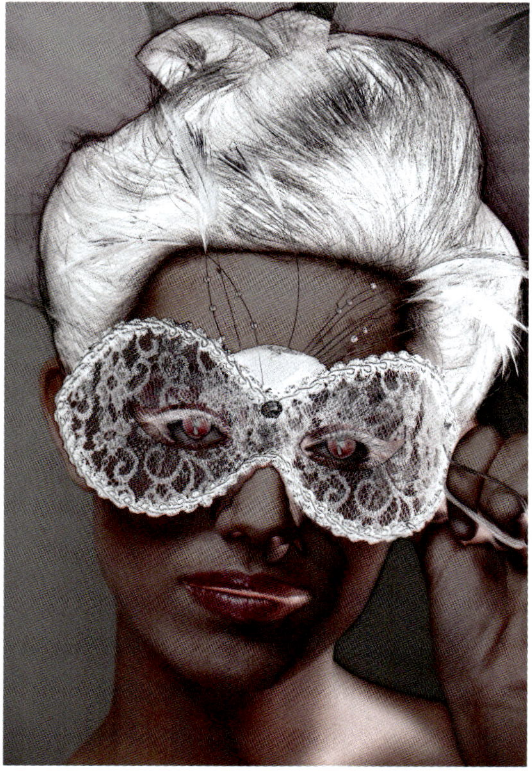

▲ I created this special effect by using LAB color to invert the luminance information contained in the photo. Essentially, this means swapping white for black, and black for white—with truly neutral gray staying gray. You can see the original version of the photo before the effect was applied on page 6.

135mm, 1/160 of a second at f/8 and ISO 100, hand held

▶ This was a pretty typical studio shot of a model dressed in a white camisole on a white background. In Photoshop, I used LAB color to invert the L channel to create the special effect you see. Black has become white, and white has become black. The world of a gorgeous model is now strange and eerie.

200mm, 1/160 of a second at f/9 and ISO 100, hand held

There are many ways to apply special effects in Photoshop. It's fun to experiment with the many filters that come with Photoshop—and there are also a great many third-party filters. For more information about third-party filters specifically designed for use with portraiture, see the samples on pages 210–217 and page 235 in the Resources section.

Personally, when it comes to special effects, I often like to go back to basics. There's a great deal you can do in Photoshop using simple concepts like color spaces, channels, and adjustments. One of my favorite techniques—shown in the examples here—is to invert a channel in LAB color. Sometimes this is an easy way to create fantastic special effects—and it is all up to your own creativity when using these simple techniques, not the pre-packaged visual ideas from a software vendor.

Using a special effect in portrait photography is not for everybody, or for every photo. Sometimes straightforward is best. But when you are in the mood to reverse colors and create fantastic creatures where before there were only humans, consider playing with some of the myriad options available in Photoshop—and specifically with the creative color control that the LAB color space gives you.

You'll find complete information about creatively using LAB color in my *Photoshop Darkroom* books (see page 234).

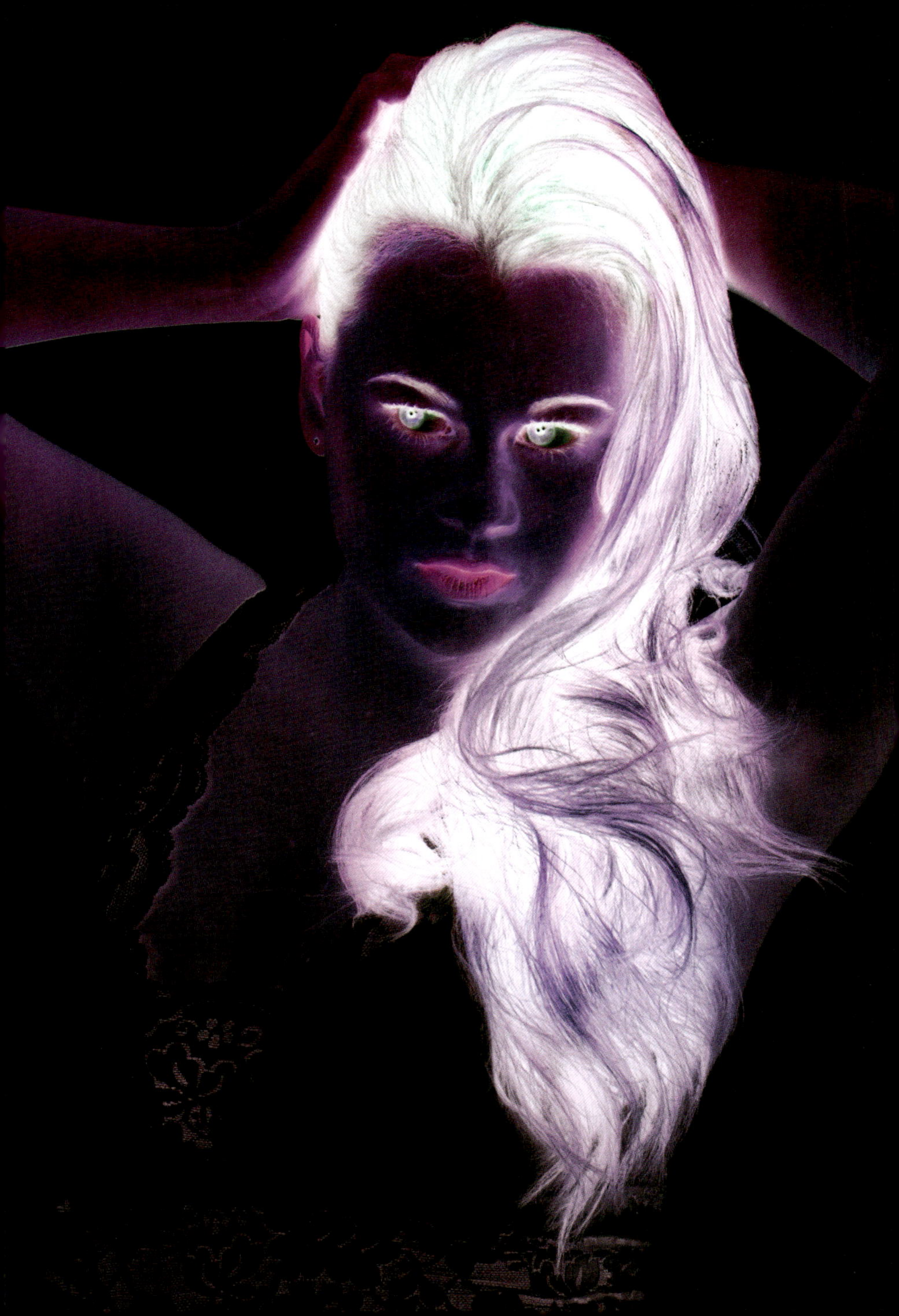

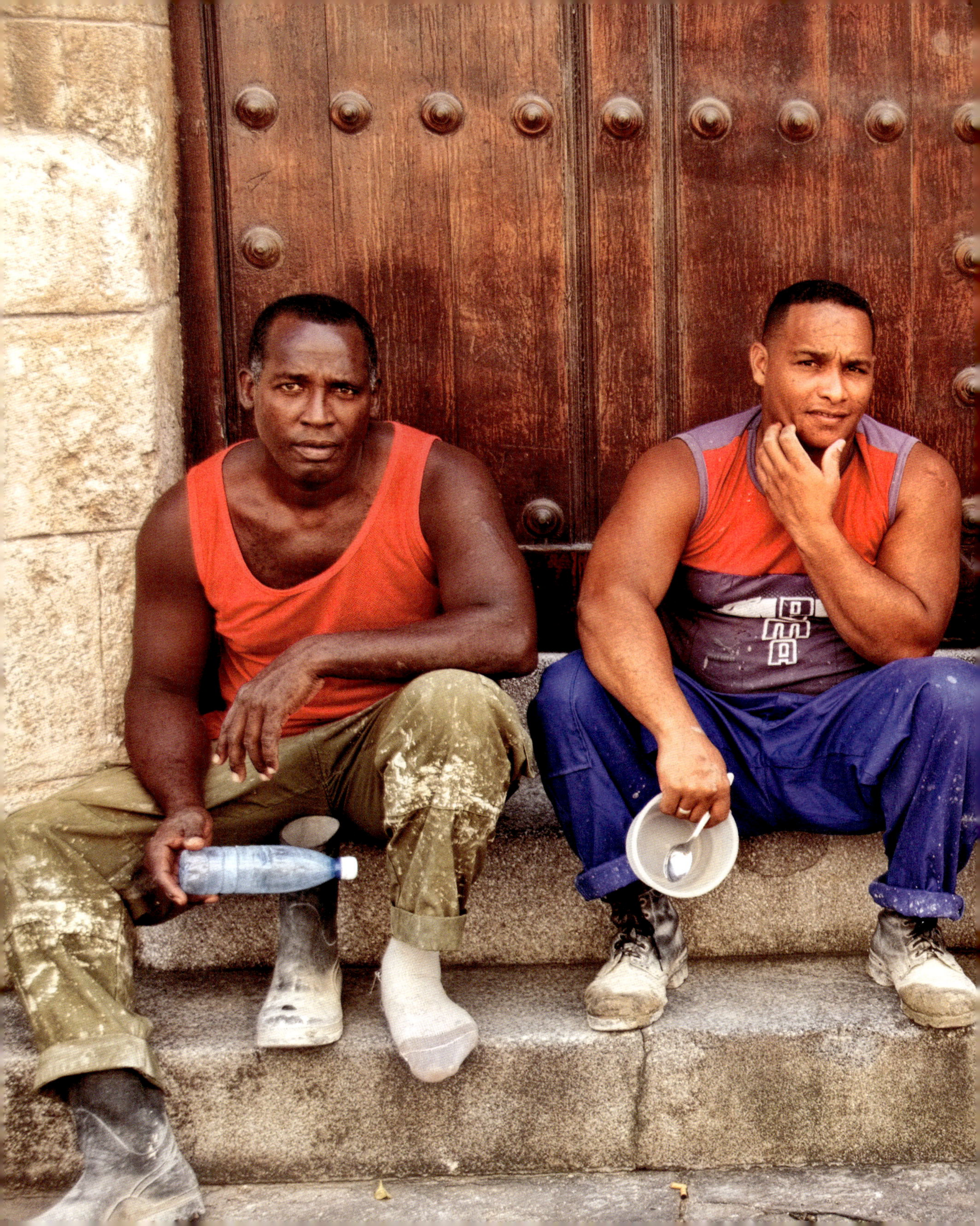

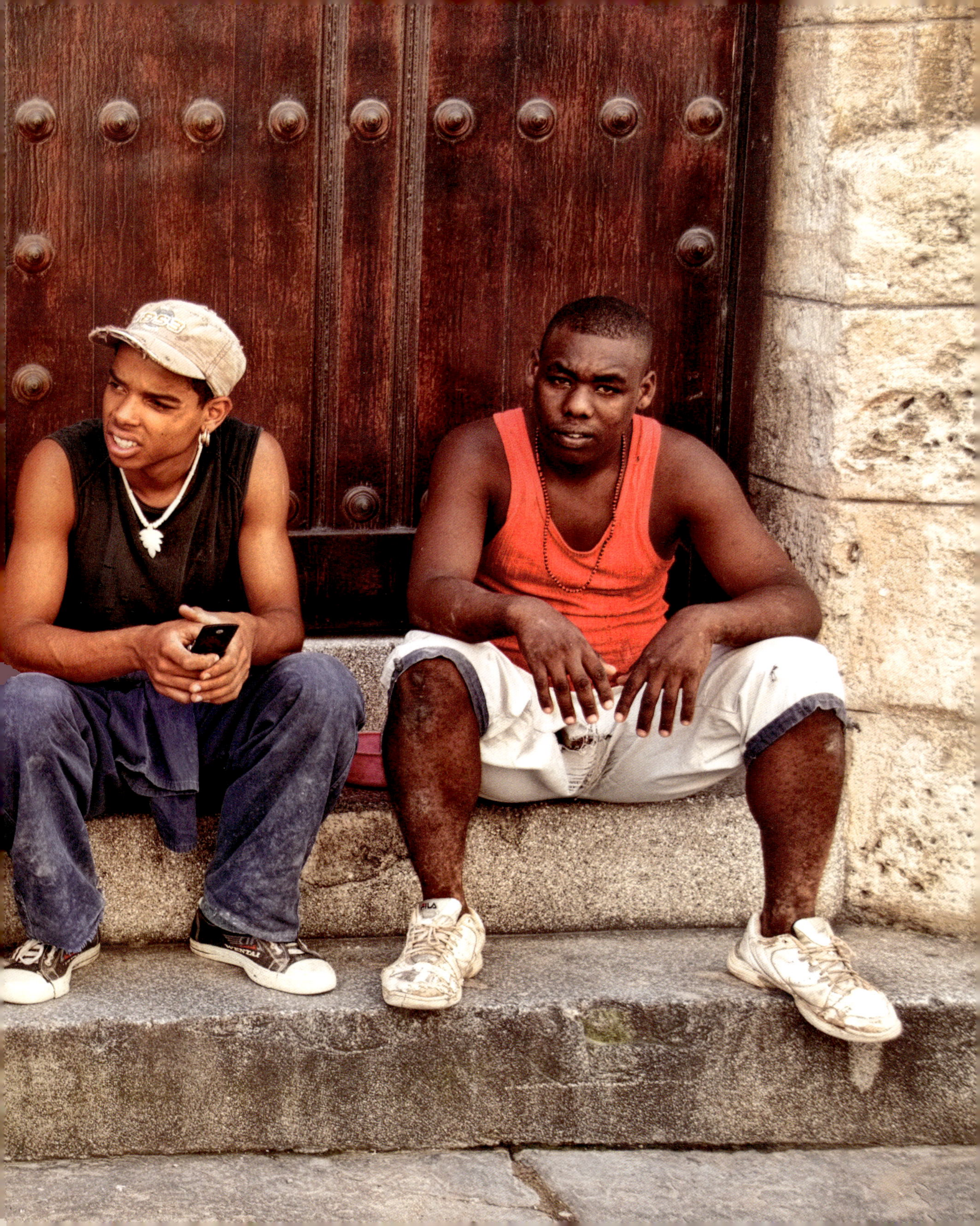
FILA

Notes and Resources

Further Reading

If you've enjoyed *Creative Portraits: Digital Photography Tips & Techniques,* I think you'll also find some of my other books useful because they cover areas of photography related to portraiture that I don't explain in detail in this book, particularly:

Creative Black & White: Digital Tips & Techniques (Wiley, 2010)

Creative Composition: Digital Tips & Techniques (Wiley, 2010)

Creative Lighting: Digital Tips & Techniques (Wiley, 2011)

Practical Artistry: Light & Exposure for Digital Photographers (O'Reilly, 2008)

One of the best ways to learn about portrait photography is to look at the work of great portrait photographers. I'd suggest taking a look at the work of Richard Avedon, Henri Cartier-Bresson, Arnold Newman, and Irving Penn. Some specific books I recommend are:

Richard Avedon: Photographs 1946–2004 (Louisiana Museum of Modern Art, 2007)

Henri Cartier-Bresson: The Modern Century (Museum of Modern Art, New York, 2010)

Arnold Newman (Louisiana Museum of Modern Art, 2007)

Irving Penn Portraits (Abrams, 2010)

You might also want to take a look at the following collection of interesting and effective portraits:

Vanity Fair: The Portraits: A Century of Iconic Images (Abrams, 2008)

There are many how-to books aimed at professional photographers and serious amateurs that explain studio portraiture and flash and strobe-lighting techniques. Among these books, my top picks are:

Michael Greco, *Lighting and the Dramatic Portrait: The Art of Celebrity and Editorial Photography* (Amphoto, 2006)

Joe McNally, *The Hot Shoe Diaries: Big Light from Small Flashes* (New Riders Press, 2009)

Kirk Tuck, *Minimalist Lighting: Professional Techniques for Studio Photography* (Amherst Media, 2009)

You'll also find Lee Varis's excellent book *Skin: The Complete Guide to Digitally Lighting, Photographing, and Retouching Faces and Bodies*, 2nd Edition (Sybex, 2010) very useful. *Skin* goes into great detail about lighting and how to effectively post-process the human epidermis (and eyes and hair and so on). Highly recommended.

Learning Photoshop

Creative Portraits: Digital Tips & Techniques is not a book about Photoshop—it's a book about learning how to see and photograph people. That said, some of the book is concerned with finding the best strategy in Photoshop to process and retouch specific images in a way that lives up to your expectations when the image was pre-visualized.

I've tried to include enough Photoshop information so that you can use the techniques with your own photos.

At the same time, I haven't included information on basic Photoshop techniques. If you need to brush up on Photoshop concepts and techniques, I think you might find one of my other books helpful. Please check out *The Photoshop Darkroom: Creative Digital Post-Processing* (Focal Press, 2010) and *The Photoshop Darkroom 2: Creative Digital Transformations* (Focal Press, 2011).

Sensor Size and Focal Length

Not all sensors are the same size. The smaller the sensor, the closer a given focal length lens brings you to your subject. For example, if a sensor has half the area of another sensor, then a specific focal length lens will bring you twice as close on a camera with the smaller sensor.

Since different cameras have different sized sensors, it is not possible to have a uniform vocabulary of lens focal lengths. So people compare focal lengths to their 35mm film equivalent by adjusting for the sensor size.

To make the comparison with 35mm film focal lengths, you need to know the ratio of your sensor to a frame of 35mm film, which is called the *focal-length equivalency.* Unless otherwise noted, the photos in this book were created using Nikon DSLRs with a 1.5 times 35mm focal-length equivalency. To find out how the focal lengths I used compare with 35mm focal lengths, multiply my focal lengths by 1.5.

To compute the comparable focal lengths on your own camera if your sensor has a different size than mine, you need to know the focal-length equivalency factor of your sensor. Check your camera manual for this information.

For example, I took the photo of the construction workers in old Havana shown on page 232–233 using a 32mm focal length with my 1.5X sensor size Nikon DSLR. The 35mm equivalence is therefore 32 x 1.5 = 48mm.

Software

In the *Portraits in the Digital Darkroom* section of this book, I discuss a number of software programs that I use in the digital darkroom for post-processing portraits. Here's the software that I mention, along with each publisher's website for more information, or to download trial versions:

Adobe Lightroom and Adobe Photoshop: www.adobe.com

Auto FX Software, Mystical Lighting: www.autofx.com

Imagenomic, Portraiture: www.imagenomic.com

Nik Software, Color Efex Pro 3.0 and Silver Efex Pro: www.niksoftware.com

PictureCode, Noise Ninja: www.picturecode.com

Topaz Labs, Topaz Adjust 4: www.topazlabs.com

▲ Pages 232–233: I was walking down the narrow streets of old Havana, Cuba, when I saw these construction workers on their break. I was struck by the contrast between the colorful, modern clothing and the ancient wood doors behind these men. I asked if I could take their photo and they replied "Si!" Then they went right back to their break-time conversation.

32mm, 1/100 of a second at F/5 and ISO 100, hand held

Glossary

Ambient light: The available, or existing, light that naturally surrounds a scene.

Aperture: The size of the opening in the iris of a lens. Apertures are designated by f-numbers. The smaller the f-number, the larger the aperture and the more light that hits the sensor.

Barn Doors: Black metal folding doors that attach to a light and are used to control the width of the beam of light.

Beauty Dish: Circular light modifier with an opaque center that softens light, particularly useful in creating attractive portraits.

Bracket: To shoot more than one exposure at different exposure settings.

Chiaroscuro: Moody lighting that shows contrasts between shadows and brightness.

CMYK: Cyan, Magenta, Yellow, and Black; the four-color color model used for most offset printing.

Color space: A color space—sometimes called a color model—is the mechanism used to display the colors we see in the world in print or on a monitor. CMYK, LAB, and RGB are examples of color spaces.

Composite: Multiple images that are combined to create a new composition.

Cucoloris: A wood, plastic, or cardboard sheet with cut-outs that can be placed over a light source to create a patterned effect.

Depth-of-field: The field in front of and behind a subject that is in focus.

Diffraction: Bending of light rays; unwanted diffraction can cause loss of optical sharpness at small apertures.

DSLR: Digital Single Lens Reflex, a camera in which photos are composed through the lens that will be used to take the actual image.

Dynamic range: The difference between the lightest tonal values and the darkest tonal values in a photo.

Ellipsoidal Spot: A spotlight that can vary both the size and focus of the spot, with the focus controlling whether the spot of light has sharp or soft edges.

Exposure: The amount of light hitting the camera sensor. Also the camera settings used to capture this incoming light.

Exposure histogram: A bar graph displayed on a camera or computer that shows the distribution of lights and darks in a photo.

Extension tube: A hollow ring that fits between a lens and the DSLR, used to achieve closer focusing.

f-number, f-stop: The size of the aperture, written f/n, where n is the f-number. The smaller the f-number, the larger the opening in the lens; the larger the f-number, the smaller the opening in the lens.

Fill card: a white or foil-covered card or board used to reflect light back into the shadow areas of a subject.

Focal length: Roughly, the distance from the end of the lens to the sensor. (The relationship of focal length to sensor size is explained on page 235.)

Framing: In a photographic composition, positioning the image in relationship to its edges.

Grayscale: Used to render images in a single color from white to black; in Photoshop a grayscale image has only one channel.

Grid: A very useful light modifier that uses a pattern to create a concentrated spot of light comparable—but more diffuse—to the light created using a snoot.

Hand HDR: The process of creating a HDR (High Dynamic Range) image from multiple photos at different exposures without using automatic software to combine the photos.

High Dynamic Range (HDR) image: Extending an image's dynamic range by combining more than one capture, either using automated software or by hand.

High key: Brightly lit photos that are predominantly white, often with an intentionally "over exposed" effect.

Hyperfocal distance: The closest distance at which a lens at a given aperture can be focused while keeping objects at infinity in focus.

Image stabilization: Also called vibration reduction, this is a high-tech system in a lens or camera that attempts to compensate for, and reduce, camera motion.

Infinity: The distance from the camera that is far enough away so that any object at that distance or beyond will be in focus when the lens is set to infinity.

Infrared (IR) photography: Captures made using infrared rather than normal, visible light.

ISO: The linear scale used to set sensitivity of a digital sensor.

JPEG: A compressed file format for photos that have been processed from an original RAW image.

Key light: Primary light used with a portrait subject.

LAB: Color model that separates luminance from color information.

Lensbaby: A special purpose lens with a flexible barrel that allows you to adjust the "sweet spot" (area in focus).

Low key: Dimly lit photos that are predominantly black, often with an intentionally "under exposed" effect.

Macro lens: A lens that is specially designed for close focusing; often a macro lens focuses close enough to enable a 1:1 magnification ratio.

Monochrome, monochromatic: A monochrome image is presented as nominally consisting of tones from white to black; however, "black and white" images can be tinted or toned, and so may vary from straight grayscale.

Multi-RAW processing: Combining two or more different versions of the same RAW file to extend the dynamic range and create a more pleasing final image.

Noise: Static in a digital image that appears as unexpected, and usually unwanted, pixels.

Open up, open wide: To open up a lens, or to set the lens wide open, means to set the aperture to a large opening, denoted with a small f-number.

Photo composite: *See* Composite.

Pre-visualization: Before making an exposure, envisioning how an image will come out after capture and processing.

RAW: A digital RAW file is a complete record of the data captured by the sensor. The details of RAW file formats vary among camera makers.

RGB: Red, Green, and Blue; the three-color color model used for displaying photos on the web and on computer monitors.

Sensitivity: Set using an ISO number; determines the sensitivity of the sensor to light.

Shutter speed: The interval of time that the shutter is open.

Snoot: A tube used as a light modifier to direct a beam of light.

Soft box: A light modifier that diffuses light; in studio lighting, generally a fairly large rectangular unit.

Stop down: To stop down a lens means to set the aperture to a small opening; denoted with a large f-number.

Sweet spot: The area that is in focus when using a Lensbaby.

Toning: In the chemical darkroom, toner such as sepia or selenium was added for visual effect; in the digital darkroom, toning simulates the impact of chemical toning.

Umbrella: A light modifier that can be used to reflect light onto the subject, or light can be directed through an umbrella to create a diffuse lighting source.

Index

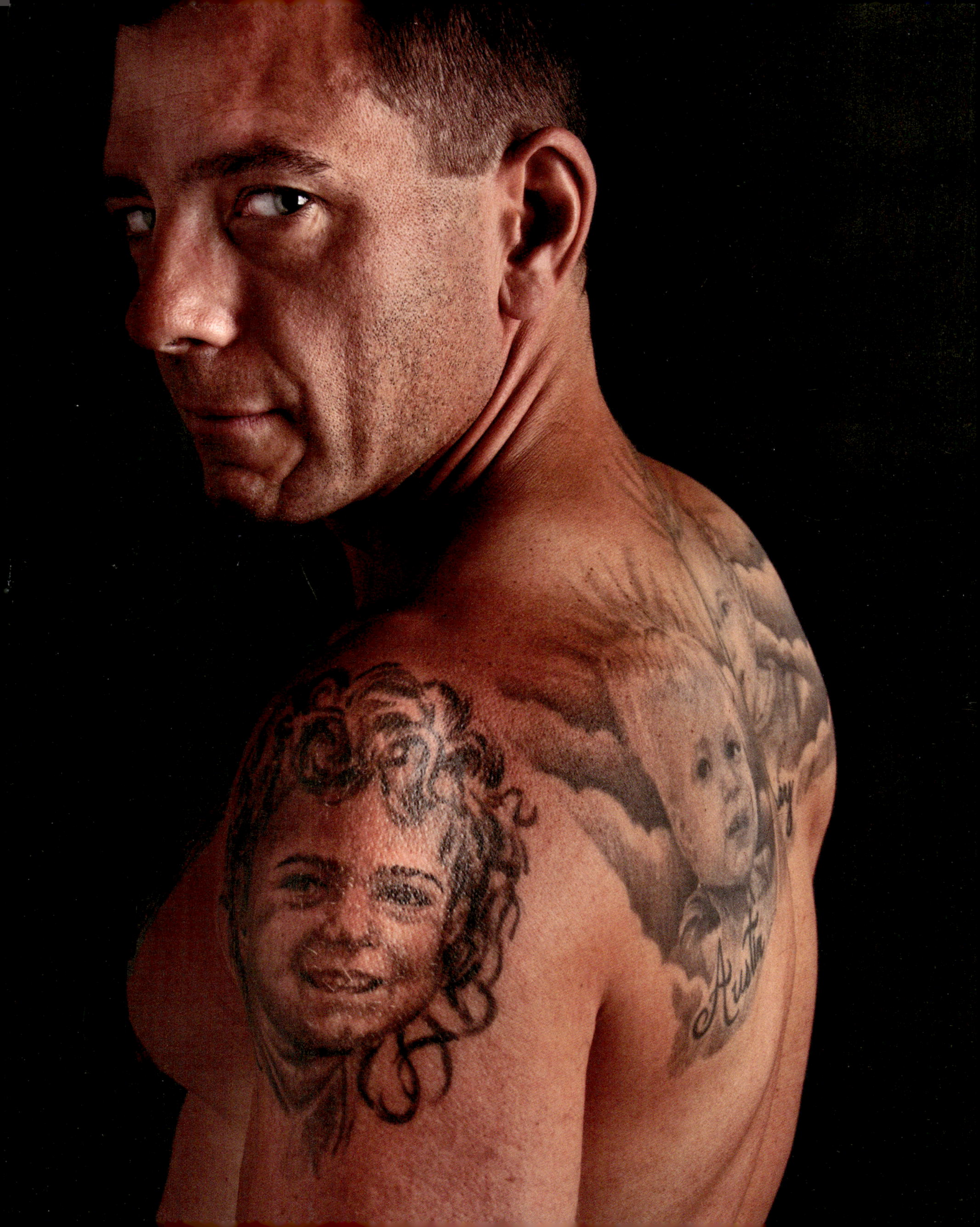